WHOM CAN WE TRUST?

WHOM CAN WE TRUST?

How Groups, Networks, and Institutions Make Trust Possible

Karen S. Cook, Margaret Levi,
and Russell Hardin
Editors

A VOLUME IN THE RUSSELL SAGE FOUNDATION SERIES ON TRUST

Russell Sage Foundation • New York

The Russell Sage Foundation

The Russell Sage Foundation, one of the oldest of America's general purpose foundations, was established in 1907 by Mrs. Margaret Olivia Sage for "the improvement of social and living conditions in the United States." The Foundation seeks to fulfill this mandate by fostering the development and dissemination of knowledge about the country's political, social, and economic problems. While the Foundation endeavors to assure the accuracy and objectivity of each book it publishes, the conclusions and interpretations in Russell Sage Foundation publications are those of the authors and not of the Foundation, its Trustees, or its staff. Publication by Russell Sage, therefore, does not imply Foundation endorsement.

Library of Congress Cataloging-in-Publication Data

Whom can we trust? : how groups, networks, and institutions make trust possible / Karen S. Cook, Margaret Levi, and Russell Hardin, editors.
p. cm.—(A volume in the Russell Sage Foundation series on trust)
Includes bibliographical references and index.
ISBN 978-0-87154-315-8 (alk. paper)
1. Trust. 2. Reliability. 3. Social networks. 4. Group identity. I. Cook, Karen S. II. Levi, Margaret. III. Hardin, Russell, 1940-
BF575.T7W56 2009
302.3'5—dc22

2009016759

The paper used in this publication meets the minimum requirements of American National Standard for Information Sciences—Permanence of Paper for Printed Library Materials. ANSI Z39.48-1992.

Text design by Suzanne Nichols.

RUSSELL SAGE FOUNDATION
112 East 64th Street, New York, New York 10065
10 9 8 7 6 5 4 3 2 1

The Russell Sage Foundation Series on Trust

The Russell Sage Foundation Series on Trust examines the conceptual structure and the empirical basis of claims concerning the role of trust and trustworthiness in establishing and maintaining cooperative behavior in a wide variety of social, economic, and political contexts. The focus is on concepts, methods, and findings that will enrich social science and inform public policy.

The books in the series raise questions about how trust can be distinguished from other means of promoting cooperation and explore those analytic and empirical issues that advance our comprehension of the roles and limits of trust in social, political, and economic life. Because trust is at the core of understandings of social order from varied disciplinary perspectives, the series offers the best work of scholars from diverse backgrounds and, through the edited volumes, encourages engagement across disciplines and orientations. The goal of the series is to improve the current state of trust research by providing a clear theoretical account of the causal role of trust within given institutional, organizational, and interpersonal situations, developing sound measures of trust to test theoretical claims within relevant settings, and establishing some common ground among concerned scholars and policymakers.

Karen S. Cook
Russell Hardin
Margaret Levi

SERIES EDITORS

Previous Volumes in the Series

Coethnicity: Diversity and the Dilemmas of Collective Action
James Habyarimana, Macartan Humphreys, Daniel N. Posner, and Jeremy M. Weinstein

Cooperation Without Trust?
Karen S. Cook, Russell Hardin, and Margaret Levi

Democracy and the Culture of Skepticism: Political Trust in Argentina and Mexico
Matthew R. Cleary and Susan Stokes

Distrust
Russell Hardin, editor

eTrust: Forming Relationships in the Online World
Karen S. Cook, Chris Snijders, Vincent Buskens, and Coye Cheshire, editors

Evolution and the Capacity for Commitment
Randolph N. Nesse, editor

Streetwise: How Taxi Drivers Establish Their Customers' Trustworthiness
Diego Gambetta and Heather Hammill

Trust and Distrust in Organizations: Dilemmas and Approaches
Roderick M. Kramer and Karen S. Cook, editors

Trust and Governance
Valerie Braithwaite and Margaret Levi, editors

Trust and Reciprocity: Interdisciplinary Lessons from Experimental Research
Elinor Ostrom and James Walker, editors

Trust and Trustworthiness
Russell Hardin

Trust in Society
Karen S. Cook, editor

Trust in the Law: Encouraging Public Cooperation with the Police and Courts
Tom R. Tyler and Yuen J. Huo

Contents

About the Authors

Karen S. Cook is Ray Lyman Wilbur Professor of Sociology, current chair of the Department of Sociology, and director of the Institute for Research in the Social Sciences at Stanford University.

Margaret Levi is Jere L. Bacharach Professor of International Studies in the Department of Political Science and director of the CHAOS (Comparative Historical Analysis of Organizations and States) Center at the University of Washington, Seattle, and holds the chair in U.S. politics at the U.S. Studies Centre at the University of Sydney.

Russell Hardin is professor of politics at New York University.

Abigail Barr is research officer at the Centre for the Study of African Economies, Oxford University.

Bruce G. Carruthers is Gerald F. and Marjorie G. Fitzgerald Professor of Economic History in the Department of Sociology at Northwestern University.

Matthew R. Cleary is assistant professor of political science in the Maxwell School at Syracuse University.

Jean Ensminger is Edie and Lew Wasserman Professor of Anthropology at the California Institute of Technology.

Henry Farrell is associate professor in the Department of Political Science and Elliott School of International Affairs at George Washington University.

Margaret Foddy is associate professor of psychology at La Trobe University in Melbourne, Australia.

Corina Graif is Ph.D. candidate in sociology at Harvard University and dissertation fellow with the Center for American Political Studies.

James Habyarimana is assistant professor at the Georgetown Public Policy Institute (GPPI).

Philip T. Hoffman is Rea A. and Lela G. Axline Professor of Business Economics and professor of history at the California Institute of Technology.

Macartan Humphreys is associate professor of Political Science at Columbia University and research scholar at the Center for Globalization and Sustainable Development at the Earth Institute.

Jeffrey C. Johnson is professor of sociology at East Carolina University and senior scientist at the Institute for Coastal and Marine Resources.

Roderick Kramer is visiting professor of public policy at the John F. Kennedy School of Government at Harvard University and is William R. Kimball Professor of Organizational Behavior at Stanford Business School.

Stefanie Mollborn is assistant professor of sociology at the University of Colorado–Boulder.

Gabriella R. Montinola is associate professor of political science at the University of California–Davis.

Elinor Ostrom is Arthur F. Bentley Professor of Political Science and senior research director of the Workshop in Political Theory and Policy Analysis at Indiana University.

Daniel N. Posner is associate professor of political science at the University of California–Los Angeles.

Gilles Postel-Vinay is director of studies at L'École des Hautes Études en Sciences Sociales and director of research at the INRA.

Jean-Laurent Rosenthal is Rea A. and Lela G. Axline Professor of Economics at the California Institute of Technology.

Robert J. Sampson is Henry Ford II Professor of the Social Sciences and department chair at Harvard University.

Irena Stepanikova is assistant professor at the University of South Carolina.

Susan C. Stokes is John S. Saden Professor of Political Science at Yale University and director of the Yale Program on Democracy.

David Thom is professor-in-residence and director of research at the University of California–San Francisco (UCSF), and director of Evidence Based Medicine for the UCSF Family Medicine Residency Program.

James Walker is professor of economics and co-director of the Workshop in Political Theory and Policy Analysis at Indiana University.

Jeremy M. Weinstein is associate professor of political science at Stanford University.

Toshio Yamagishi is professor in the Graduate School of Letters at Hokkaido University, Japan.

Preface

RENEWED INTEREST in understanding the role of trust in society over the past few decades has been inspired by several major works in sociology, political science, and history. Diego Gambetta's 1988 edited volume was an interdisciplinary effort to explore the meaning of trust both theoretically and empirically. James Coleman in 1990 and Robert Putnam in 1993 gave trust a key role in their work on social capital, and the historian Francis Fukuyama impelled trust to center stage in 1995 with the publication of his widely circulated book *Trust: The Social Virtues and the Creation of Prosperity*. Many theoretical discussions of the role of trust in society followed in the immediate wake of these publications, but empirical investigations that clarified the specific role trust played in varied social settings were less numerous. In what sense was trust central to social order, as some had claimed, and, if it was, under what conditions? What work does trust do in securing social, political, and economic transactions, and when? What are the limits to trust as a mechanism of social control and when do social organizations rely on trust in the absence of monitoring and sanctioning? What are the cultural roots of trust and trustworthiness and how do they differ? What are the consequences of distrust and how is trust restored when violated? These and other questions required sustained investigation using multiple methods in various contexts.

The Russell Sage Foundation responded by funding a working group and a program of research on the role of trust in society from 1995 until 2005 to facilitate multidisciplinary work on this important topic. The full list of funded projects is available on the foundation's website, but the chapters in this volume report on some of the most significant findings from these investigations. Although only about a third of the projects are represented here, we believe that this volume provides a window into the types of phenomena analyzed by teams of researchers funded under this initiative from across the social sciences, including psychology, anthropology, political science, economics, and sociology.

The commitment of the Russell Sage Foundation to sustained efforts of this type make it unique in the world of social science funding. The well-known success of an earlier (and continuing) initiative on behavioral economics is a testimony to the significance of this funding strategy. We thank Eric Wanner, president of the Russell Sage Foundation, for his foresight and his unusual capacity to identify topics of central importance in the social sciences, which he is willing to fund.

We also thank the Center for Advanced Study in the Social and Behavioral Sciences (CASBS) where various investigators, including the editors of this volume, were able to bring some of this work to fruition. In particular, we acknowledge the Rockefeller Foundation, which funded a team residency for the editors in Bellagio at the beginning of this project and subsequently an important conference on distrust. These fellowships and awards resulted in several of the books published in the trust series. Finally, we thank the authors whose work is included in this volume for their commitment to writing chapters that clearly summarize some of the most important findings from their research investigating trust in varied settings, ranging from the streets of Chicago and the offices of physicians in California to the countryside of Kenya, the countries of Mexico and Argentina, and even the dusty archives of small villages in France.

Introduction

As Matthew Cleary and Susan Stokes have noted (2006), the Russell Sage Foundation Trust Project has produced three key innovations: the change in focus from trust to trustworthiness (Hardin 2002; Cook, Hardin, and Levi 2005), the recognition that trust is only one of many potential sources of cooperative behavior (Cook, Hardin, and Levi 2005), and the reminder that in many strategic situations actors are better served by skepticism or a healthy level of distrust than trust (Braithwaite and Levi 1998; Cleary and Stokes 2006; Cook, Hardin, and Levi 2005). The chapters in this volume develop these themes by exploring them in a wide array of settings, at very different levels of analysis, and with varied disciplinary lenses.

Theorists often assume that trust is critical to managing everyday affairs in politics, business, and social life. Some even go as far as declaring trust as necessary and good. But these claims, both empirical and normative, have not been fully put to the test in the social science of trust. Trust cannot be good in contexts in which it is not merited. To trust strangers, for example, is taking a risk that may end badly, as many of those who enter social or economic relationships mediated by the Internet can attest. And certainly we would not say in normative language that trust in such contexts is inherently of value. As Russell Hardin clearly argued, we might desire those we interact with to be trustworthy, and that might generally be good for society, but we can make no such general claim about trust (2002). The chapters included in part I of this volume develop this insight more fully by clarifying the conditions under which we find others to be trustworthy and on what bases. Part II treats trust as mediated by organizations and networks providing the context in which trust extends our capacity to engage with one another over matters of substance. Part III moves up a level of analysis to spell out the institutional backing required for relations of trust and cooperation more generally. Here we also see the causal role of trust at the macro level addressed. There is a natural progression of the work reported in this volume, from interpersonal and intergroup relations to larger scale organizations, social networks, and institutions. At each level, the authors address key issues in the formation and role of trust in various social and cultural contexts.

Too much of the recent literature on trust treats trust as necessary for cooperation. The more nuanced understanding of trust advanced in the Russell Sage Foundation research program reveals the multiple sources of cooperation. It also provides an advance in understanding what sources are likely to matter under what conditions and with what sets of actors. By more adequately theorizing interpersonal trust, it is obvious that it is but one among many sources of cooperation. Moreover, it is neither always available nor always preferable as a basis for cooperation. In some circumstances, interpersonal trust may actually be an impediment.

Although the distinction between bonding and bridging social capital captures one aspect of when networks of trust and reciprocity produce exclusionary cooperation (Putnam 2000), it does not go far enough in revealing the dynamics of interaction and intergroup relations. Here the considerable advances in social psychology, particularly those derived from the experimental tradition of research represented in part I, provide clear evidence of the conditions under which relations of trust emerge between persons and members of groups distinguished by different status markers.

One of the major emphases of the Trust Project has been on situations in which ethnic, racial, or other markers facilitate certain kinds of trust relationships while inhibiting others and when they do not. For example, evidence of the trustworthiness of white police in black neighborhoods (Tyler and Huo 2002) or of middle-class government agents with working class clients (Peel 1998) may foster cooperation and ameliorate power relationships between street-level bureaucrats and those they are meant to serve (Lipsky 1980). In other instances, intraethnic relationships are themselves problematic. Often when immigrants are victimized it is by the conationals on whom the newer arrivals depend and whom they initially believed trustworthy (Nee and Sanders 2000). Sometimes the immigrants are simply calculating that the potential return is worth the risk of exploitation. Sometimes they have no choice given conditions in their home countries, but sometimes they are mistaken in their assessments of the trustworthiness of those with whom they are dealing.

Why is it that cultural markers sometimes are indicators of trustworthiness and facilitate cooperation, and what accounts for the abuse of these same markers to take advantage of others? The documentation of variation is a first step, but we also need an explanation of why we should have different expectations in different contexts. The markers some once thought might be good bases for trusting relationships may be deceptive—at least under certain circumstances.

Cost-benefit calculations take us some distance. When there are great returns from deception and relatively little punishment for exploitative behavior, we expect more of it. But the cost-benefit calculation is not always straightforward. A strategic reason to cooperate may in fact stimulate the creation of institutions for monitoring and sanctioning. Historical research on long-distance medieval trade suggests that the Maghrebi traders developed a set of rules and procedures to govern their interactions with each other, and this enabled them to form beliefs about the credible trustworthiness of other traders (Greif 1994). The motivation for establishing such arrangements was the profitability of the trade. The effectiveness of these arrangements rested on a shared written language and the high likelihood of loss of status and friends, as well as income, in cases of betrayal.

Field experiments on trust relations, ethnic markers, and cooperation add even more context. It seems that it may be easier to locate a coethnic in a complex setting, and that they are also likely to be more cooperative given the existence of ingroup norms and sanctions (Habyarimana et al. 2009; see also chapter 2, this volume). Other field experiments suggest that the more economically developed a society, the more likely it is that individuals will cooperate (Barr 2004; Henrich et al. 2004). Thus it seems that when there is mutual advantage to cooperation and enforceable ingroup norms, cultural markers may well serve as bases of trustworthiness that facilitate cooperation. These findings are consistent with the increased emphasis on cooperation generated by the iterated and long-term relationships embodied in some communities and networks (Putnam 2000; Taylor 1987 [1976]).

It is not simply identity per se that matters. It is typically the norms and sanctions that accompany group membership that motivate cooperation (Cook and Hardin 2001) and the expectation of generalized exchange (chapter 1, this volume). Coethnics who exploit immigrants not only derive economic advantage from doing so, they have also come to belong to a different normative community or none whatsoever. Thus it would be a mistake to assume that those who share a cultural marker can always trust each other, and it is equally wrong to assume that those whose markers are different can never trust one another.

The Trust Project has focused considerable attention on sources of cooperation other than trust relations as well as developing better evidence concerning how trustworthiness is assessed especially in high-risk settings. Sophisticated models of signaling (Bacharach and Gambetta 2000), combined with empirical research to test these models (Gambetta and Hamill

2005), suggest that individuals can cultivate a capacity to recognize who is likely to be trustworthy, even when theft of property and loss of life are the potential consequences of ill-chosen transactional partners. Of course, the tendency to misread signals still exists, as does the possibility of making tragic mistakes.

As history reminds us, however, institutions generally provide the best defense against the untrustworthy. According to Margaret Levi, "good defenses make good neighbors" (2000). The argument that trust is not the only, let alone always the best, source of cooperative behavior has a long intellectual history, dating back at least to the early work of David Hume and James Madison. Both men emphasized the institutional bases of reaching agreements and resolving disputes, and that the major source of such institutions in complex societies is government.

State institutions encourage cooperation by providing third-party enforcement to insure personal safety and the security of exchange. The more government actors elicit confidence in the government's capacity to enforce the laws relatively fairly and without too great a cost, the more likely they are to elicit cooperation and compliance with the state (Cook, Hardin, and Levi 2005; Levi 1997; Tyler 1990). The more the state demonstrates the reliability and neutrality of its institutions, the more it is able to facilitate the establishment of personal trustworthiness by allowing individuals to begin relationships with relatively small risks as they learn about each other, and by providing insurance against failed trust. Increased civic engagement, improved economic growth, and widespread compliance with government policies are among the possible consequences.

In an earlier volume, we offered an account of how, why, and when state institutions produce cooperative behavior with positive outcomes for the polity and society (Cook, Hardin, and Levi 2005, chapter 8). In the process, we contradicted the de Tocqueville thesis, as revised by Putnam, that civic association is the principal mechanism for promoting democracy and better government generally. There is some empirical evidence of a correlation between dense civic associational life and effective government, but not the clear causal link that de Tocqueville suggested or is central to Putnam's social capital argument. Our claim is that a responsive, fair, competent, and benevolent state is a reliable and even trustworthy one and thus likely to successfully elicit compliance and consent from citizens. It is in this sense that state effectiveness depends on the acquiescence and confidence of citizens. As Cleary and Stokes argue in chapter 11 of this volume, government is a key player in bringing this result about, not just a beneficiary of existing trust within the polity.

Simultaneously, we argue for the liberal view advocating institutionalized distrust of government (see also Braithwaite 1998; Hardin 2002; Pettit 1998). Healthy skepticism keeps constituents alert and public officials therefore responsive, but only if transparency is designed into state institutions so that wary citizens may be constructively vigilant. It is likely that widespread, deep distrust of government, going well beyond healthy skepticism, can undermine the state's institutional arrangements and provoke a breakdown in general cooperativeness, as several chapters in the third part of this volume suggest.

Part I. Social Relations, Groups, and Trust

One of the major puzzles in the work on trust is how we determine who is trustworthy when there is little evidence on which to base such judgments and on the extent to which we trust those we assume trustworthy based on stereotypes or group-based assessments. In part I of this volume, social psychologists, anthropologists, economists, and political scientists working in different but related research traditions address these questions and begin to identify the conditions under which such judgments are group based or derive from institutional contexts that provide confidence in such assessments.

In chapter 1, Margaret Foddy and Toshio Yamagishi investigate the sources of group-based trust examining the argument that ingroup trust is high, even in the absence of personal contact, because of a belief in the superiority of the group to which one belongs. Hypothesized alternative sources of such an ingroup bias in trustworthiness assessments include the expectation of generalized exchange among group members (that is, the expectation that reciprocity norms apply within group boundaries thus the expectation of fair and favorable treatment is justified), and the simple expectation that people reciprocate the goodwill of their fellow group members (referred to as the ingroup) more than they will that of members of outgroups. In comparisons of these hypothesized effects, the results suggest that the primary mechanism supporting ingroup favoritism was a belief in and the expectation of generalized exchange and not simply an ingroup stereotype response.

In general, the findings reported in chapter 1 indicate that category-based judgments and the related ingroup biases that the participants in these studies demonstrate are more likely to derive from the social expectation of generalized exchange than from a purely cognitive stereotype about a relevant category of membership. These findings link to some of the evolutionary arguments that James Walker and Elinor Ostrom address in chapter 4, in which the possible bases of cooperation are examined more fully. As the authors conclude, whatever the basis for group-based trust, it has important implications for social relations. To the extent that group boundaries are broadly defined, trusting relations are more likely to be established that lead to cooperation even among those who do not initially know each other within the group. However, if such boundaries are narrowly drawn, within group trust can lead to selective exclusion and potentially distrust of those on the outside. In this context, ingroup trust can produce greater fragmentation and even intergroup conflict especially when resources are scarce.

Building on the work related to stereotyping and cognitive categorization in chapter 2, James Habyarimana, Macartan Humphreys, Daniel Posner, and Jeremy Weinstein investigate the link between ethnic diversity and the provision of public goods. Using experimental games much like those in chapter 1, they demonstrate in field experiments (outside the laboratory) that category-based trust is weak, supporting the laboratory results reported in chapter 1. Drawing on economics and political science, Habyarimana and his colleagues identify a different set of mechanisms they consider likely to result in within group favoritism—the likelihood that trust is higher within homogeneous groups than across groups. They focus on contributions to a public good that benefited the group based on ethnic similarity. For Foddy and Yamagishi in chapter 1, the similarity was based on same department or university affiliation (a weaker source of group-based identity), rather than on similarity of ethnicity.

Habyarimana and his collaborators identify three general mechanisms through which trust and cooperation among coethnics might operate what Habyarimana and his colleagues termed other-regarding preferences, incentives, and competence. The investigators use distinct experimental games to isolate these mechanisms to see which ones accounted for cooperative behavior among members of different ethnic groups (from a random sample) in the urban neighborhoods of Mulago and Kyebando in Kampala, Uganda. The results suggest that ethnic-based ingroup favoritism in this context is not based on simple preference for positive relations with similar others or on task competence beliefs. Instead, it depends on norms of cooperation (and the relevant socially generated incentives) reinforced by group members, in much the way that Foddy and Yamagishi found in chapter 1 that expectations of generalized exchange operate to support cooperative behavior among ingroup members. In this context, successful trust-based collective action was derived from incentives and the ingroup norms that facilitated the sanctioning of noncontributors and thus reduced the likelihood of exploitation. The authors conclude on the positive note that their findings provide some hope that institutions that provide incentives for universal norms of trustworthiness might foster cross-group cooperation and potentially over time displace subgroup norms based on ethnicity and ingroup favoritism.

In chapter 3, Abigail Barr, Jean Ensminger, and Jeffrey Johnson use experimental trust games in field experiments in Africa to investigate the links between the social network position of individuals and trust and trustworthiness controlling for the demographic characteristics of the participants. Although they find no consistent relationship between these sociodemographic variables such as age, gender, education, income, and wealth on trust, they do find support for the hypothesized effect of centrality of social network position on trust and levels of trustworthiness.

In particular, Barr, Ensminger, and Johnson find in their urban Ghanaian study support for the hypothesis that those most central in the social network, measured in two ways, are more trusting. In their rural Kenyan study, they find support for this hypothesis and even stronger support for a positive correlation between network centrality and trustworthy behavior. The theoretical explanation they offer is based on Ronald Burt's work on brokerage (1992, 2005). Brokers can use their centrality in a network, in particular their "betweenness," to engage in strategic behavior as political entrepreneurs, which grants them access to trustworthy partners and to positions of power in the network, that is, to information that enables them to minimize risk. They are thus more likely to locate trustworthy partners and thus to engage in less risky transactions. Barr and her colleagues argue that more research on the role of social networks in facilitating trust and reinforcing trustworthiness in a variety of cultural contexts is required.

Chapter 4, by James Walker and Elinor Ostrom, concludes part I and provides a general overview of the experimental research on cooperation, trust, and the provision of public goods. Walker and Ostrom focus on the role of the social norm of reciprocity in the evolution of cooperation within groups, echoing themes in chapter 1 on generalized exchange as the primary motive behind ingroup favoritism and in chapter 2 on normative pressures within groups. Walker and Ostrom argue that the results of many laboratory experiments are corroborated by field experiments and support the role of reciprocity considerations. Their results are evidence that successful and sustainable cooperation must be built on a foundation of trust and reciprocity. Institutions that facilitate communication of information about the trustworthiness of others and that merit trust make cooperation possible and even efficient in many contexts.

Walker and Ostrom emphasize the key role of institutions in managing a wide range of problems of cooperation and collective action more reliably, and provide not only information but also assurance about the expected actions of others. In many situations, individuals must rely on norms of trust and reciprocity not only in repeated interaction situations but also in single transactions (one-shot settings) in which future interaction does not provide the opportunity for reciprocal cooperation. The authors lament the lack of a single formula for building environments in which cooperation can be sustained. They also lament that government or market-based attempts to create incentives for the efficient use of commonly held resources, under some conditions, hinder efforts to build trust and foster cooperation. In particular, asymmetric payoffs from cooperation, limited communication, incomplete group-level agreements, and the requirement for too much redistribution make cooperation at best fragile.

The findings discussed in part I of this volume provide the grounding for subsequent discussions in parts II and III on the specific social structures and institutional mechanisms that often emerge in a variety of contexts to produce cooperation in settings in which trust may fail.

Part II. Networks, Organizations, and Trust

Trust at the interpersonal level is often not enough to generate widespread cooperation in social settings, especially in communities and organizations. Other mechanisms can be brought to bear. In addition, at levels of analysis that involve larger social settings, even institutions, trust is often based on assessments of reliability, trustworthiness of the organization's representatives or agents, or simply the confidence that these individuals and institutions will be fair and consistent.

In chapter 5, Henry Farrell builds on the conceptualization of trust as encapsulated interest that Hardin proposed (2002) and Cook, Hardin, and Levi expanded (2005). He suggests that network theory is a useful complement to the analysis of trust at both the interpersonal and the macro level. He emphasizes the need for constructing mid-level theories of trust, arguing that there is a gap in the conceptualization of trust that only the careful analysis of networks and institutions can fill. He claims that there is relatively little detailed theoretical work on how meso-level social structures shape the ways individuals do or do not trust each other. He demonstrates how these social structures can have substantial consequences for trusting relations.

Farrell's work moves beyond the encapsulated interest model of trust suggesting that networks do not fully explain observed forms of trust and cooperation. What is missing, he argues, is the recognition that individuals need informal rules to govern a particular community on who may be trusted under which circumstances. He maintains that individuals often make category-based assessments when the information is embedded in institutions. Informal rules or norms are based not only on information derived from interpersonal relations (or direct experience with the organization, as Gabriella Montinola suggests in chapter 10), but also on longstanding practices often institutionalized in rules passed through networks that produce an independent effect on trust assessments. Empirical work on mid-range organizations and social settings is critical to this agenda.

Chapter 6 addresses physician-patient trust and provides some empirical evidence to support Farrell's claim about the importance of investigating meso-level structures as they influence micro-level interactions and macro-level outcomes related to trust. Irena Stepanikova, Karen Cook, David Thom, Roderick Kramer, and Stephanie Mollborn report the findings of a study of physician-patient trust, highlighting the factors that increase or decrease trust in these relationships as it affects outcomes for patients and work satisfaction for physicians. Results from interviews and focus groups in which trust was the central topic of discussion provide insights into the organizational and institutional factors that respondents cite as inhibiting or facilitating trust relations.

In particular, Stepanikova and her colleagues focus on the features of managed care practices that alter the nature of the trust relations between physicians and patients. An example is the role of perceived conflict of interest when physicians prescribe medicines or require tests performed in laboratories (or derived from companies) in which they have a financial interest. Among the strategies physicians use to build trust are to make medical decisions independent of insurance rules and financial concerns and to "team up" with patients in attitudinal opposition to managed care and insurance companies. Stepanikova and her colleagues conclude with an assessment of some of the consequences of high and low trust relations for the delivery of health care. In so doing, they present clear evidence that examining the role of trust in interpersonal relationships embedded in organizational settings can provide valuable insights into the actual mechanisms at work in such settings.

In chapter 7, Robert Sampson and Corina Graif further expand the notion that trust and its effects must also be examined at the network and organization level. Exploring the contextual properties of trust among institutional leaders and the residents of contemporary Chicago, the authors focus on social network ties and community-level processes, allowing the network data to serve as a proxy for social mechanisms between individuals connected by ties that have implications for communities. Sampson and Graif provide evidence to support Farrell's claim that much is to be learned from filling in the gap between persons and institutions.

The data these investigators use are drawn from a two-wave panel of more than 1,000 positional leaders in Chicago sampled from six institutional domains—law, politics, business, community organizations, education, and religion—across a stratified sample of thirty communities. As part of this study, Sampson and Graif developed an instrument that allows the social networks that link community leaders in achieving community goals, along with leaders' perceptions of the working trust characterizing these ties, to be assessed. In two independent studies of the same communities, the authors also assess multiple aspects of social cohesion, including resident trust in neighbors and institutions. Sampson and Graif find, disturbingly, that durable and increasing poverty has long lasting consequences, including lower neighborhood-level feelings of collective efficacy and higher levels of mistrust. The only ray of hope they provide is the belief that cohesive networks of community leaders may induce neighborhood social change for the better over time.

The chapters in part II provide the much-needed empirical support for multilevel analyses of the role of trust in society. In the final section of the book, claims about trust and its working at the institutional level are examined more closely with data that are typically very hard to come by.

Part III. Institutions and Trust

A major reason for interest in trust is the presumption that it has consequences that affect the whole of society. Trust, embodied in social capital or in attitudes that induce cooperation, is said to improve the quality of law and order, the economy, and the government. Most of the research for this perspective uses survey data, and findings rely on a few correlations that then become part of the common understanding. Although much of this work offers a causal story, the key relationships remain untested. A major line of argument in the Russell Sage Foundation Trust Project is that institutions and social networks are what produce the essential forms of cooperation. The chapters in part III offer compelling additional evidence for the causal role of institutions that provide not only information but also incentives for transparency, monitoring, and enforcing rules and laws. The authors find that for societies, markets, and governments, trust may not be the leavening agent Kenneth Arrow suggested it is for organizations (1974).

One way to get at the direction of causation, that is, whether trusting relations improve institutions or institutions are the source of trust-like behaviors, is to consider the development and maintenance of credit. What determines to whom a lender will extend credit clearly has to do with lender confidence in the ability of borrowers to repay loans. This, on the face of it, seems a crucible issue of establishing trust and building trustworthiness. Both chapter 8, by Bruce Carruthers, and chapter 9, by Philip Hoffman, Gilles Postel-Vinay, and Jean-Laurent Rosenthal, consider credit institutions and financial markets over time, but do so with different methods and with somewhat different conclusions about the role that trust plays.

Carruthers details the historical transformation of borrowing and lending in the Anglo American commercial world. Evaluations of creditworthiness were once based on bilateral ties between individuals but now depend on multilateral ties. Reliance on informal social networks and qualitative knowledge concerning the reputation of individuals has given way to formal institutions and quantitative knowledge. The acquisition of information by the lender about the borrower remains key, but the sources of that information have changed radically.

The result is that bankers can now collect highly individualized data to form the basis for their assessments of creditworthiness. Such information makes it possible to lend to people outside their social networks, but it is also biased against those without the right kind of financial biographies. That rotating credit associations and other such mechanisms based on social networks still exist suggests that impersonal institutions cannot fully replace more personalized social networks. Moreover, as Carruthers notes, "a striking (and somewhat ironic) historical change has been the extent to which credit now depends on a complex set of social, legal, and economic institutions whose own internal operations are mostly non-transparent." Thus it should be no surprise to Carruthers that these institutions can provide insurance for greedy creditors who choose to make problematic loans, as the current housing crisis suggests. Although institutions are key to information that extends the capacity of lenders to offer credit, such institutions are not necessarily reliable or equitable. Improving the conditions for credit does not in itself improve the quality of financial markets.

Hoffman, Postel-Vinay, and Rosenthal investigate more than a hundred French credit markets between 1740 and 1899. They combine history with an economic model to derive hypotheses about the relationship between social capital, trust, and the flourishing of financial markets. They then test their model statistically and hypothesize that social capital should increase trust and therefore the quality of financial markets. They find little evidence of this effect; however, economic variables explain the extent to which lenders trust borrowers as well or better than social capital does. Further, they discover that trust really matters only in situations characterized by widespread corruption, civil unrest, ethnic discrimination, or other circumstances in which formal institutions are weak. Institutions, not social capital or trust, are the major determinants of the quality of financial markets. Those that improve the quality of information, the same institutional role Carruthers emphasized, are essential. However, for Hoffman, Postel-Vinay, and Rosenthal, the ability to detect borrowers' misbehavior is as important as the capacity to evaluate their creditworthiness initially. Also important are those institutions that promote savings and thus make individuals more creditworthy.

In chapter 10, Gabriella Montinola examines the courts in the Philippines and argues that citizens use information about local institutions when assessing the trustworthiness of the larger institutions, which they reflect (for example, government). She tests the hypothesis that the reform of local institutions may generate higher levels of trust even if other institutions are problematic, to use her phrasing. In this view, citizens' assessments are actually data-driven and experience with the local institutions cements views on reliability, fairness, and consistency. Such experience grants citizens a basis for updating their assessments of the organizations and institutions they confront in their daily lives, in ways in which they may not confront national-level organizations. The alternative, Montinola argues, is the notion that generalized trustworthiness judgments transfer from one organization to the next and there is little experience-based updating of such assessments.

To evaluate these claims, Montinola uses survey data from citizens with and without court experience and compares their assessments of the trustworthiness of the courts. She argues that her findings are important for emerging democracies in which resources are constrained in such a way that reforms are limited and thus must be focused on those organizations that can be transformed to increase citizen compliance based on increased perceived legitimacy. Montinola's work also has implications for the study of trust in specific government institutions. Do trustworthiness assessments transfer across institutions based on information derived from experience as reflected in some research, or are they simply reflections of generalized (and stable) tendencies to trust government at all levels? Montinola concludes that such research should be of great interest to organizations like USAIS and the World Bank, which are targeting their assistance to the reform of judicial systems on the hope that this strategy will strengthen the rule of law in emerging democracies.

In chapter 11, which concludes this volume, Matthew Cleary and Susan Stokes turn our attention from markets to government and, in particular, the role of trust in promoting democratic government. They review the survey evidence that links trust and the quality of democracy, especially in Latin America. Based on their own surveys, supplemented by in-depth qualitative research, they conclude that much of the research misinterprets the data. They recognize that correlations exist between low levels of trust and low levels of political participation and social cooperation, factors that contribute to the quality of democracy, but find trust to be a symptom, not a cause, of democratic performance. They argue that institutions that enhance monitoring of government and its accountability are also likely to enhance citizen responsiveness in the form of participation and social cooperation and, therefore, democratic quality. They conclude, in keeping with Hume and Madison, that healthy skepticism, not trust, is at the heart of the citizens' relationship to government in a democracy.

It is our hope that this volume provides invaluable theoretical insights and stimulates further empirical research on the complexities and limits of the role of trust in society. The research program motivating this volume illuminates the contexts in which trust relations facilitate cooperation and when they do not. It reveals the importance of networks and institutions in making trusting relations possible, but also suggests when networks and institutions inhibit cooperation. The role government plays also appears to be more complicated than originally theorized. Yet there is no question that the capacity to govern is improved when the citizenry expresses basic confidence in the governing apparatus while maintaining a critical stance and willingness to protest particular policies and actions. Government illustrates but one instance of the effect of power relations on interpersonal interactions, networks, organizations, and institutions. This volume reveals how much power relations can create challenges for the creation of trustworthiness and cooperation. The essays contribute to unraveling those challenges and to laying out a fruitful agenda for future research.

References

Arrow, Kenneth J. 1974. *The Limits of Organization.* New York: W. W. Norton & Co.

Bacharach, Michael, and Diego Gambetta. 2000. "Trust in Signs." In *Trust in Society,* edited by Karen S. Cook. New York: Russell Sage Foundation.

Barr, Abigail. 2004. "Kinship, Familiarity, and Trust: An Experimental Investigation." In *Foundations of Human Sociality,* edited by Joseph Henrich, Robert Boyd, Samuel Bowles, Colin Camerer, Ernst Fehr, and Herbert Gintis. New York: Oxford University Press.

Braithwaite, John. 1998. "Institutionalizing Distrust, Enculturating Trust." In *Trust and Governance,* edited by Valerie Braithwaite and Margaret Levi. New York: Russell Sage Foundation.

Braithwaite, Valerie, and Margaret Levi. 1998. *Trust and Governance.* New York: Russell Sage Foundation.

Burt, Ronald S. 1992. *Structural Holes: The Social Structure of Competition.* Cambridge, Mass.: Harvard University Press.

———. 2005. *Brokerage and Closure: An Introduction to Social Capital.* Oxford: Oxford University Press.

Cleary, Matthew R., and Susan C. Stokes. 2006. *Democracy and the Culture of Skepticism: Political Trust in Argentina and Mexico.* New York: Russell Sage Foundation.

Coleman, James S. 1990. *Foundations of Social Theory.* Cambridge, Mass.: Harvard University Press.

Cook, Karen S., and Russell Hardin. 2001. "Networks, Norms, and Trustworthiness." In *Social Norms,* edited by Michael Hechter and Karl Dieter-Opp. New York: Russell Sage Foundation.

Cook, Karen S., Russell Hardin, and Margaret Levi. 2005. *Cooperation Without Trust?* New York: Russell Sage Foundation.

Fukuyama, Francis. 1995. *Trust.* New York: Basic Books.

Gambetta, Diego. 1988. *Trust: Making and Breaking Cooperative Relations.* New York: Blackwell Publishing.

Gambetta, Diego, and Heather Hamill. 2005. *Streetwise: How Taxi Drivers Establish Their Customers' Trustworthiness.* New York: Russell Sage Foundation.

Greif, Avner. 1994. "Cultural Beliefs and the Organization of Society: A Historical and Theoretical Reflection on Collectivist and Individualist Societies." *Journal of Political Economy* 102(5): 912–50.

Habyarimana, James, Macartan Humphreys, Daniel N. Posner, and Jeremy M. Weinstein. 2009. *Coethnicity: Diversity and the Dilemmas of Collective Action,* edited by Karen S. Cook, Russell Hardin, and Margaret Levi. New York: Russell Sage Foundation.

Hardin, Russell. 2002. *Trust and Trustworthiness.* New York: Russell Sage Foundation.

Henrich, Joseph, Robert Boyd, Samuel Bowles, Colin Camerer, Ernst Fehr, Herbert Gintis, and Richard McElreath. 2004. "Overview and Synthesis."

In *Foundations of Human Sociality*, edited by Joseph Henrich, Robert Boyd, Samuel Bowles, Colin Camerer, Ernst Fehr, and Herbert Gintis. New York: Oxford University Press.

Levi, Margaret. 1997. *Consent, Dissent and Patriotism.* New York: Cambridge University Press.

———. 2000. "When Good Defenses Make Good Neighbors." In *Institutions, Contracts, and Organizations: Perspectives from New Institutional Economics*, edited by Claude Menard. Colchester: Edward Elgar.

Lipsky, Michael. 1980. *Street-Level Bureaucracy.* New York: Russell Sage Foundation.

Nee, Victor, and Jimmy Sanders. 2000. "Trust in Ethnic Ties: Social Capital and Immigrants." In *Trust in Society*, edited by Karen S. Cook. New York: Russell Sage Foundation.

Peel, Mark. 1998. "Trusting Disadvantaged Citizens." In *Trust and Governance*, edited by Valerie Braithwaite and Margaret Levi. New York: Russell Sage Foundation.

Pettit, Philip. 1998. "Republican Theory and Political Trust." In *Trust and Governance*, edited by Valerie Braithwaite and Margaret Levi. New York: Russell Sage Foundation.

Putnam, Robert D. 1993. *Making Democracy Work: Civic Traditions in Modern Italy.* Princeton, N.J.: Princeton University Press.

———. 2000. *Bowling Alone: The Collapse and Renewal of American Community.* New York: Simon & Schuster.

Taylor, Michael. 1987 [1976]. *The Possibility of Cooperation.* Cambridge: Cambridge University Press.

Tyler, Tom R. 1990. *Why People Obey the Law.* New Haven, Conn.: Yale University Press.

Tyler, Tom R., and Yuen J. Huo. 2002. *Trust in the Law: Encouraging Public Cooperation with the Police and Courts*. New York: Russell Sage Foundation.

PART I

SOCIAL RELATIONS, GROUPS, AND TRUST

Chapter 1

Group-Based Trust

MARGARET FODDY AND TOSHIO YAMAGISHI

THE CONCEPT OF trust and, in particular, trust in strangers has attracted increasing attention in social psychology and related disciplines (Buskens and Raub 2002; Cook 2001; Fukuyama 1995; Gambetta 1988; Hollis 1998; Kramer 1999; Kramer and Tyler 1996; Ostrom 1998; Riegelsberger, Sasse, and McCarthy 2003; Yamagishi and Yamagishi 1994; Tyler 2001; Tyler and Huo 2002). In part, this reflects the emergence of new forms of social and economic relationships made possible through electronic communication, such as the Internet and virtual organizations (Braithwaite and Levi 1998; Kollock 1997; Kramer 1999; McKenna and Bargh 2000; Smith and Kollock 1999; Tyler and Huo 2002), and developments in global economic and political systems (Hardin 2001; Kramer 1999; Yamagishi and Yamagishi 1994), in which the establishment of "fast trust" among strangers is critical (Kramer and Tyler 1996). Our uncertainty about the behavior of strangers leads us to seek out, identify, and attend to information that informs us of their potential trustworthiness (Brann and Foddy 1987; Kramer 1999).

In this chapter, trust is defined as an expectation of beneficent reciprocity from others in uncertain or risky situations (Brann and Foddy 1987). Trust reflects a belief that others will act in a way to benefit or at least not harm us, before we know the outcome of their behaviors (Dasgupta 1988). Trust is not required when others' interests are totally allied with our own; this is the domain of assurance (for example, Hardin 2001; Buskens and Raub 2002). Rather, trust is needed when another person has the potential to gain at our expense, but can choose not to do so (Yamagishi and Yamagishi 1994; see also Knight 2001). Trust is most important in uncertain, not certain, relationships (Cook et al. 2005).

Although there is reasonable consensus about how trust is defined, the same cannot be said for how it develops and is maintained (Hardin 2001; Kramer 1999). Debate exists over whether trust is a feature of the truster, in the form of personality trait, moral commitment, or cognitive bias, or a reflection of the trustworthiness of the other, established through a history of interaction, third-party reputation, or normative constraints associated with roles occupied by the other person (see, for example, Cook 2001; Hardin 2001; chapter 4, this volume). An emerging view is that trust develops from the nature of the relationship between interactants, including shared group membership. Marilynn Brewer argued, for example, that shared membership in a social category can "serve as a rule for defining the boundaries of low-risk interpersonal trust that bypasses the need for personal knowledge and the costs of negotiating reciprocity" (1981, 356). Indeed, we argue that shared group membership is the key factor to understanding trust in strangers (see also Kramer 1999; McAllister 1995; Tyler 2001).

Conceptualizing Group-Based Trust

The large literature on ingroup favoritism is one starting point for understanding group-based trust. Evidence is extensive that categorizing people into one of two mutually exclusive groups (even arbitrary groups) can lead them to hold more favorable evaluations of their group relative to the other (Paris et al. 1972), and to distribute resources to favor the ingroup (Tajfel 1970; Tajfel et al. 1971; Hogg and Abrams 1988; Gaertner and Insko 2000; Jetten, Spears, and Manstead 1996). Making salient shared group membership also increases cooperation in a range of social dilemmas (see Brewer and Kramer 1986; Foddy and Hogg 1999; Wit and Wilke 1992). Such responses do not seem to depend on anticipated or continuing interaction with a specific person, nor on specific information about members of the shared category (Bourhis, Turner, and Gagnon 1997; Platow, McClintock, and Liebrand 1990). Other research in this tradition suggests that group members place their faith (if not their fate) more confidently in the hands of ingroup than in those of outgroup members. Group members, one, expect fellow ingroup members to favor the ingroup over an outgroup in the allocation of resources (Jetten, Spears, and Manstead 1996; Moy and Ng 1996), two, approve of individuals who do favor the ingroup over an outgroup (Platow et al. 1995), and, three, judge allocations favoring the ingroup to be fair (Platow et al. 1995; Platow et al. 1997).

Although ingroup favoritism is not the same as trust, both may arise from recognition of shared group membership (Yamagishi and Kiyonari 2000). Ingroup favoritism reflects in part a perception of self as an interchangeable exemplar of the group (Turner et al. 1987). Through this perception, "others' interests become our own interests" and people are motivated to evaluate positively, bestow favors on, and cooperate with other group members (Bourhis, Turner, and Gagnon 1997, 282). Accordingly, people think well of their groups and want their groups to do well, for the same intrinsic reason that they want to regard themselves positively and to do well. Although less attention has been given to group-based trust than to ingroup favoritism, it is not difficult to suggest possible mechanisms that might lead to higher trust in members of a shared category or group. We focus on two we label stereotype-based trust, and on generalized expectations about the behavior of ingroup members to others in their group. These two mechanisms are not necessarily mutually exclusive, but they lead, under specifiable conditions, to different consequences.

Stereotype-Based Trust

The frequently demonstrated positive evaluation of strangers who are ingroup members may be a basis for differential trust. We may trust them simply because we think they have positive qualities per se—the ingroup stereotype is globally positive and contains an array of positively construed specific traits that usually outnumber the negative (for example, Brewer 1981). Among the positive attributes are that they are more generous, trustworthy, and fair (McAllister 1995), qualities important in settings that oblige people to put their fates into the hands of strangers. Michael Platow, Charles McClintock, and Wim Liebrand found, for example, that ingroup members are rated as more trustworthy than outgroup members (1990). Similarly, Janet Boldizar and David Messick observed that the behavior of ingroup members is expected to be more fair than that of members of a relevant outgroup (1988). A corollary of this argument is that, in cases where the ingroup stereotype is more negative, trust in fellow group members should be weak (for example, Doosje et al. 1998; Mlicki and Ellemers 1996).

Expectation of Generalized Reciprocity

A second basis for trust in strangers from one's own group is that group members may have expectations of altruistic behavior from ingroup members independent of the valence of ingroup evaluations (Buchan, Croson, and Dawes 2002; Yamagishi and Kiyonari 2000; see also Kiyonari 2002; Yamagishi, Jin, and Kiyonari 1999). Describing their work with the minimal group paradigm (MGP), Toshio Yamagishi, Nobuhito Jin, and Toko Kiyonari referred to a *group heuristic*, an expectation of generalized or indirect reciprocity within the bounds of a salient social group (Yamagishi, Jin, and Kiyonari 1999, 186; see also Nowak and Sigmund 1998). This view differs from the stereotype in that it claims that cooperation with and trust in other ingroup members depends on a naïve theory of groups, according to which people understand that members of a group help each other to further each others' interests. Yamagishi, Jin, and Kiyonari (1999) argued that environmental cues that suggest interdependent relations within a group trigger the group heuristic as a guide for behavior. Once the naïve theory is easily accessible, group members expect fellow ingroup members to act favorably toward them. Insofar as group members expect this, they respond with benevolent treatment of other ingroup members.

Expectations of ingroup-favoring behavior are postulated to be acquired through repeated experience in groups, and are not tied to stereotypes of either any particular group or the ingroup. Thus members of a negatively stereotyped group might have strong expectations of positive treatment from fellow group members (trust) at the same time that they may agree with a general stereotype of the group as untrustworthy and dangerous. What is critical to reciprocal behavior favoring ingroups is the expectation that people can be depended on to treat others within the group benevolently, rather than positive evaluations and feelings of closeness, sameness, or liking (Kiyonari, Foddy, and Yamagishi 2007; Knight 2001; Yamagishi and Kiyonari 2000). Although positive sentiments often accompany trust, they are not a necessary condition for it—the only similarity required is a shared belief that group members will act on the basis of a norm of generalized group-bound reciprocity. On this account, the intensity with which a person identifies with a group is not as important as mutual recognition of shared group membership and the obligations that this entails for oneself and other group members (Yamagishi, Jin, and Kiyonari 1999). Stereotype-based trust, on the other hand, does not require mutual recognition of common identity—the assumption of the goodness of ingroup members can be made when only the perceiver is aware of the commonality, and should vary with the degree of ingroup identification (Foddy, Platow, and Yamagishi 2009).

In the studies presented, we first examine whether people do in fact trust ingroup members more than outgroup members in a situation that requires a decision about where to entrust one's interests. We then contrast the explanation that trust is mediated by positive ingroup stereotypes, with the explanation based on an expectation of bounded generalized reciprocity. Unlike work on ingroup favoritism, in which the focus is on a person who has the ability to distribute rewards and make evaluations, our work changes the focus to the potential recipients of fair or unfair treatment.

Experimental Studies

We define an *ingroup member* as someone who shares a salient social category membership with self, and an *outgroup member* as someone who does not (that is, is a member of a different, salient social category).

We first deal with the simple question of whether higher trust is placed with ingroup or outgroup strangers. It is consistent with either of the mechanisms posited. Specifically, we tested the following hypothesis:

> Ingroup trust hypothesis. When shared category membership is salient, people will trust and prefer to enter into a relationship of dependence with someone from their group rather with someone from another group.

We have posited two possible mechanisms that may generate higher ingroup trust: the attribution of more positive characteristics to the ingroup (that is, stereotype-based trust), and the stronger reciprocity expectations between ingroup members. Because these mechanisms are not mutually exclusive, they may operate additively or interactively, but it is possible that one is more important than the other. At this point, it is premature to specify how the two processes might combine. We thus offer two hypotheses related to the bases of ingroup trust:

> Group heuristic hypothesis. Trust in and preference for relationships with ingroup members depend on expectations of relatively better treatment from ingroup than from outgroup members. Independent of the valence of the ingroup stereotype, these expectations are part of the obligations of group members to one another, when there is mutual recognition of membership. Ingroup trust will be inhibited when shared group membership cannot be recognized by one party.
>
> Stereotype hypothesis. Trust in and preference for relationships with ingroup members depend on an ingroup stereotype that is more positive or less negative than that of the outgroup. Expectations of better treatment from ingroup members will arise from attributions of relevant positive characteristics associated with the ingroup, including greater trustworthiness and fairness. This hypothesis suggests that the positive evaluative bias for ingroup members produces trust. A relatively more positive stereotype of an outgroup will undermine or displace ingroup trust. Mutual recognition of shared group membership will not be a necessary condition for stereotype-based trust.

After an initial experiment, in which we test the existence of higher trust in strangers from one's own group (ingroup trust hypothesis), we examine the heuristic and stereotype hypotheses. Our strategy is to create conditions that allow or block expectations of group-based fairness and reciprocity, and to examine the role of these expectations in group-based trust (heuristic hypothesis). In the first three studies, we compare groups with similar stereotype valences (established in previous studies), but also measure individual perceptions of ingroup and outgroup (study 3). In the second three, we vary the relative valence of the ingroup and outgroup stereotypes (stereotype hypothesis) to determine whether ingroup trust persists when the ingroup has a relatively more negative stereotype, or whether people place more trust in people from an outgroup with more positive, trust-related characteristics.

Overview of the Experimental Paradigm

For our allocator paradigm, we adapted a variant of a trust game that Toko Kiyonari and Toshio Yamagishi once used to investigate trust in strangers (1999). In their study, Kiyonari and Yamagishi offered naïve participants (recipients) a choice between a sure thing payment of $X, and the alternative of accepting a share of money from an unknown allocator, who had been given an amount $Y, where $Y was more than $2X, by the experimenter (not by the recipient as in the standard trust game) to allocate between self and the recipient. They found substantial willingness on the part of recipients to put their outcomes in the hands of the allocator, and with good reason—allocators shared close to half of their endowments with the unknown recipient.

In all of the experiments we report, we changed Kiyonari and Yamagishi's paradigm in two important ways (Foddy, Yamagishi, and Platow 2009). First, we offered participants a choice between two allocators, with no sure-thing option. One allocator was identified as being from the recipient's ingroup (either the same university or the same college major), and the other from a salient outgroup (different university or different major). In this paradigm, the recipient had no power and no opportunity to engage in strategy or signaling to influence the allocator, or to affect the allocators' outcomes. Thus it is particularly useful for assessing differential trust in strangers—the recipients had to decide which of two allocators could be trusted more to treat them fairly, or at least to take the recipient's interests into account. The removal of the sure thing or opting out alternative and its replacement with a choice of allocator means that our focus is on relative trust in two types of strangers, not on absolute trust, and our research does not address the question of whether people with a sure thing option would be more willing to put their fates into the hands of an ingroup stranger. In the studies reported here, we explore differential expectations of fair treatment that arise from shared group membership.

From the perspective of strict economic rationality, there is no reason for the recipient to expect any share of the allocator's endowment; the allocator had unilateral fate control (Thibaut and Kelley 1959). Thus there is no reason to prefer one allocator over the other. We were interested in whether participants would nevertheless be more willing to trust allocators with whom they shared a salient category membership. Variations in the paradigm made it possible to investigate possible reasons for such differential trust. In particular, we varied, first, whether the allocator and recipient had mutual knowledge of their shared and unshared category memberships, a necessary precondition for expectations of mutual obligation and ingroup fairness, and, second, whether the outgroup stereotype was relatively more positive or negative than that of the ingroup. The first variation addressed the question of whether blocking mutual knowledge of shared group membership would eliminate differential trust in the ingroup—a person who cannot recognize you as a fellow group member cannot be expected to treat you benevolently. The second allowed us to investigate whether group-based trust depends on positive stereotypes of the ingroup, and the trust-inducing traits of ingroup members.

Our focus in these studies is on the recipients' choices, and on their expectations about how they will be treated by ingroup and outgroup members. In all cases, there were in fact no allocators; their distribution of money was said to have been made in a previous phase of the study, and were based on a previous study that included both allocators and recipients. In all of the experiments, we measured recipients' expectations about what they would receive from each allocator, chosen and not chosen by the recipient, and asked them to write free response reasons for making their choices.

Do People Trust Ingroup Members More than Outgroup Members?

In the first study, category membership was defined in terms of being a student at one or the other of two universities in Melbourne, Australia, where there are eight universities. Participants in the study were all from one university (La Trobe University); pilot work had shown that students from this population regarded students at the other university (Melbourne University) as a relevant outgroup, and they held both positive and negative stereotypes about both groups.[1] Participants were forty-seven first-year university student volunteers.[2]

The procedure for the first study is given in detail because it was identical in all following experiments except for manipulation of additional independent variables, and addition of measures that are noted where relevant.

Participants were tested in groups ranging from three to six students in cubicles within a larger room. Questionnaires were distributed to participants as they became ready to complete them.

Initially, the experimenter introduced the study by explaining that it involved making decisions regarding the distribution of money (a total of AU$16) between students of two universities, La Trobe University (ingroup) and Melbourne University (outgroup). The fifteen-item social identity scale was administered and then the experimenter explained that a research grant had made available funds for an experiment involving two different universities. Participants were given a copy of these instructions, which described the study as a situation involving allocators and recipients. All participants were informed that they would be recipients.

The social identity scale was used to make salient the ingroup identity, and provided a measure of the degree to which the salient ingroups were in fact important to the participants.

Participants were informed that in a previous experimental session some students from the ingroup and outgroup had already acted as allocators. They were told that the allocators had each been given AU$16.00 to divide between themselves and the recipients; allocators had to decide whether to allocate some, all, or no money to a recipient. It was emphasized that the allocators did not know the personal identity of any recipient, although they did know the university from which the recipients came (group identity). Recipients were given a copy of the instructions purportedly given to the two groups of allocators on an earlier occasion. This reinforced the information that the allocators had identical information, and knew the university affiliation of the recipient to whom they could allocate a share of AU$16.

While explaining the procedure followed by the allocators, the experimenter held up two boxes labeled La Trobe University and Melbourne University that contained the allocators' envelopes with money inside them. Showing participants the envelopes emphasized that the allocators had already made their decisions and that real money was involved. Participants were instructed that, as recipients, they each had the choice between two options: to accept the amount allocated by the (ingroup) La Trobe University allocator or the (outgroup) Melbourne University allocator. At the end of these instructions, participants filled out a questionnaire indicating their choice of allocator, indicated how much money they believed they would receive from each allocator had they chosen that person, and answered an open-ended question on the reasons for their choice. Participants then filled out the six-item trust scale (Yamagishi and Yamagishi 1994). The sessions took about thirty minutes.[3]

The results of primary interest are the recipients' choices of allocator and their expected share of the allocators' endowment; in all cases they made predictions about what they expected from both allocators (chosen and nonchosen). Because our focus is on the comparison of expectations for ingroup and outgroup allocators, regardless of choice, these predictions were also coded according to group membership of the allocator.

Participants showed an overwhelming preference for the ingroup allocator: forty-one of forty-seven, or 87 percent, chose to receive the unknown amount provided by someone from their own university. This proportion differed significantly from the random proportion of 50 percent, $x^2(1, N = 47) = 26.06, p < .001$).

Recipients' predictions of what they would receive from the ingroup and outgroup allocator (regardless of choice) were compared using a paired t-test (t (46) = 6.36, $p < .001$.). The mean expected proportion from the ingroup allocator (.46) was significantly higher than for the allocator from the outgroup (.29). Recipients choosing the ingroup allocator expected less from the outgroup allocator (median = .38, $M = .27$), and the few choosing the outgroup allocator did not have differential expectations: median expectations were .50 for both outgroup and ingroup allocators, means also equal (.47). Recipients clearly did not believe that either allocator would give them nothing.

Is Mutual Knowledge Necessary for Ingroup Trust?

To test whether common knowledge of shared category membership is necessary to activate group-based trust (Heuristic Hypothesis), we created a condition in which a new group of participants were told that allocators knew only that the recipients were from either the ingroup or the outgroup; the probability of each option was not specified. If preference for an ingroup stranger is based on positive stereotypes and liking for the ingroup, it should make no difference to the recipients whether the allocator recognizes shared membership (or lack of it). However, if, as the Heuristic Hypothesis predicts, the group heuristic is activated only under conditions of mutual awareness, then there should be no preference for the ingroup allocator when this awareness is absent.

For comparability with the first study, university affiliation was used as the shared category membership for twenty-seven participants, recruited from the general volunteer pool at La Trobe University. The procedure was identical to the first study, except that when the recipients were shown the instructions purportedly given to the two allocators, there was an explicit statement that the recipient might be from either La Trobe University (ingroup) or Melbourne University, but that the allocator did not know which.

Recipients did not show a significant preference for the ingroup allocator: fifteen of twenty-seven students (56 percent) chose an allocator from the same university, whereas twelve of twenty-seven (44 percent) preferred the outgroup ($x^2(1) = .33, p = .56$, versus the random proportion of .50). The preference for the ingroup allocator found under conditions of mutual knowledge (87 percent in study 1) did not extend to the unilateral knowledge condition, suggesting that mutual recognition of shared group identity is necessary for ingroup trust. Recipients' expectations of the share they would receive from the ingroup and outgroup allocators (regardless of choice) were virtually identical: .36 and .35 respectively, again consistent with the heuristic hypothesis.

Does the Stereotype of Outgroup Members Matter in the Decision to Trust Them? The first two studies provided compelling evidence that people will trust ingroup members more when faced with a decision to put their fate into the hands of an ingroup or an outgroup member, and that this trust is based on expectations of fair treatment from ingroup allocators. The evidence did not support the role of positive ingroup stereotypes as the basis of this trust. To further explore the role or lack of role that stereotype bias might play, we decided to introduce a more systematic experimental manipulation of the valence of ingroup and outgroup stereotypes. This was done by first identifying groups with relatively more positive or more negative stereotypes than the ingroup, to assess whether choice of allocator is determined by the valence or content of these stereotypes under the mutual knowledge conditions. The fourth and the final study is a replication of the third study with the additional manipulation of valence of the outgroup stereotype.

To manipulate stereotype valence of the outgroup in respect to the ingroup, we used shared membership in undergraduate degree enrollment as a relevant category, with psychology students as the focal ingroup. In second-year laboratory classes, fifty-seven students were asked to provide free-response stereotypes (not necessarily personal beliefs) about their ingroup (psychology students), and one of three outgroups: students in engineering ($n = 18$), nursing ($n = 20$), and economics ($n = 19$). These groups had been chosen from group discussions with psychology students who were asked to identify groups on campus that had positive and negative stereotypes. Participants listed up to ten words they thought were descriptive of psychology students, and of one of the other three student categories (nursing, engineering, economics). They were then asked to rate each item on the two lists as being positive, negative, or neutral. Participants placed their anonymous responses in a box in the classroom.

For each participant, the proportion of positive, negative, and neutral items generated for both the psychology group and the relevant outgroup was calculated; the positive and negative proportions were then used in a comparison of the valence of stereotypes of psychology students with each of the other groups. The stereotype of nursing students relative to the ingroup stereotype (psychology) was much more positive and less negative. The reverse was true for the comparison with economics students; here the ingroup stereotype contained a higher proportion of positive stereotypes and a lower proportion of negative items. We concluded that the positively evaluated outgroup (nursing) and the negatively evaluated outgroup (economics) were appropriate to use to manipulate stereotype valence of the outgroup.[4]

In the third study, we examined whether our participants trust outgroup more than ingroup allocators when the stereotype valence of the outgroup is more positive than that of the ingroup. If ingroup trust rests on positive stereotyping, then, in the event that outgroup members are seen to have more positive traits, there should be greater trust in the outgroup than in the ingroup. In our allocator choice paradigm, more recipients should

Table 1.1 Subjects Who Chose an Ingroup Allocator

Mutual Knowledge Condition (Study 3)		Unilateral Knowledge Condition (Study 4)	
Economics Allocator	Nursing Allocator	Economics Allocator	Nursing Allocator
.94 (15/16)	.80 (12/15)	.62 (10/16)	.57 (8/14)

Source: Authors' compilation.

therefore choose to put their fates in the hands of an allocator from another group when the stereotype of that group is relatively more positive, or contains more traits relevant to trustworthiness (such as kindness, helpfulness, fairness). This should hold true under conditions of mutual and nonmutual knowledge.

We offered a separate sample of psychology students at La Trobe University a choice between ingroup and outgroup allocators when the outgroup allocator was from either economics or nursing. Sixty-three participants were randomly assigned to the two outgroup conditions. Two participants were dropped from the study when their responses to validity checks showed that they had not understood the knowledge manipulation. The experiment was a 2 (identity of outgroup) X 2 (mutual knowledge, unilateral knowledge) factorial design. Participants were assigned randomly to knowledge and outgroup conditions.

Results of study 3 were consistent with those of studies 1 and 2 (see table 1.1). In the mutual knowledge condition, participants overwhelmingly preferred the ingroup allocator regardless of the valence of outgroup stereotype: 94 percent (fifteen of sixteen) when economics students were the outgroup, and 80 percent (twelve of fifteen) when nursing students were the outgroup. In the unilateral knowledge condition, however, their preference for the ingroup allocator was weak and nonsignificant: 62 percent (ten of sixteen) in the economics outgroup condition, and 57 percent (eight of

Table 1.2 Proportion of Endowment Psychology Participants Expected to Receive from Allocator, Regardless of Choice

	Mutual Knowledge		Unilateral Knowledge	
	Economics	Nursing	Economics	Nursing
Ingroup	.31 (.18)	.36 (.15)	.32 (.17)	.45 (.08)
Outgroup	.41 (.13)	.43 (.08)	.36 (.20)	.41 (.09)

Source: Authors' compilation.
Note: Standard deviations in parentheses.

fourteen) in the nursing outgroup condition. In a knowledge manipulation x valence of outgroup log-linear analysis of the preference for ingroup allocator, only the main effect of the knowledge manipulation was significant (x^2 (1) = 5.32, p = .021). Neither the main effect of the stereotype valence (x^2 (1) = 1.17, p = .280) nor the interaction of the two (x^2 (1) = .06, p = .442) was significant. Preference for ingroup allocator in the mutual knowledge condition was significantly greater than the 50 percent split: $x^2(1) = 17.06, p < .001$. In the unilateral knowledge condition, it was only slightly and nonsignificantly more than half (60 percent, or eighteen of thirty): $x^2(1, n = 30) = 1.20$, not significant. Consistent with the earlier studies, these results clearly indicate that preference for the ingroup allocator emerges only in the mutual knowledge condition. Valence of outgroup stereotype did not have a significant effect.

Recipients provided estimates of the amounts they would receive from the ingroup and outgroup allocator, regardless of choice (see table 1.2 for the average estimates). We calculated the difference in expectation from the ingroup and the outgroup allocator, and this difference—ingroup-bias in expectation—was analyzed with an ANOVA in which the independent factors were knowledge manipulation x outgroup identity. The result of this analysis was consistent with the result of preference for ingroup allocator. The only significant effect was for the knowledge manipulation: participants expected relatively more from the ingroup allocator when there was mutual knowledge of shared identity: F (1, 60) = 2.45, p =.01. There were no main effects for valence of the outgroup, and no interaction effect. The ingroup-bias in expectation was significantly greater than zero in the mutual knowledge condition: $t(30) = 3.84, p < .001$. It was not significantly different from zero in the unilateral knowledge condition: $t(29) = .01, p = .922$.

Do People Trust Ingroup Members When the Ingroup Stereotype Is Negative? All of our pilot studies, and the experimental studies, showed that the stereotype of economics students is more negative than that of psychology or nursing students, and, as it happens, worse than any group we tried (engineering and education students), and economics students agree with this negative stereotype in terms of trust (greedy, self-interested, uncaring, mathematical, rational, untrustworthy). We took a small sample of twenty-one economics students at La Trobe University. In the allocator choice study, students chose the ingroup over an outgroup (psychology) allocator 67 percent of the time (fourteen of twenty-one). Participants knew that the economics allocator knew the group membership of the recipient. We did not manipulate membership knowledge; that is, participants knew the group membership of other participants. Furthermore, the data show that economics students expected more favorable allocation from another economics student (an average of 30 percent of the endowment) than from a psychology student (25 percent) despite the less positive stereotype of economic students. The choice of the ingroup allocator, then, is certainly not based on the negative stereotype of the ingroup.

Do Allocators Trust Members of Their Own Group More than Members of Another Group? So far we have demonstrated that our participants trust members of their own group more than members of another group when, and only when, both the allocator and the recipient knew their group identities. These consistent findings let us reject the ingroup stereotype hypothesis—that people trust ingroup members more than outgroup members because they believe that the ingroup have morally superior qualities. Rather, the results support the group heuristic hypothesis—people trust ingroup members more because they believe that people generally treat ingroup members more favorably than outgroup members, that generalized exchange takes place in the group. Is this belief well founded? Do people in fact generally treat ingroup members more favorably even when no future interactions are expected? If so, does the commonality of membership knowledge matter, and why? Yamagishi and Mifune addressed these questions using a dictator game (2008).

In an effort to answer these questions, Yamagishi and Mifune extended the conception of group heuristic to a more general form. As mentioned earlier, people have a naïve theory of how groups operate, and one important feature of this theory is the belief that the group accommodates a system of generalized exchange. In a generalized exchange, no direct reciprocation of favors between particular partners takes place, and yet people who give out benefits to others receive benefits from someone in the system. Most generalized exchanges, except those formally organized in industrial societies such as blood banks, take place in naturally occurring groups. One important function of groups is that they serve as venues for generalized exchange or resource sharing (Kaplan and Hill 1985; Woodburn 1982; Yamagishi and Kiyonari 2000; Yamagishi et al. 2007).

The group heuristic is a set of beliefs and decision rules that people use, by default, when they face a group situation. It is ecologically rational (Gigerenzer 2000; Gigerenzer and Todd 1999) for those whose survival depends on resources provided by systems of generalized exchange. How critical generalized exchange is for human survival may be seen in the miserable situation that people face when they are denied access to resources provided through generalized exchange in the community. The group heuristic induces people to behave in such a way to minimize the risk of exclusion from a system of generalized exchange. Being nice to other members of a system of generalized exchange so as to avoid accumulating the reputation of a free rider (and eventually being ostracized from the system) is the basic principle for group living. To adapt to such group living, it is safe to assume that a system of generalized exchange exists when one faces a group situation. Erroneously assuming the absence of generalized exchange and behaving selfishly incurs a risk of bad reputation and eventual ostracism from the system. This risk should be minimized even at a cost of being cooperative or altruistic when no reputation is at stake. Assuming the existence of generalized exchange, by default, when facing a group situation, is thus an ecologically rational strategy for those whose livelihood depends so much on generalized exchange (for the logic of this error management, see Yamagishi, Jin, and Kiyonari 1999; Yamagishi et al. 2007).

According to the group heuristic as Yamagishi and Nobuhiro Mifune reformulated and elaborated it (2008), people facing a group situation assume, by default (that is, when no salient cue indicating otherwise is available), that social interactions that take place in the group involve generalized exchange, and thus they behave in a way to minimize the risk of developing a bad reputation among the members of their group. One important implication is cooperative and altruistic behavior toward members of the same group. According to this approach, such behavior is a kind of admission ticket to a generalized exchange system. Once admitted, people can enjoy the benefit of generalized exchange when they are in need. Those who do not pay for the ticket, that is, those who do not provide their resources to the system, will be denied access to the system. Even egoists, who surely want to enjoy the fruits of the system without paying the admission fee, will refrain from the free-riding attempt when the chances of detection for such cheating behavior are not negligible. The group heuristic is based on a default assumption of generalized exchange that does not require repeated interactions. Generalized exchange takes place even in a one-shot game, such as a one-shot social dilemma: when every member unilaterally decides whether to cooperate, each can share the benefits of other members' cooperation—a good example of generalized exchange. The group heuristic is not a conscious strategy based on calculation of future benefits of the current cooperation or defection.

Based on the reformulation of the group heuristic, Yamagishi and Mifune proposed that being altruistic to ingroup members is a default strategy to enhance good reputations and avoid receiving bad reputations among members of one's own group (2008). This default strategy applies both in the prisoner's dilemma game and the dictator game. A dictator game is played by two players, an allocator and a recipient. The allocator has total control of the division of a shared resource. Taking the lion's share of the resource, leaving the minimum to the recipient, will certainly be considered socially undesirable and earn one a bad reputation when such a behavior is observed by ingroup members who can identify the allocator as a member of their group. Being observed by people who cannot identify the allocator avoids the threat of a bad reputation. This logic led Yamagishi and Mifune to predict that allocators would provide ingroup recipients with a fairer share of the endowment than outgroup recipients only in the mutual knowledge condition. By contrast, threat to reputation does not exist in the unilateral knowledge condition in which the allocator cannot be identified by ingroup members as being one of them; group membership of the recipient was thus predicted not to affect the amount the allocator would give to the recipient.

The results of their experiment supported these predictions (Yamagishi and Mifune 2008). In it, 155 Japanese participants were assigned to one of two minimal groups based on their preferences for two painters, Paul Klee and Wassily Kandinsky. As predicted by both the group heuristic hypothesis and the ingroup stereotype hypothesis, participants in the common knowledge condition gave a fair allocation to an ingroup recipient more frequently than to an outgroup recipient, 65.8 percent versus 40.0 percent: $x^2(1) = 5.08$, $p = .024$. In contrast, participants in the unilateral knowledge condition gave a fair allocation to an ingroup recipient (47.5 percent) slightly less frequently than to an outgroup recipient (54.1 percent), though the difference was not statistically significant: $x^2(1) = .33$, $p = .566$. The latter finding is consistent with the group heuristic hypothesis, but not with the ingroup stereotype hypothesis.

The belief that people would treat members of their own group more fairly and altruistically than members of other groups, which presumably was behind participants' expectations in the first four studies, was thus shown to be founded on reality. Participants of Yamagishi and Mifune's study did in fact treat members of their own group more fairly when and only when the group membership of the allocator was known to the recipient (2008). When their group membership was not known, they did not.

A recent, unpublished study by Michael Platow and his colleagues places some closure on the reasoning behind the Yamagishi and Mifune results (2008). Using the allocator choice paradigm, Platow and his associates manipulated group membership first, as existing groups (for example, university major), and later, by arbitrary assignment to ad hoc groups (red group and blue group). Recipients could choose an allocation of $16 from an ingroup or an outgroup allocator. Ingroup and outgroup were operationalized as same or a different college major and then as same or different minimal group, that is, red or blue. These allocators had purportedly made a distribution to an ingroup or an outgroup recipient, while understanding that the recipient was either aware or not aware of their membership (unilateral and mutual knowledge conditions). A third-choice option, a sure-thing allocation of $6 was also offered. According to the generalized trust theory, recipients should trust ingroup allocators more than outgroup allocators, and prefer that ingroup allocator to the sure thing. Further, they should prefer an allocation from an ingroup allocator, but only under the common knowledge condition. If there is not common knowledge of group identity, the recipient cannot rely on the group-based expectations of higher shares of funds available, making the sure thing relatively more attractive.

The results of this study showed that participants did not overwhelmingly choose the sure-thing option. When there was mutual knowledge of shared group membership (existing categories or minimal groups), participants preferred to place their fates in the hands of a fellow group member. Although not predicted, choice of the sure thing was high only under unilateral knowledge conditions and when the groups were ad hoc social categories. Nevertheless, shared group memberships, even in ad hoc social categories, provided a significant basis for people to place their trust in others, particularly if these fellow ingroup members knew of the shared group membership as well.

Do People Reciprocate Ingroup Favors More Than Outgroup? The last question we address is whether the group heuristic concerns only generalized exchange or also includes direct exchange between two people. Margaret Foddy and Robyn Dawes provided an answer to this question when their participants reciprocated trust (or entrustment) from ingroup members more than from outgroup members (2007). Participants in this study played a variant of the investment game called the Berg game (Berg, Dickhaut, and McCabe 1995). Each player was given an endowment of $5. The sender decided how much of this to send to (entrust in) the recipient. The money sent was tripled by the experimenter and then given to the recipient. The recipient was instructed to decide how much of the total to return to the sender. At all points in the study, senders and receivers did not see one another, and were identified only by role (sender or receiver) and group membership (ingroup or outgroup).

The results showed that, on average, senders sent more to the ingroup recipient ($3.57) than to the outgroup recipient ($2.80). Recipients, in turn, reciprocated a greater proportion of what they received to the ingroup sender (41 percent) than to the outgroup sender (28 percent). Furthermore, a sender who initiated the exchange with a higher proportion of the endowment (showing higher entrustment) was rewarded with a higher proportion of the receivers' funds. This relationship between the amount sent and the amount returned existed when the recipient was an ingroup member, but not when an outgroup member. Foddy and Dawes thus demonstrated that their participants not only trust ingroup members more than outgroup members, but also reciprocate trust from ingroup members more than from outgroup members (2007).

The study, however, does not explain why recipients reciprocated trust from an ingroup member more than from an outgroup person, because it involved only the mutual knowledge condition (Foddy and Dawes 2007). Yutaka Horita and Yamagishi addressed the question by analyzing the behavior of a sequentially played prisoner's dilemma game (2007). In such a game, two players make their decisions in sequence. The first player makes a decision, which is relayed to the second player before he or she makes a decision. According to the group heuristic hypothesis in its original form, the second player's choice should not be affected by the group membership of the first player, given that the first player's choice is already known to the second player, and thus the second player does not need to expect that the first player's choice would be based on the group membership of the second player (Yamagishi, Jin, and Kiyonari 1999). On the other hand, the reformulated version of the group heuristic produces a different prediction (Yamagishi and Mifune 2008). This is because not reciprocating the goodwill of the first player is socially undesirable and thus a source of bad reputation. This argument led them to a hypothesis that such a behavior will be avoided only when the second player is identified by ingroup members as one of them—the same prediction applied to the allocator's behavior in the Yamagishi and Mifune study (2008).

The result of the Horita and Yamagishi study supported the prediction based on the revised version of the group heuristic hypothesis (2007). Their participants were eighty-nine Japanese students who had been assigned to one of two minimal groups based on their preferences for the two painters by the same method Yamagishi and Mifune used (2008). Participants were first informed that their partner fully cooperated (that is, gave all of his or her endowment of ¥600), and then decided how much of the endowment of ¥600 they would want to give their partner. The amount given by the player, either the first or the second, was doubled and given to the partner.

The second player cooperated more frequently with an ingroup partner than with an outgroup partner only in the mutual knowledge condition. In that circumstance, the second player gave an average of ¥543 to the ingroup first player, and an average of ¥336 to an outgroup partner. In contrast, the average amounts of money given to an ingroup partner and an outgroup partner in the unilateral knowledge condition were ¥493 and ¥470, respectively. The second player reciprocated more strongly when the first player was a member of the same group only when the responder knew that the truster regarded him or her as a member of the same group. The group heuristic is thus shown to apply to direct exchange as well as to generalized exchange.

Cultural Differences If the principles of trust in generalized exchange as outlined here are broadly applicable, one should expect the results described to be replicable in a wide range of groups and in many cultures. Details of the sorts of group that may activate group-based trust and the sorts of positive behaviors toward ingroup members may differ across cultures, but the more general principles of ingroup trust should remain constant. The work reported so far has not focused on comparing cultures, but some research is relevant. We note also that the studies we report were done in several countries, namely, Japan, Canada, and Australia.

Naoto Suzuki, Yuske Konno, and Yamagishi examined whether the group heuristic produces group-based trust in another Japanese culture (2007). They replicated the choice of allocator game used in studies 1 through 4 with minimal groups instead of schools or departments as groups and with eighty-one (fifty-two male and twenty-nine female) Japanese participants (first-year Hokkaido University students). They first divided their participants into one of two minimal groups based on their preferences for the paintings by Paul Klee and Wassily Kandinsky. They also manipulated the commonality of the group membership knowledge as in the studies reported earlier. In the mutual knowledge condition, three-quarters (78 percent, that is, thirty-one of forty) of the participants chose the ingroup allocator, whereas in the unilateral knowledge condition, only half (51 percent, that is, twenty-one of forty-one) did so. These findings are consistent with the others in this chapter.

Although the findings were almost perfectly replicated when minimal groups were used, they were not when university affiliations were used instead. In an unpublished study, Masafumi Matsuda and Yamagishi replicated the choice of allocator game (Suzuki, Konno, and Yamagishi 2007). They asked their participants—students of Hokkaido University—to choose an allocator either from students of their own school or from another (Tokyo University or Hokkaido University of Education, a between-participants factor). Matsuda and Yamagishi chose these two outgroups because Hokkaido University's prestige is lower than that of Tokyo University and higher than that of Hokkaido University of Education. Students at Hokkaido generally consider their counterparts at Tokyo University smart but self-absorbed and those at Hokkaido University of Education less smart but honest and caring. The results of this study showed, first, that the knowledge manipulation did not produce any effect, and, second, that their choice of the allocator was strongly affected by the stereotype of the school, not by the ingroup bias. That is, when the outgroup was Tokyo University, 61 percent of the participants chose the ingroup allocator. The proportion of the ingroup choice was not affected by the knowledge manipulation. When the outgroup was Hokkaido University of Education, 56 percent chose the outgroup allocator. Again, knowledge manipulation had no effect. The same pattern was observed in the amounts of money they expected from the ingroup and the outgroup allocators, specifically, more from Hokkaido University than Tokyo University and from Hokkaido University of Education than Hokkaido University, in both conditions.

The inconsistency is interesting. First, it suggests that the group heuristic has a strong effect when the groups are generic—the heuristic is about the generic nature of group-ness, that the group is the venue of generalized exchange through which members help each other. Second, the social category of university works as the generic group or the basis of the group heuristic in Australia, but not as much in Japan. It seems that the social category of university is inseparably intertwined with the substance of the group. This difference seems to reflect the difference in the nature of groupness in the East and the West, as Masaki Yuki and his colleagues discussed (2005)—groups in the West are argued to be category-based, and those in the East more relationship-based. How different types of groups work as the basis of the group heuristic and as the basis of stereotypes is an important topic for future study. Equally important are comparisons of group-based trust in different forms of group—minimal, categorical, existing interacting groups, and so on. To the extent that the frequency of occurrence of different types of groups differs across cultures, cultural differences, if they exist, may be explained in part by the distribution of group types, and, more broadly, by the prevailing concept of group, about which expectations of bounded reciprocity and trust may form.

Discussion

The aim of our research was to establish, first, whether shared category membership provides a basis for trust and, second, to explore two possible mechanisms for such trust. The results showed higher trust in members of the ingroup than of the outgroup. This preference was equally strong whether the relevant category was university affiliation, or course of enrollment at university, or minimal groups. The results point to expectations of ingroup favoring behavior as the key to group-based trust, rather than more positive ingroup stereotypes and evaluations. Two separate but converging outcomes led us to this conclusion.

First, preference for the ingroup allocator was high under mutual knowledge conditions, regardless of whether the stereotype of the ingroup was relatively more positive or negative than that of the outgroup. Even when it was negative (economics student participants), the majority of recipients preferred the ingroup allocator. Predicted share of the allocators' money showed that recipients expected better treatment from a stranger from their own group even when stereotype of the ingroup was less positive than that of the outgroup.

Second, when the allocator did not have knowledge of the shared group membership, expectations of ingroup favoring behavior were blocked—the allocator could not act on the basis of information she or he did not have. In this situation, we argue, recipients needed to form expectations on the basis of other information. There are at least two related possibilities. Recipients could take into consideration the traits most associated with the stereotypes of both the ingroup and outgroup as a basis for predicting what the allocator would do. Participants did not seem to use stereotypes as a basis of their trust, or used it only very slightly if at all, even when they trusted ingroup more than outgroup allocators.

It is important that the expectation of reasonable treatment from both allocator-strangers in all studies was high. There was little evidence that participants endorsed the rational choice prediction that neither allocator would give them anything. Rather, recipients seemed confident in their use of both the group heuristic and, when it was blocked, their knowledge of group stereotypes to inform their decisions. As an extension of our arguments about the importance of a group heuristic, we predict a range of naïve theories of group behavior, including an expectation that outgroup members will treat each other fairly, cooperatively, and so on. Such a belief may coexist with generally more negative stereotypes known to be held about outgroups (Yamagishi and Kiyonari 2000). Another implication is that the relationship between individuals, such as common group membership, is important in interpreting information used to establish trust and trustworthiness, such as knowledge of the pattern of a person's past behavior toward others, or reputation. That a person has been fair in the past is no guarantee of fairness to oneself, but may depend on whether the target of the fairness was a member of the same group.

Our theoretical position and empirical results add to the growing consensus that some form of group heuristic has ecological rationality (Brewer 1999; Gigerenzer and Todd 1999). The person who has internalized the group heuristic is more likely to gain from the risky but potentially beneficial relationships with strangers, but has to forgo the chance of a free ride by showing trust, initiating cooperation, and being vulnerable. The person who does not adopt the group heuristic will avoid these potentially positive relationships in fear of exploitation. To the extent that conditions within the boundaries of the group include reciprocity and benevolence to fellow group members, the person embracing the group heuristic will be advantaged. Marilynn Brewer suggested, in a similar evolutionary vein, that "contingent altruism" within the bounds of a group provides a mechanism to deliver the benefits of cooperative interdependence while avoiding the costs of indiscriminate trust (1999, 43).

The basis for group-based trust, whatever it is, has important implications for selective interaction and intergroup relations. If the boundaries of group inclusiveness are broad, trust in strangers from the group can produce generalized trust and cooperative relations (Yamagishi and Yamagishi 1994; Brewer 2003; Foddy and Dawes 2007). However, trust limited to narrower boundaries can lead to selective exclusion as well as inclusion, and related resentment and distrust between members of different groups.

Finally, group-based trust has both positive and negative consequences. We have focused on the positive aspects: group-based trust in strangers facilitates the formation of new relationships, probably signals trust and positive evaluations by the trustee, and is usually well founded. Trust between groups, though, may as a result be difficult to generate. Selective preference for ingroup members, however slight, may appear as rejection and exclusion to members of the outgroup. Successful interactions with ingroup members increases the probability that they will continue, at the expense of others. Such a bias can then aggregate, creating resentment and hostility (Foddy 1989).

The two Yamagishi studies—demonstrating that people reveal more altruism and reciprocity toward members of their own group, even when the group is purely categorical and thus devoid of social interaction, than toward members of another group—are evidence that group heuristic applies even when expectations of ingroup favoring behavior are irrelevant (Yamagishi and Mifune 2008; Horita and Yamagishi 2007). Based on these findings, Yamagishi and his colleagues argued that expectation-based generalized reciprocity is only one application of a more general form of group heuristic, which they define as a set of default strategies designed to adapt to group life. Groups are indispensable as a way to recruit resources for survival and reproduction. This fundamental fact has been overlooked in recent studies of groups in social psychology.

Notes

1. Students, twelve male and twenty-six female, were asked to list their impressions of students from the two universities in a free response format, and to indicate whether the items listed were positive, neutral, or negative. The most frequent positive items for the ingroup (La Trobe) were easygoing, smart, sociable, and diverse; the most frequent negative items were lazy, party animals, irresponsible, and poor. For the outgroup (Melbourne), the most frequent positive items were smart-intelligent, serious-responsible, rich, and successful; the negative stereotype centered around snobby, conservative, and nerdy. The overall valence of the ingroup (La Trobe) stereotype was somewhat higher than for the outgroup, but the content of the stereotypes did not seem to differentiate the groups in terms of trustworthiness.
2. Participants were recruited from the first-year psychology volunteer pool, and from a pool of volunteers from a wide range of courses across the university. Comparisons of the psychology students and the nonpsychology volunteers on all the dependent measures showed no significant differences and so their results were combined.
3. Participants were offered a written description of the rationale and results from the study once all the data were collected. Those who chose this option provided their contact details on a separate sheet of paper.
4. For space reasons, we do not present the results of an ANOVA on these data. There was good separation of the mean proportions of positive and negative stereotypes of the relevant outgroups (nursing and economics), and the mean

proportions of positive and negative stereotypes of engineers did not differ from those for the ingroup (psychology).

References

Berg, Joyce, John Dickhaut, and Kevin McCabe. 1995. "Trust, Reciprocity, and Social History." *Games and Economic Behavior* 10(1): 122–42.

Boldizar, Janet P., and David M. Messick. 1988. "Intergroup Fairness Biases: Is Ours the Fairer Sex?" *Social Justice Research* 2(2): 95–111.

Bourhis, Richard Y., John C. Turner, and Andre Gagnon. 1997. "Interdependence, Social Identity and Discrimination." In *The Social Psychology of Stereotyping and Group Life,* edited by Russell Spears, Naomi Ellemers, Penelope J. Oakes, and S. Alexander Haslam. Oxford: Blackwell Publishing.

Braithwaite, Valerie, and Margaret Levi, eds. 1998. *Trust and Governance.* New York: Russell Sage Foundation.

Brann, Peter, and Margaret Foddy. 1987. "Trust and the Consumption of a Deteriorating Common Resource." *Journal of Conflict Resolution* 31(4): 615–30.

Brewer, Marilynn B. 1981. "Ethnocentrism and Its Role in Interpersonal Trust." In *Scientific Inquiry and the Social Sciences,* edited by Marilynn B. Brewer and Barry E. Collins. San Francisco: Jossey-Bass.

———. 1999. "The Psychology of Prejudice: In-Group Love or Out-Group Hate." *Journal of Social Issues* 55(3): 429–44.

———. 2003. *Intergroup Relations,* 2nd ed. Buckingham, U.K.: Oxford University Press.

Brewer, Marilynn B., and Roderick M. Kramer. 1986. "Choice Behavior in Social Dilemmas: Effects of Social Identity, Group Size, and Decision Framing." *Journal of Personality and Social Psychology* 50(3): 543–49.

Buchan, Nancy R., Rachel T. A. Croson, and Robyn M. Dawes. 2002. "Swift Neighbors and Persistent Strangers: A Cross-Cultural Investigation of Trust and Reciprocation in Social Exchange." *American Journal of Sociology* 108(1): 168–206.

Buskens, Vincent, and Werner Raub. 2002. "Embedded Trust: Control and Learning." In *Advances in Group Processes,* vol. 19, *Group Cohesion, Trust, and Solidarity,* edited by Shane R. Thye and Edward J. Lawler. Oxford: Elsevier.

Cook, Karen S., ed. 2001. *Trust in Society.* New York: Russell Sage Foundation.

Cook, Karen S., Toshio Yamagishi, Coye Cheshire, Robin Cooper, Masafumi Matsuda, and Rie Mashima. 2005. "Trust Building via Risk Taking: A Cross-Societal Experiment." *Social Psychology Quarterly* 68(2): 121–42.

Dasgupta, Partha. 1988. "Trust as a Commodity." In *Trust: Making or Braking Cooperative Relations,* edited by Diego Gambetta. Oxford: Blackwell Publishing.

Doosje, Bertjan, Nvla R. Branscombe, Russell Spears, and Antony S. R. Manstead. 1998. "Guilty by Association: When One's Group Has a Negative History." *Journal of Personality and Social Psychology* 75(4): 872–86.

Foddy, Margaret. 1989. "Information Control as a Bargaining Tactic in Social Exchange." In *Advances in Group Processes,* vol. 6, edited by Edward J. Lawler, Barry Markovsky, and Karen Heimer. Greenwich, Conn.: JAI Press.

Foddy, Margaret, and Robyn D. Dawes. 2007. "Group-Based Trust in Social Dilemmas." In *New Issues and Paradigms in Research on Social Dilemmas,* edited

by Anders Biel, Daniel Eek, Tommy Gaqrling, and Mathias Gustafson. New York: Springer.
Foddy, Margaret, and Michael Hogg. 1999. "Impact of Leaders on Resource Consumption in Social Dilemmas: The Intergroup Context." In *Resolving Social Dilemmas,* edited by Margaret Foddy, Michael Smithson, Sherry Schneider, and Michael Hogg. Philadelphia, Pa.: Psychology Press.
Foddy, Margaret, Michael J. Platow, and Toshio Yamagishi. 2009. "Group-Based Trust in Strangers: The Role of Stereotypes and Expectations." *Psychological Science* 20(4): 419–22.
Fukuyama, Francis. 1995. *Trust: The Social Virtues and the Creation of Prosperity.* New York: Free Press.
Gaertner, Lowell, and Chester A. Insko. 2000. "Intergroup Discrimination in the Minimal Group Paradigm: Categorization, Reciprocation, or Fear?" *Journal of Personality and Social Psychology* 79(1): 77–94.
Gambetta, Diego, ed. 1988. *Trust: Making and Breaking Cooperative Relations.* Oxford: Blackwell Publishing.
Gigerenzer, Gerd. 2000. *Adaptive Thinking: Rationality in the Real World.* Oxford: Oxford University Press.
Gigerenzer, Gerd, and Peter M. Todd. 1999. "Fast and Frugal Heuristics: The Adaptive Toolbox." In *Simple Heuristics That Make Us Smart,* edited by Gerd Gigerenzer, Peter M. Todd, and the ABC Research Group. Oxford: Oxford University Press.
Hardin, Russell. 2001. "Conceptions and Explanations of Trust." In *Trust in Society,* edited by Karen S. Cook. New York: Russell Sage Foundation.
Hogg, Michael A., and Dominic Abrams. 1988. *Social Identifications: A Social Psychology of Intergroup Relations and Group Processes.* London: Routledge.
Hollis, Martin. 1998. *Trust Within Reason.* Cambridge: Cambridge University Press.
Horita, Yutaka, and Toshio Yamagishi. 2007. "The Effect of Group Membership on Direct Reciprocity." *CEFOM/21* working paper 70 (in Japanese). Hokkaido: Hokkaido University.
Jetten, Jolanda, Russell Spears, and Antony S. R. Manstead. 1996. "Intergroup Norms and Intergroup Discrimination: Distinctive Self-Categorization and Social Identity Effects." *Journal of Personality and Social Psychology* 71(6): 1222–33.
Kaplan, Hillard, and Kim Hill. 1985. "Food Sharing Among Ache Foragers: Tests of Explanatory Hypotheses." *Current Anthropology* 26(2): 223–46.
Kiyonari, Toko. 2002. "Expectations of a Generalized Exchange System and Ingroup Favoritism: An Experimental Study of Bounded Reciprocity." *Japanese Journal of Psychology* 73(1): 1–9.
Kiyonari, Toko, and Toshio Yamagishi. 1999. "A Comparative Study of Trust and Trustworthiness Using the Game of Enthronement."*Japanese Journal of Social Psychology* 15(2): 100–9.
Kiyonari, Toko, Margaret Foddy, and Toshio Yamagishi. 2007. "Effects of Direct and Indirect Exchange on Trust of In-Group Members" (in Japanese). *Japanese Journal of Psychology* 77(6): 519–27.
Knight, Jack. 2001. "Social Norms and the Rule of Law: Fostering Trust in a Socially Diverse Society." In *Trust in Society,* edited by Karen S. Cook. New York: Russell Sage Foundation.

Kollock, Peter. 1997. "Transforming Social Dilemmas: Group Identity and Cooperation." In *Modeling Rational and Moral Agents,* edited by Peter Danielson. Oxford: Oxford University Press.

Kramer, Roderick M. 1999. "Trust and Distrust in Organizations." *Annual Review of Psychology* 50(1999): 569–98.

Kramer, Roderick M., and Tom R. Tyler, eds. 1996. *Trust in Organizations: Frontiers of Theory and Research.* Thousand Oaks, Calif.: Sage Publications.

McAllister, Daniel J. 1995. "Affect- and Cognition-Based Trust as Foundations for Interpersonal Cooperation in Organizations." *Academy of Management Journal* 38(1): 24–59.

McKenna, Katelyn Y. A., and John A. Bargh. 2000. "Plan 9 from Cyberspace: The Implications of the Internet for Personality and Social Psychology." *Personality and Social Psychology Review* 4(1): 57–75.

Mlicki, Pawel P., and Naomi Ellemers. 1996. "Being Different or Being Better? National Stereotypes and Identifications of Polish and Dutch Students." *European Journal of Social Psychology* 26(1): 97–114.

Moy, Jonathan, and Sik Hung Ng. 1996. "Expectation of Outgroup Behaviour: Can You Trust the Outgroup?" *European Journal of Social Psychology* 26(2): 333–40.

Nowak, Martin A., and Karl Sigmund. 1998. "Evolution of Indirect Reciprocity by Image Scoring." *Nature* 393(June): 573–77.

Ostrom, Elinor. 1998. "A Behavioral Approach to the Rational Choice Theory of Collective Action." *American Political Science Review* 92(1): 1–22.

Paris, W. Doise, G. Csepeli Budapest, H. D. Dann Konstanz, C. Gouge Bristol, K. Larsen Oregon, A. Ostell Stirling. 1972. "An Experimental Investigation into the Formation of Intergroup Representations." *European Journal of Social Psychology* 2(2): 202–4.

Platow, Michael J., Charles G. McClintock, and Wim B. G. Liebrand. 1990. "Predicting Intergroup Fairness and Ingroup Bias in the Minimal Group Paradigm." *European Journal of Social Psychology* 20(3): 221–39.

Platow, Michael J., Aaron O'Connell, Roger Shave, and Peter Hanning. 1995. "Social Evaluations of Fair and Unfair Allocators in Interpersonal and Intergroup Situations." *British Journal of Social Psychology* 34(4): 363–81.

Platow, Michael J., Margaret Foddy, Toshio Yamagishi, L. Lim, and A. Krebeck. 2009. "Human Trust in the Absence of Known Reciprocity and Kin Relations." Unpublished manuscript.

Platow, Michael J., Stephanie Hoar, Scott Reid, Keryn Harley, and Dianne Morrison. 1997. "Endorsement of Distributively Fair and Unfair Leaders in Interpersonal and Intergroup Situations." *European Journal of Social Psychology* 27(4): 465–94.

Riegelsberger, Jens, M. Angela Sasse, and John D. McCarthy. 2003. "Shiny Happy People Building Trust? Photos on E-Commerce Websites and Consumer Trust." In *Proceedings of the SIGCHI Conference on Human Factors in Computing Systems,* chaired by Panu Korhonen, 121–28. New York: ACM.

Smith, Marc A., and Peter Kollock, eds. 1999. *Communities in Cyberspace.* London: Routledge.

Suzuki, Naoto, Yuske Konno, and Toshio Yamagishi. 2007. "In-Group Bias in Trusting Behavior: A Choice of Allocator Experiment with Minimal Groups" (in Japanese). *Japanese Journal of Psychology* 78(1): 17–24.

Tajfel, Henri. 1970. "Experiments in Intergroup Discrimination." *Scientific American* 223(November): 96–102.

Tajfel, Henri, M. G. Billig, R. P. Bundy, and Claude Flament. 1971. "Social Categorization in Intergroup Behaviour." *European Journal of Social Psychology* 1(2): 149–78.

Thibaut, John W., and Harold H. Kelley. 1959. *The Social Psychology of Groups.* New York: John Wiley and Sons.

Turner, John C., Michael A. Hogg, Penelope J. Oakes, Stephen D. Reicher, and Margaret S. Wetherell. 1987. *Rediscovering the Social Group: A Self-Categorization Theory.* Oxford: Blackwell Publishing.

Tyler, Tom R. 2001. "Why Do People Rely on Others? Social Identity and the Social Aspects of Trust." In *Trust in Society,* edited by Karen S. Cook. New York: Russell Sage Foundation.

Tyler, Tom R., and Yuen J. Huo. 2002. *Trust in the Law: Encouraging Public Cooperation with the Police and Court.* New York: Russell Sage Foundation.

Wit, Arjaan P., and Henk A. M. Wilke. 1992. "The Effect of Social Categorization on Cooperation in Three Types of Social Dilemmas." *Journal of Economic Psychology* 13(1): 135–51.

Woodburn, James. 1982. "Egalitarian Societies." *Man* 17(3): 431–51.

Yamagishi, Toshio, and Toko Kiyonari. 2000. "The Group as the Container of Generalized Reciprocity." *Social Psychology Quarterly* 63(2): 116–32.

Yamagishi, Toshio, and Nobuhiro Mifune. 2008. "Does Shared Group Membership Promote Altruism? Fear, Greed and Reputation." *Rationality and Society* 20(1): 5–30.

Yamagishi, Toshio, and Midori Yamagishi. 1994. "Trust and Commitment in the United States and Japan." *Motivation and Emotion* 18(2): 129–66.

Yamagishi, Toshio, Nobuhito Jin, and Toko Kiyonari. 1999. "Bounded Generalized Reciprocity: In-Group Boasting and In-Group Favoritism." In *Advances in Group Processes,* vol. 16, edited by Edward J. Lawler, Michael W. Macy, and Shane R. Thye. Greenwich, Conn.: JAI Press.

Yamagishi, Toshio, Sigeru Terai, Toko Kiyonari, Nobuhiro Mifune, and Satoshi Kanazawa. 2007. "The Social Exchange Heuristic: Managing Errors in Social Exchange." *Rationality and Society* 19(3): 259–91.

Yuki, Masaki, William W. Maddux, Marilyn B. Brewer, and Kosuke Takemura. 2005. "Cross-Cultural Differences in Relationship- and Group-Based Trust." *Personality and Social Psychology Bulletin* 31(1): 48–62.

Chapter 2

Coethnicity and Trust

James Habyarimana, Macartan Humphreys, Daniel N. Posner, and Jeremy M. Weinstein

Scholarship on trust emphasizes the beliefs individuals hold about actions that others will take.[1] In such accounts, trust is a belief that the other person will take an action in one's own interest, perhaps in response to a trusting action. It is a belief that the other is trustworthy. But where do these beliefs come from? Why are some people trusted in this way and others not?

We examine one of the many answers that have been offered to this question: people are more likely to trust someone from the same ethnic group. This assumption can be found throughout the literature on ethnicity (see Brewer 1981; Cohen 1969; Fearon and Laitin 1996; Landa 1994; Macharia 1988), and finds empirical support in both experimental studies (see Fershtman and Gneezy 2001; Burns 2003; Petrie 2003; Barr 2004; Karlan 2005; chapter 1, this volume) and survey findings.[2] For example, the Afrobarometer survey project includes a standard question in which respondents are asked how much they trust others, including "people from your ethnic group" and "people from other ethnic groups." While 50.6 percent of respondents indicate that they trust coethnics "somewhat" or "a lot," only 38.3 percent say the same of noncoethnics.[3] This chapter probes the sources of this connection between coethnicity and greater perceived trustworthiness. The goal is not to document that people are more likely to perceive coethnics as more worthy of trust—we follow the literature cited in assuming this is the case—but to contribute to an understanding of why this is so.

We examine three possible explanations.[4] The first is the *other-regarding preferences rationale,* in which trust stems from the belief that the trustee cares about the truster. The second is the *incentives rationale,* in which trust derives from the belief that the trustee is motivated to act in the interests of the truster. The third is the *competence rationale,* in which trust stems from the belief that the trustee is capable of acting in the interests of the truster. Each rationale provides a different answer to the question of why a person might believe that a coethnic is more trustworthy than a noncoethnic.

A major impediment to figuring out which of these rationales best accounts for the greater expectations of trustworthiness among coethnics is that, though theoretically distinct, the three mechanisms are often observationally equivalent. If we ascertain, through a survey, for example, that a respondent believes that a coethnic is more trustworthy than a noncoethnic, is it because she believes the coethnic cares more about her than the noncoethnic does? Or is it because she simply thinks that the coethnic has stronger incentives, or is better able, to take an action in her interest? It is impossible to know based solely on reported levels of trust.

Our approach to this inferential problem is to use a series of experiments designed to test each of the rationales independently of one another. Specifically, we compare patterns of play among coethnics and noncoethnics across different experimental games, each designed to isolate a single rationale. When coethnics and noncoethnics play differently in a particular game, we interpret it as evidence for the salience of the rationale that the game was designed to capture. In the case of some games, we extract direct statements about beliefs. In others, we infer beliefs from behavior under the assumption that players' beliefs are consistent, on average, with how others behave.

Although this chapter deals with the general question of why people believe coethnics to be more trustworthy, our empirical analysis is grounded in a specific multiethnic setting—that of the urban neighborhoods of Mulago and Kyebando in Kampala, Uganda.[5] Uganda is a good place to study why ethnicity affects beliefs about trustworthiness. The Afrobarometer findings cited earlier regarding levels of trust for coethnics and noncoethnics suggest a trust gap between in-group and out-group interactions in Africa of about 12 percentage points. In Uganda, the gap is nearly double that size. Whereas 60.9 percent of Ugandans in the round 3 survey reported trusting people from their own ethnic group "somewhat" or "a lot," just 39.4 percent reported equal levels of trust for people from other ethnic communities.[6]

The particular neighborhoods in Uganda we study offer a good laboratory for examining interethnic interactions and the beliefs that shape them. Mulago-Kyebando has been the site of heavy in-migration over the past two decades, driven in part by strong ties to sending areas and the availability of cheap accommodation (and even land) in the area. In a pre-survey of 594 randomly selected individuals in Kawempe, the broader division of the city in which Mulago-Kyebando is located, more than 50 percent of respondents reported that they had lived in their current neighborhood less than five years. Nearly 80 percent described their community as composed largely of people born outside of Kampala who had moved to the capital. The consequence of this steady stream of migrants has been a dramatic increase in the level of ethnic heterogeneity. Whereas Mulago-Kyebando were once dominated demographically by the Baganda, the largest ethnic group in Uganda and the group whose historical kingdom is centered in Kampala, Baganda now comprise only a little more than 50 percent of the local population. The ethnic fractionalization value for Uganda as a whole is approximately 0.9, though the figure for Mulago-Kyebando is somewhat lower given the still dominant place of the Baganda.[7]

Ethnic differences in Mulago-Kyebando are not only present but also highly salient in everyday social interactions. Many ethnic groups have formed homogeneous associations for accumulating savings, providing access to credit, and meeting other practical needs. In focus groups and interviews with local council leaders, participants frequently used ethnic or regional labels to refer to factions within the community: "the Bafumbira do this," we would commonly be told, and "people from the Northeast do that." Failures of community-level collective action were often explained in terms of the inability of members of different ethnic groups to work together. Although Mulago-Kyebando's extreme ethnic heterogeneity has never led to intergroup violence, it is nevertheless a central feature of daily life. This is important insofar as it permits us to rule out the possibility that the nonfindings we report stem from the lack of salience of ethnic divisions per se within the community.

Our empirical strategy rests on a sequential examination of game play between coethnics and noncoethnics. In the sections that follow, we examine evidence for each of the three rationales described above. First we investigate whether other-regarding preferences are, in fact, structured along ethnic lines. Our strategy is to use a dictator game with an anonymous offerer to examine whether individuals take account of the welfare of in-group members more than out-group members. Such behavior would provide a basis for a belief that coethnics are more likely to have one's interests at heart. Next, we explore whether individuals are incentivized to act in the interests of coethnics. We first draw on survey data to examine whether preferences over outcomes are aligned in ways that would provide a basis to expect that coethnics have incentives to support initiatives consistent with one's own interests. Then we use the results of a dictator game with a *non*-anonymous offerer to examine whether the prospect of social sanctions affects the actions of offerers or the beliefs of receivers about those offers. The final section addresses the third rationale: that individuals have greater trust in the capacity of coethnics to solve problems with them. We explore this possibility by examining the choices players make about partners in a new game, which we call the "lockbox game," that is designed to incentivize players to accomplish a joint task. By examining partner selection in this game, we can gain insight into subjects' beliefs about the competence of different potential partners.

Experimental Framework

We took a set of experimental games, typically played in laboratory environments, to the field in Kampala, Uganda.[8] We began by randomly sampling 300 individuals from Mulago-Kyebando.[9] Like the underlying population from which they were recruited, our subjects were extremely diverse. Forty-four percent were Baganda, with declining shares of Banyankole (9 percent), Bafumbira (7 percent), Batoro, Banyarwanda, Bakiga (roughly 5 percent each), and other groups. They were also largely uneducated: 23 percent had not completed primary school, and more than 70 percent had completed at most only some secondary school. Just 17 percent reported holding formal sector jobs; roughly half were either unemployed or working in the informal sector. Fewer than 30 percent owned their dwelling. Thirty-six percent reported not having electricity and 87 percent reported not having piped water in their homes. Ownership of assets such as refrigerators (28 percent), electric irons (53 percent), televisions (51 percent), bicycles (13 percent), and cars or trucks (10 percent) was also very low. Our subjects were also overwhelmingly migrants or children of migrants: just 22 percent reported having been born in Kampala.

Before playing the experimental games, we recorded a series of five digital images of each subject (a headshot and four brief video clips) each providing a different level of information that an observer might use to ascertain the subject's ethnic background. In the analyses presented here, we treat all five levels of information equally and distinguish only between situations in which players have no information about the identities of their partners and situations for which they have some information.

Public Information Box and General Set-Up

All but one of the games we describe were played using a computer interface.[10] Players could make inferences about the ethnic backgrounds of the other players from pictures or video clips made available to them in what we call the public information box (PIB). The key attribute of the PIB is that, as its name suggests, the information provided about the players in the game was provided publicly. Before each round of each game, all the players in the round were shown the same PIB containing images of all of the players in that round—including themselves—with the images of the players ordered in the same way. Underneath the PIB, each player

Figure 2.1 Public Information Box with Nonanonymous Offerer

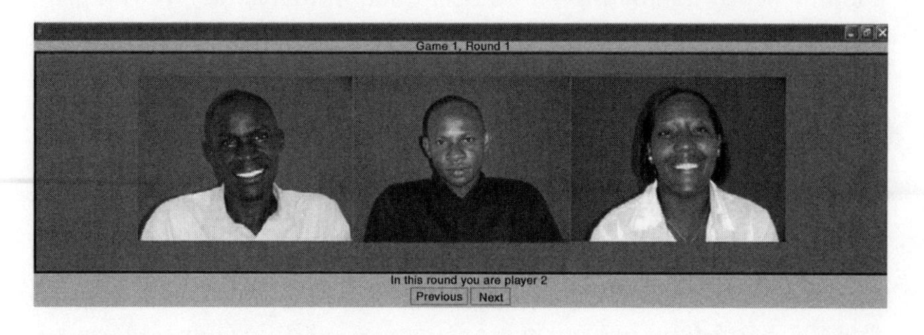

Source: Author-provided screenshots.
Notes: Player 2, the offerer, is "seen" by all players. Images are for illustration purposes only and are not the images of actual subjects.

saw a note indicating which player number he or she was for that round. Figure 2.1 presents a sample screenshot of a PIB.

Beyond providing the information that players could use to ascertain the ethnicity of the other players, described in more detail in the next section, the PIB played three roles in the computer-based experiments. First, it made the interaction more realistic by increasing the credibility of the existence of the other players (Bohnet and Frey 1999; Eckel and Wilson 2006). Second, it provided common information: each player was provided not just with information about who the other players were but also about what the other players knew about them, and that the other players knew what they knew about the others, and so on. Third, its design allowed us to manipulate the anonymity of the players in the game. Compare, for example, figures 2.1 and 2.2. In figure 2.1, the middle player's picture is shown to the other players. That player will therefore play the game knowing that the other players can see who he is. In figure 2.2, however, the middle player's picture is not shown. He still has information about the other players and knows that they have no information about him. He will therefore play the game knowing that he is doing so anonymously. Exploiting this manipulation turns out to be extremely valuable for distinguishing behavior motivated by other-regarding preferences from behavior motivated by incentives.

Although subjects were shown images of the other players in the game, the games were designed to study interactions among strangers. Therefore, after viewing the PIB, subjects were asked to report whether they knew either of the other players whose images they had just been shown. About 6 percent of all rounds involved subjects who said they knew one or more of the other players. All results reported in this chapter are robust to the exclusion of such rounds. Each subject played all of the games multiple

Figure 2.2 Public Information Box with Anonymous Offerer

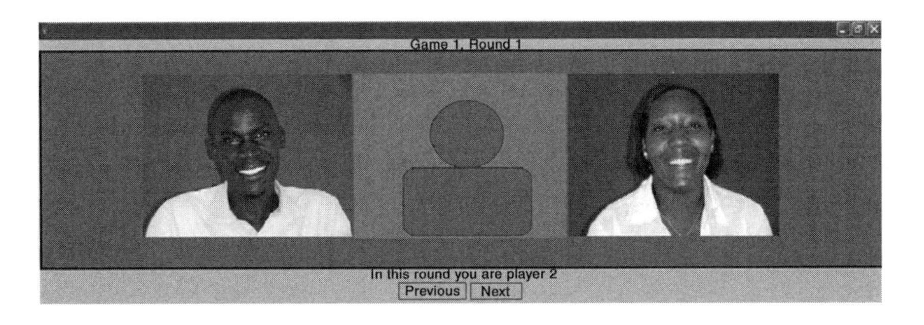

Source: Author-provided screenshots.
Notes: Player 2, the offerer, is anonymous. Images are for illustration purposes only and are not the images of our subjects.

times but, as they were informed, never more than once with any other player. Furthermore, although they played multiple times, with different partners, players were not given feedback about play until they had completed all games. This limited learning as well as the players' ability to use repeated interaction to establish coordination procedures, norms, or different forms of other-regarding preferences within the context of the game (Crawford and Haller 1990).

Coding Coethnicity

The empirical strategy we adopt in this chapter depends on our ability to distinguish interactions among coethnics from interactions among noncoethnics.[11] A simple rule—analogous to the practice employed in most studies of cross-race, -gender, and -ethnic interactions in the experimental literature—is to code as coethnics any pair of players that identified themselves as belonging to the same ethnic category in our pre-experiment questionnaire. Using this rule, we generate what we term a benchmark measure of coethnicity. However, this measure runs into the problem that the way a person self-identifies may not correspond with the way he or she is perceived. Thus, if two subjects who identified themselves in the pre-experiment questionnaire as members of group X were paired in a game, then, under the benchmark measure, the pairing would be coded as coethnic. But if each subject believed that the other was not really a member of group X (whether because of imperfect information or different notions of group boundaries), they would each behave as if they were playing with a noncoethnic, and our inferences about the impact of shared ethnicity on their actions would be wrong.

To overcome this problem, we used a relatively straightforward exercise to generate a subjective measure of coethnicity based on how our subjects perceived the ethnic backgrounds of the players with whom they were interacting. After all the games had been played, and the danger of priming subjects to ethnicity had passed, we showed our subjects a series of images of other subjects (in most cases players they had been randomly matched with earlier) and invited them to guess their ethnic identities. To motivate the guessers, correct guesses (corresponding to how the person had self-identified in the pre-experiment questionnaire) were rewarded with a small payment. To ensure that everyone had the same prior beliefs about the distribution of ethnic groups in the sample of images, we told the subjects that the ethnic demography of the sample population matched that of Mulago-Kyebando, and we read aloud a breakdown of shares of the major ethnic groups in Mulago-Kyebando based on 2001 census figures.

To generate estimates of subjective coethnicity, we collected data on a total of 15,265 guesses by 274 subjects. Overall, we found that individuals were able to correctly identify the ethnic backgrounds of others only about 50 percent of the time—a result that underscores the inferential problem we would have faced had we limited ourselves to the benchmark measure. We used the results of the identification exercise to generate, for every information level, an estimate of the likelihood that an individual of group A believes that an individual of group B is a coethnic for each possible information level.[12] The resulting measure (ranging from 0 to 1) provides a measure of subjective coethnicity. For all games that use the PIB, we report results using both the benchmark and the subjective measures of coethnicity.

We also parse the results in yet another way to reflect the fact that in Uganda, as elsewhere, ethnic categorization may operate at multiple levels (Mozaffar, Scarritt, and Galaich 2003; Posner 2005) and that we, the researchers, do not know ex ante what the salient dimension of cultural cleavage may be for a given interaction. To deal with this issue, we present the results of all games in terms of coethnicity defined by shared ethnic group membership and by an additional, broader notion of coethnicity based on the region of origin of these ethnic groups, that is, central, east, north, and west.

Other-Regarding Preferences Rationale

The first rationale we explore is other-regarding preferences. High levels of other-regarding preferences may produce expectations of trustworthiness by making a potential truster believe that the trustee has the truster's interests at heart. If other-regarding preferences are stronger (or believed to be so) between coethnics than between noncoethnics, then this could provide a basis for beliefs about the greater trustworthiness of coethnics.[13]

To test whether such a basis exists, we had subjects play a version of the standard dictator game in which the offerer is anonymous and the receivers' identities are known (Kahneman, Knetsch, and Thaler 1986). We then attribute observed difference in patterns of play between situations in which the offerer and receiver are coethnics and in which they are not to differential levels of altruism toward ingroup and outgroup members. Because our focus is on detecting ethnic discrimination, the dictator game our subjects played differs from more commonly used versions in two ways. First, we play in trios rather than in pairs. This permits us to evaluate situations where offerers must decide between allocating a sum to a coethnic and a noncoethnic. Second, the sum to be allocated is "lumpy." Instead of being given a continuous endowment to divide among the players, offerers were given two coins and told that no player (including themselves) was permitted to receive more than one coin. This forced the offerer to discriminate between the two receivers, or, if the offerer chose to give away both coins, against him or herself. Hence we refer to this as the discrimination game.[14]

Each round began with subjects, who in this game only play the role of offerer, seated in front of a laptop computer. The screen showed a PIB containing images of the two other players (the receivers) and a dummy for the subject, as in figure 2.2. In front of the computer were three ballot boxes, each directly below one of the pictures in the PIB. Subjects were given two 500-USh coins (about US$0.60, approximately the per capita daily income in Uganda) and asked to divide this sum as described. Subjects were told to put the amount they wanted to keep directly into their pockets and to put the amounts they wanted to allocate to each of the other players into envelopes and deposit them in the ballot boxes below the players' pictures. Subjects were told that the envelopes would be delivered to their intended recipients at a later date, which they were. An enumerator manipulated the computer to show the PIB for the given round and handed the subject the money, but then stepped away and waited behind a screen while the subject completed his or her allocation. When the subject was finished making the allocation, he or she signaled the enumerator, who returned from behind the screen and set up play for the next round.[15]

Each subject played multiple rounds (an average of 2.7) of the game. In all, we have data from 782 rounds (1,564 individual choices). The modal strategy (played in 73 percent of rounds) was to keep one 500-USh coin and to allocate the other coin to another player. Nonetheless, in 23 percent of the rounds, subjects allocated both coins to the other players. These offers can be compared with a baseline strategy of random allocation, under which subjects would keep one coin two-thirds of the time.

We now turn to the question of whether subjects displayed different degrees of other-regardingness toward coethnics and noncoethnics. We restrict our analysis to rounds in which a player was or believed he or she was playing with one coethnic partner and one noncoethnic partner, and in which he or she also elected to discriminate.[16] Row 1 of table 2.1 reports

Table 2.1 Discrimination Rates in Dictator Game

	Benchmark Coethnicity	Benchmark Coregion	Subjective Coethnicity	Subjective Coregion
Effect of in-group membership when offerer is anonymous	–0.03 (0.10)	0.06 (0.08)	0.08 (0.15)	0.08 (0.14)
Effect of in-group membership when offerer is seen	0.12* (0.07)	0.14*** (0.06)	0.28** (0.13)	0.24*** (0.11)
Difference	0.15 (0.12)	0.08 (0.09)	0.19 (0.21)	0.16 (0.18)
Observations	628	962	310	432

Source: Authors' calculations.
Notes: Standard errors in parentheses, calculated using weighted OLS regression with weights to account for different assignment probabilities across groups. Disturbance terms are clustered for each player across all of his or her games. Cells in first two rows report average treatment effects on the treated (ATT) using exact matching to average over treatment effects obtained for offerers for each ethnic or regional group. Cells in third row report interaction terms from an OLS regression with weights to take account of different assignment probabilities for different groups.
*significant at 10 percent; **significant at 5 percent; ***significant at 1 percent.

the average effect of coethnicity on the likelihood that players discriminated in favor of coethnics when they played anonymously.[17] We find no evidence of any coethnic effect. Contrary to the expectations of the other-regarding preferences rationale, there is no statistically significant difference in the likelihood that players discriminate in favor of coethnics.

These results do not directly establish what individuals believe about the other-regarding preferences of coethnic and noncoethnic partners. To establish beliefs directly, we would like to have been able to ask our receivers to predict the offers made by coethnic and noncoethnic offerers. However, playing such a back end to this game would have required either asking respondents hypothetical questions or showing receivers pictures of the offerers, who had been told that they were making their allocations anonymously, a violation of the experimental norm of no deception. Nonetheless, the results suggest that other-regarding preferences are not structured along ethnic lines, and any belief to the contrary would be sharply at odds with this observed behavior.

Incentives Rationale

Next we turn to the incentives rationale. An individual may have an incentive to be trustworthy even if he or she does not have the interests of the truster at heart for a variety of reasons. One possibility is that the preferences of the two agents over outcomes are aligned—the truster in this case knows that the trustee will take the right action because that action is also in the interest of the trustee. A second is social norms. In this case, the truster believes that the trustee will take the right action because he or she knows that the trustee will be violating a norm if he or she does not, a violation that could come at a cost to the violator. In either case, the existence of incentives for the trustee to be trustworthy, if known to the truster, would lead the truster to have higher expectations of the trustee's trustworthiness.

Preferences over Outcomes

In a trivial sense, the other-regarding preferences rationale we discussed in the last section may be thought of as an incentive rationale. But other preference rationales may be less trivially linked to incentives. In the classic example provided by Adam Smith, I can rely on a serviceman to deliver goods not because he likes me but because he, like me, benefits from the trade (Smith 1776/1994). What matters is not preferences over the welfare of others but that the welfare of each person is correlated across outcomes. If the preferences of coethnics are relatively more aligned in this way, this could lead to higher levels of trust among coethnics and greater expectations that coethnics will be trustworthy.

To probe the plausibility of this argument for Mulago-Kyebando, we use simple survey techniques to test whether preferences over public goods outcomes do in fact correlate with ethnic group membership. Insofar as they do, individuals have incentives to trust each other in the joint production of these goods. We examine two types of survey questions. First, to what types of public goods do individuals attach the highest priority (security, drainage maintenance, or garbage collection)? Second, how should these goods be provided, for example, should private or public resources be used? We focus on these issues—how projects are prioritized and provided—because they were identified by community members in interviews and focus group discussions as being among the most salient concerns in Mulago-Kyebando.

Table 2.2 reports the results from *F*-tests derived from a simple analysis of variance (ANOVA) and from the nonparametric Kruskal-Wallis test, which is more appropriate when the outcome measure is categorical. We cannot reject the null hypothesis of no systematic variation across ethnic or regional groups for any of the six questions. More detailed analysis further suggests that clustering on any given group is minimal and that what clustering exists can be accounted for by locality-fixed effects. In short, we do not find empirical support for the argument that members of ethnic groups have correlated preferences over political outcomes in Mulago-Kyebando.

Table 2.2 Within-Group Clustering of Policy Preferences

	Ethnicity		Region	
I	ANOVA F-test (p)	Kruskal-Wallis x^2 test (with Ties) (p)	ANOVA F-test (p)	Kruskal-Wallis x^2 test (with Ties) (p)
II				
First priority for public goods provision				
Drainage	0.25	0.25	0.91	0.91
Garbage collection	0.70	0.69	0.39	0.39
Security	0.67	0.66	0.25	0.25
III				
How public goods are to be provided				
Preference for fee-based garbage collection, over free but lower quality provision	0.88	0.66	0.51	0.72
It's better not to have to pay anything or to volunteer for patrols, even if that means security is low	0.35	0.23	0.73	0.80
It's better to have well-maintained drainage channels, even if we have to make contributions of money or labor	0.41	0.22	0.44	0.48

Source: Authors' calculations.
Notes: Analysis is limited to ten largest groups.

Preferences can be correlated across groups in many ways, of course. We have examined just one and cannot rule out such correlations in general. The key point in assessing these results is that the questions we examine were identified as being locally salient in communities. The main implication is that for these salient issues we cannot find evidence that the failure to coordinate across groups can be attributed to groups wanting different outcomes.

Social Norms

A second source of beliefs about trustworthiness is social norms and the social sanctioning that may take place if those norms are violated. If individuals know that a norm exists that one should act in a trustworthy way, and that one is subject to sanctioning in the event that they fail to abide by this norm, they are more likely to be trustworthy and increase their expectations of trustworthiness in others who adhere to this norm. In principle, such norms could exist within but not across ethnic groups: if coethnics expect that cooperation with coethnics will be reciprocated under threat of sanctioning but that cooperation with noncoethnics will not, expectations of trustworthiness will be higher among coethnics.

To test for such a norm—and for its differential strength among coethnics and noncoethnics—we explored what happened to the offerers' behavior in the dictator game when the offerers were no longer anonymous: the PIB shifts from the one depicted in figure 2.2 to the one depicted in figure 2.1. In such a setting, the offerer's behavior can be interpreted as a function of his or her relative other-regardingness toward the receiver, as it was in the anonymous version of the game, and his or her concern about being seen to violate a social norm requiring cooperation. This latter concern is irrelevant when the offerer is anonymous, but becomes potentially important when the offerer is seen and in principle can be sanctioned if his or her actions breach the norm against failing to contribute. To evaluate whether such a norm exists, we can therefore compare patterns of play in dictator games where the offerer is and is not seen. To evaluate whether the norm exists more strongly for coethnics than noncoethnics—the central claim of the incentives rationale that we seek to test here—we can compare the results of anonymous and nonanonymous dictator games played among coethnics and noncoethnics.[18]

Each subject played approximately four rounds of the nonanonymous version of the dictator game, yielding a total of 1,226 rounds (2,452 choices). Aggregate patterns of play were similar to those found in the dictator game with the anonymous offerer. Subjects kept one 500-USh coin and allocated the other to another player 70 percent of the time. They gave both coins away 24 percent of the time.

The effects of coethnicity on offers can be seen in the second row of table 2.1. Again, for our analysis, we focus only on cases in which players actually discriminate (that is, choose to give the coin to one player and not another) when they are or believe they are facing one coethnic and one noncoethnic. In nonanonymous games, we find systematic differences in the way subjects played with coethnics and noncoethnics. Using the benchmark measure, coethnicity increases the likelihood that a partner will be favored by 12 percentage points; using our subjective coding, a zero to one change in subjective coethnicity is associated with a 28 percentage point increase in the likelihood of favoritism. Results for shared group membership defined by common regional background are similarly large, 14 and 24 percentage points respectively.

The contrast between these findings and those reported in the first row of table 2.1 is striking. When they are making their offers anonymously, subjects give no more to coethnics than to noncoethnics. But when they know that they can be seen, they give significantly more. Like the findings presented in chapter 1 of this volume, these results provide evidence that trust-facilitating norms exist within ethnic groups (see also Yamagishi and Mifune 2008). Although we find a significant effect of coethnicity in the nonanonymous games and not in the anonymous games, we cannot distinguish the difference between these marginal effects from zero with confidence (see the second to last row of table 2.1).[19]

Beliefs

These results support the claim that individuals take the interests of others into account in response to socially generated incentives. They do not, however, establish that individuals believe that others respond this way. They provide only a basis for drawing a conclusion about beliefs of trustworthiness if we assume consistency of beliefs—that is, that people's beliefs about trustworthiness follow directly from behavior that is in fact trustworthy. We turn now to a more direct investigation of whether individuals believe that others will act in a trustworthy way. Specifically, we test whether, in nonanonymous dictator games, players expect to receive more from coethnics than from noncoethnics. Because we condition on cases in which play is nonanonymous, this test does not permit us to determine whether the source of these beliefs lies in presumptions about the trustee's other-regardingness toward the truster or in incentives that increase the likelihood that the trustee will behave in a trustworthy way. However, if players do expect to receive more from coethnics, then our claim that the threat of punishment is credible when such expectations are not met—the rationale for which we have found empirical support—stands on stronger grounds.

To assess player's expectations, we examine data gathered during the back end of the nonanonymous dictator game. Subjects played the back end after all dictator games had been completed but, of course, before they learned what they received from each offerer. Capturing an accurate reading of people's expectations is a challenge. We did not want subjects to provide their guesses directly to our enumerators for fear that that it might bias our results. Instead, we gave each receiver the exact endowment of cash that had been provided to offerers in the front end of the game (two 500-USh coins) and asked them to indicate how they believed the offerer had allocated the coins among the three players. To do this, we showed them PIBs for each round of each game in which they had been a receiver and, for each one, asked them to place coins in envelopes and put them in the boxes corresponding to the pictures of each player on the

Table 2.3 Receivers' Expectations in Dictator Game

Marginal Effect	Dictator Game (Back End) (p)	n
Benchmark coethnicity	.12 (.11)	385
Benchmark coregion	.07 (.04)*	684
Subjective coethnicity	.21 (.15)	385
Subjective coregion	.15 (.06)**	675

Source: Authors' calculations.
Notes: Standard errors in parentheses, calculated using weighted OLS regression with weights to account for different assignment probabilities across groups. Disturbance terms are clustered for each player across all of his or her games. Cells report average treatment effects on treated (ATT) using exact matching to average over treatment effects obtained for offerers for each ethnic or regional group.

computer screen exactly as they thought the offerer had allocated the coins.[20] As incentives, players were given 500 USh if their guesses about the offerer's allocation were correct.

In general, our subjects were wishful thinkers. Players guessed that the offerer would keep one coin and give them the other in about half the games, but that the second coin would go to the other receiver only 28 percent of the time. In 17 percent of cases, receivers believed that the offerer would give away both coins, and that the offerer would keep them (against the rules of the game) in about 4 percent.

In table 2.3, we explore whether players conditioned their expectations on the match between the offerer's ethnic background and their own. We limit the analysis to games in which guessers expected offerers to keep one coin and give the other away, and in which one of the receivers was a member of the offerer's ethnic group and the other was not. By conditioning on players who always keep one coin, no offerer is more or less generous than another; the question is simply who they chose to benefit. The results suggest that individuals expect coethnic offerers to discriminate in their favor. This effect is especially strong with respect to region. Coregionists are between 7 and 15 percentage points more likely to expect to be benefitted than their counterparts; the substantive magnitudes for coethnic pairings are even larger, but these results do not obtain statistical significance. These findings offer some additional support to the results reported earlier regarding the role of sanctioning and social norms in generating trustworthy behavior: in nonanonymous settings, players favor their coethnics and their coethnics expect them to do so.[21]

Competence Rationale

A third rationale for why some people will be believed to be more trustworthy than others derives from beliefs about their ability to deliver what has been promised. As the myriad stereotypes about the natural abilities of members of particular groups to perform certain tasks attest (that is, Italians are good at making shoes, Nubians make good soldiers, and the like), perceived competence in particular domains is frequently associated with different ethnic groups. However, such stereotyping would not produce higher levels of perceived trustworthiness among coethnics per se. Only if competence is or is perceived to be relational—that is, that individuals believe that coethnics, though perhaps no more competent overall, are better able to work together with them—will beliefs about competence provide a foundation for differential expectations of trustworthiness among coethnics and noncoethnics.

To test the possibility that our subjects had differential beliefs about the abilities of others (and specifically the ability of others to work effectively with them), we created a game in which players had to select from among a set of partners to perform a joint task. Because rewards accrued only to teams that successfully completed the task, players had an incentive to select partners with whom they believed they would be most likely to succeed.

The game we examine here—the lockbox game—involves two people working together to open a combination lock on a box containing cash. Pairs that successfully open the box share the money. Partners were matched by randomly dividing six subjects in a given session into two groups of three: one group was designated to play the role of Player 1, the other to play the role of Player 2. Player 1 is taught how to open the combination lock; he or she must then provide oral instructions to Player 2, who actually manipulates the lock.

After receiving instructions about how the game would be played, one subject was selected at random from the Player 1 pool, shown pictures of the three subjects in the Player 2 pool and asked to select one to be his or her partner in the game. A second subject was then selected at random from the Player 1 pool, shown pictures of the two remaining subjects in the Player 2 pool, and asked to select one to be his or her partner. The final subject in the Player 1 pool had no choice and was simply assigned to play the game with the last remaining subject in the Player 2 pool. In this way it was randomly determined whether a given player faced a choice between one, two, or three potential partners.

Each subject played the game only once, so only half of our subjects played in the position of Player 1. Thirty-one subjects could choose a partner from among three partners, fifty-one from among just two, and sixty-six had no choice. To the extent that they could identify coethnics from looking at their pictures, did subjects select them as partners?

Table 2.4 Partner Selection in Lockbox Game

	Share of Players Selecting Ingroup Members		
Case	Ethnicity (*N*)	Region (*N*)	Expected Share Given Random Selection
One coethnic, one noncoethnic	0.55 (11)	0.53 (19)	0.50
One coethnic, two noncoethnics	0.39 (8)	0.33 (12)	0.33
Two coethnics, one noncoethnic	0.6 (5)	0.67 (6)	0.67

Source: Authors' calculations.

The basic results are as follows. First, there is no evidence that competence in this task is relational. Coethnic pairs were no more likely than noncoethnic pairs to succeed in the game: success rates were 0.63 for coethnics ($n = 32$) and 0.63 for noncoethnics ($n = 114$). When group membership is defined in terms of region, success rates are even lower for coethnics, 0.59 ($n = 51$) to 0.61 ($n = 83$) for noncoethnics (difference not significant).[22] This is true both when players had a choice in partner selection and when they did not.

Given this pattern, it is perhaps not surprising that players appear not to have believed that coethnics would be better able to work with them. Table 2.4 presents data on partner selection for those cases in which a player could select a partner from among a pool of coethnics and noncoethnics. Although the *n* is low for all these cases, we see that player selections are as close as possible to random given integer constraints. The same pattern also emerges from a more general analysis (not shown) that uses an alternative-specific multinomial probit model to check for coethnicity effects. This model is appropriate for settings in which an individual chooses one option from a set of alternatives (with the number of options possibly varying) for which each option has distinct characteristics. In this analysis, we looked to see whether any ethnic cues were used. It is possible, and consistent, for example, with findings of Chaim Fershtman and Uri Gneezy (2001), that individuals find it optimal to work with some particular ethnic groups though not necessarily their own. Again, we find no evidence to support this view and fail to reject the null that the selection is independent of the ethnic composition of the pool of potential partners.

One possible challenge to our strategy is that players may select partners in part because, independent of success rates, they simply do or do not prefer working alongside individuals of a given group. If players had preferences to work alongside coethnics, this would bias the results toward finding coethnic selection even if there were no competence advantage of coethnic pairings. That we do not find such selection strengthens our results, to the extent that we expect procedural preferences to be positively correlated with coethnicity.

As with our discussion of correlated preferences over outcomes, there are of course many types of joint tasks we could consider and multiple domains in which differential competence might matter. We cannot infer from these results that there are no competence concerns in other domains. Indeed, in another study, we report more positive evidence for relational effects for a different task for which we do not allow partner selection (Habyarimana et al. 2009). In this sense, our results should be interpreted as absence of evidence for, rather than evidence of the absence of, a competence rationale.

Conclusion

One problem with many approaches to the question of why some people are believed to be more trustworthy than others is that they do not distinguish among competing accounts for the observed outcome. Suppose we observe an individual handing over a monetary contribution to a political campaign in the belief that this money will not be misspent. What is the source of this person's trusting belief? One possibility is that the individual believes that the trustee cares about the welfare of the truster and so is motivated to act in her interests. Another is that the trustee is motivated to act in the trustee's interests, perhaps because she seeks the same outcomes or perhaps because she expects to be sanctioned if she misuses the funds. A third is that the person believes that the trustee has the skills to spend the campaign funds successfully. These rationales can account for absolute levels of trust but also for differences in trust across groups.

Parsing these explanations is of substantive importance, but is difficult using standard methods. We have used experimental techniques to test these explanations. Our focus was on why people believe that coethnics are more trustworthy than noncoethnics. Our results suggest that, at least in Mulago-Kyebando, the reason is the expectation that, owing to norms of reciprocity that bind more strongly in within-group than in cross-group interactions, coethnics have greater incentives than noncoethnics to respond to trusting overtures in a trustworthy way. The competing rationales find weaker empirical support.

We end with a note of caution and a note of optimism. A skeptical reader might question the generality of our conclusions. The salience of each of the rationales we study, a critic might argue, might depend on the context of the trusting decision. We concur. Other regarding preferences may plausibly be more important in settings where ethnic differences have been a source of violence. A competence rationale may underlie trusting actions in settings where, unlike in Mulago-Kyebando, no lingua franca exists or where success in specific tasks depends more directly on shared group attributes. Experimental protocols that involve explicitly priming subjects to ethnicity (which our protocols do not) may also generate different conclusions about the relative importance of the three rationales.

It is possible, however, that incentives explanations may be of overriding importance for generating trust in a broad class of settings—at this stage, we simply do not have enough evidence to know. To the extent that they are, a hopeful implication is that the distrust that sometimes characterizes cross-ethnic interactions need not be insurmountable. It is difficult to make people care about the welfare of others if they do not do so already. Expectations that collaboration with certain types of people are also not likely to be successful are difficult to change, particularly if they are well founded. But incentives may be more malleable. Formal institutions that penalize people who respond uncooperatively to trusting behavior might generate universal norms about trustworthiness that can displace the ethnic ones that may otherwise predominate.

The authors thank Claire Adida, Bernd Beber, Pepine Bulambo, Deo Byabagambi, Elizabeth Carlson, Chris Crabbe, Kenneth Ekode, Nathan Falck, Alex Kunobwa, Sylvester Mubiru, Douglas Musonga, Winfred Nabulo, Ruth Nagawa, Susan Najjuuko, Brenda Nakkazi, Harriet Nambi, Winfred Naziwa, Livingstone Ntensibe, Alex Odwong, Alexandra Scacco, Geoff Sentongo, Simon Ssenyimba, Elizabeth Suubi, Alex Tindyebwa, Sheila Watuwa, and Daniel Young for their extraordinary research assistance; the Harvard Academy for International and Area Studies, the Russell Sage Foundation, and the Harry Frank Guggenheim Foundation for financial support; and Karen Cook, Jean Ensminger, Henry Farrell, Russell Hardin, Margaret Levi, Susan Stokes, James Walker, and Rick Wilson for their helpful comments on this chapter.

Notes

1. We recognize that in some accounts trust is not a belief: it is possible, for example, to interpret trust as pertaining to the taking of trusting actions. For our purposes here, however, we equate trusting with a belief of trustworthiness.

2. Iris Bohnet and Fiona Greig are an exception (2006). They do not find evidence that coethnicity matters in a trust game played with subjects from a slum in Nairobi, although their sample may exhibit too little ethnic variation to identify an effect.

3. Based on an analysis of pooled data from round 3 of the Afrobarometer, collected in 2005 and 2006. The sample includes 25,397 respondents from eighteen African countries.

4. These explanations parallel those of Margaret Levi and Laura Stoker (2000). Levi and Stoker also identify a fourth rationale, the morality rationale, which hinges on a belief that the trustee adheres to moral values that emphasize promise keeping. We do not have the data to explore this rationale, and we leave it aside in this chapter. We also cannot distinguish the social norms–sanctioning explanation we discuss from an explanation in which trusting beliefs are generated by strong reciprocity within but not between ethnic groups (Gintis 2000).

5. Our study area is comprised of four adjacent parishes (LC2s) in the poorest of Kampala's five divisions, Kawempe: Mulago I, Mulago II, Mulago III, and Kyebando. We refer to them collectively in the text as Mulago-Kyebando.

6. Figures are based on an analysis of round 3 Afrobarometer data for Uganda only ($N = 2{,}400$).

7. The ethnic fractionalization index measures the likelihood that two people selected at random will be from different ethnic groups. Communities with values of 0 are completely homogeneous; communities with values approaching 1 are extremely heterogeneous (for further details of the demography of our study site, see Habyarimana et al. 2009).

8. The full protocols for all the experiments described in this chapter are available from the authors on request.

9. Simple random sampling was used within local neighborhoods (LC1s). The number of subjects for each LC1, however, was set using targets that diverged modestly from proportionate-to-size to oversample the second and third largest ethnic groups (for detail, see Habyarimana et al. 2009). More than 75 percent of those we contacted agreed to participate in the study. Of those who chose to enter the study, more than 95 percent attended all sessions.

10. The lockbox game is played live. However, the partner selection process we study in that game does involve showing players pictures of other subjects, which is similar to the computer interface we describe here.

11. Given the large number of different ethnic groups in our sample, a treatment of dyadic pairings of groups would have been too complex, so we limit our analysis to the more general difference between coethnic and noncoethnic interactions.

12. Note that by using this rule, an individual *i* is coded as a subjective coethnic of individual *j* if individual *j* believes that *i* would code herself in the same group as *j* codes herself. A stricter definition would require that *j* codes *i* in the same group as *j* codes herself under *j*'s own (rather than under *i*'s) classification criteria. Our requirement for a single criterion of "correct" identification to use as a basis for allocating rewards to players precluded us from generating this more precise measure of subjective coethnicity.

13. A variant on this mechanism, which some social scientists refer to as quasi-magical thinking, depends on the other-regardingness of the truster toward the trustee. That is, if the truster has the trustee's interests at heart, he or she assumes that the reverse is true as well. By contrast, the mechanism we focus on here depends only on the other-regardingness that the trustee has for the truster, and on the truster's beliefs about the trustee's other-regardingness.

14. We also played a nondiscrimination version of the dictator game with ten coins instead of two. The results, reported elsewhere, are very similar to those described here (see Habyarimana et al. 2007).

15. We instituted various checks to ensure that our subjects understood the games they were playing. Most important, before beginning play, subjects were tested on their comprehension of the rules of the game and the set of strategies available to them. Subjects who failed this test were given additional instruction until they could explain the game on their own. In addition, we organized a back-translation of the games in which an educated Ugandan with no connection to the project met with a group of our subjects and tried to elicit from them enough information about the various games they were playing that he could describe the details of the games back to the experimenters. The success of this back-translation exercise gave us confidence that our subjects understood the underlying behaviors that each game sought to assess.

16. In the subjective coethnicity analysis, a player was coded as believing that he or she was facing one coethnic partner and one noncoethnic partner if the difference in his or her estimated beliefs that each of the two partners was a coethnic exceeded .5. Including the set of games in which there is no discrimination weakens all results marginally but does not affect the conclusions of this chapter.

17. As with all coethnic effects reported in this chapter, average treatment effects are estimated by using exact matching to average over the treatment effects obtained for offerers for each ethnic or regional group. Averaging over differences between treated and untreated subjects within groups ensures that the results are not confounded by main effects that could result from treatment assignment probabilities varying across groups. The results are robust to the inclusion of a battery of controls for age, education, income, gender, and other characteristics (which, by design, are uncorrelated with the experimental treatment).

    Because the game is played with two partners for each offerer, we stack the data and code a dependent variable that captures whether a given receiver was favored. We thus double the number of observations in our regressions. Our results—both those reported here and those in the next section—are robust to treating each game as a single game. In analyses using nonstacked data (not shown), we can reject the null hypothesis that players select between a coethnic and a noncoethnic randomly at the 99 percent level for coethnicity and the 95 percent level for coregion using a subjective coding of coethnic pairings.

18. Our decision to interpret the dictator game where the offerer is seen as a situation where the offerer can be punished for the violation of a social norm

requires explanation, because the game is a one-shot interaction that, by construction, does not allow for punishment within the game. Our logic, following Elizabeth Hoffman, Kevin McCabe, and Vernon Smith is that players "are accustomed to operate in an environment in which there is ongoing social interaction" and as a result "may be concerned about the extent to which their decisions have post-experimental consequences, or that others may judge them by their decisions" (Hoffman, McCabe, and Smith 1996, 655). Thus, although punishment may not be possible within the game, players behave as if it is. This interpretation is supported by the findings of Kevin Haley and Daniel Fessler, who reported strikingly different results in dictator games when players believe they can and cannot be seen, even in a context where the identity of the would-be punisher is undefined (2005). A similar logic is also employed in a study of voter behavior in the United States (Gerber, Green, and Larimer 2008).

19. We identify a similar pattern of no coethnic bias in anonymous games and coethnic favoritism in nonanonymous games in a version of the dictator game our subjects played with ten 100-USh coins (reported in Habyarimana et al. 2007). In that game, subjects were free to choose from a wide range of potential allocations, including many that permitted them to treat each of the other players equally. In the 100-USh version of the game, we have greater power and can demonstrate that an important subgroup of players favor coethnics if and only if they are observed.
20. One natural concern with this approach is that the action of placing coins in one's own box might predispose subjects toward wishful thinking: they might always guess that they received more. This might be especially the case if the subject had trouble comprehending the game. This possibility could potentially swamp some of the subtle effects with which we are concerned. However, it should not bias the findings either toward or against a coethnic effect.
21. These results survive the inclusion of fixed effects for all receiver (guesser) groups. They do not, however, survive the inclusion of fixed effects for the offerer.
22. The *n*'s and global means differ in these two cases because of differences in our ability to find matches for treated observations based on ethnicity and for region.

References

Barr, Abigail. 2004. "Kinship, Familiarity and Trust: An Experimental Investigation." In *Foundations of Human Sociality: Economic Experiments and Ethnographic Evidence from Fifteen Small-Scale Societies,* edited by Joseph Henrich, Robert Boyd, Samuel Bowles, Colin Camerer, Ernst Fehr, and Herbert Gintis. New York: Oxford University Press.

Bohnet, Iris, and Bruno Frey. 1999. "Social Distance and Other-Regarding Behavior in Dictator Games: Comment." *American Economic Review* 89(March): 335–39.

Bohnet, Iris, and Fiona Greig. 2006. "Why Women Cooperate with Women and Not Men: Evidence from a Slum in Nairobi, Kenya." Mimeo, Kennedy School of Government, Harvard University.

Brewer, Marilynn B. 1981. "Ethnocentrism and Its Role in Interpersonal Trust." In *Scientific Inquiry and the Social Sciences*, edited by Marilynn Brewer and Barry E. Collins. San Francisco: Jossey-Bass.

Burns, Justine. 2003. "Insider-Outsider Distinctions in South Africa: The Impact of Race on the Behavior of High School Students." Unpublished paper. University of Cape Town.

Cohen, Avner. 1969. *Custom and Politics in Urban Africa: A Study of Hausa Migrants in Yoruba Towns.* Berkeley: University of California Press.

Crawford, Vincent P., and Hans Haller. 1990. "Learning How to Cooperate: Optimal Play in Repeated Coordination Games." *Econometrica* 58(May): 571–95.

Eckel, Catherine C.. and Rick K. Wilson. 2006. "Internet Cautions: Experimental Games with Internet Partners." *Experimental Economics* 9(1): 53–66.

Fearon, James D., and David D. Laitin. 1996. "Explaining Interethnic Cooperation." *American Political Science Review* 90(December): 715–35.

Fershtman, Chaim, and Uri Gneezy. 2001. "Discrimination in a Segmented Society: An Experimental Approach." *Quarterly Journal of Economics* 116(February): 351–77.

Gerber, Alan S., Donald P. Green, and Christopher W. Larimer. 2008. "Social Pressure and Voter Turnout: Evidence from a Large-Scale Field Experiment." *American Political Science Review* 102(1): 33–48.

Gintis, Herbert. 2000. "Strong Reciprocity and Human Sociality." *Journal of Theoretical Biology* 206(2): 169–79.

Habyarimana, James, Macartan Humphreys, Daniel N. Posner, and Jeremy M. Weinstein. 2007. "Why Does Ethnic Diversity Undermine Public Goods Provision?" *American Political Science Review* 101(November): 709–25.

———. 2009. *Coethnicity: Diversity and the Dilemmas of Collective Action.* New York: Russell Sage Foundation.

Haley, Kevin and Daniel Fessler. 2005. "Nobody's Watching? Subtle Cues Affect Generosity in an Anonymous Economic Game." *Evolution and Human Behavior* 26(May): 245–56.

Hoffman, Elizabeth, Kevin McCabe, and Vernon L. Smith. 1996. "Social Distance and Other-Regarding Behavior in Dictator Games." *American Economic Review* 86(June): 653–60.

Kahneman, Daniel, Jack Knetsch, and Richard Thaler. 1986. "Fairness as a Constraint on Profit Seeking: Entitlements in the Market." *American Economic Review* 76(September): 728–41.

Karlan, Dean. 2005. "Using Experimental Economics to Measure Social Capital and Predict Financial Decisions." *American Economic Review* 95(5; December): 1688–99.

Landa, Janet Tai. 1994. *Trust, Ethnicity, and Identity: Beyond the New Institutional Economics of Ethnic Trading Networks, Contract Law, and Gift-Exchange.* Ann Arbor: University of Michigan Press.

Levi, Margaret, and Laura Stoker. 2000. "Political Trust and Trustworthiness." *Annual Review of Political Science* 3(1): 475–507.

Macharia, Kinuthia. 1988. "Social Networks: Ethnicity and the Informal Sector in Nairobi." *Institute for Development Studies* working paper 463. Nairobi: University of Nairobi.
Mozaffar, Shaheen, James R. Scarritt, and Glen Galaich. 2003. "Electoral Institutions, Ethnopolitical Cleavages, and Party Systems in Africa's Emerging Democracies." *American Political Science Review* 97(August): 379–90.
Petrie, Ragan. 2003. "Trusting Appearances and Reciprocating Looks: Experimental Evidence on Gender and Race Preferences." Unpublished paper. Georgia State University.
Posner, Daniel N. 2005. *Institutions and Ethnic Politics in Africa.* New York: Cambridge University Press.
Smith, Adam. 1776/1994. *The Wealth of Nations.* New York: The Modern Library.
Yamagishi, Toshio, and Nobuhiro Mifune. 2008. "Does Shared Group Membership Promote Altruism? Fear, Greed and Reputation." *Rationality & Society* 20(1): 5–30.

Chapter 3

Social Networks and Trust in Cross-Cultural Economic Experiments

ABIGAIL BARR, JEAN ENSMINGER, AND JEFFREY C. JOHNSON

IN THIS CHAPTER, we present two datasets from Africa, one rural and one urban, in which we examine the correlates of individual-level demographics and trusting and trustworthy behavior in economic experiments. We use a slightly modified version of the Joyce Berg, John Dickhaut, and Kevin McCabe investment game (1995). Our primary original contribution is to include in these demographics data on each individual's standing in their social network (compare Alesina and La Ferrara 2002; Anderson, Mellor, and Milyo 2005a, 2005b; Bouckaert and Dhaene 2003; Burns 2004; Chaudhury and Gangadharan 2003; Croson and Buchan 1999; DeBruine 2002; Eckel and Wilson 2003, 2004). We hypothesize that those who are pivotally and centrally located in social networks hold such positions because they have established and maintained reputations as successful social and political entrepreneurs, and that such positions are achieved in part by demonstrating trustworthiness. We define political entrepreneurs as those who strategically cultivate, create, and invest in social relationships to enhance their bargaining power and political brokerage abilities in areas such as conflict management and institutional change (compare Schneider and Teske 1992). This is a quality we believe is well identified by conventional measures of social network centrality (compare Christopoulos 2006). Further, we hypothesize that such entrepreneurs are risk takers by nature, and that this propels them to risk trusting to reap the rewards of cooperation that stem from such behavior. Inclinations to trust are further reinforced by the greater access to information, including information concerning who is worthy of trust, that such pivotal positions in the social network afford.

Social networks are central to the concept of social capital as most people use the term, but studies of social capital have suffered from a lack of conceptual clarity. The metaphorical use of the concept and the looseness with which the term social capital has been operationalized, together with the power with which some have endowed an ill-defined version of the concept, has lead to some discounting the entire concept. In this chapter, we seek to differentiate individual from group-level concepts of social capital and attempt to restore some clarity to the concept. We then take the individual component of social capital that exists as social or political entrepreneurship, and use social network analysis to provide precise measures of this individual-level trait. Finally, we derive specific predictions about the relationship between network position and the relative level of trust and trustworthiness exhibited by individuals within a given society.

Concepts of Social Capital

We are certainly not the first to attempt to make a link between social capital and trust and trustworthiness, nor are we the first to recognize the lack of consistency in providing a clear operational definition of social capital. Over the next few sections we take a brief look at the concept of social capital particularly as it relates to social networks and economic experimental games. There has been considerable discussion in the trust literature concerning the vagueness surrounding the various definitions, measures and applications of the concept of social capital (Durlauf 2002; Carpenter, Daniere, and Takahashi 2004). Further, and more important, is the general recognition of problems stemming from confusion surrounding the analytical levels at which social capital has been theoretically conceptualized. As others have noted, the important distinction among societal, organizational, group- and individual-level notions of social capital has often been either obscured or not well articulated (Cook, Hardin, and Levi 2005; Glaeser, Laibson, and Sacerdote 2002; Carpenter, Daniere, and Takahashi 2004; Guillén et al. 2002; Lin, Cook, and Burt 2001). Yet such a distinction is critical to gaining a more realistic understanding of the role of social capital in accounting for individual-level variation in trust and trustworthiness.

Group-Level Social Capital

Much of the work examining the relationship between trust and social capital has been at the community or aggregate level (Glaeser, Laibson, and Sacerdote 2002). One general use in the literature has to do with the degree to which an actor is embedded in a dense set of social relations—the denser an actor's relations, the higher their social capital (Coleman 1990; Portes and Sensenbrenner 1993). This group-oriented conceptualization stands in stark contrast to the individual-level social capital. Here density provides security for individual group members in that it protects them from potentially negative outside influences (for example, outgroup conflicts) and promotes a more certain social environment (social norms are clear). In addition to protection, such dense, cohesive networks foster cooperation and provide members with a sense of belonging and identity (Portes and Sensenbrenner 1993)—that is, they have the potential to imbue actors with prosocial preferences. Some see this form of group-level social capital as both reflecting and creating the degree of trust in a given society (Putnam 1993, 2000). It comes at a cost, however. Such dense, redundant social relations often entail various social obligations and restrictive norms (Portes and Landolt 1996). In addition, this more macro-level conceptualization of social capital does not lend itself well to understanding individual-level factors accounting for intrasocietal variation in actors' game playing behavior. We focus in this chapter on the individual-level concept of social capital as captured by individual measures of one's network centrality.

Individual-Level Social Capital

Interest in the role of more individual-oriented forms of social capital in understanding trust is on the increase (Carpenter, Daniere, and Takahashi 2004). Edward Glaeser, David Laibson, and Bruce Sacerdote, for example, saw individual-level social capital in terms of the characteristics of actors with regard to such things as interpersonal skills, charm, and "the size of his Rolodex" (2002, 438). This more network-oriented view, depending on the type of relation or relations, can be thought of as a kind of "social or political entrepreneurship" that varies as a function of the degree to which an actor has the ability to bring together, bridge, or broker among a wide range of other actors who are themselves not connected (Burt 1992, 1997, 2001, 2005; Lin 1999, 2001; Lin, Cook, and Burt 2001). Referred to as bridging social capital by Joel Sobel (2002), such a structural position may allow an individual to influence the flow of information and control knowledge that can facilitate an individual's economic, political, or social advantage. It should be pointed out, however, that this does not necessarily predict more self-interested behavior, because it may not be possible to maintain such a position if one abuses it. It may predict strategic talents or acuity; however, as such actors need to be strategic not only to get where they are, but to stay there. Whatever their preferences, we may expect them to be more adept at calculation, have higher levels of social knowledge (Johnson and Orbach 2002), greater social shrewdness (Yamagishi 2001) or display an outsider orientation, seek authority, and thrive on advocacy and change (Burt, Jannotta, and Mahoney 1998). Such individuals may be both providing public goods through their organizational capacities, and steering social norms and institutions toward their own ends (Ensminger and Knight 1997).

Trust and Social Networks

An important question concerns individual motivations for behaving in a trusting way across a variety of contexts. What underlies individual variation in an actor's capacity for trust (Cook and Cooper 2003)? What do actors bring with them into a given context that might account for both their motivations and capacity to trust, and, ultimately, their behavior? One important consideration relates to the benefits associated with the capacity for trust, and conversely the possible costs incurred by a lack of such capacity, or the possibility of being caught up in a vicious cycle of distrust (Yamagishi 2001).

Russell Hardin linked the capacity to trust and the ability to assess trustworthiness to a range of potential benefits (2002). More important, he recognized that an individual actor who lacks such capacity will be a "relative loser" (116). Critical to this is the idea that actors endowed with this capacity are by their very nature risk takers, given that it is only through the taking of risks that one can accrue greater gain. As Hardin noted, "Being an optimistic risk taker or cooperator opens up the opportunity for great loss and for great gain, neither of which might be possible without risking cooperation" (116).

The factors usually considered in understanding how individual actors develop the propensity to trust have primarily focused on a variety of sociological and psychological influences. These include such things as the way an actor was raised, an actor's social class background, an actor's religious training, and a variety of other life experiences. What has generally been missing is how an actor is embedded in a social network. Although a great deal of work has addressed how social networks are important for creating an environment of trust, little has looked at variations in the influences of network dynamics at the individual actor level in the development and maintenance of trust and trustworthiness. In individual-level approaches, the focus has been primarily on the impact of different community- or societal-level social capital on individuals as exemplified by the work of Robert Putnam, James Coleman, and Alejandro Portes. In society-level approaches, trust arises from the density of social relations, participation in civil society that engenders social connections, or the degree of network closure. These factors influence the extent of normative constraints, social obligations, and the capacity for social sanctions. In this case, the ties that bind foster trust and lower the risk associated with engaging in trustworthy behaviors because strong normative constraints tend to limit the potential for defection. However, the societal-level approaches have no mechanism to account for intra-societal variation in trust and trustworthiness. If all actors are embedded in a set of dense relations, then by definition we should expect little individual variation in levels of trust and trustworthiness because all actors are constrained in similar ways. This kind of invariant notion may work at the macro level in terms of comparisons of trust across groups or societies, where some societies have denser networks than others and, therefore, may have higher levels of trust, as in Putnam's civil society. But it does little for helping us in understanding intragroup, intracultural, or intrasocietal variation in trust or trustworthiness, and, in particular, how individual differences, even in highly dense networks, shape an actor's approach to repeated social interactions.

Recently, Ronald Burt addressed aspects of this issue in attempting to account for the presence of brokerage within network closure or within highly redundant networks (2005). The two reigning views of social capital discussed earlier, that is, group-level social capital through dense networks, and individual social capital as social or political entrepreneurship (brokerage and bridging structural holes), have seemingly been at odds with one another, particularly with respect to aspects of trust. Clearly, trust is higher and trusting others is less risky when there is network closure (that is, high density and tie redundancy). Extracting value from such trust, however, falls within the realm of brokerage or the ability of an actor to connect people in the network not otherwise connected to one another. As Burt put it, "bridging a structural hole can create value, but delivering the value requires the closed network of a cohesive team around the bridge" (2005, 79). Thus the successful social entrepreneur requires closure of a kind to limit the risk inherent in trusting, yet needs to span structural holes to cash in on this trust, because coordination of bridging relations, though of significant value, is potentially riddled with risk. So it is within this context that we might find the underlying factors contributing to variations in the capacity or propensity to trust no matter the structural density of a given group or society. For nonbrokers, there is less to gain from risking trust because they are not structurally positioned to exploit and therefore benefit from structural opportunities that brokerage affords. For brokers better positioned structurally, on the other hand, risks have higher potential payoffs.

Evidence is clear that advantages do accrue to those who span such structural holes (Burt 2001, 2005; Guillén et al. 2002). These political entrepreneurs must recognize, build, and exploit structural holes to develop individual-level social capital. Further, they must engage in repeated activities that maintain their network position and reputation and hence sustain their social capital (Burt 2002). Both developing and maintaining social capital in this entrepreneurial form requires the repeated risk-taking that results from trusting in others. This process is enhanced, and risks somewhat reduced, if there is a social safety net in the form of network closure around the bridge. In addition, risks are further reduced by the tendency for actor's with entrepreneurial or bridging social capital to have a better understanding of the social and political landscape (Johnson and Orbach 2002).

A significant contributor to maintaining social capital is the parallel development and maintenance of reputation. Reputation is essential for sustaining social capital, given that its very nature is future oriented (Burt 2005; Hardin 2002). A reputation for trustworthiness stems from a history of repeated interactions with others in which there is a clear perception on the part of others that one can be trusted (Kramer 1999). This has important implications with regard to both the perception of trust and trustworthiness by others and various aspects of individual self-perception at both a conscious and an unconscious level (Hartung 1988). As such, risk-taking in the form of trusting and being trusted are critical to fostering one's reputation. In addition, it becomes a behavior expected by others (Burt 2005). In other words, we would predict that those actors with bridging ties are also trustworthy.

An interesting query concerns the extent to which these expectations are internalized and translate into behaviors across a variety of contexts, including playing experimental games. That is, expectations become psychologically internalized, leading to the propensity for trusting and trustworthy behaviors, whether conscious or unconscious, in a variety of contexts, including economic experiments (for a discussion of this in understanding self perceptions as adaptive mechanisms, see Johnson and Orbach 2002; Hartung 1988).

Networks and Social Capital

Although social networks have become an important concept in experimental research on the relationship between trust and social capital, they have been measured and operationalized in wildly different ways (Durlauf 2002). The more conventional measure has been indirect proxies, particularly with regard to group-level measures, whereby respondents are asked to report on such things as participation in community projects or membership in clubs and organizations (Carpenter, Daniere, and Takahashi 2004). Edward Glaeser and his colleagues used a decidedly network approach when they asked subjects paired in trust experiments to provide a count of the number of acquaintances they had in common (2000). This reflects a kind of personal network approach (McCarty 2002) for understanding overlap in individual's social networks and how this overlap might influence behavior in trust experiments. Virtually none of the experimental research looking at social capital and trust, however, has measured social capital directly using a whole or complete social network approach (Wasserman and Faust 1994). This is somewhat understandable given the difficulty and cost involved in collecting the entire network of a large social group and the boundary specification problems inherent in such data. However, understanding the way in which an actor is embedded in a social network or networks is crucial to understanding the ways in which an actor's greater social world influences their capacity to trust and be trustworthy.

Study Sites

This project was part of the second phase of a cross-cultural experimental project studying small-scale societies around the world that began in 1998 in collaboration with many anthropologists and economists. That project has yielded two volumes (Henrich et al. 2004; Henrich and Ensminger forthcoming) and a number of papers summarizing the group's data (see especially Henrich et al. 2005; Henrich et al. 2006).

In this chapter, we report on the coordinated effort of two researchers from this project to use similar methods to combine the Berg, Dickhaut, and McCabe (1995) investment game with data on social network analysis for the same populations. Ensminger conducted this research among a community of Orma pastoral livestock herders in Eastern Africa, and Barr did similar analyses among several communities of urban coworkers in Accra, Ghana. The two studies provide an opportunity to examine how the hypothesized effect of network position on trust and trustworthiness holds in two contrasting populations in Africa. One is a population of pastoralists in a more remote and less developed region and the other is a population of mostly migrants working in various small-scale production enterprises in an urban setting. Despite these considerable differences in populations, we find tentative support for the effect of individual level measures of social network centrality on trusting behavior.

Orma

The Orma are pastoral livestock herders living in the arid Tana River district of eastern Kenya (see Ensminger 1992). Although roughly one-third of the population is still nomadic, two-thirds are sedentary and heavily integrated into the market economy. The entire economy is closely tied to livestock, though most sedentary households now practice some opportunistic flood-plain agriculture and many individuals have casual labor jobs or engage in small-scale trading activities. The wealthiest households are those with civil service jobs or involved in cattle trading and retail shopkeeping. Despite this high level of market integration, the population lives almost entirely in grass houses, education is limited, and the area has no running water, no electricity, and only one seasonal and highly unreliable road. In short, the area is remote and undeveloped by Kenyan standards, but the population is quite market savvy and entrepreneurial.

Members of this community who display high network centrality are typically active political and economic entrepreneurs from sedentary rather than nomadic households. They are also often senior male elders in the community who have central roles in dispute resolution and carry much influence in the community. Typically they are elders at the heads of large kinship groups and either are or have been successful livestock owners, livestock traders, shopkeepers, religious leaders, or headmen of the village. They command broad respect and are able to lobby others in the community to sway public opinion on a broad range of decision making and dispute resolution matters as diverse as domestic disputes, property rights conflicts, community development, and criminal complaints. These positions are not hereditary, however, and there is considerable fluidity in economic and political fortunes across generations and great variability among siblings in terms of their success in these roles. It is more accurate to characterize these individuals as self-made political brokers who are to some degree held accountable for their deeds. Those who score lowest in network centrality tend to be marginal community members, typically newcomers without strong kin connections in the area, women or young men who are not the sons of the power elite, and those with limited economic resources and who depend on the generosity of the top political and economic entrepreneurs.

Ghana

The Ghanaian sample was drawn from four enterprises, a bakery, a textiles and garment manufacturer, and two metal workshops, all in Accra, the capital city. The enterprises had fifteen, nine, twenty, and twenty-five employees respectively. The sample included fifty men and women. All were full-time employees and derived all of their personal income from their employment in these enterprises. Only one of the metal workshops could be described as a formal sector business, operating (roughly) in accordance with government regulations on taxation, trading, financial operations, and employment. The implication is that the individuals from the other three enterprises did not pay taxes and their employment was effectively unregulated by the government.

A key difference between the Orma and Ghanaian samples is that the Ghanaian social networks are both restricted to the workplace and far smaller and less dense than the Orma sample. Thus, though the Ghanaian network captures political dynamics within the firm, it does not capture all of the social and political dynamics of the Orma context.

Experimental Design

The measure of trust used in this chapter comes from experimental data collected in line with the investment game protocol designed by Berg, Dickhaut, and McCabe (1995; for the script, see the appendix). The game has two players. At the start of the game, both players receive an equal initial cash endowment equivalent to roughly one day's wage among the Orma and two days' among the urban Ghanaian workers. The first player decides how much of her cash to pass to the second player. In these games, for the purpose of simplicity and understanding, we limited the options to offers of 0, 25, 50, 75, and 100 percent. The amount player 1 passes is tripled by the experimenter and then given to the second player. The second player then decides how much to pass back to the first player. The first player's final payoff is thus the amount not sent, plus anything that was returned by player 2. The second player's final payoff is their original endowment, plus the portion received from player 1 (including the tripling done by the experimenter), less anything which player 2 returned to player 1. Under the classical assumptions of selfish money maximization, the second player returns nothing and, expecting this, the first player sends nothing.

In both sites the protocol for the game was back-translated into the native language of the participants. This process requires two bilingual speakers. One person unfamiliar with the game translates the text from English to the local language and another uninformed bilingual speaker translates the new text back into English. Any discrepancies in translation are then sorted out to the satisfaction of all speakers. The players were randomly selected from the community or workplace pool and invited to participate in the experiment at a set time and place. Among the Ghanaian workers, this occurred after work hours in schools near the employees' places of work. Roughly twenty individuals at a time were called for the game and monitored for the duration to ensure that they did not have contact with outsiders and did not talk among themselves about the game. They were instructed in the game according to identical scripts at both sites that included examples that were played out on a game board showing the payoffs to both players for each offer and response.

The players were then called one at a time to play the game. For the Orma population, this was always Ensminger and a native-speaking research assistant and, for the Ghanaian population, a native-speaking research assistant sometimes alone and sometimes with Barr. In these interviews, the players were taught the game once more, were verbally tested on their understanding of the game, and then played. Finally, they were directed to wait in a second isolated location until everyone had played and they could receive their payoffs. Both the description of the game presented in the first instance and the one-on-one interviews were scripted. If subjects asked questions, the relevant part of the script was repeated. Monitors were posted to prevent players awaiting their turn to play talking after learning the game but before making their decisions. Both roles and pairs were randomly assigned. The first players (the trusters) played in random order. The second players (the trustees) then played, again in random order. Each player was informed that they were playing with one of their covillagers or coworkers who had come for the game that day but none of the players knew the identity of their playing partner.

While subjects were waiting to play the game before the Ghanaian experiment, the sociodemographic data used in the analysis were collected. For the Orma, the income and wealth data were collected in a large-scale survey before the play, but other demographic data were collected at the time of the experiments. The interviews followed a structured questionnaire designed to elicit data on age, sex, education, income, and wealth. We used these data as controls in the regression analyses.

A word is in order on the use of experiments to capture trusting and trustworthy behavior among anonymous partners. We operate from the assumption that economic experiments often capture people playing out rules of thumb and behaving in ways consistent with their underlying experiences and social norms, even though such behaviors may not appear to make sense in an anonymous experiment (Ensminger 2004). For example, we posit that political entrepreneurs who have often taken the risk of trust in their daily lives and had such risk rewarded bring this experience into the game and invoke similar behavior more often than those who have not had the same experience. Similar principles apply to the role of trustworthy behavior in everyday life. People internalize societal norms and create habituated individual behaviors based on repeated experiences. When confronted with abstract games they often ask themselves, "What does this remind me of," and then use that analogy to guide their behavior in the experiment.

Network Data and Measures

Among both the Orma villagers and the Ghanaian workers, we used the same instrument to measure the social network. Among the Orma, twelve villages in one highly integrated market and political unit were surveyed and a closed network of 899 individuals was identified. All adult males and females in the area were asked the same question: "Who do you usually talk to about any kind of problem in this village?" Subjects listed as many individuals as they chose, within or outside their village. Because we bound the network in terms only of those interviewed, some who were mentioned but not interviewed were dropped from the network. This was a relatively small number, however, and usually did not include those named by anyone else, thus they were marginal with respect to this network.

Among the Orma, the network analysis was carried out two years after the trust experiments. Given the stability of kinship ties and network relationships in these communities, it is not expected that the centrality measures would have changed significantly over such a relatively short span. The results of these network measures are highly consistent with twenty-five years of ethnographic knowledge of the population and longitudinal observations of the power brokers within the society. It is quite common for the same elders to command these positions for a generation or more.

In the Ghanaian sample, the network analysis was carried out for each work site separately on the day of but before the experiments were conducted. Four firms were surveyed and the method used was identical to that used for the Orma except for the variation on the question: "Who do you usually talk to about any kind of problem in this workplace?"

The type of network relation used here was the result of careful consideration of the applicability and meaning of network relations for a larger cross-cultural study (Henrich et al. 2006). The network relation for use across study sites had to be relatively meaningful for cultures that were radically different economically, politically, socially, and geographically. The social relation for the go-to person with respect to problems was the one deemed the most applicable and meaningful whether we were dealing with social organization at the band, village, or workplace level. It also reflected social relations with the potential to in turn reflect elements of power, control, and political or social activity and influence, all important for understanding aspects of political and social entrepreneurship.

The primary network measures of interest include indegree and betweenness centrality as indicators of social capital (Freeman 1979; Johnson and Parks 1998). Indegree centrality as measured here reflects the extent to which an actor is a political go-to person for discussing or solving problems in the villages or factories. It reflects those actors people see as important for addressing village or workplace political or social problems and likely captures some element of those who are trusted or are viewed as trustworthy within segments of the network. Betweenness centrality reflects an actor's bridging or brokering social capital or the extent to which an actor spans structural holes in these problem-oriented communication networks (Burt 1992, 2005). This measure captures the degree to which individuals hold strategic positions as bridges between otherwise weakly connected segments of the network.

The $n \times n$ binary matrices of social relations X_{ij} for each culture group is defined as

$$X_{ij} = \begin{cases} 1 \text{ if } i \text{ goes to } j \text{ to discuss village or workplace problems,} \\ 0 \text{ otherwise} \end{cases}$$

The equation for betweenness centrality follows Freeman (1979), where the betweenness centrality $C_B(k)$ of node k is

$$C_B(k) = 2\left(\sum_{i-1}^{n}\sum_{j=1}^{n}\left[\frac{g_{ij}(k)}{g_{ij}}\right]\right)$$

Where for all unordered triples $i, j, k (i < j$, and $i \neq j \neq k)$, n is the number of nodes in the network, g_{ij} is the number of geodesics or shortest paths between node i and j, and $g_{ij}(k)$ is the number of shortest paths from i to j that include k. Similarly, the equation for indegree C_{DI} follows Freeman (1979):

$$C_{DI}(i) = \sum_{j=1}^{n} a_{ij}$$

Where for node i, a_{ji} is 1 if there is an edge from node j to i, 0 otherwise. These are simply a count of the number of incoming ties to a given node.

We include both indegree and betweenness centrality for determining social capital in this context on the basis of the political nature of the network relation elicited. Newman noted that betweenness and indegree are often closely related (2005). In terms of the relationship between the two measures in our study, we find in the Orma case a 0.83 correlation between log transformed indegree and betweenness centralities, indicating that the two measures are picking up much the same phenomena. In the Ghanaian sample, the correlation is 0.47. Newman also noted, however, that despite these similarities in terms of correlations there are often important subtle structural differences between the two measures. We include both measures. Indegree centrality reflects the importance of an actor in terms of the sheer number of people who cite an individual. This says nothing, however, about the nature of the ties to which a central actor is connected. Such ties could be with actors within or not within close social proximity. Thus it is quite possible that all ties to an actor with high indegree are highly localized (for example, with members that all know one another). In contrast, betweenness centrality has the potential to capture elements of the network global properties of an individual actor. Actors with high betweenness centrality are more likely to be tied to actors who are themselves not tied to one another, thus spanning structural holes. We therefore examine the contribution of each centrality measure to our understanding of variations in game playing behaviors separately in the models.

Experimental Data

In figure 3.1 we see the histogram of player 1 offers for the trust experiment among the Orma. The population splits roughly between offers of 25 and 50 percent of their stake. The mean offer for the entire group is 41 percent. Figure 3.2 displays the returns by player 2 as a percentage of what was received after the amount given by player 1 was tripled by the experimenter. Among the Orma, we see that though they repaid the trust (returns average 107 percent), many in the player 2 group pocketed the entire surplus from the tripling effect. Fifty percent of the players returned what player 1 sent and kept the two-thirds surplus. Nevertheless, the sample

Figure 3.1 Orma Trust, $N = 37$

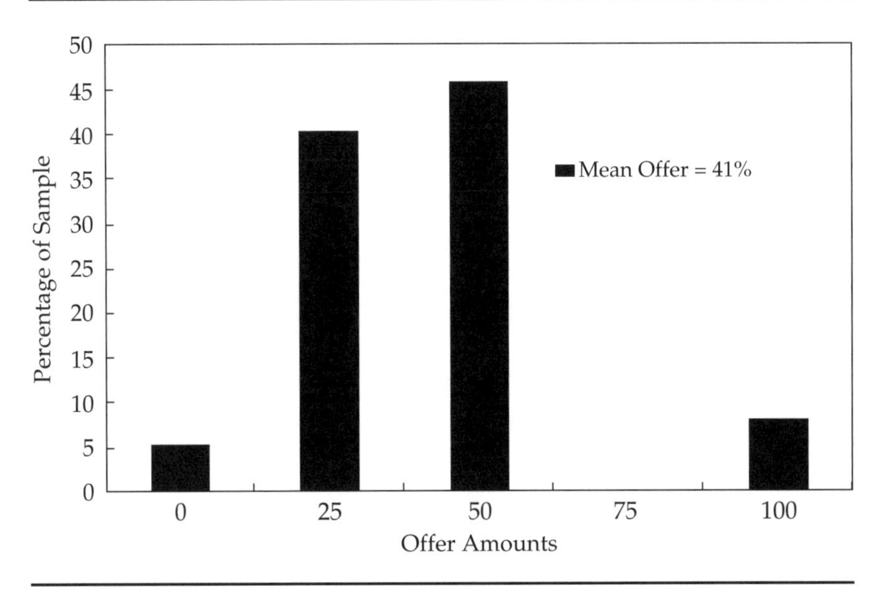

Source: Authors' calculations.
Note: Player 1 offers.

Figure 3.2 Orma Trustworthiness, $N = 30$

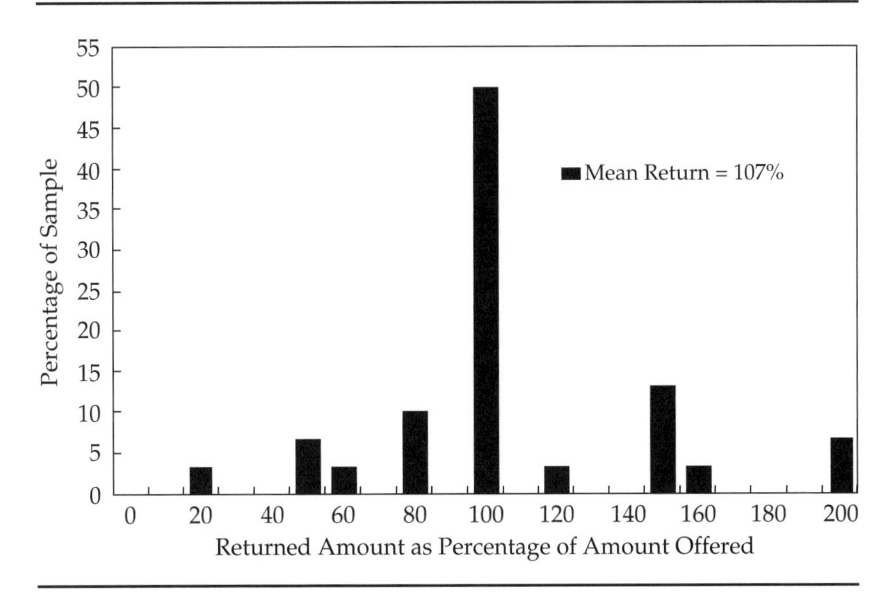

Source: Authors' calculations.
Note: Player 2 percentage return.

Figure 3.3 Ghana Trust, $N = 25$

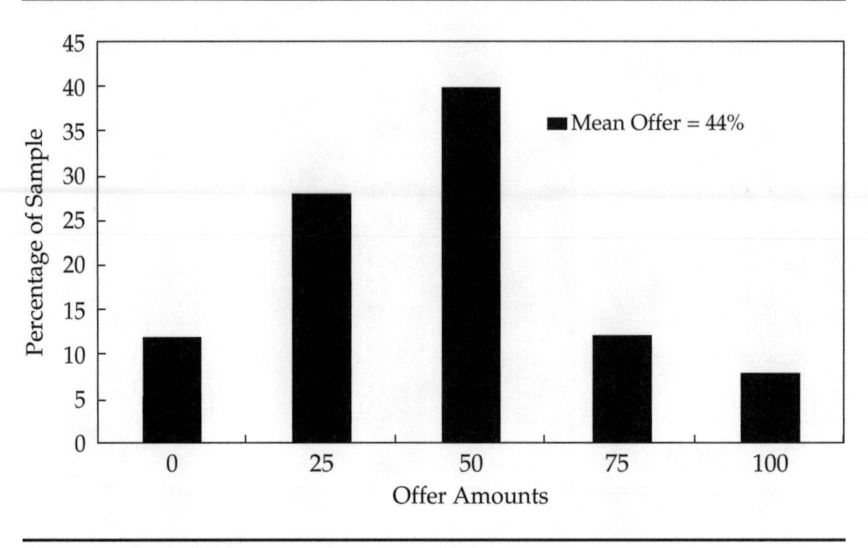

Source: Authors' calculations.
Note: Player 1 offers.

returns vary, from 20 percent to 200 percent, which is what results when all the money is split equitably between players 1 and 2.

In the Ghanaian sample, we see in figure 3.3 that the trust behavior of player 1s follows a pattern similar to that of the Orma, with a mean of 44 percent, but with somewhat more variation in behavior. However, they are significantly more trustworthy, as reflected in player 2 behavior in figure 3.4. Almost 45 percent returned the perfect equity amount of 200 percent, and 25 percent played more like the Orma and returned exactly the amount sent, but none of the surplus. Most of the remainder (about 25 percent) returned more than the amount sent, thereby providing their playing partners with a positive return on their trusting acts, while securing a higher final payoff for themselves.

In the regression tables (tables 3.1 through 3.5), we see the relative impact of demographic variables, including the players' social network positions. To counteract any nonnormality problems, network centrality measures have been log transformed. Gender has been dropped from the Orma regressions because it is inversely correlated with indegree –0.72. Based on the correlation measures, multicollinearity does not appear to be a problem for other variables.

Both network centrality as measured by indegree (those consulted on other's problems) and betweenness (social and political brokers) are significant predictors of trust and trustworthiness in these analyses. However, the

Figure 3.4 Ghana Trustworthiness, $N = 25$

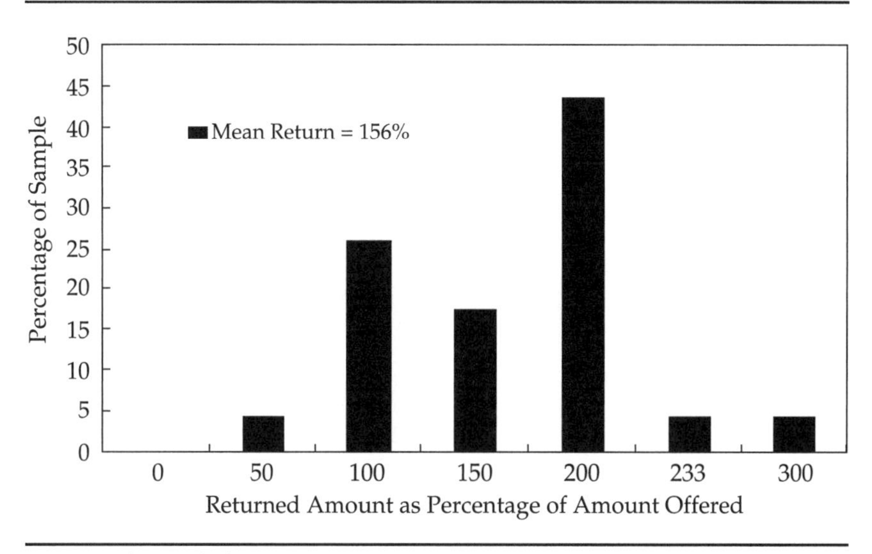

Source: Authors' calculations.
Note: Player 2 percentage return.

Table 3.1 Orma Trust and Network Centrality (Indegree), Player 1 Offers

Variable Divided by SD	Model 1	Model 2
Age	–0.760	
	(3.296)	
Education	15.650†	15.401*
	(8.090)	(7.505)
Household wealth	2.966	
	(3.952)	
Income	–6.851***	–6.193***
	(1.831)	(1.620)
Centrality: ln indegree	6.136†	6.078*
Sign. = one-tailed test	(4.773)	(3.066)
Constant	35.265***	33.697***
	(7.856)	(4.378)
Observations	37	37
R^2	.372***	.366***
Model significance	.001	.001

Source: Authors' calculations.
Note: Robust standard errors in parentheses.
$^{***}p = 0.001$, $^{**}p = 0.01$, $^{*}p = 0.05$, $^{\dagger}p = 0.1$

Table 3.2 Orma Trust and Network Centrality (Betweenness), Player 1 Offers

Variable Divided by SD	Model 1	Model 2
Age	2.167	
	(2.106)	
Education	18.589*	17.077*
	(7.523)	(7.275)
Household wealth	3.555	
	(4.424)	
Income	–6.042***	–4.839**
	(1.521)	(1.792)
Centrality: ln betweenness	1.103	1.793†
Sign. = one-tailed test	(1.532)	(1.400)
Constant	26.217*	29.017**
	(10.142)	(9.294)
Observations	37	37
R^2	.341***	.320**
Model significance	.001	.004

Source: Authors' calculations.
Note: Robust standard errors in parentheses.
***$p = 0.001$, **$p = 0.01$ *$p = 0.05$ †$p = 0.1$

sample sizes in both studies are small, the statistical significance is sometimes marginal and not robust across both samples, and consequently these findings should be interpreted more as inspiration for future work rather than as definitive evidence of the effect we are highlighting. Among the Orma, we see evidence that network centrality, measured as both indegree (table 3.1) and betweenness (table 3.2) are marginally correlated with higher levels of trusting behavior. In table 3.3, we find that the same effect holds among the workers in Ghana when we measure betweenness (both logged and unlogged). Although the coefficient is positive for indegree in Ghana, it is not statistically significant, and we have not included these results.

We extend Burt's theory relating network spanning to social entrepreneurship to suggest that those who bridge structural holes (high betweenness individuals), should be more likely to engage in trusting behavior (2005). This relationship is suggested by our data in the direction predicted.

We turn now to the indices of trustworthiness, as measured by how much of the tripled offer player 2 chooses to return to player 1. We suggested that those who achieve positions of social and political entrepreneurship—that is, those who bridge structural holes (high betweenness) and those to whom others turn for advice (high indegree)—are likely to earn these positions in part by demonstrating that they are

Table 3.3 Ghana Trust and Network Centrality (Betweenness), Player 1 Offers

Variable Divided by SD	Model 1	Model 2	Model 3
Age	0.559		
	(6.015)		
Female	−14.480		
	(11.496)		
Education	0.091		
	(3.112)		
Household wealth	5.018		
	(9.120)		
Income	3.673		
	(2.849)		
Centrality: betweenness	2.066*	2.538**	
Sign. in one-tailed test	(1.218)	(0.791)	
Centrality: ln betweenness			10.356*
Sign. in one-tailed test			(5.403)
Constant	35.285†	33.848***	32.237***
	(20.508)	(5.839)	(6.700)
Observations	25	25	25
R^2	.300**	.201**	.154†
Model significance	.002	.004	.068

Source: Author's calculations.
Note: Robust standard errors in parentheses.
***$p = 0.001$, **$p = 0.01$, *$p = 0.05$, †$p = 0.1$

trustworthy. Our Orma data support this hypothesis strongly, but our Ghanaian data do not. In table 3.4, we see that for the Orma indegree is a statistically significant correlate of trustworthiness. Similarly, in table 3.5 (also for the Orma), betweenness is also a statistically strong correlate of trustworthiness. Returning to the histograms of the trustworthiness offers, we see in figure 3.4 for the Ghanaian workers that their mean of 156 percent is pushing against the logical bound of 200 percent (pure equity return). It is possible that with our small sample sizes, the low level of variation in the Ghanaian data made it difficult to pick up a statistically significant effect. Alternatively, one should note that the Ghanaian firm sizes are very small (nine to twenty-five members), and it is possible that untrustworthy behavior in such small-scale environments just does not pay for anyone. Finally, as noted, the networks we capture in the Ghanaian workplaces are more circumscribed than those in the Orma villages. The Orma networks are large and dense and most likely subsume more dimensions than do those shared in the workplace. Among other things, they are more affected by kinship, which undoubtedly interacts with trust and trustworthiness.

Table 3.4 Orma Trustworthiness and Network Centrality (Indegree), Player 2 Returns

Variable Divided by SD	Model 1	Model 2
Age	–5.011	
	(9.318)	
Education	–4.272)	
	(9.039)	
Household wealth	27.975	
	(18.300)	
Income	–7.702	–8.811**
	(4.628)	(3.033)
Centrality: ln indegree	24.365**	21.461***
Sign. = one-tailed test	(9.017)	(6.268)
Constant	86.028**	81.825***
	(25.774)	(8.794)
Observations	30	30
R^2	.367**	.271**
Model significance	.012	.006

Source: Authors' calculations.
Note: Robust standard errors in parentheses.
***$p = 0.001$, **$p = 0.01$, *$p = 0.05$, †$p = 0.10$

Table 3.5 Orma Trustworthiness and Network Centrality (Betweenness), Player 2 Returns

Variable Divided by SD	Model 1	Model 2
Age	4.314	
	(8.288)	
Education	–5.728	
	(9.083)	
Household wealth	18.485	
	(17.007)	
Income	–2.611	–5.636†
	(3.227)	(2.906)
Centrality: ln betweenness	9.561*	9.134***
Sign. = one-tailed test	(4.431)	(3.829)
Constant	33.401	53.526**
	(28.137)	(20.527)
Observations	30	30
R^2	.319*	.201†
Model significance	.015	.068

Source: Authors' calculations.
Note: Robust standard errors in parentheses.
***$p = 0.001$, **$p = 0.01$, *$p = 0.05$, †$p = 0.10$

These differences may also explain some of the differences in the findings, which only more research can help tease out.

Conclusions

Much work has been published on the individual-level demographic correlates of trusting and trustworthy behavior, but this is—to the best of our knowledge—the first study to report on behavioral measures of trust together with complete social network data, although Jacob Goeree and his colleagues have done so for dictator games (forthcoming). We measure trust and trustworthiness with economic experimental data following closely the Berg, Dickhaut, and McCabe (1995) investment game. We draw two samples from Africa, one rural (the Orma of Kenya) and one urban (workers in Accra, Ghana). Controlling for age, education, income, and wealth, we find support for our theoretical argument that political entrepreneurs (as measured by two types of social network centrality) are more trusting, and in one of our studies (the Orma of Kenyan), also more trustworthy.

Our sample sizes are small, and thus the power of our findings are not high, but they point clearly in the direction of the theoretical work of Ronald Burt, who has articulated the entrepreneurial role of actors who have maneuvered into pivotal social network positions (2005). We extend this work by positing that one of the ways in which political entrepreneurs achieve and maintain their positions of network centrality is by demonstrating trustworthiness. Second, we find support for Russell Hardin, who views trusting behavior as a necessary risk in pursuit of considerable rewards (2002). Social and political entrepreneurs are more trusting in both of our samples and more trustworthy in one of our samples (the Orma).

Future research is necessary to address some of the limitations of the work as reported here. In addition to increasing the number of study participants and the number and types of cases studied, there should be attempts to understand the extent to which other types of network relations (for example, friendship) or the multiplicity of relations affect study outcomes. The results of this study certainly suggest a relationship between variation in game playing behaviors and the characteristics of an actor's network structural position, just as Jacob Goeree and his colleagues found for the dictator game (forthcoming).

Appendix: The Trust Game Script

Note to researchers: Be sure to read the general instructions that you always read before a game (see below). Players 1 and 2 should be separated in two rooms/locations before you begin this game. The risk of collusion in the holding room is greater in this game due to the tripling effect and warrants the trade-off. First instruct the player 1s in a group, then take all of their offers. Ask them to wait while you play with the player 2s and then call back the player 1s to pay them off. Remember that there is no show-up fee with the trust game because both sides are given the same initial endowment.

General Instructions

Thank you all for taking the time to come today. This game may take three to four hours, so if you think you will not be able to stay that long without leaving please let us know now. Before we begin, I want to make some general comments about what we are doing here today and explain some rules that we need to follow. We will be playing a game for real money that you will take home. You should understand that this is not [insert name of researcher]'s own money. It is money given to [him/her] by [his/her] university to use to do a research study. This is research—which will eventually be part of a book [optional: it is not part of a development project of any sort.] [Insert name of researcher] is working together with many other university professors who are carrying out the same kind of games all around the world.

Before we proceed any further, let me stress something that is very important. Many of you were invited here without understanding very much about what we are planning to do today. If at any time you find that this is something that you do not wish to participate in for any reason, you are of course free to leave regardless of whether we have started the game.

If you have heard about a game that has been played here in the past you should try to forget everything that you have been told. This is a completely different game. We are about to begin the game. It is important that you listen as carefully as possible, because only people who understand the game will actually be able to play it. [Insert name of researcher] will run through some examples here while we are all together [if you are doing this]. You cannot ask questions or talk about the game while we are here together. This is very important and please be sure that you obey this rule, because it is possible for one person to spoil the game for everyone, in which case we would not be able to play the game today. Do not worry if you do not completely understand the game as we go through the examples here in the group. Each of you will have a chance to ask questions in private with [insert name of researcher] to be sure that you understand how to play.

Trust Game Instructions

This game is played by pairs of individuals. Each pair is made up of a player 1 and a player 2. Each of you will play this game with someone from your own village. However, none of you will know exactly with whom you are playing. Only [insert name of researcher] knows who is to play with whom and [he/she] will never tell anyone else.

[Insert name of researcher] will give $4 to each player 1 and another $4 to each player 2. Player 1 then has the opportunity to give a portion of their $4 to player 2. They could give $4, or $3, or $2, or $1, or nothing. [Note: It is important to allow only five options for dividing the money—this is to simplify the game and to create the same focal points across sites.] Whatever amount player 1 decides to give to player 2 will be tripled by the researcher before it is passed on to player 2. Player 2 then has the option of returning any portion of this tripled amount to player 1.

Then the game is over.

Player 1 goes home with whatever he or she kept from their original $4, plus anything returned to them by Player 2. Player 2 goes home with their original $4, plus whatever was given to them by Player 1 and then tripled by [insert name of researcher], minus whatever they returned to Player 1.

Here are some examples [Note: you should work through these examples by having all the possibilities laid out in front of people, with player 1's options from $4 to $0 and a second column showing the effects of the tripling. As you go through each example demonstrate visually what happens to the final outcomes for each player. Be careful to remind people that player 2 always also has the original $4.]:

1. Imagine that player 1 gives $4 to player 2. [Insert name of researcher] triples this amount, so player 2 gets $12 (three times $4 equals $12) over and above their initial $4. At this point, player 1 has nothing and player 2 has $16. Then player 2 has to decide whether they wish to give anything back to player 1, and if so, how much. Suppose player 2 decides to return $3 to player 1. At the end of the game, player 1 will go home with $3 and player 2 will go home with $13.
2. Now let's try another example. Imagine that player 1 gives $3 to player 2. [Insert name of researcher] triples this amount, so player 2 gets $9 (three times $3 equals $9) over and above their initial $4. At this point, player 1 has $1 and player 2 has $13. Then player 2 has to decide whether they wish to give anything back to player 1, and if so, how much. Suppose player 2 decides to return $0 to player 1. At the end of the game, player 1 will go home with $1 and player 2 will go home with $13.
3. Now let's try another example. Imagine that player 1 gives $2 to player 2. [Insert name of researcher] triples this amount, so player 2 gets $6 (three times $2 equals $6) over and above their initial $4. At this point, player 1 has $2 and player 2 has $10. Then player 2 has to decide whether they wish to give anything back to player 1, and if so, how much. Suppose player 2 decides to return $3 to player 1. At the end of the game, player 1 will go home with $5 and player 2 will go home with $7.
4. Now let's try another example. Imagine that player 1 gives $1 to player 2. [Insert name of researcher] triples this amount, so player 2 gets $3 (three times $1 equals $3) over and above their initial $4. At this point, player 1 has $3 and player 2 has $7. Then player 2 has to decide whether they wish to give anything back to player 1, and if so, how much. Suppose player 2 decides to return $2 to player 1. At the end of the game, player 1 will go home with $5 and player 2 will go home with $5.

5. Now let's try another example. Imagine that Player 1 gives nothing to player 2. There is nothing for [insert name of researcher] to triple. Player 2 has nothing to give back and the game ends here. Player 1 goes home with $4 and player 2 goes home with $4.

Note that the larger the amount that player 1 gives to player 2, the greater the amount that can be taken away by the two players together. However, it is entirely up to player 2 to decide what to give back to player 1. The first player could end up with more than $4 or less than $4 as a result.

We will go through more examples with each of you individually when you come to play the game. In the mean time, do not talk to anyone about the game. Even if you are not sure that you understand the game, do not talk to anyone about it. This is important. If you talk to anyone about the game while you are waiting to play, we must disqualify you from playing.

[Bring in each player 1 one by one. Use as many of the examples below as necessary.]

6. Imagine that player 1 gives $4 to player 2. [Insert name of researcher] triples this amount, so player 2 gets $12 (three times $4 equals $12) <u>over and above</u> their initial $4. At this point, player 1 has nothing and player 2 has $16. Then player 2 has to decide whether they wish to give anything back to player 1, and if so, how much. Suppose player 2 decides to return $6 to player 1. At the end of the game, player 1 will go home with $6 and player 2 will go home with $10.
7. Now let's try another example. Imagine that player 1 gives $3 to player 2. [Insert name of researcher] triples this amount, so player 2 gets $9 (three times $3 equals $9) <u>over and above</u> their initial $4. At this point, player 1 has $1 and player 2 has $13. Then player 2 has to decide whether they wish to give anything back to player, and if so, how much. Suppose player 2 decides to return $11 to player 1. At the end of the game, player 1 will go home with $12 and player 2 will go home with $2.
8. Now let's try another example. Imagine that player 1 gives $2 to player 2. [Insert name of researcher] triples this amount, so player 2 gets $6 (three times $2 equals $6) <u>over and above</u> their initial $4. At this point, player 1 has $2 and player 2 has $10. Then player 2 has to decide whether they wish to give anything back to player 1, and if so, how much. Suppose player 2 decides to return $0 to player 1. At the end of the game, player 1 will go home with $2 and player 2 will go home with $10.
9. Now let's try another example. Imagine that player 1 gives $1 to player 2. [Insert name of researcher] triples this amount, so player 2 gets $3 (three times $1 equals $3) <u>over and above</u> their initial $4. At this point, player 1 has $3 and player 2 has $7. Then player 2 has to decide whether they wish to give anything back to player 1, and if so, how much. Suppose player 2 decides to return $2 to player 1. At the end of the game player 1 will go home with $5 and player 2 will go home with $5.

10. Now let's try another example. Imagine that player 1 gives nothing to player 2. There is nothing for [insert name of researcher] to triple. Player 2 has nothing to give back and the game ends here. Player 1 goes home with $4 and player 2 goes home with $4.

Now, can you work through these examples for me:

11. Imagine that player 1 gives $3 to player 2. So, player 2 gets $9 (3 times $3 equals $9) over and above their initial $4. At this point, player 1 has $1 and player 2 has $13. Suppose player 2 decides to return $5 to player 1. At the end of the game player 1 will have how much? [The initial $4 – $3 (given to player 2) = $1 + return from player 2 of $5 = $6. If they are finding it difficult, talk through the math with them and be sure to use demonstration with the actual money.] And player 2 will have how much? [Their original $4 + $9 (after the tripling of the $3 sent by player 1) – $5 they return to player 1 = $8, if they are finding it difficult, talk through the math with them.]
12. Imagine that player 1 gives $1 to player 2. So player 2 gets $3 (3 times $1 equals $3) over and above their initial $4. Then, suppose that player 2 decides to give $1 back to Player 1. At the end of the game player 1 will have how much? [The initial $4 – $1 (given to player 2) = $3 + return from player 2 of $1 = $4. If they are finding it difficult, talk through the maths with them and be sure to use demonstration with the actual money.] And player 2 will have how much? [Their original $4 + $6 (after the tripling of the $3 sent by player 1) – $1 they return to player 1 = $6, if they are finding it difficult, talk through the maths with them.]

First player: You are player 1. Here is your $4. [At this point $4 is placed on the table in front of the player.] While I [RA] am turned away, you must hand [insert researcher's name] the amount of money you want to be tripled and passed on to player 2. You can give player 2 nothing, $1, $2, $3, or $4. Player 2 will receive this amount tripled by me plus their own initial $4. Remember the more you give to player 2 the greater the amount of money at his or her disposal. While player 2 is under no obligation to give anything back, we will pass onto you whatever he or she decides to return. [Now the player hands back whatever he or she wants to have tripled and passed to player 2.]

[Note to researcher: Finish all player 1s and send them to a third holding location—they must not return to the group of player 1s who have not played and they must not join the player 2s. Once all player 1s have played you can begin to call player 2s. Player 2s can be paid off immediately after they play and sent home.]

Second player: You are player 2. First, here is your $4. [Put the $4 in front of player 2.] Let's put that to one side. [Move the $4 to one side but leave it on the table.] This pile represents player 1's initial $4. [Put this $4 in front of the researcher.] Now [insert name of researcher] will show you how much player 1 decided to give to you. It will be tripled. Then you must hand back the amount that you want returned to player 1. [Take player 1's offer out of the pile representing player 1's stake and put it down in front of player 2, near but not on top of player 2's $4. Then add to player 1's offer to get the tripled amount. Receive back player 2's response.] Remember, you can choose to give something back or not. Do what you wish. While I [RA] am turned away, you must hand [insert researcher's name] the amount of money you want to send back to player 1. [The player hands back his return for player 1.] You are now free to go home, but do not visit with any of the waiting players.

References

Alesina, Alberto, and Eliana La Ferrara. 2002. "Who Trusts Others?" *Journal of Public Economics* 85(2): 207–34.

Anderson, Lisa, Jennifer Mellor, and Jeffrey Milyo. 2005a. "Did the Devil Make Them Do It? The Effects of Religion and Religiosity in Public Goods and Trust Games." *Department of Economics* working paper 20. Williamsburg, Va.: College of William and Mary.

———. 2005b. "An Experimental Study of the Effects of Inequality and Relative Deprivation on Trusting Behavior." *Department of Economics* working paper 0502. St. Louis: University of Missouri.

Berg, Joyce, John Dickhaut, and Kevin McCabe. 1995. "Trust, Reciprocity, and Social History." *Games and Economic Behavior* 10(1): 122–42.

Bouckaert, Jan, and Geert Dhaene. 2003. "Inter-Ethnic Trust and Reciprocity: Result from and Experiment with Small Businessmen." *European Journal of Political Economy* 20(4): 869–86.

Burns, Justine. 2004. "Race and Trust in Post Apartheid South Africa." Unpublished manuscript. University of Cape Town and Santa Fe Institute.

Burt, Ronald S. 1992. *Structural Holes: The Social Structure of Competition.* Cambridge, Mass.: Harvard University Press.

———. 1997. "The Contingent Value of Social Capital." *Administrative Science Quarterly* 42(June): 339–65.

———. 2001. "Structural Holes Versus Network Closure as Social Capital." In *Social Capital: Theory and Research,* edited by Nan Lin, Karen S. Cook, and Ronald S. Burt. New York: Aldine de Gruyter.

———. 2002. "Bridge Decay." *Social Networks* 24(4): 333–63.

———. 2005. *Brokerage and Closure: An Introduction to Social Capital.* Oxford: Oxford University Press.

Burt, Ronald S., Joseph Janotta, and James Mahoney. 1998. "Personality Correlates of Structural Holes." *Social Networks* 20(1): 63–87.

Carpenter, Jeffrey P., Amrita G. Daniere, and Lois M. Takahashi. 2004. "Cooperation, Trust, and Social Capital in Southeast Asian Urban Slums." *Journal of Economic Behavior and Organization* 55(4): 533–51.

Chaudhury, Ananish, and Lata Gangadharan. 2003. "Gender Differences in Trust and Reciprocity." Working paper. Auckland: University of Auckland.

Christopoulos, Dimitrios C. 2006. "Relational Attributes of Political Entrepreneurs: A Network Perspective." *Journal of European Public Policy* 13(5): 757–78.

Coleman, James S. 1990. *Foundations of Social Theory.* Cambridge, Mass: Harvard University Press.
Cook, Karen S., and Robin M. Cooper. 2003. "Experimental Studies of Cooperation, Trust and Social Exchange." In *Trust and Reciprocity: Interdisciplinary Lessons from Experimental Research,* edited by Elinor Ostrom and James Walker. New York: Russell Sage Foundation.
Cook, Karen S., Russell Hardin, and Margaret Levi. 2005. *Cooperation Without Trust.* New York: Russell Sage Foundation.
Croson, Rachel, and Nancy Buchan. 1999. "Gender and Culture: International Experimental Evidence from Trust Games." *American Economic Review* 89(2): 386–91.
DeBruine, Lisa M. 2002. "Facial Resemblance Enhances Trust." *Proceedings of the Royal Society of London* 269(1498): 1307–312.
Durlauf, Steven N. 2002. "On the Empirics of Social Capital." *The Economic Journal* 112(483; November): 459–79.
Eckel, Catherine C., and Rick K. Wilson. 2003. "Conditional Trust: Sex, Race and Facial Expressions in a Trust Game." In *Trust and Reciprocity: Interdisciplinary Lessons from Experimental Research,* edited by Elinor Ostrom and James M. Walker. New York: Russell Sage Foundation.
———. 2004. "Is Trust a Risky Decision?" *Journal of Economic Behavior & Organization* 55(4): 447–65.
Ensminger, Jean. 1992. *Making a Market: The Institutional Transformation of an African Society.* Cambridge: Cambridge University Press.
———. 2004. "Market Integration and Fairness: Evidence from Ultimatum, Dictator, and Public Goods Experiments in East Africa." In *Foundations of Human Sociality: Economic Experiments and Ethnographic Evidence from Fifteen Small-Scale Societies,* edited by Joseph Henrich, Robert Boyd, Samuel Bowles, Colin Camerer, Ernst Fehr, and Herbert Gintis. Oxford: Oxford University Press.
Ensminger, Jean, and Jack Knight. 1997. "Changing Social Norms: Common Property, Bridewealth, and Clan Exogamy." *Current Anthropology* 38(1): 1–24.
Freeman, Linton C. 1979. "Centrality in Social Networks: Conceptual Clarification." *Social Networks* 1(3): 215–39.
Glaeser, Edward L., David I. Laibson, and Bruce Sacerdote. 2002. "An Economic Approach to Social Capital." *Economic Journal* 112(483): 437–58.
Glaeser, Edward L., David I. Laibson, Jose A. Scheinkman, and Christine L. Soutter. 2000. "Measuring Trust." *Quarterly Journal of Economics* 115(3): 811–46.
Goeree, Jacob K., Margaret A. McConnell, Tiffany Mitchell, Tracey Tromp, and Leeat Yariv. Forthcoming. "The 1/d Law of Giving." *American Economic Journal: Microeconomics.*
Guillén, Mauro F., Randall Collins, Paula England, and Marshall Meyer. 2002. *The New Economic Sociology: Developments in an Emerging Field.* New York: Russell Sage Foundation.
Hardin, Russell. 2002. *Trust and Trustworthiness.* New York: Russell Sage Foundation.
Hartung, John. 1988. "Deceiving Down: Conjectures on the Management of Subordinate Status." In *Self-Deception: An Adaptive Mechanism,* edited by Joan S. Stockard and Delroy L. Paulhus. Englewood Cliffs, N.J.: Prentice Hall.
Henrich, Joseph, and Jean Ensminger, eds. forthcoming. *Experimenting with Social Norms: Fairness and Punishment in Cross-Cultural Perspective.* New York: Russell Sage Foundation.

Henrich, Joseph, Robert Boyd, Samuel Bowles, Colin Camerer, Ernst Fehr, and Herbert Gintis, eds. 2004. *Foundations of Human Sociality: Economic Experiments and Ethnographic Evidence from Fifteen Small-Scale Societies.* Oxford: Oxford University Press.

Henrich, Joseph, Richard McElreath, Abigail Barr, Jean Ensminger, Clark Barrett, Alexander Bolyanatz, Juan Camilo Cardenas, Michael Gurven, Edwins Gwako, Natalie Henrich, Carolyn Lesorogol, Frank Marlowe, David Tracer, and John Ziker. 2006. "Costly Punishment Across Human Societies." *Science* 312(23): 1767–770.

Henrich, Joseph, Robert Boyd, Samuel Bowles, Colin Camerer, Ernst Fehr, Herbert Gintis, Richard McElreath, Michael Alvard, Abigail Barr, Jean Ensminger, Natalie Smith Henrich, Kim Hill, Francisco Gil-White, Michael Gurven, Frank Marlowe, John Q. Patton, and David Tracer. 2005. "'Economic Man' in Cross-Cultural Perspective: Behavioral Experiments in 15 Small-Scale Societies." *Behavioral and Brain Sciences* 28(6): 795–855.

Johnson, Jeffrey C., and Michael K. Orbach. 2002. "Perceiving the Political Landscape: Ego Biases in Cognitive Political Networks." *Social Networks* 24(3): 291–310.

Johnson, Jeffrey C., and Dawn Parks. 1998. "Communication Roles, Perceived Effectiveness, and Satisfaction in an Environmental Management Program." *Journal of Computational and Mathematical Organization Theory* 4(3): 223–39.

Kramer, Roderick M. 1999. "Trust and Distrust in Organizations: Emerging Perspectives, Enduring Questions." *Annual Review of Psychology* 50(February): 569–98.

Lin, Nan. 1999. "Building a Network Theory of Social Capital." *Connections* 22(1): 28–51.

———. 2001. *Social Capital: A Theory of Social Structure and Action.* New York: Cambridge University Press.

Lin, Nan, Karen Cook, and Ronald S. Burt, eds. 2001. *Social Capital: Theory and Research.* New York: Aldine de Gruyter.

McCarty, Christopher. 2002. "Structure in Personal Networks." *Journal of Social Structure* 3(1). Available at: http://www.cmu.edu/joss/content/articles/volume3/McCarty.html (accessed in 2007).

Newman, Mark E. J. 2005. "A Measure of Betweenness Based on Random Walks." *Social Networks* 27(1): 39–54.

Portes, Alejandro, and Patricia Landolt. 1996. "The Downside of Social Capital." *The American Prospect* 26(1): 18–23.

Portes, Alejandro, and Julia Sensenbrenner. 1993. "Embeddedness and Immigration: Notes on the Social Determinants of Economic Action." *American Journal of Sociology* 98(6): 1320–50.

Putnam, Robert D. 1993. "The Prosperous Community: Social Capital and Public Life." *The American Prospect* 13(spring): 35–42.

———. 2000. *Bowling Alone: The Collapse and Revival of American Community.* New York: Simon & Schuster.

Schneider, Mark, and Paul Teske. 1992. "Toward a Theory of the Entrepreneur-Evidence from Local Government." *American Political Science Review* 86(3): 737–47.

Sobel, Joel. 2002. "Can We Trust Social Capital?" *Journal of Economic Literature* 40(1): 139–54.

Wasserman, Stanley, and Katherine Faust. 1994. *Social Network Analysis: Methods and Applications.* Cambridge: Cambridge University Press.

Yamagishi, Toshio. 2001. "Trust as a Form of Social Intelligence." In *Trust in Society*, edited by Karen S. Cook. New York: Russell Sage Foundation.

Chapter 4

Trust and Reciprocity as Foundations for Cooperation

JAMES WALKER AND ELINOR OSTROM

NUMEROUS EXPERIMENTAL STUDIES conducted over the past several decades have demonstrated that individuals' decisions, in a variety of social dilemma situations, reflect complex and diverse motivations beyond simple self-income maximization (see research summarized in Camerer 2003; Camerer and Fehr 2006; Ostrom and Walker 2003). This research, replicated across multiple cultures, has led to a wide variety of models designed to reflect rich and complex social preferences. Central to many of them, and the primary focus of this chapter, is the interaction between trust and reciprocity as necessary foundations for the evolution of cooperative solutions to social dilemmas (chapter 1, this volume). We continue to use the concept of trust as we defined it in our conclusion to our earlier Russell Sage volume: "as the willingness to take some risk in relation to other individuals on the expectation that the others will reciprocate" (Ostrom and Walker 2003, 382).

In addition, an ongoing discussion among social scientists undertaking research in the field and the laboratory has focused on the extent to which clear behavioral differences in social dilemma settings can be attributed to the context in which decision makers interact—including institutional rules, incentives, and time horizons. Using results reported from the experimental laboratory and the field, the primary goal of this chapter is to provide a set of illustrative examples of many of the core findings from this research. These examples, which are based in large part on research in which we have been extensively involved with collaborators, are not meant to provide a complete overview of this extensive literature but instead insight into the importance of context as it influences trust and reciprocity, and ultimately the level and sustainability of cooperation.

Social Dilemmas

Social dilemmas characterize settings where a divergence exists between expected outcomes from individuals pursuing strategies based on narrow self-interests versus groups pursuing strategies based on the interests of the group as a whole. The presence of social dilemmas and the degree of predicted suboptimality depend on three components of the decision situation: the existence of a physical domain in which the actions of one individual imparts gains or losses on others, such as externalities in production or consumption; modes of behavior in which individuals make decisions based on individual gains rather than group gains or losses; and environments or institutional settings that do or do not create incentives for internalizing group gains or losses into individuals' decision calculus.

When individuals make choices that do not fully account for social costs or benefits, their choices lead to outcomes that are suboptimal from the perspective of the group. The empirical significance of social dilemmas thus depends on the physical characteristics of a given situation, the paradigmatic mode of behavior of individuals in that situation, and the incentives created by the institutions governing the situation. This chapter focuses primarily on behavior from three stylized social dilemma decision situations: the trust or investment game, the public goods game, and the common-pool resource game.

We briefly describe each of these games as they have been studied in experimental laboratories around the world, including examples of core behavioral results obtained in experimental studies. When feasible, we indicate efficiency measures that relate actual behavior to behavior that would yield maximum payoffs to the group. Nonlaboratory studies have also examined contexts similar to the social dilemmas examined in the laboratory. Including a brief overview of such studies enables us to comment on the robustness of results found in the laboratory that most often includes decisions made by undergraduate students.

Trust Game

The most commonly examined form of the trust game includes two players, making decisions sequentially. Each player begins with an endowment of E tokens worth Z dollars each. Subjects are randomly paired as type X and type Y. Each X decides whether to send any tokens to Y. Each token that X sends reduces the value of his or her token fund by $\$Z$, but increases the value of the token fund of Y by a multiple of $\$Z$ greater than 1. After X makes his or her decision, Y makes his or hers. Y's decision is to divide the value of the token fund he or she holds with X. That is, Y decides how much of the fund to keep for him or herself and how much to send back to X. In the most commonly examined form of this game, each player begins with an endowment of ten tokens worth $1 each, the multiplier is three, and the game is played only once. To maximize the joint payoffs, the first mover (X) would send his or her entire endowment to the second mover (Y), creating the largest possible surplus to be divided between them. The social dilemma is, however, that the first mover's pecuniary interest is to send nothing, unless he or she trusts the second mover to return a suitable amount. The pecuniary incentive of the second mover, however, is to return nothing. Thus the predicted return for both players is suboptimal in terms of what could be obtained if X trusted Y and Y reciprocated that trust.

Public Goods Games

The most commonly examined form of this game includes N players, making decisions simultaneously. Each player begins with an endowment of E tokens worth Z dollars each. Each player is allowed to allocate a portion of his or her endowment to a group fund, yielding a benefit to that player and all other players in the group, regardless of their own decision. That part of the endowment that is not allocated to the group fund is maintained in his or her private fund. Each token allocated to the group fund yields less to the contributor than its value in his or her private fund, but a greater amount to the group as a whole. For example, suppose that $N = 4$, and that each token allocated to a player's private fund is worth $.01, and that each token allocated to the group fund yields $.0075 to each player (meaning that the value to the group of a token allocated to the group fund is $.03). To maximize group earnings, all individuals would allocate their entire endowments to the group fund. If the game is played only once, however, an individual's pecuniary interest is to allocate nothing to the group fund.[1]

Common-Pool Resource Game

Like the public goods game, the typical common-pool game includes N players, making decisions simultaneously. Each player begins with an endowment of E tokens worth $\$Z$ each. Each player is allowed to invest a portion of his or her endowment into an investment opportunity—the common-pool resource—that initially yields higher returns at the margin than if these funds remain in his or her private fund. However, the marginal gain from the investment opportunity in the common pool decreases with the overall size of the aggregate group investment. Each individual receives a return from the common pool as a proportion of his or her investment relative to the aggregate investment. To maximize joint payoffs, the group invests some but not all of its endowments in the common pool. The dilemma is that each individual's pecuniary interest is to invest more than the amount that would maximize group earnings (for an example of an alternative common-pool resource setting, see Herr, Gardner, and Walker 1997).

Context

Each of these games has been studied in the laboratory under varying contextual conditions including, but not limited to, size of group, size of incentives, repetition of the game, and institutional changes that alter decision or outcome space. The varying contexts can be viewed, at least in part, as influencing the level of trust and expected reciprocity players may anticipate from their game counterparts. In some cases, based purely on pecuniary payoffs, the change in context shifts the noncooperative Nash equilibrium and subsequently expected play from a traditional theoretical perspective. The contextual influences observed in the laboratory, however, go beyond those that can be explained by purely pecuniary motives. In one sense, it is behavioral regularities that are essential to understanding the foundations of trust and cooperation and how the contextual structure of the experiment increases or decreases the likelihood of sustained levels of cooperation (for a summary of possible explanations for trust, see chapter 2, this volume).

Games of Trust

We begin with a summary presentation of trust experiments conducted during the spring of 2006 (Cox et al. 2009). All experiments were conducted using double-blind procedures and follow a decision format that parallels that discussed in the introduction. Figure 4.1 presents a bar graph and summary statistics for key behavioral measures for the decisions. The *x*-axis displays decisions for each *X*-*Y* pair, ordered from high to low in regard to the *X*-decision. The first behavioral result to notice is the extreme heterogeneity in decisions by *X* and *Y* players.

Recall, the decision that maximizes joint payoffs in this game is for *X* to send all ten tokens to *Y*, increasing the value of *Y*'s token fund by $30, and yielding a maximum of $40 to be allocated among the two players. This is relative to the minimum of $20 the players would earn if *X* sent zero tokens (because both players begin the game with endowments of $10). In these experiments, the average *X* decision (amount sent) is $5.65, increasing *Y*'s token fund by $16.95. From the perspective of efficiency or the gains from trust, on average, the players in this game split $31.30 ($4.35 + $16.95 + $10) in comparison to the maximum of $40. Incorporating the fact that the players begin the game with minimum possible earnings of $20 in endowments, average efficiency observed in this game is 56 per-

Figure 4.1 Two-Person Trust Game Decisions and Descriptive Statistics

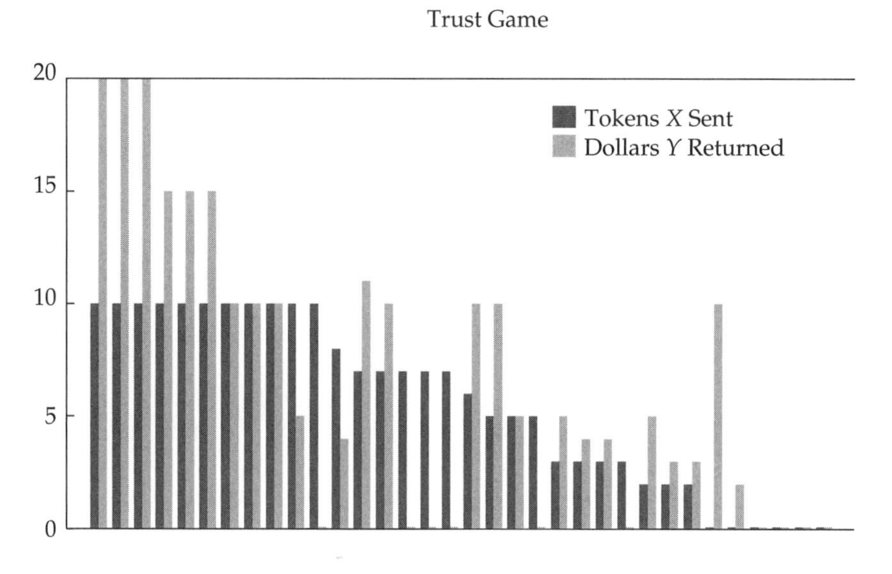

Two-Person Investment Game Type X and Type Y – N = 34				
	Mean	SD	Minimum	Maximum
Tokens X sent	5.65	3.83	0	10
$ Y returned	6.65	6.43	0	20
$ X earned	11.00	5.08	0	20
$ Y earned	20.29	9.09	0	40

Source: Authors' adaptation from Cox et al. (2009, 964).

cent ($11.30/$20), compared to 0 percent at the most inefficient outcome, where the first mover sends $0 to the second mover.

Of course, beyond efficiency, there is the issue of the degree to which Y reciprocates actions of X. On average, the Y decision (amount returned) is only $6.65 of the $16.95 created by X on the average investment of $5.65. Thus, on average, trust pays (though not by a large amount).[2] This behavior is consistent with an extensive number of experiments conducted by many scholars (see Berg, Dickhaut, and McCabe 1995; see also Ostrom and Walker 2003, chapters 8–13; chapter 3, this volume).[3]

The analysis James Cox and his colleagues present also includes an analysis of motivations for decisions based on postexperiment questionnaires that contain questions tied to level of trust and fairness (2009). In summary, the response to the survey question regarding trust is highly significant and in the expected direction. Thus those who responded that most people could be trusted sent more tokens than those who disagreed with the statement. Similarly, those who responded that most people would try to be fair also sent significantly more tokens to those who disagreed. For second movers, as expected, the amount sent by the first mover had a significant effect on the amount returned. Interestingly, the gender effect is highly statistically significant. Controlling for the amount sent by first movers, males who are second movers, returned less. Also, as expected, the qualitative variables for trust and fairness are both of the expected sign and statistically significant.

These results are consistent with several other studies in this literature. Iris Bohnet and Rachel Croson provide an excellent review (2004). Two other articles are particularly useful for understanding the role of trust and its relation to contextual variables. Nava Ashraf, Iris Bohnet, and Nikita Piankov investigated an experimental design created to decompose trust and trustworthiness (2006). Examining a within-subject design, they investigated behavior in both a trust and dictator game, in which the subjects allocated an endowment between themselves and an anonymous second individual. Ashraf, Bohnet, and Piankov provided evidence that motivations for first movers in the trust game are beyond expecting a positive return on what they send the second mover. That is, they argued that subjects "enjoy the act of trusting and being kind to others, even to anonymous strangers" (2006, 204). Interestingly, their results suggest that trustworthiness is based both on reciprocity and unconditional kindness, with unconditional kindness serving as a better predictor of variation in trustworthiness. This result is consistent with the findings of James Cox, in which a triadic design is used to decompose reciprocity from other-regarding behavior (2004).

In a related study, building on psychological game theory, Gary Charness and Martin Dufwenberg examined a notion of guilt aversion, in which players feel guilt from actions they perceive as letting other players down (2006). Studying a version of the trust game, first movers are presumed to have beliefs about the probability of second movers' play. Second movers are presumed to have beliefs about the beliefs of first movers: "A guilt-averse player suffers from guilt to the extent he believes he hurts others relative to what they believe they will get" (1583). Subjects' beliefs about the play of others are solicited. Consistent with their guilt aversion model, Charness and Dufwenberg's experiments with and without preplay nonbinding written communication reveal strong correlation between beliefs and game behavior.

Clearly, the trust game implies a degree of risk on the part of any first mover. On the other hand, the trust game is not framed, as many games of risk (gambles) are. Further, there is no reason to believe that individuals would have common expectations over the level of risk involved (the expected response by second movers). Thus, the expected risk and the attitude toward taking that risk may be quite different across subjects. Several studies have examined the degree to which trust is linked to measurable characteristics of risk attitude, but the results are anything but conclusive. Catherine Eckel and Rick Wilson surveyed much of this literature and reported results from a set of experiments designed to address the question (2004). In summary, they reported that they found "little evidence that trust is related to survey or decision measures of general risk aversion" (463).

On the other hand, Laura Schechter made a strong argument about the interaction between trust and risk preferences (2007). Using subjects from rural villages in Paraguay, she conducted both the trust game and a gambling game designed to be similar in framing and protocol. She found strong evidence that play in the gambling game is a significant predicator of play by first movers in the trust game. Research by Dean Karlan is also useful on this issue (2005). He argued that although trust is risky by construction, a social capital perspective of the motivations of first movers focuses more on an ability for social norms and relationships to mitigate risks inherent in informal contracts, rather than simply on a gambling decision. His experiments, using subjects drawn from a Peruvian microcredit program, found a strong correlation between the decision of first movers and propensity to take risks. He also found evidence to support a social capital hypothesis of trust. Higher levels of trust emerge when both players are indigenous, live near their partner, and attend the same church.

Public Goods Games

The experimental literature on public goods games is vast and extensively covers the behavioral responses to changes in institutional rules, pecuniary incentives, group size, and repetition of the game. The most commonly studied public goods games, as discussed earlier, is designed so that the prediction of traditional game theory, based strictly on an individual's pecuniary returns, is zero provision of the public good. The observed behavior is inconsistent with this prediction, which is not surprising in light of the behavior discussed for the stark environment of a trust game played a single time, using double-blind procedures. How subjects respond to context in the case of the public goods game, however, is central to understanding the interplay between trust in others and the link between trust and reciprocity.

We turn first to a brief summary of results from public goods experiments in an environment that has become known as the voluntary contribution mechanism (VCM). The primary focus is on experiments in which one of the authors, James Walker, has been involved. These results have been found to be quite robust across studies by numerous other researchers (for an excellent review, see Ledyard 1995).

VCM Environment

The results begin with observations Mark Isaac, James Walker, and Arlington Williams reported (1994). Subjects in this setting faced the following VCM decision problem. Each individual was endowed with fifty tokens per decision round. Tokens could be allocated to an individual account that paid the subject $.01 per token. Alternatively, tokens could be allocated to a group account that paid each group member $.003 or $.0075 per token, depending on the experimental design. In the discussion that follows, the results are organized around the concept of marginal per capita return (MPCR) from the group account relative to the private account. In these experiments, this is simply 0.3 and 0.75. Groups numbered 4, 10, 40, or 100. As noted earlier, in these decision environments, allocating all tokens to the group account maximized group earnings. Thus efficiency is directly related to the level of allocations to the group account.

Before play, subjects were informed of the number of decision rounds, that all decisions were anonymous, and that each subject would be paid in private at the end of the experiment. Between rounds, subjects learned of the total allocations to the group account in the previous round and their earnings for the previous round. The information conditions were such that no subject could deduce the individual earnings of other group members. Finally, group composition was constant between rounds.

Four general findings emerge from this research. First, allocations to the group account and efficiency are inversely related to MPCR. Second, holding MPCR constant, allocations to the group account and efficiency are positively related to group size. Third, increasing group size in conjunction with a decrease in MPCR leads to lower allocations to the group account and a decrease in overall efficiency. Last, allocations to the group account and efficiency are well above those predicted by models of behavior based purely on private pecuniary incentives, but well below the allocation that would maximize group earnings.

Figures 4.2 through 4.4 display evidence related to each of these findings. Reported are mean levels of allocations as a percentage of optimum (total endowment) across decision rounds. Figure 4.2 results from parametric conditions where $N = 10$ and MPCR = 0.3 or MPCR = 0.75. Note the general increase in allocations to the group account for the MPCR = 0.75 condition. Figure 4.3 presents results from conditions where MPCR = 0.3 and $N = 10$ or $N = 100$. Contrary to many of the generalizations found in textbook discussions of public goods, holding MPCR constant, one observes an increase in allocations to the group account (less free riding) with the larger group size. However, evidence is also found to support some textbook discussions of the free-rider phenomena, in which authors explicitly

Figure 4.2 **VCM Group Allocations—MPCR = 0.30, N = 10 Versus MPCR = 0.75**

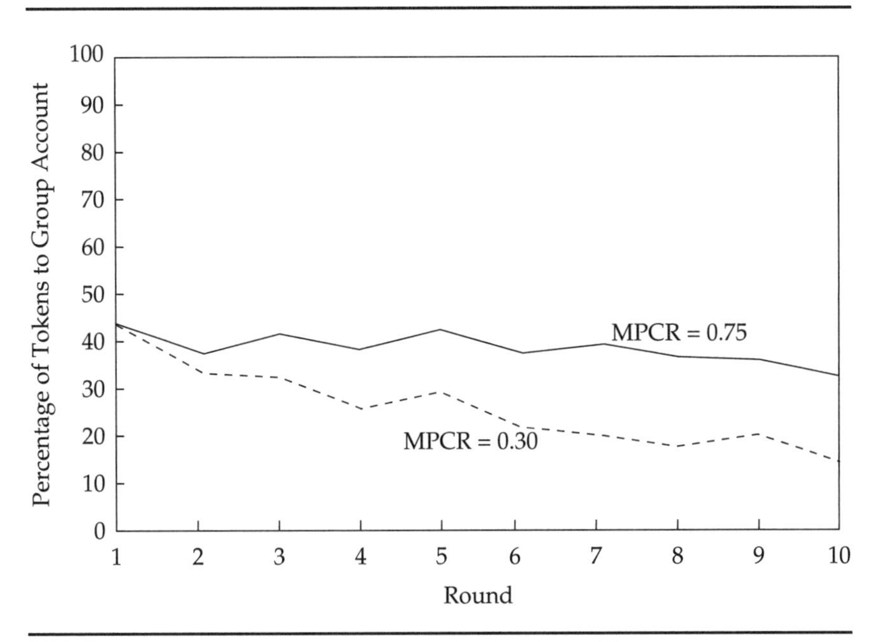

Source: Authors' adaptation from Noussair and Walker (1999, 56).

Figure 4.3 **VCM Group Allocations—MPCR = 0.30, N = 10 Versus N = 100**

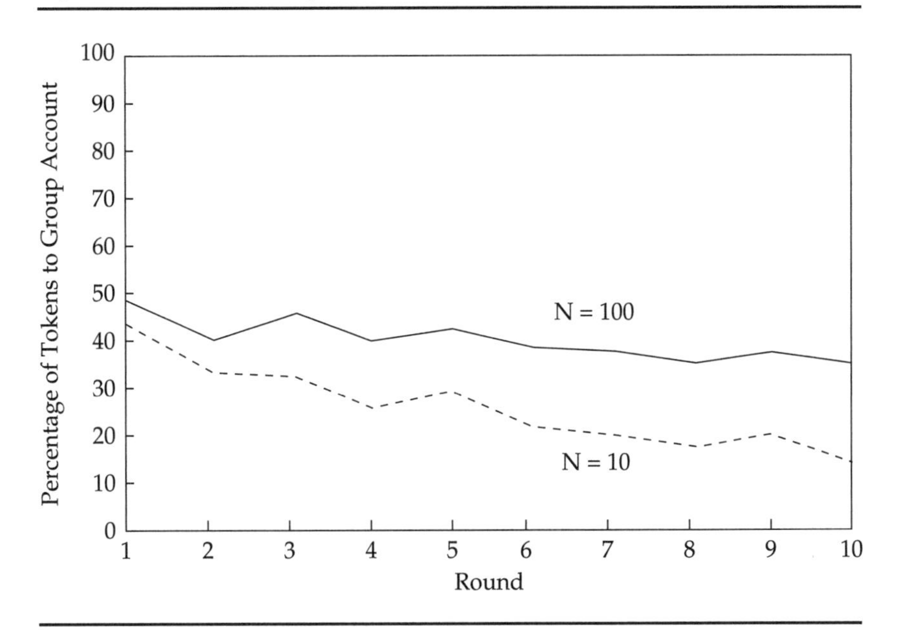

Source: Authors' adaptation from Noussair and Walker (1999, 56).

Figure 4.4 VCM Group Allocations—MPCR = 0.30, N = 10 Versus MPCR = 0.03, N = 40

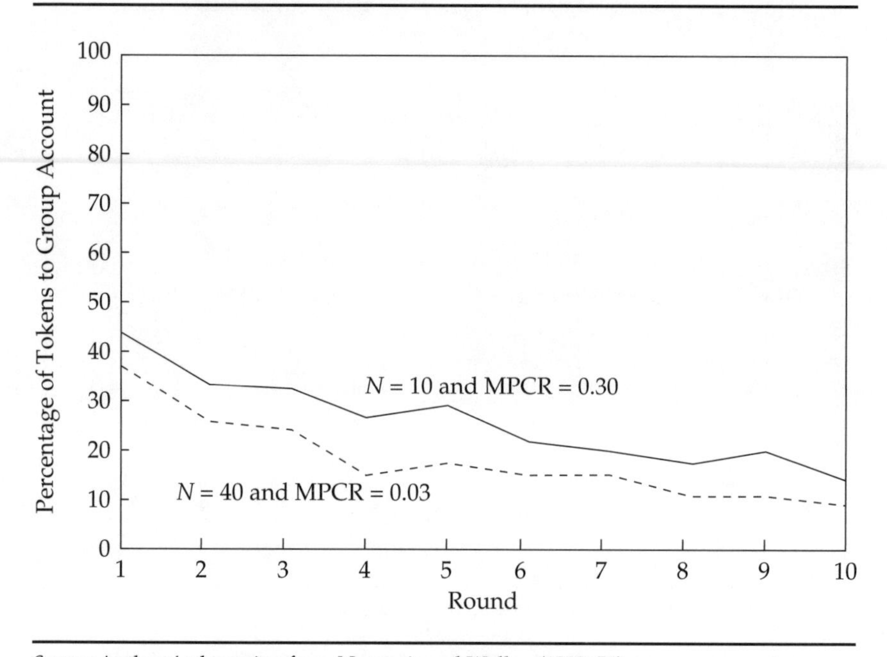

Source: Authors' adaptation from Noussair and Walker (1999, 56).

illustrate group size effects with specific arguments related to decreases in the marginal value of the public good in conjunction with increases in group size (crowding effects) or illustrations of large group, public goods settings with inherently small marginal valuations. Figure 4.4 displays results from the conditions where $N = 10$, MPCR = 0.3 and $N = 40$, MPCR = 0.03. With an increase in group size, the value of the public good at the margin decreases to group members. In this case, one observes a validation of the proposition that an increase in group size leads to a decrease in the level of public goods provision.

The experiments reported next were conducted to examine the effects of giving subjects more explicit instructions related to the strategic nature of the game, as well as examining the effect of gaining experience in the decision environment. All experiments were conducted with $N = 10$ and MPCR = 0.30. There are two design changes. First, subjects were provided with a handout explicitly stating the conditions in which an individual receives the maximum possible earnings, an individual receives the minimum possible earnings, the group as a whole receives the maximum possible earnings, and the group as a whole receives the minimum possible earnings. Second, the number of decision rounds varied from ten in three experiments to forty in two experiments to sixty in one experiment. The subjects in the forty-round experiments were drawn from a pool of subjects with experience in VCM ten-round experiments. The subjects in the sixty-round experiment were drawn from the two forty-round experiments.

These experiments support the results from earlier experiments in several interesting ways. Even with a richer information environment, highly experienced subject groups continue to follow a pattern of behavior inconsistent with the predictions of models based purely on one's own pecuniary incentives. Further, the rate of decay of allocations to the group account is inversely related to the number of decision rounds. This result is inconsistent with backward induction models, and purely adaptive or learning models based on the number of rounds completed. This aspect of the data, however, is consistent with a forward-looking modeling approach based on reciprocity and the gains from cooperation. It is this link between cooperation, trust, and reciprocity to which we now turn.

Trust and Reciprocity in the VCM Environment

The evidence from all social dilemma games suggests a high level of heterogeneity in individual behavior. The public goods setting allows one to observe the role of this heterogeneity as it impacts group dynamics in the sense of interaction between players. Categorizing subjects into strategic types is quite complicated because of the complexity of these interactions. However, there is strong evidence of four basic types: players who appear to be very trustful and consistently cooperate; players who are more cautious, but respond as reciprocators; players who are more strategic, signaling a high level of cooperativeness (through a high group allocation), then respond to reciprocity of others with very low group allocations; and players who are clearly noncooperative and willing to free ride on the cooperativeness of others.

Of particular importance to the discussion here are two behavioral issues: the role of consistent cooperators and the degree of reciprocity among players (Croson 2007). For both issues, an additional question relates to the role of context. Mark Weber and Keith Murnighan offered an invaluable look at these issues (2006). Building on the literature, their basic premise is that the consistent cooperation of a single or relatively small number of individuals can significantly improve rates of cooperation within groups. As they noted, "philosophers have suggested that Kantian actors who apply a moral maxim of unconditional cooperation 'may be a necessary condition for the emergence of conditional cooperators. These, in turn, may bring the level of participation up to the point at which new people join because they would be ashamed of being free riders'" (Elster 1985, cited in Weber and Murnighan 2006, 6). They focused on three mechanisms by which cooperation by an individual affects others: risk reduction, signaling that cooperation is individually appropriate and may constitute an appropriate group norm, and the activation of feelings of obligation that in turn result in reciprocity. It is argued that these mechanisms may affect others differently, depending on social motivation (Messick and McClintock 1968). Weber and Murnighan examined these hypotheses with a meta-analysis drawing from a diverse set of public goods experiments and found strong support for the role of consistent cooperators as catalysts for promoting group cooperation. They also provided strong evidence supporting the hypothesis that all three mechanisms play an important causal role in these higher levels of cooperation. Further, because of the effect on contribution levels of others, consistent contributors suffer no apparent cost from their actions relative to their counterparts.

Toh-Kyeong Ahn and his colleagues added further evidence related to trust and reciprocity in public goods experiments (2007). They examined the role of asymmetry in payoffs and the interaction of asymmetry with decisions that are made simultaneously or sequentially in binary choice, two-person VCM games that also have the payoff properties of prisoner dilemma games. Two principal findings emerge from this research. First, asymmetry has a clear negative effect on cooperation (efficiency) in simultaneous decision settings. In games with symmetric payoffs, 32 percent of participants cooperate, whereas in those with asymmetric payoffs, cooperation rates fall to 13 percent. They hypothesize that asymmetric payoffs increase uncertainty about the intentions of the other person with whom one is matched, leading to reduced cooperation. Second, the impact of asymmetry on cooperation rates interacts with order of play in sequential settings. First movers who are payoff advantaged are less likely to cooperate than their counterparts in a simultaneous game setting. In one game the researchers investigate, the second mover is payoff disadvantaged and has the larger incentive to defect. The advantaged first movers appear to anticipate this incentive for the second mover, and act accordingly with decreased levels of cooperation (21 percent). By contrast, in the sequential game, in which the advantaged player moves second and has less incentive to defect, Ahn and his colleagues observed higher levels of cooperation by payoff disadvantaged first movers (45 percent). Here, the first mover, the disadvantaged player, may be less fearful of defection (more trusting of the motives) by the second mover and thus choose to cooperate. Cooperation rates for second movers are consistent with the first mover choices. Advantaged players cooperate more than disadvantaged players when first movers have cooperated. In sum, the evidence supports the conclusion that players in sequential asymmetric games respond both to their own incentives and those of the person with whom they are matched, as if anticipating the trustworthiness of their counterparts based on that subject's incentives.

These results are consistent with earlier discussions of the role of guilt. If a player has feelings of guilt from lowering the other player's payoff (defecting when the other person cooperates), anticipation of such feelings will allow for reciprocity. In addition, it seems quite natural to conceive of the degree of guilt interacting with the asymmetry in payoffs and having an impact on the player's play and expectations of play of the other player. To the extent that players are concerned about fairness or guilt, the differences in incentives of advantaged and disadvantaged players will affect the level of cooperation and interact with order of play. This study complements the work of Gary Charness and Martin Dufwenberg (2006), discussed earlier, and is consistent with that of Sue Crawford and Elinor Ostrom (2005).

Institutional Changes in VCM

The VCM decision environment is relatively constrained in the sense of behavioral options available to decision makers. In the last two decades, the experimental literature has exploded with a vast array of studies examining public goods environments that allowed subjects greater behavioral opportunities that relate to both trust and reciprocity. We now focus on two such environments: face-to-face communication and sanctions and rewards.

Face-to-Face Communication When face-to-face communication is allowed, subjects are brought together in a common area in the laboratory. They are told they can discuss anything they choose, except that no private information can be exchanged (such as individual decisions in past rounds or individual returns from the private account), no physical threats can be made and no side-payments can be discussed, and their discussions will be monitored for compliance to these conditions.

A study by Mark Isaac and James Walker typifies the findings from VCM environments with face-to-face communication (1988a). With groups of size four and repeated decisions rounds, they investigated three treatment conditions in which ten decision rounds were conducted under one condition and a second ten rounds under either the same or a different condition: NC/NC, where no communication was allowed in either condition; NC/C, where ten initial rounds of no communication were followed by ten rounds in which communication was allowed between every round; and C/NC, where ten initial rounds with communication were followed by ten rounds with none. In the NC/NC treatment, cooperation tended to decay with repetition. By the final rounds of the second sequence, group allocations average below 10 percent of optimum. In the NC/C treatment, communication had an immediate positive effect on allocations to the group account and that effect increased with repetition. During the second communication phase, average levels of group allocations rose from approximately 60 percent to more than 90 percent. In the C/NC treatment, communication had a significant positive effect on cooperation during the first ten rounds and there was a strong hysteresis effect in the rounds that followed where no communication was allowed. In fact, in the four experiments included in this condition, only one experiment had a significant decay in group allocations during the last ten rounds. In three of the four experiments, the groups reached efficiencies of 98 percent or higher in all ten rounds of the no-communication condition.

In another study, Isaac and Walker also investigated a setting where communication is available to the subjects, but at a cost (1991). Before the start of the experiment, it was explained that the subjects would have the opportunity to meet before each decision round, if they purchased the opportunity to do so. The opportunity to communicate was funded as a provision point public good. Groups were all of size $N = 6$. If at least four individuals chose to contribute $.10, the group was allowed to meet. In effect, this setting created a second-order dilemma game in which individuals were required to expend resources to provide a mechanism that might change the strategic nature of a first-order dilemma game. The results from these sets of experiments can be summarized as follows. Of six groups, only two succeeded in funding the communication opportunity in the first round. By the fourth round, however, all groups were successful. The groups used the opportunity to communicate to make allocation commitments to the group good and to solve the second-order efficiency problem, not having to fund the opportunity to meet every round. That is, the subjects explicitly discussed this problem and made multiperiod commitments. In the decisions that followed the first opportunity to communicate for each group, average efficiency in providing the public good was 91 percent. There was, however, an end-period effect in which efficiencies dropped significantly in four of six experiments.

The results from these experiments with face-to-face communication are consistent with those observed by earlier experiments in the social psychology literature (Dawes et al. 1986; Dawes 1988). In addition, with further experiments from a wide array of researchers, they are some of the most robust results reported in the social dilemma literature. Among the conclusions is that face-to-face communication allows subjects to make credible commitments of cooperation that increase the level of trust among group members. On the other hand, as the experimental setting is made more complex, group confidence in commitments appears to decrease, leading to a decrease in cooperation.

Rewards and Sanctions The VCM experimental setting allows for trust and reciprocity through a limited choice space—contributions to the group good. Based on the research Martin Sefton, Robert Shupp, and James Walker reported (2007), we next discuss experiments that maintain the same basic structure as the baseline VCM environment, except that a second stage is added to the decision problem where individuals may reward or sanction other group members.

In many team situations, workers repeatedly interact while observing the efforts of their coworkers. An individual worker has rich opportunities for reacting to a coworker's behavior in ways that may impose costs or benefits on both parties. Abundant evidence exists that individuals sanction those who engage in selfish activities at the expense of other group members. For example, people who violate social norms are often ostracized. Similarly, there is strong evidence that people are prepared to make sacrifices to help others on a quid pro quo basis.

In the experiments we summarize next, subjects participated in a series of standard VCM games (matched with the same group of subjects throughout), and then participated in a second series of decision rounds that allowed for sanctions or rewards. We focus here on these latter decisions. At the beginning of the round, each subject was endowed with six tokens to be allocated between their private account and the group account. For each token placed in his or her private account, a subject received $.10. For each token placed in the group account, every group member received $.05 (an MPCR = 0.5). After all subjects had made their decisions for the round, they were informed of the aggregate allocations to the group account, the allocation of each member of their group to the group account, and their own earnings for the round. Individual decisions were not linked to subject identifiers, however, and the order in which other group member's decisions were presented was randomized. Thus, it was impossible for subject-specific reputations to develop.

In the sanction treatment, the first stage of the round involved a VCM game identical in structure to that used in the first sequence of rounds. In the second stage, each subject was endowed with six additional tokens, which could be allocated to a private account, from which the subject earned $.10 per token, or used to sanction other group members. The computer screen informing subjects of the individual decisions of other group members was used for imposing sanctions. Alongside each of the other group member's decisions, subjects could indicate how many of their six tokens they wished to use to sanction the group member making that decision. Subjects could thus sanction on the basis of current round decisions, but would not be able, for instance, to sanction subjects for their earlier round decisions. For each token used to sanction another group member, that group member's earnings were reduced by $.10. The cost to the sanctioner was the forgone earnings from his or her private account. A feature of the sanction treatment, therefore, is that each token used for sanctioning reduces group earnings by $.20. The reward treatment was identical to the sanction treatment, except that instead of using tokens to sanction other group members, subjects could reward other group members. As with the sanction treatment, subjects using tokens to reward other group members incurred a cost in the form of forgone earnings. However, for each token used to reward a group member, that group member received $.10. Rewards thus constituted a pure redistribution of earnings and had no direct effect on total group earnings. The combined treatment allowed both rewards and sanctions.

The results from these experiments can be summarized as follows. In the sanction treatment, subjects began by allocating on average 31 percent of their endowment of tokens to sanctions, but this percentage fell to 16 percent by the final round. In the reward treatment, tokens used for rewarding others fell sharply from 41 percent of endowment to 3 percent. In the combined treatment, subjects seemed to initially prefer using rewards to sanctions. Initially, 42 percent of tokens were allocated to rewards and only 8 percent to sanctions. This pattern did not survive, however. In the final round, only 8 percent of token endowments were used for rewarding other subjects, and 10 percent for sanctioning. Focusing on contributions to the group good, the time trends of average group allocations diverged across treatments. The baseline condition showed a continued decline in average group allocations, falling to approximately 30 percent by the final round. Average group allocations in all three treatment conditions moved above those observed in a baseline condition. The combined treatment showed the largest increase in group allocations, averaging approximately 75 percent of optimum in the ten rounds of the second stage. Further, the reward treatment led to an interesting dynamic near the end of the experiments, in that contribution levels fell abruptly to approximately 20 percent of optimum.

Overall, these experiments support the supposition of a behavioral asymmetry in how rewards and sanctions can be used to facilitate cooperation. Sanctions may be necessary to promote cooperation initially, but the viable threat of sanctions may be enough to sustain cooperation after a history of sanctioning has been established. In contrast, a reward system may require the continued use of rewards.

The results from the sanction treatment of the Martin Sefton, Robert Shupp, and James Walker study (2007) are qualitatively consistent with those of Ernst Fehr and Simon Gächter (2000) and other recent research that examines sanctioning: subjects use sanctions and aggregate group allocations increase. A primary difference among the studies is the degree to which sanctions increase group allocations and the extent to which increased group allocations succeed in increasing overall earnings. Structural variations among the studies may account for this difference. In particular, some studies followed Fehr and Gächter and use parameterizations in which subjects faced convex costs of imposing sanctions

(Carpenter 2007; Masclet et al. 2003). In these studies, it was relatively inexpensive to assign a few sanctions to another group member. Further, each unit of sanction reduced earnings by a fixed percentage. Thus, in absolute terms, sanctions reduced earnings more for high earners. Others, like the study here, use a simpler linear framework (Yamagishi 1986; Page and Putterman 2000). In this case, there is a one-to-one mapping from costs of imposing a sanction to the magnitude of the sanction. The weaker effect of sanctions in our study may reflect the intuitive notion that sanctions will be more readily used when they are less costly to impose, and will be more effective when they impose greater costs on those sanctioned.

All of these studies demonstrate a clear behavioral norm of the willingness of a large proportion of subjects to make decisions, at a monetary cost to themselves, that can be viewed as a reciprocal response to the play of others.[4] In fact, some players are willing to make such decisions even in the final round of play. Norms of fairness and reciprocity appear to shape the expectations of these group members beyond purely strategic responses. In support of this argument, Walker and Matthew Halloran examined the sanction and reward setting in a one-shot game setting (2004). Subjects are allowed to reward or sanction other group members after observing group allocations. They find extensive use of sanction and rewards in this one-shot setting even though subjects know that such sanction and rewards can have no impact on play.

Common-Pool Resource Games

Several versions of common-pool resource (CPR) games have been examined in the literature. These variations incorporate changes in the basic underlying structure of the game that include time dependency in the productive nature of the CPR, alternative forms of externalities created by harvesting, and the potential for destruction of the CPR. The focus here is on the repeated time independent game that Ostrom, Gardner, and Walker examined extensively, in which the productive potential of the CPR is fully replenished after each decision round (1994).

Ostrom, Gardner, and Walker Game

In the Ostrom, Gardner, and Walker CPR game, subjects are endowed each decision round with a specified number of tokens to be divided between two markets. Market 1 is described as an investment opportunity in which each token yields a constant marginal (additional) output and each unit of output yields a constant marginal return. Market 2 (the CPR) is described as a market that yields a rate of average and marginal output per token that diminishes as the total number of tokens invested by the group increases.

Investments in market 2 are intended to represent the appropriation of units from the CPR. Subjects are informed that they will receive a level of output from market 2 equivalent to the percentage of total group tokens they invest. Further, subjects know that each unit of output from market 2 yields a constant average and marginal rate of return. Before each decision round, subjects know the number of decision makers in the group, that individual endowments are equal, and the total investments in market 2 for all previous decision rounds.

In the experiments summarized here, the CPR is operationalized with eight appropriators ($N = 8$) and a quadratic production function $F(\Sigma x_i)$ for market 2, where

$$F(\Sigma x_i) = 23\Sigma x_i - .25(\Sigma x_t)^2$$

with a return from market 2 of $.01 per unit of output. Subjects are endowed each round with either ten or twenty-five tokens and receive a return from market 1 of $.05 per token invested. With these payoff parameters, a group investment of thirty-six tokens yields the optimal or group payoff maximizing level of investment. The complete information symmetric noncooperative Nash equilibrium, based purely on individuals pursuing their own pecuniary returns, is for each subject to invest eight tokens in market 2 regardless of the endowment condition—for a total group investment in market 2 of sixty-four tokens. The negative externality imbedded in this game is a result of the production function used for market 2. As an individual invests tokens in market 2, the marginal and average return to that individual and all other individuals is reduced for market 2. A decision maker focusing purely on his or her pecuniary return is assumed to make investment decisions that take into account the impact on his or her own investments, but that disregard the negative return imposed on others.

Instead of focusing on total payoffs in the experiments and resulting efficiencies, to more closely follow the standard economics literature for natural resource exploitation, the experimental results for the game have generally focused on what is termed *maximum net yield* from the CPR. This measure captures the degree of optimal yield earned from the CPR only. Dissipation of maximum net yield from the CPR is known in the resource literature as *rent* dissipation. As a benchmark, the Nash equilibrium investment of eight tokens per subject yields 39 percent of maximum potential rents, or resource efficiency.

Several key behavior results from early CPR experiments can be summarized as follows. Subjects appropriated from the CPR made investments in market 2 well above optimum, which led to significant inefficiencies in accrued rents, averaging 37 percent in the ten-token endowment setting and –3 percent in the twenty-five. Investments in market 2 were characterized by a pulsing pattern: investments increased and yields decreased, at which point investors tended to reduce their investments, and yields again increased. This pattern reoccurred across rounds within an experiment and variation across rounds tended to diminish as the experiment continued. Note that the endowment effect is not predicted by standard game theory. However, in the twenty-five-token setting, individuals had more resources to exploit the CPR. That is, when individual decisions were not coordinated, individual exploitation increased and efficiency decreased.

This stark environment yields results that fall far from the cooperative outcome. In fact, in a broad sense, the behavior is much less cooperative than that observed in both trust games and public goods games—yet the subjects in these games are drawn from the same subject population. Several conjectures can be made about these results and how they tie back to trust and reciprocity. First, the CPR game is more complex. The cooperative outcome may be obscured by the complexity of the decision setting. Second, this complexity may reduce the ability of subjects to readily calculate desired reciprocal actions. Finally, and possibly most important, cooperation by a subset of individuals in the CPR game can be hidden and negated by subsets of subjects who play noncooperatively. Unlike the public goods game, surplus or rents generated by cooperative players can be captured by noncooperators.

Changes in the CPR Game

Using the CPR environment, Ostrom and Walker (1991) conducted a set of experiments that allowed for communication parallel to those Isaac and Walker conducted (1988a, 1988b).

Face-to-Face Communication Ostrom and Walker focused initially on the ten-token endowment setting. In this setting, the opportunity to communicate followed a series of no-communication rounds. Communication was allowed in each decision round before investments were made. All four experiments showed a strong shift toward maximum rents beginning in the first round that allowed communication. In the first ten periods, the mean level of rents (30 percent) was nearly identical to the baseline experiments. In periods eleven through twenty, rents shifted dramatically upward, to an average of 98 percent, compared to 35 percent in periods eleven through twenty of baseline experiments without communication. Clearly, the ability to communicate translated into a shift in efficiency to near optimality.

To examine the robustness of the initial experiments, Ostrom, Gardner, and Walker extended this analysis to a twenty-five-token setting (1994). They found that subjects in repeated, high-endowment CPR games with only one opportunity to communicate obtained higher yields than those in baseline experiments without communication (55 percent to 21 percent).

In the same setting, with repeated opportunities to communicate before every decision period, subjects obtained yields substantially above those in baseline experiments without communication (73 percent to 21 percent). In addition, repeated communication opportunities led to lower defection rates on agreements in comparison to one-shot opportunities to communicate (13 percent as compared to 25 percent).

Additional experiments were also conducted with a nested public goods problem similar to that of Isaac and Walker (1991). In these experiments, the opportunity to communicate was a costly public good that subjects first had to provide through anonymous voluntary contributions. As Ostrom and Walker noted, the provision problem players faced in the costly communication experiments was not trivial and did in fact create a barrier (1991). In all experiments with costly communication, the problem of providing the institution for communication diminished the success of either having the ability to develop a coordinated strategy or dealing with players who cheated on a previous agreement. On the other hand, all groups succeeded to some degree in providing the communication mechanism and in dealing with the CPR dilemma. On average, efficiency in these groups increased from approximately 42 percent to 80 percent.

Heterogeneity In previous CPR experiments, individuals were homogeneous in game attributes. It is possible that the strong efficiency-enhancing properties of face-to-face communication significantly depend on homogeneity. In fact, the literature provides several arguments that point to heterogeneity as a serious deterrent to cooperation (Hardin 1982; Johnson and Libecap 1982; Libecap and Wiggins 1984; Isaac and Walker 1988a; Wiggins and Libecap 1985, 1987; Ostrom 1990; Kanbur 1992; Hackett 1992). The task of agreeing to and sustaining agreements is more difficult for heterogeneous individuals because of the distributional conflict associated with alternative sharing rules. In heterogeneous settings, different sharing rules generally produce diverse distributions of earnings across individuals. Although all individuals may be made better off by cooperating, depending on the sharing rule chosen, some benefit more than others. Consequently, individuals may fail to cooperate on the adoption of a sharing rule because they cannot agree on what would constitute a fair distribution of benefits produced by cooperating.

Steven Hackett, Edella Schlager, and James Walker extended the parameter and institutional environment of the CPR setting to examine the role of heterogeneity, introducing heterogeneity by varying the input endowments of the subjects (1994). Heterogeneities in endowments imply that alternative rules adopted to reduce overappropriation from the CPR will have differential effects on earnings across subjects. Hackett, Schlager, and Walker found that, even with heterogeneity, face-to-face communication remained effective in increasing efficiency. Investigating two designs, one in which heterogeneities in endowments were assigned randomly and one through an auction mechanism under which subjects purchased the rights to higher endowments, both treatment conditions led to significant increases in net yield. Hackett, Schlager, and Walker reported rent levels in no-communication conditions relatively close to those predicted by the Nash equilibrium (49 percent). When communication was allowed, average rents increased to more than 94 percent across treatment conditions.

In addition, Pamela Schmitt, Kurtis Swope, and Walker (2000) investigated face-to-face communication in the Ostrom, Gardner, and Walker setting, but allowed for communication to be held among only a subset of the subjects. Remaining subjects were outsiders to the communication opportunity. Recall that a subject's marginal return from the resource depends on their own investment in harvesting the resource, and marginal returns are declining in aggregate group harvesting. One important aspect of this environment is therefore that reductions in harvesting by some group members lead to greater opportunities for others. The results of this study indicate that communication is less likely to be effective in preventing rent dissipation in CPR environments in which a subset of appropriators either cannot or will not participate in collective action. Three protocols were investigated, varying the investment constraints on the outsiders and whether the outsiders were computerized or humans. Protocol 2 created the most difficult environment for cooperation among insiders. In it, using human outsiders, the only limit on outsider investments were their endowments. Rents averaged only 6 percent during communication rounds, the agreement rates among insiders was only 31 percent, and the defection rate on agreements was 50 percent. This compares to average rents of 73 percent, agreement rates of 95 percent, and defection rates of 13 percent in the parallel Ostrom, Gardner, and Walker high-endowment experiments that allowed for communication among all subjects in the group. In the experiments with outsiders, outsiders responded strategically to reductions in appropriation by cooperating group members. Further, the lack of outsider commitment to a cooperative appropriation strategy agreed to by insiders was compounded by the fact that insiders were more likely to deviate from agreements. Finally, groups anticipated the potential problems and had difficulty reaching agreements or committing to a specific appropriation rule.

As in public goods experiments with face-to-face communication, then, the CPR experiments demonstrate the role of trust and reciprocity as fundamental to cooperation. When groups are able to develop clear understandings and verbal commitments to a cooperative agreement, they are quite capable of reaching a near optimal solution. However, as demonstrated by the two studies that created more complex settings, the sustainability of such agreements can be undermined by issues related to payoff distributions that some subjects may see as unfair or situations in which collective action proceeds with only a subset of participating actors.

Sanctioning in CPRs No well-specified theoretical model explains the diverse types of sanctioning behavior observed in field settings. In many instances, theory predicts that individuals will not self-monitor and impose sanctions on others that are costly to the sanctioner. Understanding internally imposed monitoring and sanctioning behavior more thoroughly is a key to understanding endogenous solutions to collective-action dilemmas. In another study, Ostrom, Walker, and Gardner examined variations of sanctioning institutions in which the institution was imposed on decision makers, and a setting with face-to-face communication in which decision makers were allowed to choose whether to use a sanctioning mechanism (1992).

As in some public goods settings, the sanctioning mechanism required that each subject incur a cost when sanctioning another. In experiments without communication, the researchers drew the following conclusions. Significantly more sanctioning occurred than predicted by games based purely on pecuniary gains and subgame perfection, and the frequency was inversely related to cost. Sanctioning primarily focused on heavy market 2 (CPR) investors. A nontrivial amount of sanctioning, however, can be classified as error, lagged punishment, or blind revenge. Average net yield increased from 21 percent with no sanctioning to 37 percent with sanctioning. When the costs of fees and fines are subtracted from average net yield, however, net yield dropped to 9 percent.

Subjects thus overused the sanctioning mechanism, and sanctioning without communication reduced net yield. When communication and sanctioning were combined, on the other hand, the results were quite positive. With an imposed sanctioning mechanism and a single opportunity to communicate, subjects achieved an average net yield of 85 percent. When the costs of fees and fines were subtracted, average net yield was still 67 percent. Both are substantial gains over the baseline net yield, which averaged 21 percent. With the right to choose a sanctioning mechanism and a single opportunity to communicate, subjects who adopted a sanctioning mechanism achieved an average net yield of 93 percent. When the costs of fees and fines were subtracted, average net yield was still 90 percent. In addition, the defection rate from agreements was only 4 percent. With the right to choose a sanctioning mechanism and a single opportunity to communicate, subjects who did not adopt a sanctioning mechanism achieved an average net yield of only 56 percent. In addition, the defection rate from agreements was 42 percent.

Thus, subjects who used the opportunity to communicate to agree to a cooperative strategy and chose their own sanctioning mechanism achieved close to optimal results based entirely on the promises they made, their own efforts to monitor, and their investments in sanctioning.[5] This is especially impressive in the high-endowment environment, where defection by a few subjects is very disruptive.

Evidence from Outside the Laboratory

The most common setting for social science experimental research is with undergraduate students as subjects. Most of our own experiments, for example, have been conducted with undergraduate students as paid subjects on the Bloomington campus of Indiana University. Although most social scientists recognize the internal validity of experimental research, many are skeptical of the external validity of experiments that rely heavily on a pool of undergraduate students. In regard to the critical role of trust and reciprocity in achieving sustained cooperation within groups facing social dilemmas in diverse contexts, evidence from field research is also highly supportive of the findings from the laboratory. Four types of empirical studies are relevant to the work we report: experiments drawing from a broader population of subjects, case studies of self-organized resource regimes, case studies of reactions to external stress, and macro-level studies of trust.

Taking Laboratory Experiments to the Field

The first class of studies relies on experimental methods, but does so using subjects from alternative field settings (Carpenter, Harrison, and List 2005). For example, Juan-Camilo Cárdenas has conducted a series of experiments in Colombia with subjects drawn from village populations facing issues of harvesting from field CPRs. His experiments use the analytical structure of the CPR game, but change the instructions to make them more relevant and understandable to resource users living in the countryside (Cárdenas, Stranlund, and Willis 2000; Cárdenas 2003; Rodriguez-Sickert, Guzman, and Cárdenas 2008). These experiments strongly support the results from the laboratory CPR experiments: high levels of rent dissipation in settings without communication and the positive impact of face-to-face communication on cooperation.

In addition, one of Cárdenas's surprising findings supports the importance of local norms of trust and reciprocity. In this experiment, subjects were told, after an initial set of rounds involving no communication, that a new set of rules was to be introduced in the game involving an external regulation, the purpose of which was to improve the group's earnings. The participants were accurately informed of the strategy that would yield them the payoff maximizing outcome, but that the rules of play did not require them to follow that particular harvesting amount. To achieve this outcome, the subjects were told that the monitor would randomly audit one of the players with a probability of 1:16 in each round, a somewhat high probability compared to real field conditions. If a player chose to harvest more than the optimal strategy, a penalty was subtracted from his or her final earnings, depending on the amount of harvesting above the designated rule. This external regulation was designed such that the expected cost of violation of the rule would induce behavior consistent with an improvement in efficiency. In early decision rounds, after the harvesting strategy was introduced, subjects did conform and improve payoffs. In subsequent rounds, however, the gains rapidly eroded as subjects increased their harvesting levels. The level of harvesting toward the end of the imposed regulations was in fact greater than in the no-communication rounds before the introduction of the rule (Cárdenas, Stranlund, and Willis 2000).

More recently, a major set of experimental studies was conducted with the assistance of field anthropologists from fifteen small communities where the scholars had already conducted field research (Henrich et al. 2004). These experiments examined three games—ultimatum, dictator, and public goods. Although variation in the behavior of community members recruited to participate in these experiments was considerable, the broad findings in laboratory investigations were replicated. The authors concluded that models based purely on individual pecuniary gains failed to consistently explain behavior. Behavior across societies varied systematically with group-level differences in economic organization and the structure of social interactions.

Individual-level economic and demographic variables did not adequately explain game behavior, and in many cases behavior reflected personal interactions related to patterns of everyday life (for further evidence related to communication and sanctioning behavior in the field and the laboratory, see Henrich et al. 2006; Camerer and Fehr 2006). In support of this last finding, Jeffrey Carpenter and Erika Seki reported on a public goods experiment conducted with three types of workers in the fishery industry of a Japanese coastal community (2006). They found considerable contributions to a public good. The contribution levels, however, vary systematically with the level of competition that workers face in their daily jobs. Contributions to the public good are highest for those who work in a more cooperative environment.

In addition to experiments conducted using subjects from field settings, a second type of experiment—referred to by some authors as natural field experiments (see Bandiera, Barankay, and Rasul 2006)—has been growing in its applications (for a review, see the 2006 special issue of *Advances in Economic Analysis and Policy*). Oriana Bandiera, Iwan Barankay, and Imran Rasul, for example, measured the change of cooperative norms and behavior over time among British farm workers paid for a fruit-harvesting season according to two formulae: a piece rate versus a relative incentive scheme in which a worker's increased productivity increased his or her own wage but reduced the common pool of wages (2005, 2006). Although the piece rate had no effect on productivity over time, the relative incentive scheme led workers to cooperate more and more over time with each other by reducing their individual productivity. At the end of the season, the total payment given to the workers in the two natural field experiments lay between the Nash equilibrium, under which each worker maximized individual pay, and the optimal group payment, under which all worked at a lower speed.

In his review of natural field experiments, John List urged for the expansion of such studies in the literature (2006). List based his argument not on the conventional critique of laboratory experiments—that the subject population is generally too restrictive. Instead, he focuses on the representativeness of the decision environment as the crucial variable in interpreting the generalizability of results. The actual design of the natural field experiment has taken place long before the researcher enters the study. In a true natural experiment, the participants have no knowledge that they have even been in an experiment. Such field experiments complement well-designed laboratory experiments. They allow researchers to examine diverse institutional and contextual factors in complex settings, often more observationally rich than those considered in theoretical models or laboratory settings.

Case Studies of Self-Organized Resource Regimes

The second type of research is the case study, that is, small sample size intensive field research, examining contextual factors that enable individuals to overcome social dilemmas. We recognize such studies as being closely related to natural field experiments, but often without the level of information or control over key variables of interest. From a research perspective, it is often the synthesis of information across time or multiple case studies that allows for drawing inferences.

Multiple case studies have demonstrated that many, but certainly not all, resource users facing social dilemmas have crafted institutions to govern a resource and create settings where trust and reciprocity can be sustained over time (National Research Council 1986, 2002; McCay and Acheson 1987; Wade 1988; Agrawal 2005; Acheson 2003; Gibson, McKean, and Ostrom 2000). For example, Ostrom, Gardner, and Walker included several chapters devoted to examining the conditions under which parallel populations of CPR users in the field have (or have not) successfully crafted institutions that allow for the creation of joint strategies, monitoring and sanctioning systems, and the design of arbitration systems for settling disputes (1994). These and similar cross-sample studies have given rise to design principles that characterize robust, sustainable, and institutional arrangements for the governance of common-pool resources and helped identify conditions under which users have been unsuccessful in finding cooperative solutions (see Ostrom 1990, 1999, 2005; Abernathy and Sally 2000; Weinstein 2000; De Moor, Shaw-Taylor, and Warde 2002; Dietz, Ostrom, and Stern 2003).

Long-surviving, self-organized resource governance systems do not in general resemble textbook versions of either a government or a private-for-profit firm because they use a wide diversity of specific boundary, harvesting, and maintenance rules crafted to fit a particular biophysical resource and the values and norms of the participants. Given the immense variety of resource structures and local norms, it is not surprising that rules designed by resource users tend to reinforce local norms and enable participants to gather information about the behavior of others and to sanction behavior that does not follow local rules and norms (Ostrom and Nagendra 2006; Gibson, Williams, and Ostrom 2005). Because many policy analysis and government officials have not understood the important role of trust and reciprocity in sustaining collective action over time, evidence of accelerated overharvesting of forests and other natural resources after national governments have challenged the legitimacy of the norms and rules of evolved systems is considerable (Ascher 1995; Fitzpatrick 2006).

Cases Involving Reactions to External Stresses

A third class of field research related to the laboratory experiments are studies focusing on an external stressful event that affects a group within a natural setting and investigates whether contextual variables affect the level of cooperation achieved among individuals facing an emergency situation. These studies isolate several key structural variables while holding other potential variables relatively constant. Two studies used the occasion of a water shortage, for example, to examine the variables that affect respondent's attitudes and behavior. Tom Tyler and Peter Degoey undertook a random sample of four hundred respondents during a California water shortage (1995). They found that respondents were more willing than in normal times to endow leaders with substantial control over how water resources would be allocated in the community. They also found that respondents who had pride in their local community and trusted local officials were more interested in community outcomes than strictly personal ones. Tyler and Degoey concluded that the authority of local officials is strongly "linked to the nature of their social bonds with community members" (482). Mark Van Vugt and Charles Samuelson also conducted a study in a setting that was experiencing a severe water shortage (1999). They found both individual and structure variables affecting conservation behavior. Respondents who perceived the shortage as severe and lived in households with water meters were more likely to undertake conservation efforts than respondents, regardless of their evaluation of the shortage, whose water did not come from a metered system.

Macro-Level Studies of Trust

A fourth type of research involves macro-level examinations of trust in helping to develop and sustain highly productive societies. In addition to his experimental studies of trust in Sweden and Romania, Bo Rothstein (2005) addressed why citizens of Sweden and other Nordic countries are able to build higher levels of social capital and with more productive economies than citizens of eastern Europe and Russia. His explanation is based on the importance of institutional design to enhance the sense of citizens in the trustworthiness and credibility of officials and the likely reciprocity of other citizens. Charles Tilly explored an even broader sweep of history to examine the delicate relationships between the trust networks that citizens develop and their relationships with rulers leading either toward more democratic or less democratic functioning (2005). Among the important studies that stress the importance of trust in the development of macro social and economic structures are those of Margaret Levi (1998), Robert Putnam (2000), and Eric Uslaner (2002).

Conclusion

The general findings from laboratory experiments are that subjects faced with a variety of social dilemmas, including the trust game, the public goods game, and the common-pool resource game, are able to achieve outcomes with higher efficiencies than those predicted by game-theoretic equilibriums based solely on individuals maximizing their own pecuniary benefits. The extent to which these outcomes represent efficiencies over inefficient equilibriums, however, depends on the parametric and institutional context of the decision setting. Further, robust results are found that the same subjects are able to achieve and sustain more cooperative outcomes when the context of the game facilitates individuals gaining information that others are trustworthy enough that they can themselves increase their trust in the others. These results add significantly to the argument that successful and sustainable cooperation must be built on a foundation of trust and reciprocity. On the other hand, experiments that allow for more complex decision settings, such as asymmetry in payoffs or incompleteness in opportunities for group agreements, reveal the fragile nature of cooperative solutions.

Evidence from the field points to the robustness of the findings from the laboratory. There is clearly no single formula for building environments in which cooperation is sustained. Market or government solutions may provide a positive influence in creating incentives for more efficient use of commonly held resources or the provision of public goods. They are, however, clearly not the only solutions. Further, in some contextual situations, they hinder efforts at building trust and cooperation. Current research in the laboratory and the field acknowledges the importance of theoretical and empirical approaches that account for institutional differences between social dilemma settings. These approaches also point to the importance of understanding the role of shared norms.

Although the findings summarized here are consistent with those of many researchers, contemporary social scientists face a substantial theoretical puzzle as to why and how individuals are able to solve social dilemmas in some contexts and not in others. What is important is that the context in which individuals can build knowledge about the intentions and behavior of other participants enables them to increase their trust and reciprocity and achieve greater cooperation. People are not simply selfish maximizers of immediate benefits, nor are they always altruistic seekers of group benefits. When the context makes it feasible for individuals to develop trust in others in the same setting, sustainable solutions to social dilemmas may also be feasible. But, as the research demonstrates, the structural context of the situation—for example, the incentives of the decision setting and the institutions crafted to solve dilemmas—is essential to understanding the conditions under which sustainable cooperative agreements may be reached.

Support from the National Science Foundation for the conduct of many of the experiments discussed in this paper is gratefully acknowledged. The editing assistance of Patty Lezotte, and comments from Arlington Williams, Margaret Levi, Juergen Bracht, and participants in the Capstone Meeting, are gratefully appreciated.

Notes

1. The commonly known prisoner's dilemma game can be structured as a public goods game with $N = 2$ and suitable payoffs constructed as described.
2. Providing evidence related to context, Cox and his colleagues also investigated an alternative framing of the trust game, in which pairs of subjects begin with a joint fund (2009). The first mover's decision is what part of the fund to remove for him or herself (each dollar removed reduces the joint fund by $3). The second mover's decision is to allocate remaining group funds. In this environment, first movers on average leave a larger surplus than in the standard game ($6.71) and receive a higher return ($8.76).
3. The trust game, as initially designed by Berg, Dickhaut, and McCabe (1995), has been replicated in numerous countries, including Germany (Jacobsen and

Sadrieh 1966), Bulgaria (Koford 1998), France and Germany (Willinger et al. 2003), Zimbabwe (Barr 2003), France and China (Buchan and Croson 2004), Vietnam and Thailand (Carpenter, Daniere, and Takahashi 2004), Sweden and Tanzania (Holm and Danielson 2005), Bangladesh and Maluccio (Johansson-Stenman, Mahmud, and Martinsson 2006), Sweden and Romania (Rothstein and Eek 2006), Namibia and South Africa (Vollan 2008), and Tanzania (Danielson and Holm 2007). A good synthesis of findings from the trust game is provided in Colin Camerer's *Behavioral Game Theory* (2003). The most general finding is that a large proportion of first movers do send a substantial portion of their endowments to the second mover. Second movers do not tend to repay the level of trust invested in them by the first movers. Findings vary by country and the specific experimental design, but there is more congruence across experiments than disparity. In their general review, Fiona Greig and Iris Bohnet concluded that the norm of conditional reciprocity is more prevalent in the western industrialized world (2008). Here, if the first mover invests more money, the amounts returned by the second mover increase. The returns of the second player in developing countries, they concluded, is mostly balanced where the amount returned tends to equal the amount invested, no matter the level.

4. See the recent experiments by Michael Kosfeld, Akira Okada, and Arno Riedl (2006), in which they give subjects an opportunity to vote on an institution that will punish participants who do not contribute optimally to a public good. Despite this second-order public goods problem, subjects tend to create the new organization and achieve much higher returns.

5. Ivo Bischoff also found that communication strongly improves outcomes in a CPR experiment (2007). Groups used the opportunity to communicate to reach a binding harvesting quota and to greatly increase their individual and joint outcomes. Groups given the additional opportunity to choose a costly patrolling institution, however, did not do as well as those who did not have such an option.

References

Abernathy, Charles L., and Hilmy Sally. 2000. "Experiments of Some Government-Sponsored Organizations of Irrigators in Niger and Burkina Faso, West Africa." *Journal of Applied Irrigation Studies* 35(2): 177–205.

Acheson, James. 2003. *Capturing the Commons: Devising Institutions to Manage the Maine Lobster Industry*. Hanover, N.H.: University Press of New England.

Agrawal, Arun. 2005. *Environmentality: Technologies of Government and the Making of Subjects*. Durham, N.C.: Duke University Press.

Ahn, Toh-Kyeong, Myungsuk Lee, Lore Ruttan, and James Walker. 2007. "Asymmetric Payoffs in Simultaneous and Sequential Prisoner's Dilemma Games." *Public Choice* 132(3): 353–66.

Ascher, William. 1995. *Communities and Sustainable Forestry in Developing Countries*. San Francisco: ICS Press.

Ashraf, Nava, Iris Bohnet, and Nikita Piankov. 2006. "Decomposing Trust and Trustworthiness." *Experimental Economics* 9(1): 193–208.

Bandiera, Oriana, Iwan Barankay, and Imran Rasul. 2005. "Social Preferences and the Response to Incentives: Evidence from Personnel Data." *Quarterly Journal of Economics* 120(3): 917–62.

———. 2006. "The Evolution of Cooperative Norms: Evidence from a Natural Field Experiment." *Advances in Economic Analysis & Policy* 6(2): article 4.

Barr, Abigail. 2003. "Trust and Expected Trustworthiness: Experimental Evidence from Zimbabwean Villages." *The Economic Journal* 113(489): 614–30.

Berg, Joyce, John Dickhaut, and Kevin McCabe. 1995. "Trust, Reciprocity, and Social History." *Games and Economic Behavior* 10(1): 122–42.

Bischoff, Ivo. 2007. "Institutional Choice Versus Communication in Social Dilemmas: An Experimental Approach." *Journal of Economic Behavior and Organization* 62(1; January): 20–36.

Bohnet, Iris, and Rachel Croson. 2004. "Introduction to Special Issue on Trust and Trustworthiness." *Journal of Economic Behavior and Organization* 55(4): 443–45.

Buchan, Nancy R., and Rachel Croson. 2004. "The Boundaries of Trust: Own and Others' Actions in the U.S. and China." *Journal of Economic Behavior and Organization* 55(4): 485–504.

Camerer, Colin F. 2003. *Behavioral Game Theory: Experiments in Strategic Interaction.* Princeton, N.J.: Princeton University Press.

Camerer, Colin F., and Ernst Fehr. 2006. "When Does 'Economic Man' Dominate Social Behavior?" *Science* 311(January): 47–52.

Cárdenas, Juan-Camilo. 2003. "Real Wealth and Experimental Cooperation: Evidence from Field Experiments." *Journal of Development Economics* 70(2): 263–89.

Cárdenas, Juan-Camilo, John K. Stranlund, and Cleve E. Willis. 2000. "Local Environmental Control and Institutional Crowding-Out." *World Development* 28(10): 1719–733.

Carpenter, Jeffrey P. 2007. "Punishing Free-Riders: How Group Size Affects Mutual Monitoring and the Provision of Public Goods." *Games and Economic Behavior* 60(1): 31–51.

Carpenter, Jeffrey P., Amrita G. Daniere, and Lois M. Takahashi. 2004. "Cooperation, Trust, and Social Capital in Southeast Asian Urban Slums." *Journal of Economic Behavior and Organization* 55(4): 533–51.

Carpenter, Jeffrey P., Glenn W. Harrison, and John A. List, eds. 2005. *Research in Experimental Economics,* vol. 10, *Field Experiments in Economics.* Amsterdam: Elsevier.

Carpenter, Jeffrey P., and Erika Seki. 2006. "Competitive Work Environments and Social Preferences: Field Experimental Evidence from a Japanese Fishing Community." *Advances in Economic Analysis & Policy* 5(2): 1460.

Charness, Gary, and Martin Dufwenberg. 2006. "Promises and Partnership." *Econometrica* 74(6): 1579–601.

Cox, James. 2004. "How to Identify Trust and Reciprocity." *Games and Economic Behavior* 46(2): 260–81.

Cox, James, Elinor Ostrom, James Walker, Antonio Jamie Castillo, Eric Coleman, Robert Holahan, Michael Schoon, and Brian Steed. 2009. "Trust in Private and Common Property Experiments." *Southern Economic Journal* 75(4): 957–75.

Crawford, Sue E. S., and Elinor Ostrom. 2005. "A Grammar of Institutions." In *Understanding Institutional Diversity*, edited by Elinor Ostrom. Princeton, N.J.: Princeton University Press.

Croson, Rachel. 2007. "Theories of Commitment, Altruism, and Reciprocity: Evidence from Linear Public Goods Games." *Economic Inquiry* 45(2): 199–216.

Danielson, Anders J., and Hakan J. Holm. 2007. "Do You Trust Your Brethren: Eliciting Trust Attitudes and Trust Behavior in a Tanzanian Congregation." *Journal of Economic Behavior and Organization* 62(2; February): 255–71.

Dawes, Robyn M. 1988. *Rational Choice in an Uncertain World.* Chicago: Harcourt Brace Jovanovich.

Dawes, Robyn M., John M. Orbell, Randy Simmons, and Alphons van de Kragt. 1986. "Organizing Groups for Collective Action." *American Political Science Review* 80(4): 1171–185.

De Moor, Martina, Leigh Shaw-Taylor, and Paul Warde, eds. 2002. *The Management of Common Land in North West Europe, c. 1500–1850.* Turnhout, Belgium: BREPOLS Publishers.

Dietz, Thomas, Elinor Ostrom, and Paul Stern. 2003. "The Struggle to Govern the Commons." *Science* 302(5652): 1907–912.

Eckel, Catherine C., and Rick K. Wilson. 2004. "Is Trust a Risky Decision?" *Journal of Economic Behavior & Organization* 55(4): 447–65.

Elster, Jon. 1985. *Sour Grapes: Studies in the Subversion of Rationality.* Cambridge: Cambridge University Press.

Fehr, Ernst, and Simon Gächter. 2000. "Cooperation and Punishment in Public Goods Experiments." *American Economic Review* 90(4): 980–94.

Fitzpatrick, Daniel. 2006. "Evolution and Chaos in Property Rights Systems: The Third World Tragedy of Contested Access." *Yale Law Review* 115(5): 996–1048.

Gibson, Clark, John Williams, and Elinor Ostrom. 2005. "Local Enforcement and Better Forests." *World Development* 33(2): 273–84.

Gibson, Clark, Margaret McKean, and Elinor Ostrom, eds. 2000. *People and Forests: Communities, Institutions, and Governance.* Cambridge, Mass.: MIT Press.

Greig, Fiona, and Iris Bohnet. 2008. "Is There Reciprocity in a Reciprocal-Exchange Economy? Evidence of Gendered Norms from a Slum in Nairobi, Kenya." *Economic Inquiry* 46(1): 77–83.

Hackett, Steven. 1992. "Heterogeneity and the Provision of Governance for Common-Pool Resources." *Journal of Theoretical Politics* 4(3): 325–42.

Hackett, Steven, Edella Schlager, and James Walker. 1994. "The Role of Communication in Resolving Commons Dilemmas: Experimental Evidence with Heterogeneous Appropriators." *Journal of Environmental Economics and Management* 27(2): 99–126.

Hardin, Russell. 1982. *Collective Action.* Baltimore, Md.: Johns Hopkins University Press.

Henrich, Joseph, Robert Boyd, Samuel Bowles, Colin Camerer, Ernst Fehr, and Herbert Gintis, eds. 2004. *Foundations of Human Sociality: Economic Experiments and Ethnographic Evidence from Fifteen Small-Scale Societies.* Oxford: Oxford University Press.

Henrich, Joseph, Richard McElreath, Abigail Barr, Jean Ensminger, Clark Barrett, Alexander Bolyanatz, Juan-Camilo Cárdenas, Michael Gurven, Edwins Gwako, Natalie Henrich, Carolyn Lesorogol, Frank Marlowe, David Tracer, and John

Ziker. 2006. "Costly Punishment Across Human Societies." *Science* 312(5781): 1767–70.

Herr, Andrew, Roy Gardner, and James Walker. 1997. "An Experimental Study of Time-Independent and Time-Dependent Externalities in the Commons." *Games and Economic Behavior* 19(1): 77–96.

Holm, Hakan J., and Anders J. Danielson. 2005. "Tropic Trust Versus Nordic Trust: Experimental Evidence from Tanzania and Sweden." *The Economic Journal* 115(503): 505–32.

Isaac, R. Mark, and James Walker. 1988a. "Communication and Free-Riding Behavior: The Voluntary Contribution Mechanism." *Economic Inquiry* 26(4): 585–608.

———. 1988b. "Group Size Effects in Public Goods Provision: The Voluntary Contributions Mechanism." *Quarterly Journal of Economics* 103(1): 179–99.

———. 1991. "Costly Communication: An Experiment in a Nested Public Goods Problem." In *Laboratory Research in Political Economy*, edited by Thomas R. Palfrey. Ann Arbor: University of Michigan Press.

Isaac, R. Mark, James Walker, and Arlington Williams. 1994. "Group Size and the Voluntary Provision of Public Goods: Experimental Evidence Utilizing Large Groups." *Journal of Public Economics* 54(1): 1–36.

Jacobsen, Eva, and Abdolkarim Sadrieh. 1966. "Experimental Proof for the Motivational Importance of Reciprocity." Discussion paper B-386. Bonn: University of Bonn.

Johansson-Stenman, Olof, Minhaj Mahmud, and Peter Martinsson. 2006. "Trust, Trust Games and Stated Trust: Evidence from Rural Bangladesh." Department of Economics working paper. Göteborg, Sweden: Göteborg University.

Johnson, Ronald N., and Gary D. Libecap. 1982. "Contracting Problems and Regulation: The Case of the Fishery." *American Economic Review* 72(5): 1005–23.

Kanbur, Ravi. 1992. "Heterogeneity, Distribution, and Cooperation in Common Property Resource Management." *1992 World Development Report* background paper. Washington, D.C.: The World Bank.

Karlan, Dean. 2005. "Using Experimental Economics to Measure Social Capital and Predict Financial Decisions." *American Economic Review* 95(5): 1688–699.

Koford, Kenneth. 1998. "Trust and Reciprocity in Bulgaria: A Replication of Berg, Dickhaut and McCabe (1995)." *Department of Economics* working paper. Newark: University of Delaware.

Kosfeld, Michael, Akira Okada, and Arno Riedl. 2006. "Institution Formation in Public Goods Games." *Institute for Empirical Research in Economics* working paper. Zurich: University of Zurich.

Ledyard, John O. 1995. "Public Goods: A Survey of Experimental Research." In *Handbook of Experimental Economics*, edited by John H. Kagel and Alvin E. Roth. Princeton, N.J.: Princeton University Press.

Levi, Margaret. 1998. *Consent, Dissent, and Patriotism.* Cambridge, Mass.: Cambridge University Press.

Libecap, Gary D., and Steven N. Wiggins. 1984. "Contractual Responses to the Common Pool: Prorationing of Crude Oil Production." *American Economic Review* 74(1): 87–98.

List, John A. 2006. "Field Experiments: A Bridge Between Lab and Naturally Occurring Data." *Advances in Economic Analysis & Policy* 6(2): article 8. Available at: http://www.bepress.com/bejeap/advances/vol6/iss2/art8 (accessed September 1, 2009).

Masclet, David, Charles Noussair, Steven Tucker, and Marie-Claire Villeval. 2003. "Monetary and Non-Monetary Punishment in the Voluntary Contributions Mechanism." *American Economic Review* 93(1): 366–80.

McCay, Bonnie, and James Acheson. 1987. *The Question of the Commons.* Tucson: University of Arizona Press.

Messick, David M., and Charles G. McClintock. 1968. "Motivational Bases of Choice in Experimental Games." *Journal of Experimental Social Psychology* 4(1): 1–25.

National Research Council. 1986. *Proceedings of the Conference on Common Property Resource Management.* Washington, D.C.: National Academies Press.

———. 2002. *The Drama of the Commons,* edited by Elinor Ostrom, Thomas Dietz, Nives Dolšak, Paul Stern, Susan Stonich, and Elke Weber. Committee on the Human Dimensions of Global Change. Washington, D.C.: National Academies Press.

Noussair, Charles, and James Walker. 1999. "Student Decision Making as Active Learning: Experimental Economics in the Classroom." In *Teaching Economics to Undergraduates: Alternatives to Chalk and Talk,* edited by William Becker and Michael Watts. Cheltenham, U.K.: Edward Elgar.

Ostrom, Elinor. 1990. *Governing the Commons: The Evolution of Institutions for Collective Action.* New York: Cambridge University Press.

———. 1999. "Coping with Tragedies of the Commons." *Annual Review of Political Science* 2(1999): 493–535.

———. 2005. *Understanding Institutional Diversity.* Princeton, N.J.: Princeton University Press.

Ostrom, Elinor, and Harini Nagendra. 2006. "Insights on Linking Forests, Trees, and People from the Air, on the Ground, and in the Laboratory." *Proceedings of the National Academy of Sciences* 103(51): 19224–231.

Ostrom, Elinor, and James Walker. 1991. "Communication in a Commons: Cooperation Without External Enforcement." In *Laboratory Research in Political Economy,* edited by Thomas R. Palfrey. Ann Arbor: University of Michigan Press.

———, eds. 2003. *Trust and Reciprocity: Interdisciplinary Lessons from Experimental Research.* New York: Russell Sage Foundation.

Ostrom, Elinor, Roy Gardner, and James Walker. 1994. *Rules, Games, and Common-Pool Resources.* Ann Arbor: University of Michigan Press.

Ostrom, Elinor, James Walker, and Roy Gardner. 1992. "Covenants with and without a Sword: Self-Governance Is Possible." *American Political Science Review* 86(2): 404–17.

Page, Talbot, and Louis Putterman. 2000. "Cheap Talk and Punishment in Voluntary Contribution Experiments (An Interim Report)." Paper presented at the Economic Science Association conference. New York (June 17, 2000).

Putnam, Robert D. 2000. *Bowling Alone: The Collapse and Revival of American Community.* New York: Simon & Schuster.

Rodriguez-Sickert, Carlos, Ricardo Guzman, and Juan-Camilo Cárdenas. 2008. "Institutions Influence Preferences: Evidence from a Common Pool Resource Experiment." *Journal of Economic Behavior and Organization* 67(1): 215–27.

Rothstein, Bo. 2005. *Social Traps and the Problem of Trust*. Cambridge: Cambridge University Press.
Rothstein, Bo, and Daniel Eek. 2006. "Political Corruption and Social Trust: An Experimental Approach." Paper presented at the American Political Science Association meeting. Philadelphia, Pa. (August 31–September 3, 2006).
Schechter, Laura. 2007. "Traditional Trust Measurement and the Risk Confound: An Experiment in Rural Paraguay." *Journal of Economic Behavior and Organization* 62(2): 272–92.
Schmitt, Pamela, Kurtis Swope, and James Walker. 2000. "Collective Action with Incomplete Commitment: Experimental Evidence." *Southern Economic Journal* 66(4): 829–54.
Sefton, Martin, Robert Shupp, and James Walker. 2007. "The Effect of Rewards and Sanctions in Provision of Public Goods." *Economic Inquiry* 45(4): 671–90.
Tilly, Charles. 2005. *Trust and Rule*. Cambridge: Cambridge University Press.
Tyler, Tom R., and Peter Degoey. 1995. "Collective Restraint in Social Dilemmas: Procedural Justice and Social Identification Effects on Support for Authorities." *Journal of Personality and Social Psychology* 69(3): 482–97.
Uslaner, Eric M. 2002. *The Moral Foundation of Trust*. New York: Cambridge University Press.
Van Vugt, Mark, and Charles D. Samuelson. 1999. "The Impact of Personal Metering in the Management of a Natural Resource Crisis: A Social Dilemma Analysis." *Personality and Social Psychology Bulletin* 25(6): 731–45.
Vollan, Bjorn. 2008. "Socio-Ecological Explanations for Crowding-Out Effects from Economic Field Experiments in Southern Africa." *Ecological Economics* 67(4): 560–73.
Wade, Robert. 1988. "The Management of Irrigation Systems: How to Evoke Trust and Avoid Prisoners' Dilemma." *World Development* 16(4): 489–500.
Walker, James, and Matthew Halloran. 2004. "Rewards and Sanctions and the Provision of Public Goods in One-Shot Settings." *Experimental Economics* 7(3): 235–47.
Weber, J. Mark, and J. Keith Murnighan. 2006. "Suckers No More: Consistent Contributors Can Solve the Cooperation Problem." Working paper. Evanston, Ill.: Northwestern University.
Weinstein, Martin S. 2000. "Pieces of the Puzzle: Solutions for Community-Based Fisheries Management from Native Canadians, Japanese Cooperatives, and Common Property Researchers." *Georgetown International Environmental Law Review* 12(2): 375–412.
Wiggins, Steven N., and Gary D. Libecap. 1985. "Oil Field Unitization: Contractual Failure in the Presence of Imperfect Information." *American Economic Review* 75(3): 368–85.
———. 1987. "Firm Heterogeneities and Cartelization Efforts in Domestic Crude Oil." *Journal of Law, Economics, and Organization* 3(1): 1–25.
Willinger, Marc, Claudia Keser, Christopher Lohmann, and Jean-Claude Usunier. 2003. "A Comparison of Trust and Reciprocity Between France and Germany: Experimental Investigation Based on the Investment Game." *Journal of Economic Psychology* 24(4): 447–66.
Yamagishi, Toshio. 1986. "The Provision of a Sanctioning System as a Public Good." *Journal of Personality and Social Psychology* 51(1): 110–16.

PART II

NETWORKS, ORGANIZATIONS, AND TRUST

Chapter 5

Institutions and Midlevel Explanations of Trust

HENRY FARRELL

THE LAST FIFTEEN years have seen an explosion in research on trust, but there are still important gaps in our understanding of its sources and consequences.[1] In particular, we know relatively little about the relationship between trust and the other sources of cooperation that social scientists have identified, most prominently institutions, the sets of rules that shape the behavior of communities of actors by providing individuals with information about the likely social consequences of their actions. How do we map out the relationship between midlevel phenomena, such as institutional rules, and micro-level expectations, such as those involved in trust?

It is hard to answer these questions because debates about trust have emerged in partial isolation from broader social science debates about the respective roles of institutions (Knight 1998) and other midlevel social phenomena in supporting cooperation. The result is that even though scholars of trust are surely interested in the empirical question of how trust operates within environments shaped by institutions, they do not have the intellectual tools that would help them investigate this and related questions easily.

On the one hand, it is surely appropriate to draw distinctions between trust-based cooperation and other forms of cooperation, where such distinctions are warranted. Scholars in the broad rational choice tradition have articulated a powerful critique of overly broad and simplistic accounts of trust found in, for example, the economics literature. Karen Cook, Russell Hardin, and Margaret Levi speak to the utility of distinguishing between trust and mere institution-induced cooperation (2005).

Many forms of cooperation in modern societies rest on institutions but do not involve trust. For some purposes, it may be useful to refer to the contractual relationship between a bank and a firm it lends to as involving trust, but there is a clear difference between the kinds of expectations that depend on contract and those that depend on personal relationships (see, for example, chapter 8, this volume).

On the other hand, there is considerable murkiness and confusion about where institutions (and other structural forces) end and where trust begins. The encapsulated interest account, as currently formulated, says relatively little about how institutions might affect the more personal and intimate forms of trust it is most directly concerned with. Political culture theorists, for their part, acknowledge that institutions and the set of cultural values that includes trust shape each other. However, they remain quite vague about what this involves in practice, either stating that they co-constitute each other without seeking to disentangle the relationships further (Inglehart 1990) or lumping trust and institutions together under the generalized rubric of social capital (Putnam 1993).

These and other confusions stem from gaps in our underlying theory. We do not have a properly developed theoretical account of how trust and institutions interact. Ideally, such an account would do at least three things. First, it would distinguish clearly between trust and institutions as sources of cooperation, disentangling their relative causal roles. Second, it would identify possible interaction effects between trust and institutions, identifying circumstances under which these effects are likely to support or to undermine trust. Finally, it would provide an explanation of those midrange forms of trust, which are poorly served in the current debate—forms of trust that are neither purely individual, nor at the highly abstract level of generality that, say, political culture accounts of diffuse interpersonal trust invoke. Midrange expectations of this kind play a key role in most complex societies, allowing actors from different social groups to navigate relations in contexts where broadly based impersonal institutions offer imperfect guidance as to what they should or should not do.

Rational choice accounts of trust in particular would benefit from such an approach. Currently the most sophisticated rational choice accounts of trust are vulnerable to the critique that they neither encompass forms of trust beyond the purely personal nor explain how broad factors such as social and political inequality can affect trust (Uslaner 2004). Although there is no reason that rational choice is incapable of explaining such relationships, these critics rightly point to the need to develop an approach that can link aggregate social factors to trust and distrust between individuals.

In this chapter, I map out the beginnings of a midrange rational choice approach that would allow us both to draw the necessary distinctions between trust and simple institution-induced expectations as sources of cooperation and to identify possible relationships between institutions and trust. I call this a midrange theory because it both emphasizes the importance of midrange factors such as institutions to the explanation of trust, and discusses how trust may itself be a midrange expectation among individuals who don't know each other personally, but who trust each other in more specific ways than political culture accounts of diffuse impersonal trust might suggest. I build on the foundation of existing work on trust, specifically the encapsulated interest account of trust Russell Hardin and his colleagues, and seeking to modify their arguments somewhat so as better to incorporate the effects of institutions on trust (Cook, Hardin, and Levi 2005).

After outlining two closely related causal accounts of the sources of trust, I show how the second causal account allows us to understand how institutions (and in particular informal institutions) may affect trust between actors, arguing that this account can explain causal relationships between inequality and trust that extend beyond the purely personal.

My goal is to make two contributions to the literature. The first is to extend the reach of rational choice–based accounts to encompass midrange forms of trust and related social expectations. The second is to set out an account of the relationship between social structure and trust, which will show how social structures may indeed affect trust but still allow one to distinguish between trust and the more impersonal forms of social expectation that underpin many forms of exchange in advanced industrial societies. This would preserve valuable conceptual distinctions yet provide a theoretical way to bridge a set of literatures largely disconnected from one another.

Two Related Accounts of Trust

Trust is a notoriously difficult concept to pin down. In the following discussion, I start from Russell Hardin's argument that trust is a kind of expectation (2002), grounded in reason, about whether another party or parties will cooperate in the future. Treating trust as an expectation allows us to make two important distinctions. First, we can distinguish between trust and cooperation on the basis of trust; although trust facilitates certain kinds of action, it is not an action itself. Second, we may distinguish between trust and trustworthiness. Trust is a set of expectations about whether another party may be expected to behave in a trustworthy manner over a particular issue or set of issues.

Not all reasoned expectations about the propensity of others to cooperate fall under the rubric of trust, however. When actors have good reason to be certain that others will cooperate, the resulting expectations cannot really be described as trust. More specifically, as Edward Lorenz argued, trust involves the expectation that another will cooperate ex post in circumstances that cannot readily be anticipated ex ante (1999). This is key to the distinction between confidence and trust. When I know that another will behave honestly in a predetermined and well-anticipated situation, this knowledge is better described as confidence than trust. Trust is involved only where there is the possibility of an unanticipated, or only imperfectly anticipated, situation arising, in which there is a real risk of default.

What are the sources of trust? In this chapter, I lay out two complementary mechanisms through which individuals may come to trust each other. The first is a somewhat simplified version of the standard encapsulated interest account of trust, in which personal relationships provide a grounding for trust. The second is a variant in which broader social expectations over the likely behavior of classes of actors serves as the necessary grounding.

First, the encapsulated interest account of trust developed by Russell Hardin and his colleagues (2005), particularly Margaret Levi and Karen Cook, focuses on forms of trust derived from personal knowledge and experience. Under this account, I trust you with regard to a particular matter to the extent that I believe that your interests encapsulate my own on that matter; more formally, I, as actor *a*, trust another actor *b*, with regard to matter *x* to the extent that *b*'s interests encapsulate my own. In other words, I trust you to the extent that I believe that you have a particular reason to pay attention to my interests. Typically, that interest will arise from our ongoing relationship. I may know (or at least believe) that you have an interest in respecting my interests with regard to a specific matter because you know that untrustworthy behavior will cause me to break off our relationship, and because our relationship is valuable to you. This will cause me to trust you; I will believe that your interests encapsulate my own with regard to the relevant matter. If the relationship is similarly valuable to me, you may trust me over a specific matter or variety of such matters.

As Hardin (2004) argues, the encapsulated interest account of trust is relational; that is, it suggests that trust is primarily grounded in ongoing personal relations between individuals who know each other well. Relationships may provide both the appropriate incentives and the appropriate knowledge to support trust. The appropriate incentives will arise if an ongoing relationship is valuable enough, and is likely to be terminated or otherwise made less valuable should one party prove untrustworthy. The appropriate knowledge will arise among actors who have engaged in repeated personalized interactions, and who should know each other well enough to underpin trust, though this knowledge will not be perfect, and trust may always be mistaken.

A few important features of the encapsulated interest account are worth highlighting. First, in contrast to many theories of trust, it focuses relentlessly on the specific, rather than seeking to explain diffuse forms of interpersonal trust in which the identity of actors and of the matter being trusted over are discounted (indeed, it suggests that a high degree of skepticism regarding such concepts is warranted). Because of this specificity, it allows for variation in the trustor, trusted, and matter of trust. To adapt Hardin's notation slightly, actor *a* may trust actor *b* with regard to matter *x*. Actor *a* may not trust actor *b* with regard to another matter, *y*. However, another actor, *c*, may trust *b* with regard to *y* but not with regard to *x*. Thus the theory can capture quite fine-grained trust relationships.

Second, although the encapsulated interest account is broadly compatible with a rational choice account of human behavior, it does not require that individuals be narrowly rational, that is, concerned only with material gain (Hardin 1982). The theory suggests that individuals will trust each other when their trust is anchored in valuable relationships. The relationship, however, may be valuable because of affective ties rather than material interests. One may perhaps trust a family member or close friend because one knows that the relationship is emotionally valuable to the other person; there need not be any material benefits involved in the relationship.

Finally, the degree to which one party trusts another may vary according to the power relations between them, an argument I developed at length in earlier work (Farrell 2004). There is no necessary reason that both actors should place the same value on a relationship for them to trust each other, and the actor who values the relationship less is likely to have more power ipso facto. Here, power is best conceived of as bargaining power, which is in turn the product of the attractiveness of the options that each actor has if they don't reach an agreement. Actors with better options are likely to be more indifferent as to the success or otherwise of a particular instance of bargaining than actors with worse options. Actors with more bargaining power are in a better position both to demand trustworthy behavior from other less powerful actors, and to behave untrustworthily themselves and to get away with it.

However, we may envisage circumstances under which power asymmetries are so extreme that trust is driven out. If one actor is so much more powerful than the other as to have no need to take account of the other's interests, then the less powerful actor has no reason to trust the more powerful one under a straightforward encapsulated interest account. Less obviously, the more powerful actor will have no reason to trust the less powerful one; because their future relationship has no value for the less powerful actor, given that the more powerful actor has no reason to respect the less powerful actor's interests, it does not serve as an anchor for trustworthy behavior. We may expect the less powerful actor to cooperate with the more powerful one only if absolutely necessary.

The encapsulated interest account of trust draws several valuable conceptual distinctions. However, to draw a clear line between trust and institution-induced cooperation, the encapsulated interest account focuses overwhelmingly on the personal. Hardin and his colleagues (2005) argue that as broadly based institutions to support impersonal cooperation have developed in advanced industrial democracies, the citizens of these democracies have less need for trust. Thus Cook, Hardin, and Levi (2005) maintain that scholars should pay less attention to trust and more to cooperation without trust.

This emphasis means that the encapsulated interest account is not ideally suited in its current form to explaining those broader forms of trust that seem neither entirely personalized, nor yet purely impersonal (grounded in institutions such as contract law or the kinds of diffuse impersonal trust to which scholars of political culture refer). It surely can accommodate some institutional effects, even in its unmodified form. Institutions certainly can mitigate or eliminate distrust by raising the costs of untrustworthy actions, and thus perhaps contribute indirectly to trust formation. It is unclear, however, how or whether institutions can play a direct causal role.

Thus, I suggest that Hardin's encapsulated interest account of the sources of trust should be supplemented by a second account, which modifies encapsulated interest to focus on the ways in which individuals may come to trust actors who belong to broader classes. For convenience, I dub the usual encapsulated interest account the *relational* version of encapsulated interest, and the second the *class-based* version of encapsulated interest. Consider a situation where *b* is personally unknown to *a*. Under these circumstances, *b* does not have any reasons grounded in an ongoing relationship to take *a*'s interests into account with regard to *x*, or indeed to any other matter. Hence the relational account would suggest that *a* will not trust *b* on the basis of their relationship; *a* has no reason to believe that *b*'s interests encapsulate her own.

However, *a* may come to trust *b* through a related mechanism. Person *a* may consider whether *b* belongs to a broader class or type of actor, which we will dub *B*, which has some reason to behave in a trustworthy fashion to members of the broader class of actors, *A*, to which *a* herself belongs. More precisely, if *a* knows that actors of type *B* have good reason to be trustworthy toward actors of type *A* in situations that resemble *x*, *a* may infer that *b* is likely to behave trustworthily in this instance. Hence *a* may come to trust *b*, not because of a specific relationship between *a* and *b* but because *a* knows that actors of type *B* behave trustworthily toward actors of type *A* in situations that resemble *x*.

Under this class-based account, individuals can indeed trust each other without previously having known each other. To take one example, well-dressed whites driving expensive cars in the United States are usually not pulled over by the police without good cause. They furthermore have good reason to believe that the police will behave trustworthily toward them across a wide variety of situations because they belong to a group (well-to-do whites) whom the police have reason to behave trustworthily toward across many situations. More formally, each member *a* of the larger class of well-to-do whites (*A*) knows that individual members *b*, who belong to the broader class of police officers (*B*) will have good reason to behave trustworthily across a wide variety of situations $x_1 \ldots x_n$.

However, we may expect that members of a different class of actors, those who belong to specific ethnic minorities, will have quite different expectations compared with well-dressed whites. They may expect to be pulled over by the police, often without good reason, and perhaps especially often when they are driving expensive cars. More generally, they will have less reason than well-to-do whites to trust the police. Indeed, they may expect that any cooperation they offer will be abused under many plausible circumstances. More formally, each member of a relevant ethnic minority (*c*) may expect that an individual member of the police force (*b*) will behave untrustworthily across many situations because *b* is a member of *B*, *c* is a member of *C*, and members of class *C* habitually abuse the trust of members of class *B* across a variety of situations *x*.

In chapter 2 of this volume, James Habyarimana and his colleagues provide another example when they discuss trust relations within and between different ethnic groups in Uganda. As they describe it, a member of a particular ethnic group is likely to behave more trustworthily toward coethnics than to noncoethnics because of informal norms. Strikingly, they find that subjects playing the dictator game give no more to coethnics than to noncoethnics when their behavior is unobservable, suggesting that this informal norm depends on the two-way provision of information, rather than, say, being a particular internalized concern for the well-being of coethnics. In the language of this chapter, coethnics of group *A* expect that when they cooperate (by providing a larger reward) with others of group *A* that their cooperation will be rewarded (or not punished), as long as their cooperation is observable to the relevant coethnics.

Thus I argue that individuals' trust or distrust of each other can be grounded in other kinds of expectations than those stemming from personal relationships. It can also be grounded in broader forms of social knowledge regarding the ways in which various classes of actors are likely to interact with each other across various social situations. Individuals may instead reason that they are members of a specific class, that they are dealing with an individual or individuals who are also identifiably members of a specific class, and that they know how these two classes of actors may be expected to interact with each other across a variety of social situations. This may be enough knowledge to ground trust relationships (when social knowledge regarding the relevant class of actors suggests that members of one class may be expected to behave trustworthily toward another in relevant situations), or to create grounds for distrust (where social knowledge suggests that members of one class are likely to betray the interests of members of another in relevant situations).

I note in passing that these two forms of encapsulated interest–based trust may interact in interesting ways. For example, in chapter 6 of this volume, Irena Stepanikova and her colleagues find evidence that some doctors working in HMOs seek to combat patient distrust in them as members of the general class of HMO doctors by building specific relationships with patients based on their willingness to fight the HMOs for benefits.

Institutions and Social Knowledge over Classes

Where are individuals likely to discover how different classes of actors should behave toward each other? The most plausible answer is the plethora of institutional rules that govern a host of interactions in all societies of even moderate complexity. Institutional rules, properly considered, are important to the understanding of human behavior precisely because they instantiate knowledge about how different classes of actors are likely to behave toward each other. Under the best developed rational choice accounts, institutions have no independent causal force in shaping human action beyond their informational aspects.[2] Instead, they are important because they provide individuals with information about how others are likely to respond to their actions across a variety of circumstances. They thus guide strategic behavior.

The kind of information that institutions provide is specific, though not in terms of how specific named individuals behave (a rule of thumb that one shouldn't bother Henry before his morning coffee because he's liable to snap at you is not an institution under any reasonable definition of the term). Instead, they provide knowledge regarding broader social categories or classifications. They shape strategic behavior allowing individuals: to identify specific individuals, acts, and situations as belonging to broader categories; to identify any relevant rules governing behavior thus classified; to recognize how others are likely to respond to specific actions given the existence of these rules; and to tailor their own actions accordingly. As Herbert L. A. Hart said of the law, which may be considered a body of formal institutions, "its successful operation over vast areas of social life depends on a widely diffused capacity to recognize particular acts, things, and circumstances as instances of the general classifications which the law makes" (1994, 124).

Hart's point extends beyond the law. It also extends to cover classifications of persons, which he does not mention. Institutions are rules over how broad categories of actors should interact in specific situations. Institutions thus commonly take a form something like the following: when actors of class *A* and actors of class *B* interact in situation *X*, the appropriate action for the actor of class *A* is *H*, and the appropriate action for the actor of class *B* is *I*.[3]

This shows us how institutions may affect trust between actors under the class-based version of the encapsulated interest account. Actors may refer to the social knowledge instantiated in institutions to understand how broad classes of actors are supposed to interact. They may then infer that others belonging to specific classes of actors are likely to be trustworthy or untrustworthy. For example, if actor *a* belonging to class *A* and actor *b* belonging to class *B* find themselves in a situation *x* of type *X* where there is a relevant institutional rule providing guidance that actors of class *A* should take action *H* and actors of class *B* should take action *I*, they may have grounds for trust or distrust of each other.[4] If action *I* involves behaving trustworthily, then the institution may allow actor *a* reasonably to surmise that actor *b* will act in a trustworthy fashion and thus perhaps will give reason to trust her.

However, not all forms of institution-based expectations will involve trust. Most obviously, where action *I* involves untrustworthy behavior, *a* will have strong grounds to distrust rather than to trust *b*. However, even where institutions conduct cooperative behavior, they may not produce trust as such. Recall Lorenz's claim that trust is an expectation that another will cooperate after the fact in circumstances that cannot readily be anticipated. Many forms of institution-induced cooperation will involve circumstances that have been anticipated, and that are fully spelled out under the existing institutional rules. Thus, to return to the example of a bank loan, the bank providing a loan to a firm doesn't trust the firm; instead, it relies on a contractual agreement that is densely specified, that is backed by a court system, and that seeks to cover an extensive range of possible contingencies to provide the firm with enough incentive to pay back the loan. It has sought to leverage contract law to anticipate the future as fully as possible (given the impossibility of drafting a complete contract) so as to ensure that unforeseeable situations (in which the borrower might perhaps be able to wriggle out of the loan) do not develop. Trust is not usually implicated—instead, the bank seeks to induce cooperation directly through appropriate institutional structures. As Bruce Carruthers argues in chapter 8 of this volume, this is a relatively recent historical development; lending practices used to be grounded in trust relations at the community or personal level.

To understand the circumstances under which institutions directly induce cooperation, and under which they instead work through trust, it is necessary to return to (or, more precisely, to reinvent[5]) Hart. In *The Concept of Law* (1994), Hart distinguishes between the *core* of a law; that is, the area in which it has direct and uncontroversial effect, and the *penumbra;* that is, the shadow that it casts over situations to which it may be relevant but is not unambiguously applicable. He also referred to the persistent difficulties of reasoning from abstract rules to concrete situations; general rules about classes of events, actors, actions, and circumstances are by no means necessarily unambiguous when applied to concrete situations.

Hart's focus on the ambiguity of applying rules and his distinction between core and penumbra allow us better to distinguish between situations in which institutions (including but certainly not limited to laws) have direct consequences for cooperation, and those in which their consequences are better understood in terms of how they affect the potential for trust between actors. Adapting Hart, we may say that the core of an institution is that body of situations to which the relevant institution applies more or less unambiguously, and for which its implications for social action are relatively clear cut. The penumbra of an institution, by contrast, is that body of situations to which the relevant institution applies only ambiguously, and for which its implications for social action are to some degree uncertain.

Given this definition, we may say that situations within the core of an institution do not invoke trust in any significant sense. When the institution applies unambiguously, it directly affects the scope for cooperation between individuals. There is no uncertainty about after-the-fact behavior to provide scope for trust to develop between actors.

The penumbra of institutions, however, provides quite significant scope. In the penumbra, institutions do not induce cooperation directly; instead, they provide guidelines that may allow actors to interpret a situation in particular ways, and thus to come to trust each other. Consider the case where actors *a* and *b* find themselves in situation *x**, which is somewhat similar, but not identical to a situation covered by an institutional rule regarding how actors of classes *A* and *B* are supposed to cooperate in situation *x*. Under these circumstances, cooperation will not be induced by the institution, will not be automatic or anything like it. However, the institution does provide information regarding how actors of *A* and *B* are supposed to behave, which will provide valuable guidance for *a* and *b* in their efforts to figure out how to behave (and how others are likely to respond to their behavior). Here, the relevant institution is likely to work in the same way as the forms of corporate culture that David Kreps described (1990). It provides an important focal point guiding behavior, without at the same time itself producing anything approaching certainty regarding how others are likely to behave (Schelling 1960). Unless there is some other, more compelling focal point, actors *a* and *b* may reasonably be expected to draw on their knowledge of how actors of class *A* and class *B* are supposed to behave under the given institution. If the institution prescribes that actors of class *B* behave in a trustworthy manner, actor *a* will have some grounded reason to believe that *b* will behave trustworthily, and thus to trust *b*. Under this account, the institution doesn't induce cooperation, but instead provides actors with guidelines likely to lead them to cooperate in the absence of other compelling information about how they and others are supposed to behave.

One implication of this set of arguments is developed further in collaborative work with Jack Knight (Farrell and Knight, unpublished)—different kinds of institutions are likely to vary with respect to the relative importance of their cores and penumbrae. In particular, we may expect that formal institutions—written regulations, laws, bureaucratic codes, and the like—will usually but not invariably have relatively large cores and relatively narrow penumbrae. Such institutions are designed to provide a high degree of certainty to actors dealing with each other in well-defined situations. Informal institutions, on the other hand, are likely to have relatively small cores and relatively wide penumbrae. Their precise extent and meaning is likely to be uncodified and relatively diffuse. By the same token, however, they also cast their shadow over a broad range of situations that appear to resemble those covered by the relevant rule, even if the precise extent and effect of the rule is uncertain.

Another is perhaps more directly relevant to the task of showing how macro- and meso-level social factors may shape trust between individuals. If social institutions reflect these factors, so too may we expect the ways in which individuals do or do not trust each other to reflect them. For example, as Terry Moe argues with respect to formal institutions, and Jack Knight with respect to informal ones, we may expect that institutions will reflect both the power asymmetries and divergent distributional preferences of different classes of actors in a given society or community (Moe 1990; Knight 1992, 1995). Institutions here act as a key intermediating variable, translating differences of power between classes of actors into expectations over trustworthy and untrustworthy behavior between individuals.

This is clearly the case with formal institutions, where actors bargain with each other directly over institutional rules, and where their bargaining strength may be expected to have direct and substantial consequences for the agreed outcomes. However, it is also, as Knight demonstrates, likely to also be the case for informal institutions that emerge through decentralized processes. Informal institutions are likely to emerge from independent instances of social bargaining between actors of different classes in a manner that reflects the power relations between them. If actors belonging to one class are repeatedly better able to get their way in bargaining interactions with members of another class, then we may expect actors' expectations to crystallize over time in an informal institution that will tell them how they are supposed to behave. Thus, informal institutions are likely to crystallize existing imbalances of power.

An example may help clarify how this is likely to work in practice. African Americans in the pre–civil rights South faced a variety of forms of informally institutionalized discrimination in addition to formal laws. Bertram Doyle offers a useful contemporary account of these informal institutions, which he dubs the etiquette of race relations, even as he glides over the brutal means through which this etiquette was maintained (1937). As he notes, institutions of this kind emerge in a decentralized fashion: "Forms of deference and recognition, repeated and imitated, soon crystallize into those conventional and obligatory forms of expression we call 'etiquette,' or social ritual" (xviii).

These rules of etiquette instantiated a social equilibrium, based on the threat of violence, in which blacks were treated systematically as inferiors, expected to show deference, and to accept manifestly unfair treatment from white people without complaint. Both blacks and whites knew and understood these informal institutions, without necessarily internalizing them. African Americans could reasonably have inferred that they could expect little in the way of respect or trustworthy behavior from white people across a range of situations, including those only imperfectly covered by the rules. Hence these institutions gave them good prima facie reason to distrust white people in these situations. Joe Feagin argues on the basis of contemporary interview evidence that more subtle, forms of informal discrimination against African Americans continue to make it difficult for blacks to trust the good intentions of white people across a variety of social settings in post–civil rights America (1991). These institutions plausibly instantiate continuing power asymmetries between blacks and whites.

Thus, to summarize, institutions are a key source of social knowledge about how different classes of actors are supposed to interact with each other. This may in turn have consequences for trust. In situations (the core) unambiguously covered by the relevant social institutions, and in which those institutions have clear consequences for behavior, we may expect institutions to have direct consequences for cooperation (or lack of it). Here, there is no need to refer to the concept of trust; the impact of institutions is unmediated. In contrast, in situations (the penumbra) in which institutions have some relevance, but are ambiguous in either scope or consequences, appropriate institutions (those that suggest to actors that they should behave trustworthily to another) may guide them toward trust, whereas inappropriate ones are likely to produce distrust. Furthermore, by examining institutions and the forces that shape them, we can better understand how factors such as the distribution of power in society may have substantial consequences for the ways in which individuals do or do not trust each other.

Applying a Midrange Theory of Trust

By examining how trust between individuals may emerge from both personal relationships and the broader information about classes of actors instantiated in social institutions, we may better understand how trust works in complex societies. Specifically, as discussed earlier, we can develop better accounts of how macro- and meso-level social factors shape the ways in which individuals trust each other at a lower level of aggregation. Under the class-based version of the encapsulated interest account, institutions become a key intervening variable between broader social factors and specific forms of trust at the individual level.

This allows rational choice scholars to extend the reach of their explanations and to respond to critics who claim that the rational choice account cannot explain trust that goes beyond specific relationships with known others. Consider, for example, Eric Uslaner's claim that strategic trust is based on individual experience, and just as it "can only lead to cooperation among people you have gotten to know, so it can only resolve problems of trust among small numbers of people" (2004, 20). Scholars who use the standard encapsulated interest account might reasonably reply that their definition of trust refers not only to individuals' experience, but to their knowledge about how ongoing relationships may give them incentives to behave in a trustworthy fashion.[6] Uslaner does, however, point to a gap in the rational choice literature—there is a clear need for a better account of how broad social factors translate into specific forms of trust and distrust among individuals.

Such an account would allow rational choice scholars better to engage with the growing body of literature that discusses trust at broader levels of aggregation. Much of this literature is rather impressionistic and of dubious social-scientific value (see Fukuyama 1995). However, a more recent body of work has sought systematically to link trust, as measured through survey instruments, to macro-level variables such as inequality, corruption, economic growth, and ethnic heterogeneity (Lee 2006; Rothstein and Uslaner 2005; Zak and Knack 2001). Although currently available aggregate survey data are far from perfectly suited to the study of more particularized varieties of trust, a developed account of how broad factors may affect trust and cooperation among individuals would at least allow rational choice social scientists better to participate in these debates.

It would, furthermore, allow rational choice scholars to exploit their comparative theoretical advantages. Much macro-level scholarship starts from the assumption that diffuse, generalized trust—the willingness of individuals to trust their fellow citizens in general—is key to understanding social outcomes. Sometimes trust of this kind is contrasted with particularized trust, that is, the propensity of respondents to trust only those who are members of their subcommunity. This emphasis is in part the result of theoretical commitments, in part the product of survey instruments, which tend to ask rather generic questions about individuals' propensity to trust others in general. However, the exact causal relationship between diffuse generalized trust and cooperative outcomes is at best rather unclear. We know from everyday experience that individuals tend to not trust or to distrust others in their country or subcommunity indiscriminately; instead they are usually quite particular in their willingness or unwillingness to trust others over particular matters. One may go further; the diffuse generalized truster, who is willing to trust other community members or citizens over a wide range of matters without reference to who those others are, or what value she places on those matters, is very possibly a chimera. This is certainly not to say that data on generalized trust is worthless—the existing literature demonstrates some real correlations and suggests in very broad terms some highly intriguing causal relationships. It is to say that whether survey questions about generalized trust are imperfect measures of a discrete propensity, some rough average of respondents' willingness to trust a range of others over a range of situations, or something else entirely is not at all clear (see chapter 11, this volume).

The modified version of the encapsulated interest account I set out in this chapter provides a way for rational choice scholars to examine not only specific forms of trust between individuals who know each other, but also midrange forms of trust between individuals belonging to specific classes of actors. The latter forms of trust are more specific in their application than diffuse generalized trust—they allow individuals to discriminate both with regard to the person (or, more precisely, class of persons) being trusted, and the matter being trusted over. However, they are also better able to account for the effect of macro- and meso-level variables than purely relational forms of interpersonal trust.

I now build on the claims I have already made to argue that the class-based version of encapsulated interest provides a highly plausible explanation of how high levels of inequality are likely to lead to higher levels of distrust across society. The most prominent alternative explanation argues that we need to refer to the kind of generalized trust found in a community of shared moral values to explain this causal relationship (Uslaner 2004; Rothstein and Uslaner 2005). I show that, at a minimum, a class-based account of trust provides an alternative account of the relationship between inequality and trust that fits with the empirical evidence. Although a proper test of the respective merits of the two approaches would require a separate chapter, as well as substantial new data and research, my arguments suggest that a strong sense of moral community is not necessary for widespread social trust. If true, the suggestion offers cautious grounds for optimism regarding the possibilities for increasing trust among individuals.

We know from a variety of sources that mistrust can be historically resilient, even over the longer term (see chapter 7, this volume). We also know that deeply rooted forms of mistrust are strongly associated with structural inequality (chapter 7, this volume; Hardin 2002). However, we are still in the early stages of theorizing the mechanisms underlying this relationship and the degree to which historically rooted forms of distrust can be redressed in social contexts in which distrust has negative consequences.

In an important article, Bo Rothstein and Eric Uslaner pointed to a strong empirical relationship across countries between trust and levels of economic equality (2005). Societies with high levels of economic inequality are likely to have low levels of trust. Societies with low levels of inequality are correspondingly likely to have higher levels of trust. To explain these and related findings, Uslaner argued that we need to refer to moral trust—the kind of trust generated in a shared moral community (2004). The concept of moral trust allows us to understand how collective rather than individual experience shapes individuals' propensity to trust or distrust each other. More equal societies are likely to be those where individuals feel that they are part of a shared community of fate; they are correspondingly more likely to trust each other in the rich ways that support broadly based (rather than particularistic) forms of civic engagement and mutual respect. To quote Rothstein and Uslaner:

> When resources and opportunities are distributed more equally, people are more likely to perceive a common stake with others and to see themselves as part of a larger social order. If there is a strong skew in wealth or in the possibilities for improving one's stake in life, people at each end may feel that they have little in common with others. In highly unequal societies, people are likely to stick with their own kind. Perceptions of injustice will reinforce negative stereotypes of other groups, making social trust and accommodation more difficult. (Rothstein and Uslaner 2005, 52)

The mechanisms Rothstein and Uslaner identify are plausible. It is quite likely that individuals do see themselves, at least in some contexts, as belonging to a larger whole, and that a sense of collective solidarity may inspire them to trust each other in circumstances when they otherwise would not. It is also highly plausible that high levels of inequality will corrode whatever sense of collective solidarity exists. Yet their counsel is one, if not of complete despair, of considerable pessimism. They argue that "when people do not see themselves as part of the same moral community with a shared fate, they will not have the solidarity that is essential for building up social trust," but find little hope that societies without a sense of shared fate can build one (Rothstein and Uslaner 2005, 61). Such societies are trapped by a mutually reinforcing combination of low trust, inequality, and dysfunctional institutions, and it is very difficult to see how they can work their way out of it. Constructing a genuine moral community of shared fate from scratch is at best extraordinarily difficult.

A strategic account of trust allows us to focus on some of the same variables as Rothstein and Uslaner, but arrives at a different diagnosis and different results. Specifically, we may see how both economic and political inequality may have a powerful effect both on relationships between individuals (the relational encapsulated interest account) and on trust between different classes of actors through intermediating institutional mechanisms (the class-based encapsulated interest account). Rather than shaping perceptions of shared political fates, persistent inequalities of resources are likely to shape trusting relations through realigning specifically individual perceptions of the degree to which others can be trusted.

First, we may see that inequality is likely to shape the specific relationships individuals have with each other. Inequalities in economic resources of the kind that Rothstein and Uslaner discuss are likely to manifest themselves as inequalities in bargaining power. Individuals who are relatively poor will find themselves at a disadvantage when dealing with those who are more affluent. Richer actors in unequal societies are likely to have many more attractive options to a given relationship with a poorer actor than vice versa, granting them much greater bargaining power, so that they are likely to be relatively indifferent to the end of a particular relationship. Furthermore, economic resources are relatively fungible; they may be translated into other forms of coercion or control that allow richer actors to prevail more easily over poor ones.

This means that poor actors are likely to have relatively little reason to trust wealthier ones over a wide variety of possible relationships. Indeed, if inequality becomes very high, rich actors may have less reason to trust poor ones as well. As economically powerful actors become more nearly indifferent about the question of which poor actor they have a relationship with, relationships with more affluent actors become less valuable to poor ones, making poor actors correspondingly less likely to behave in a trustworthy fashion if they can get away with not doing so (Farrell 2004).

However, as Cook, Hardin, and Levi have pointed out, relational trust is "no longer the central pillar of social order, and . . . may not even be very important in most of our cooperative exchanges" (2005, 1). Thus the second mechanism of trust generation, the class-based version of encapsulated interest, plays a role that is arguably even more important than that of personal relations. Different expectations regarding classes of actors may also be shaped by power relations, with knock-on effects for a variety of institutionalized relationships that are much more central to the functioning of complex societies. Institutions—and especially informal institutions—are likely to reflect inequalities of wealth and power when such inequalities are pronounced, and to generate increased distrust among actors who correctly perceive that they belong to categories that are unlikely to be treated as trustworthy either by actors belonging to more powerful categories, or by purportedly neutral actors, such as state bureaucrats, who are likely to be responsive to the needs of the powerful.

More generally, under the class-based account, we may see how actor *a*, as a member of class *A*, will refer to existing institutional rules for information about how *a* may expect to be treated in interactions with actors from other classes, such as *B*. If these institutions instantiate substantial inequalities of power, such that actors of class *B* are much more powerful than actors of class *A*, and use their power to secure distributional outcomes that are favorable to them (and not to actors of class *A*, except accidentally), *a* is likely to reason that she is unlikely to be treated well across a variety of situations that are only imperfectly covered by existing institutional rules. These institutions will communicate to *a* that actors of class *B* have no substantial reason to take the interests of actors of class *A* to heart across such situations. Accordingly, we may expect that *a* will conclude that she has little reason to trust actors of class *B* across a wide variety of situations that are partly covered by the relevant institutions, and many reasons to distrust them.

If, in contrast, there are no or moderate asymmetries of power between actors of class *A* and class *B*, we may expect trust and trustworthiness to be much easier to achieve across many situations. The interests of actors of class *A* and class *B* will still very possibly clash on some matters; asymmetries of power are far from the only possible source of distrust. However, at the least, actors from class *B* will potentially have some reason to take the interests of actors of class *A* into account; the power disparities between them will not be so grave as to rule trust out in the first place.

These mechanisms help explain a number of empirical phenomena; I briefly canvas two. The problem of corruption has persuasively been linked to problems of power asymmetries; other things being equal, more corrupt societies tend to be those with high degrees of resource asymmetry between wealthy and poor, and power asymmetry between ruler and ruled. Thus, for example, Michael Johnston documents the existence of four syndromes of corruption, conceptually distinct forms of corruption in which the degree of power asymmetry largely determines the severity of the form of corruption (2005). As Johnston notes, highly corrupt societies tend to have low levels of trust. My account points to mechanisms that are likely to promote exactly this causal relationship. Corrupt societies are those in which bureaucratic norms of impartiality and fairness are effectively supplanted by informal institutionalized expectations that it is necessary to pay powerful actors off to get results. In such societies, rich individuals (who have more resources to bribe others and otherwise smooth their way) will naturally be able to do better than poor individuals, and furthermore will often be able to take advantage of poor individuals without any real risk of punishment by legal authorities. It is unsurprising that under these circumstances individuals who are rich, or who belong to classes that are protected by the state, will have little reason to take the interests of others into account. This may translate not only into poor people distrusting rich people, or powerless people distrusting powerful ones, but the reverse as well: to the extent that broad classes of people are effectively excluded from most of the benefits of cooperation, they will have little incentive to behave trustworthily in circumstances in which they are not under immediate supervision or control.

A similar logic may characterize the contrast between northern and southern Italy, which has received much discussion in the academic literature in the wake of Robert Putnam's (1993) work on regional differences in Italy. Many of these differences have less to do with aggregate differences in social capital and more with the degree of hierarchy within local communities. The economically successful communities Putnam discusses also tend to have notably low degrees of power asymmetry between different economic actors (Farrell, forthcoming). Typically, they have highly decentralized economies, dominated by small firms, in which no single set of economic actors predominates. This has allowed firms to rely not on formal contracts but instead on trust-based relationships, anchored in local institutions of fair dealing, to organize production.

Matters are very different in the south, and especially in localities dominated by the Mafia. Rocco Sciarrone details how the Mafia, which he considers a loose organization bounded by a set of common informal rules reproduces power relations within commercial communities (1998). For example, in a part of Calabria that Sciarrone has studied intensively, he finds that members of the Mafia and their very close allies enjoy a privileged position, using their penetration of state bodies and their ability to offer differential protection to extract rents on economic activity (1993). Building on Diego Gambetta's arguments, Sciarrone argues that the Mafia "dedicate themselves to increasing distrust that they are then able to alleviate, so as to maintain high demand on the market for the protection that they are selling" (1993, 71, my translation; Gambetta 1993). Most notably, the Mafia distributes their protection in a differentiated fashion. Some businesses are entirely subordinate to the Mafia, and pay protection money without receiving any benefits. Other, better-positioned businesses can collude with the Mafia to a greater or lesser extent, and can expect to have their commercial dealings with others protected.

The result is substantial power asymmetries, in which less advantaged businesses have no effective recourse against either the Mafia or its favored clients should they be cheated (beyond fantasies of flight to other regions of Italy). Local community rules about what you can and cannot do mean that everyone understands how they are supposed to behave with respect to the Mafia. However, when situations are only ambiguously covered by informal community rules in localities dominated by the Mafia, we may expect institutions to tend to conduct actors toward distrust rather than trust in each other. Accordingly, these disfavored entrepreneurs, who are in the majority, have little reason either to trust each other or those more powerful than them. As Sciarrone described it: "In this situation, the Mafia may represent the only guarantee of trust[worthiness] and entrusting oneself to the Mafia—even if it is certainly disastrous from the collective point of view—may be rational from the point of view of the individual actor" (Sciarrone 1993, 91, my translation).

Here again, we may see how substantial power asymmetries go together with high levels of distrust across many classes of actors. Furthermore, in both these cases, cursory examination suggests that the encapsulated interest account (in both variants) provides a better understanding of what is going on than accounts based on generalized trust do, even if a more comprehensive test is still necessary properly to determine their respective merits. Most particularly, by examining actors' encapsulated interests, we can disentangle the specifics of trust relations in a way that is not really possible under the assumptions of generalized or moral trust. This is especially evident in the contrast between northern and southern Italy. The problem in the south is not so much that people do not trust each other in general because of the lack of a proper moral community, as that informal institutions promote specific forms of distrust between specific classes of actors that make important forms of economic and political cooperation more difficult.

Finally, I note in passing that the rationalistic theory of trust I outline provides grounds for some qualified optimism that actors can indeed escape from low trust equilibriums. If institutions are the key intermediary variable translating between power relations and outcomes in terms of trust and cooperation, we may expect that changes in power relations, and associated changes in institutions, will have knock-on consequences for how actors trust and cooperate with each other. This is not to say that institutional change will be easy or straightforward, especially if informal institutions (which are relatively poorly understood) are key to the ways in which actors trust each other. It is to say that meaningful action to improve levels of trust is not beyond the scope of human agency.

More generally, to the extent that formal institutions and enforceable state rules may sometimes counteract malign informal institutions, the agenda outlined in Margaret Levi's discussion of the relationship between state institutions and trust is a useful starting point for thinking about which institutional changes may be best suited to increasing (appropriate) trust relations among actors (1998). Robert Sampson and Corina Graif supplement Levi's arguments by pointing to the likely importance of learning processes in increasing trust (see chapter 7, this volume). If the arguments in this chapter are on target, one may see why learning may be valuable when supplemented with meaningful structural change. If informal institutions involve learned expectations about the ways in which different classes of actors will interact, then they may persist even when underlying power relationships have shifted, causing actors to continue to behave as if the old inequalities still applied.

Conclusions

In this chapter, I have argued that there is an important gap in our theories regarding the relationship between trust and institutions. This goes hand in hand with another, more specific problem for the encapsulated interest account of trust, which is the best strategic theory we have. There is a relative dearth of work by scholars employing this approach on the relationship between macro- and meso-level causal factors and the kinds of trust and cooperation among individuals. I suggest a way of tackling these problems—developing a modified version of the encapsulated interest account that examines how trust may be based on knowledge over how classes of actors are likely to behave in given contexts, and linking this account to a theory of institutions. Finally, I provide some plausible evidence to suggest that such an account may help us better to explain the broad relationship between inequality and trust.

The modified version of encapsulated interest I describe is not a substitute for the original formulation, but a complement. It shows how different forms of expectations than those of purely personal relationships may be described as trust, and draws a distinction between trust and those expectations directly induced by institutions. Institutions may affect trust between individuals, but the core of institutions—the set of situations in which institutions produce a high degree of regularity and predictability—do not implicate trust as such. Thus, the version I present neither replaces nor encompasses the original formulation, but does show how it may be adapted to cover new causal relationships without diluting the concept of trust to the point where it cannot be distinguished from simple institutional compliance.

Finally, I suggest that the arguments canvassed here provide the beginnings of an important and interesting new research agenda—a more systematic effort to discover how institutions affect trust and trustworthiness. Some elements of this research agenda are already in train (Farrell, forthcoming; Farrell and Knight, unpublished). Others may be discovered in what I believe is the complementary work of other scholars (Levi 1998). However, these only present a quite early set of arguments and results concerning a line of enquiry that has very considerable promise over the longer term.

I am grateful to Eric Uslaner, Russell Hardin, Jack Knight, Susan Stokes, and participants in the Russell Sage capstone colloquium for comments and suggestions.

Notes

1. This chapter draws both on my own work and ideas, and on ideas developed in joint work with Jack Knight (especially, Farrell and Knight, unpublished).
2. Some rational choice accounts that treat institutions as part of the game tree duck this issue—but do not have any good account of why institutions should be considered to be an unconsidered part of social structure (see Calvert 1995). Other approaches than the rational choice approach suggest that institutions can constitute actors and their choices in more profound ways. I bracket these issues for the purposes of this discussion.
3. One may imagine more simple institutions, governing instances where actors of the same class interact. One may also imagine more complex ones in which actors from many different classes interact. Although such institutions would require some reformulation of the arguments that I make here, they would have no substantial consequences for my basic claims.
4. I deliberately leave the term *relevant institution* vague here, but develop it in this section. It is enough to say for now that a relevant institution to the development of trust is not one that precisely and unambiguously covers the situation and actors, but rather one that is only somewhat ambiguously applicable.
5. I had developed the conceptual distinction between *core* and *penumbra* discussed in early conversations with Jack Knight, before reading Hart and discovering that he had used identical terms to cover closely related ideas. I am grateful to Melissa Schwartzberg for pointing out to me that I had been speaking Hartian all my life without knowing it.
6. See in particular the reading in Russell Hardin of the story of Trifonov in Dostoyevsky's *The Brothers Karamazov* (2002, 1–3).

References

Calvert, Randall L. 1995. "Rational Actors, Equilibrium, and Social Institutions." In *Explaining Social Institutions,* edited by Jack Knight and Itai Sened. Ann Arbor: University of Michigan Press.

Cook, Karen S., Russell Hardin, and Margaret Levi. 2005. *Cooperation Without Trust.* New York: Russell Sage Foundation.

Doyle, Bertram. 1937. *The Etiquette of Race Relations in the South: A Study in Social Control.* Chicago: University of Chicago Press.

Farrell, Henry. 2004. "Trust, Distrust, and Power." In *Distrust,* edited by Russell Hardin. New York: Russell Sage Foundation.

———. Forthcoming. *The Political Economy of Trust: Institutions, Interests and Interfirm Cooperation in Italy and Germany.* Cambridge: Cambridge University Press.

Farrell, Henry, and Jack Knight. Unpublished. "Trust and Institutional Compliance." Unpublished paper.

Feagin, Joe R. 1991. "The Continuing Significance of Race: Antiblack Discrimination in Public Places." *American Sociological Review* 56(1): 101–16.

Fukuyama, Francis. 1995. *Trust: The Social Virtues and the Creation of Prosperity.* New York: Free Press.

Gambetta, Diego. 1993. *The Sicilian Mafia: The Business of Private Protection.* Cambridge, Mass.: Harvard University Press.
Hardin, Russell. 1982. *Collective Action.* Baltimore, Md.: Johns Hopkins University Press.
———. 2002. *Trust and Trustworthiness.* New York: Russell Sage Foundation.
Hart, Herbert L. A. 1994. *The Concept of Law.* Oxford: Oxford University Press.
Inglehart, Ronald. 1990. *Culture Shift in Advanced Industrial Societies.* Princeton, N.J.: Princeton University Press.
Johnston, Michael. 2005. *Syndromes of Corruption: Power, Wealth and Democracy.* New York: Cambridge University Press.
Knight, Jack. 1992. *Institutions and Social Conflict.* Cambridge: Cambridge University Press.
———. 1995. Models, Interpretations and Theories: Constructing Explanations of Institutional Emergence and Change. In *Explaining Social Institutions,* edited by Jack Knight and Itai Sened. Ann Arbor: University of Michigan Press.
———. 1998. "The Bases of Cooperation: Social Norms and the Rule of Law." *Journal of Institutional and Theoretical Economics* 154(1998): 754–63.
Kreps, David M. 1990. "Corporate Culture and Economic Theory." *In Perspectives on Positive Political Economy,* edited by James E. Alt and Kenneth A. Shepsle. Cambridge: Cambridge University Press.
Lee, Andrew. 2006. "Trust, Inequality and Ethnic Heterogeneity." *The Economic Record* 82(258): 268–80.
Levi, Margaret. 1998. "A State of Trust." In *Trust and Governance,* edited by Valerie Braithwaite and Margaret Levi. New York: Russell Sage Foundation.
Lorenz, Edward H. 1999. "Trust, Contract and Economic Cooperation." *Cambridge Journal of Economics* 23(3): 301–15.
Moe, Terry. 1990. "Political Institutions: The Neglected Side of the Story." *Journal of Law, Economics, and Organization* 6(1990): 213–54.
Putnam, Robert D. 1993. *Making Democracy Work: Civic Traditions in Modern Italy.* Princeton, N.J.: Princeton University Press.
Rothstein, Bo, and Eric Uslaner. 2005. "All for All: Equality and Social Trust." *World Politics* 58(2005): 41–72.
Schelling, Thomas C. 1960. *The Strategy of Conflict.* Cambridge, Mass.: Harvard University Press.
Sciarrone, Rocco. 1993. "Il rapporto tra mafia e imprenditorialità in un'area della Calabria." *Quaderni di Sociologia* 5(1): 68–92.
———. 1998. "Il capitale sociale della mafia. Relazioni esterne e controllo del territorio." *Quaderni di Sociologia* 18(1): 51–72.
Uslaner, Eric M. 2004. "Trust as a Moral Value." In *Handbook of Social Capital,* edited by Dario Castiglione, Jan W. Van Deth, and Gugliemo Wolleb. Oxford: Oxford University Press.
Zak, Paul J., and Stephen Knack. 2001. "Trust and Growth." *The Economic Journal* 111(470): 295–321.

Chapter 6

Trust in Managed Care Settings

IRENA STEPANIKOVA, KAREN S. COOK, DAVID THOM,
RODERICK KRAMER, AND STEFANIE MOLLBORN

AS HENRY FARRELL argues in the previous chapter, individuals' trust or distrust of each other is not grounded solely in personal relationships. Often it stems from broader social knowledge about how individuals occupying various structural positions are supposed to interact under certain circumstances. Farrell refers to these structural positions as *classes* and explains that *class-based trust* is often anchored in norms, rules, and other forms of social knowledge embodied in institutions, which govern innumerable interactions in modern societies. In this chapter, we explore how managed care institutions shape and constrain the perspectives on patient-physician trust among practicing physicians. Structural and institutional aspects of trust highlighted by Farrell are relevant for our study for at least two reasons. First, many aspects of doctor-patient relationships are institutionalized and governed by complex norms. These norms serve as a basis of trust but also contain a potential for distrust if one or both parties violate them. Patients know that doctors are supposed to behave in a certain way simply because they are doctors; if doctors fail to fulfill such expectations, patients may respond with distrust. Second, institutional contexts in which medicine is practiced constrain the behavior of both physicians and patients. Such constraints often complicate the development of trust. Under managed care, for instance, physicians have difficulties enacting some of the more traditional norms for physician-patient interaction. Time pressures imposed by managed care are a poignant example. Physicians who cannot spend enough time with their patients to make them feel that they care violate traditional norms about what physicians should do. It is also possible, however, that norms governing physician-patient relationships eventually adapt to institutional contexts in which these relationships are embedded. If actors adopt these more particularized norms (for example, those reflecting what a doctor should do and what a patient should expect under managed care), the potential for trust may increase again. Such positive outcomes, however, require abandoning some aspects of these more general norms about physician-patient relationships, which may be difficult to do, given that such norms are deeply engrained.

Managed Care Backlash

The impact of the penetration of managed care on the health-care system in the United States has been profound. Managed care is "a set of activities that health plans and others undertake to mitigate the propensity for the provision of more and more expensive services fostered by unmonitored heavily insured fee-for-service medicine" (Baker 2003, 438). The goal of managed care has been to contain rising health-care costs while providing adequate medical care for patients. David Grembowski and his colleagues (2000, 2002) argued that managed care can be best understood in terms of specific insurance policies designed to control cost. The typical managed care policies include capitation and gatekeeping. *Capitation* is a method of payment used to compensate health-care providers. Under capitation, providers receive a fixed fee per patient, usually on an annual basis, regardless of the services provided. Capitation thus transfers the financial risk for providing health-care services from insurance companies to healthcare providers. It is intended to dissuade physicians from providing marginally useful services, and to encourage them to provide preventive services that will decrease the need for future health care.

Gatekeeping is an arrangement in which health-care providers (usually primary care physicians) oversee all the services that each patient receives, both in the primary care setting and in other settings, such as specialized clinics or hospitals. To accomplish this goal, many managed care plans require patients to sign up with a contracted physician who will ration their health-care services. The physician who serves as a gatekeeper must authorize referrals before patients can receive insurance coverage for specialist visits or hospital care. Because specialty services and hospital services tend to be costly, gatekeepers receive incentives that dissuade them from providing the referral. According to David Lawrence, in traditional gatekeeping arrangements "a financial risk pool was created for each primary care physician, and every time a patient was referred to a specialist, the pool was depleted by an amount that was proportionate to the cost of the referral" (2001, 1342).

Managed care made health care more affordable, but also spurred a powerful backlash, both from dissatisfied consumers and from physicians. Consumers started to demand more choices in their health care. Physicians pushed for higher payment rates, less risk sharing, and lighter administrative loads. According to the Center for Studying Health System Change, the managed care backlash had come to full bloom in the late 1990s (2001b). By that time, about 30 percent of privately insured Americans were enrolled in plans using capitation, and about 60 percent were enrolled in plans using gatekeeping (Center for Studying Health System Change 2001a).

Consumer demands in the late 1990s and in the early 2000s led to an easing of some of the managed care restrictions and to what Bradley Strunk and James Reschovsky called "kinder and gentler" managed care (2002, 1). Health insurance plans decreased their use of capitation and direct financial incentives to influence doctors' clinical decision making, but many still required the authorization of referrals by primary care physicians and implemented some form of incentives to limit the overall cost of services per patient. They also increased the emphasis on treatment guidelines, preventive care, and patient satisfaction. At the same time, however, measures discouraging patients from seeking care, such as increases in out-of-pocket expenses, became more common (Draper and Claxton 2004).

Impact of Managed Care on Physicians and Patients

Managed care has had a profound impact on the experiences of American physicians with practicing medicine. In large surveys, physicians who work in managed care settings report increased time pressure, financial pressure, and more conflicts of interest when compared to other physicians (Stoddard et al. 2001; Sturm 2002; Linzer et al. 2000; Grumbach et al. 1998). Strong incentives to limit the cost of services to patients, typical for managed care, are especially detrimental to physician satisfaction. Compared to their colleagues, physicians whose practice settings include such incentives are more likely to report that their expectations regarding the practice of medicine have not been met (Hadley et al. 1999).

More textured evidence concerning the complexities of physician experiences under managed care comes from qualitative studies. Lucia Sommers and her colleagues, for instance, analyzed reports of managed care hassles among physicians in twenty-six practices (2001). On average, physicians working under managed care experience one hassle lasting ten minutes for every four or five patients, and report that more than 40 percent of these hassles interfered with the quality of care, the physician-patient relationship, or both. Most of these hassles are related to referrals to specialists, medication, and after-visit work. Denise Anthony showed how managed care can disrupt physicians' professional relationships with their colleagues, especially among primary care providers who face restricted specialist panels for their managed care patients, and cannot use their existing professional networks to refer their patients (2003). Ivy Bourgeault and her colleagues explored physicians' experiences negotiating care for their patients with insurance companies, and argued that, as managed care continues to limit access to care, these negotiations are becoming increasingly time consuming for physicians, increasing physicians' stress and dissatisfaction (2004). Elaine Draper cast the managed care physicians' experience in the broader context of the corporatization of medical care (2003). Based on interviews with doctors working for large medical care companies, she described their experiences of conflict between their patients' medical care needs and corporate oversight and between being both a corporate employee and an autonomous professional.

Another body of literature addresses patients' experiences with managed care. In general, evidence shows that patients who obtain their care in managed care settings are less satisfied (Reschovsky, Kemper, and Tu 2000; Shi 2000; Gillies et al. 2006), give poorer ratings of their interpersonal relationships with their physicians (Forrest et al. 2002), and report lower levels of trust in their physicians (Kao et al. 1998), especially if they have been denied coverage for their health services (Pearson 2003). A number of reviews, editorials, and opinion pieces argue that managed care threatens physician-patient relationships and makes patient-physician trust less likely to develop (Goold 1998; Blendon, Hyams, and Benson 1993; Emanuel and Dubler 1995; Mechanic and Schlesinger 1996; Mechanic 1998a, 1998b).

We do not know, however, precisely how physicians perceive and understand the effects of managed care on their relationships with patients. Even less is known about physicians' perceptions of patient-physician trust, an important aspect of physician-patient relationships, in the context of managed care (Barber 1983; Brody 1992; Mechanic and Schlesinger 1996). The purpose of this study is to provide such knowledge by exploring specifically how physicians understand the effects of managed care on their ability to develop and sustain trust with their patients.

Potential Obstacles to Trust in Managed Care Settings

A number of mainly theoretical studies have addressed the ways in which managed care arrangements may affect physician-patient relationships and trust. Although our focus is not on these effects per se but rather on the ways in which physicians experience and interpret them, we find it useful to briefly outline some previously suggested mechanisms through which managed care may be a factor in physician-patient relations. Such an outline helps situate the physicians' understandings in respect to the views of academic observers and analysts, who commonly argue that specific features of managed care potentially make creating and maintaining trust problematic.

One potential obstacle that some scholars suggest involves differences in power. The doctor-patient relationship is hierarchical, typically characterized by differences in power and dependence. These differences are underpinned by patients' vulnerability as well as by physicians' superior medical knowledge, control over information, and access to the resources patients need. Compared to relationships characterized by equal power, trust between those unequal in power and dependence may be more difficult to develop and sustain (Kramer 1996; Cook et al. 2004; Cook, Hardin, and Levi 2005). Despite the recent movement toward more consumer-oriented medicine and the fact that greater patient involvement in health care has empowered patients, the essential aspects of power differences between physicians and patients remain. In managed care settings, physician-patient relationships are further complicated by the presence of third parties represented by insurers.

Under managed care, the power difference between patients and physicians may be further increased because physicians serve as gatekeepers who regulate access to other health services (Grumbach et al. 1998; St. Peter et al. 1999). The gatekeeper role increases physicians' power over patients in that they control an important patient resource. Scholars have suggested that the larger the power differences in an interpersonal relationship, the more likely it is that actors find it problematic to negotiate and interpret the relevant roles and expectations (Kramer 1996; Cook et al. 2004; Cook, Hardin, and Levi 2005). Such difficulties may lead to lower trust, especially when the actors' interpretations do not match.

Physicians are also in relationships with various third parties (Grembowski et al. 2002). Compared to what we might find in more traditional settings, these relationships often put managed care physicians at a power disadvantage. These physicians are pressured to see large numbers of patients, perform expanded administrative duties, and have less administrative support (Sturm 2002; Schifrin et al. 2001; Grumbach et al. 1998; Groenewegen and Hutten 1999; Baker and Cantor 1993). This leaves less time for communication with their patients, shared decision making, and other behaviors associated with increased trust. In addition, shared responsibility for a single patient among several physicians and high physician and patient turnover under managed care threaten the continuity and longevity of physician-patient relationships (Mechanic 1998b). Because patient trust increases with the number of visits to a single physician and with the length of the physician-patient relationship (Kao et al. 1998; Safran et al. 1998; Thom et al. 1999a, 1999b), features of managed care that lead to more fragmented care and shorter physician-patient relationships may decrease patients' trust. In long-term physician-patient relationships, patients are more confident that physicians will use the knowledge of their health-related history built over time to deliver the best possible care (Cook et al. 2004). In short-term relationships, less trust may develop if patients fear that the physician has an incomplete picture of their health-related history. Furthermore, physicians without ongoing relationships with their patients may not recommend services and procedures requiring regular medical follow-up (Einbinder and Schulman 2000), which may also decrease patients' satisfaction and trust.

Another potential obstacle to trust involves patients' beliefs about managed care. David Mechanic and Marsha Rosenthal pointed out that physician-patient relationships are negatively affected if patients worry that their physicians' decisions are influenced by organizational constraints and incentives to limit services (1999). Negative portrayals of managed care in the media may contribute to patients' fears that they will not receive the services they need. Such fears may create a barrier to patients' trust in a physician.

In the extreme, the presence of obstacles to trust may lead to a lack of trust or even active distrust between patients and physicians. Active distrust is conceptually distinct from low trust or a lack of trust, which can be defined as little or no confidence that the physician will act in the patient's best interest (Cook et al. 2004). Distrust is not merely the absence of trust; it refers to the patient's expectation that the physician will not act in the patient's best interest. This expectation may have more damaging consequences for the physician-patient relationship than low or no trust. Low trust may engender problems in the physician-patient relationship, including lower continuity and longevity (Thom et al. 1999a, 1999b; Mainous et al. 2001; Safran et al. 1998; Safran et al. 2001), lower patient compliance with therapeutic regimens (Altice, Mostashari, and Friedland 2001), and worse health outcomes (Safran et al. 1998; Thom et al. 2002). It is plausible that distrust breeds similar problems to a greater degree. It is also possible, however, that the effects of active distrust differ substantially from those of low trust (see Cook et al. 2004; Cook, Hardin, and Levi 2005).

Contributions of this Study

A number of trust theorists have argued for the need for richer theory and data regarding how individuals actually think about trust (Gambetta and Hamill 2005; Hardin 1993, 2002; Kramer and Cook 2004). In his influential account of trust as "street-level epistemology," for example, Russell Hardin suggested that we focus on "the individual and the way the individual comes to know or believe relevant things, such as how trustworthy another person is" (2002, 116). Accordingly, our study adopted a qualitative approach to explore how physicians think about trust and distrust in their doctor-patient relationships within managed care settings.

We are specifically interested in how physicians think about trust in the context of managed care, how they perceive managed care as potentially complicating their efforts to gain the trust of their patients, and in the nature of their perceptions of concrete mechanisms that link managed care to patients' trust. The qualitative approach is well suited for our purpose because it overcomes several of the limitations of survey research. Many survey studies are unclear about whether physicians themselves see a link between the changes brought about by managed care and the relationships they have with their patients. Survey research concentrates on the association between variables rather than on the individuals' understanding and interpretation of these relationships. Qualitative data provide a more detailed understanding of physicians' interpretations of the factors that influence trust between them and their patients. To elicit physicians' perceptions, beliefs, and attitudes regarding the nature, antecedents, and consequences of physician-patient trust within managed care settings, we used semistructured, open-ended interviews after conducting focus groups.

By examining physicians' conceptions and understandings of physician-patient trust, we hope to contribute to a more general understanding of trust dynamics within unequal power relationships. These common relationships include interactions between doctors and patients, teachers and students, supervisors and employees, and parents and children. Yet little is known about the processes and mechanisms contributing to the development of trust in such relationships. The literature suggests that the process of trust development in relationships between those who are unequal in power might differ from that in relationships characterized by an equal distribution of power (Kramer 1996; Cook et al. 2004; Cook, Hardin, and Levi 2005). Our approach enables us to explore how physicians, who are the more powerful actors in physician-patient relationships, understand and interpret the factors that contribute to relational trust.

In addition, our analyses contribute to the understanding of the complex interactions between individuals and rapidly evolving sets of organizational practices. In the U.S. health-care system, managed care practices are subject to continued change. At the time of our study (2000), an increasing number of physicians were seeing a mix of capitated and fee-for-service patients, and medical groups with a significant proportion of capitated patients were struggling to develop guidelines and processes to reduce costs. Demands were being made for disclosure of physician financial incentives that could influence patient care (Levinson et al. 2005). Direct consumer marketing of pharmaceuticals and patient Internet access to medical information were beginning to raise concerns about moving toward more consumer-oriented medical care (Mintzes et al. 2003).

Individuals affected by organizational changes continuously interpret them, negotiate them, and adjust their behaviors and attitudes to their requirements. Constant changes in policies and practices that characterize many managed care environments necessitate new forms of adaptation among physicians. One study that examined the experiences of physician-employees within a nonprofit health maintenance organization (HMO) over a five-year period concluded that adapting to organizational pressures and developments is an emergent, evolutionary process, in which physicians actively respond to rapid and often unpredictable changes, but when organizational change is rapid and makes physicians more dependent on their organization, stress levels increase (Hoff 2003). These observations led us to pay particular attention to the ways in which physicians negotiate the meaning of changes in the organizational environment for themselves and for their patients, and calibrate their understandings against their everyday experiences in the context of concrete relationships with their patients.

Methods

In the spring and summer of 2000, we collected data in focus groups and in-depth interviews with physicians practicing in two clinics in an urban area of northern California. The first clinic (A) is associated with a major university teaching hospital. It includes a group of eleven family physicians and twenty-three internal medicine specialists. Clinic A is contracted with preferred physician organization (PPO) and HMO plans, and about 50 percent of their primary care is capitated. The second clinic (B) is a not-for-profit health-care organization associated with a major network of hospitals and physician organizations in northern California. It is a multiple-specialty group practice offering forty medical specialties, staffed by 290 primary and specialty care physicians. In 2000, it contracted with most leading PPO and HMO plans, with the balance heavily skewed toward HMO plans. That at the time of data collection both clinics accepted managed care as well as nonmanaged care patients gave us a unique opportunity to talk to physicians who had experience with both types of patients and could make relevant comparisons.

Focus Groups

The goal of conducting focus groups was the initial exploration of physicians' understandings of the general topic of patient-physician trust. The focus group method was suitable because we wanted to tap into group processes that encouraged participants to clarify and explore their views on trust and managed care. As Jenny Kitzinger pointed out, focus groups help people "explore the issues of importance to them, in their own vocabulary, generating their own questions and pursuing their own priorities. . . . The method is particularly useful for exploring people's knowledge and experiences and can be used to examine not only what people think but how they think and why they think that way" (1995, 299).

Participants, who were family physicians and general internists practicing in clinic A, were first approached by e-mail from one of the principal investigators, who invited them to participate in a focus group about patient-physician trust. (The focus groups were not conducted with physicians at clinic B, mainly because of the lack of research funds.) Twenty-one physicians were approached and ten responded. Two focus groups were conducted to accommodate physicians' schedules. The first focus group consisted of six physicians and three facilitators, who were the principal investigators. The second consisted of four physicians and two principal investigators, who served as facilitators. Three graduate students who served as research assistants were present, but did not take an active part in the discussions.

The groups met for about one hour in the conference room of a family practice center. Participants were asked to reflect on the nature of trust between patients and physicians and to identify factors that influence trust. Facilitators used a protocol of questions developed by the research team consisting of the authors to initiate and guide the discussion (see appendix). Participants responded spontaneously after the purpose of the study was explained. They received dinner and a small honorarium.

Interviews

Semistructured, in-depth interviews were chosen to provide more detailed information about experiences with managed care and patient trust among individual physicians. Fifty-eight family physicians and specialists practicing in clinics A and B, including the focus group participants, were approached by e-mail and invited to participate in an interview. Participants were offered a choice of lunch or a small honorarium.

Twenty-one physicians agreed to participate and were interviewed. Two had participated in a focus group earlier. Family practitioners constituted the largest group in the final sample (38 percent). Internal medicine was the second largest group (14 percent). Interviews were also conducted with a cardiologist, dermatologist, hematologist-oncologist, general surgeon, neurologist, ophthalmologist, pediatrician, physical medicine–rehabilitation specialist, psychiatrist, and radiologist. Nine females and twelve males were interviewed. Sixteen physicians self-identified as white, four as Asian, and one as Middle Eastern. On average, the participants had been practicing medicine since 1982, but the year of graduation ranged from 1961 to 1995.

Audiotaped interviews took place in physicians' offices, typically during their lunch break, and usually lasted about thirty minutes. Interviewers included the three principal investigators and three graduate research assistants in teams of two or three. A research assistant who provided technical assistance and took notes was typically present.

The interview protocol was developed by the research team and included three question sets that reflected the major foci of the study and at the same time corresponded to the topics that surfaced as important in the focus groups. The interviews were semistructured, and the interviewers used probes when needed.

Physicians were asked three sets of questions:

1. Have recent changes in the health-care system affected issues of trust in your relationships with your patients? How?
2. Describe a specific high-trust relationship with one of your patients. What experiences come to mind when you think about specific incidents, behaviors, and so on that have led to the development of a high-trust relationship between you and that patient?
3. Describe a specific low-trust relationship with one of your patients. What experiences come to mind when you think about specific incidents, behaviors, and so on that have led to the development of a low-trust relationship between you and that patient?

Two probes were used for the second and third questions. Tell us about the relationship and the experiences that formed it. What types of signs indicate problems of trust in a physician-patient relationship? What sorts of things do you see other physicians do that impair trust development?

Data from the focus groups and interviews were transcribed. The analysis of transcripts was based on hand coding and subsequent computer coding. Themes emerged from multiple readings of the transcripts by all the investigators and were developed iteratively. The focus group transcripts and answers to the key interview questions were coded in their entirety. References to managed care, health-care system changes, insurance, or the organization of care were then identified and coded in the remainder of the interview transcripts.

Results

Data presented here illustrate how physicians work to redefine the patient-physician relationship under managed care, how they understand stress and role ambiguity brought about by various dimensions of managed care, and how they experience ambivalence toward managed care and the general changes their practices bring to it. We pay particular attention to how physicians make judgments about patients' trust. We also describe cognitive and behavioral strategies physicians use to cope with conflicting pressures and interests. Our goal is to present the data as completely as possible and to keep the commentary to a minimum as we do so. We interpret our findings in the context of previous research in the discussion.

Overall Evaluation of Managed Care

In the beginning of the interview, we asked physicians whether recent changes in the health care system, especially the managed care revolution, influenced patient-physician trust. An overwhelming majority of physicians responded to this question in the affirmative. The following response of a family physician is typical:

> Not surprisingly, I think [the changes in health care] put a real squeeze on trust. I often feel like I'm spending a lot of saved-up goodwill with my patients. Making little withdrawals and spending it, and they're willing to go along with it, so the trust is there, the goodwill is there, but it's as if we're gradually depleting that and I'm not so sure how long that could go on without them, without that trust being so eroded that they would say, you're not the same physician I used to know.

A younger physician, who started to practice under managed care, related in the first focus group how his patients' trust is lower than what he expected based on his medical training: "The way HMOs bounce people around . . . the trust has gone down from what we learned would occur in medical school."

In contrast, no physician in our sample felt that managed care improved patient-physician trust. Two interviewees, however, shared that they perceived no effect of managed care on patients' trust. One of them, a neurologist, said this: "Well, I assume you're asking me to talk about my personal experience, rather than what I read about in newspapers. I think [managed care] really hasn't done a lot in my experience. I have [only] very rarely found [anyone] who thought they weren't getting what they should get or as much as they should get because of being in a managed care plan."

Some physicians saw advantages to some aspects of managed care, though not necessarily for the quality of the physician-patient relationship. Among the advantages they mentioned were cost containment, response to pressures to excessively test or prescribe beyond what is good care, and standardization that raises the average quality of care, particularly routine and preventive care. One interviewee, who evaluated HMO health care as very good overall, also talked in great detail about the skepticism and the negative images of HMOs some patients have. His comments suggested that some physicians see managed care as a desirable model, yet are concerned about the erosion of the physician-patient relationship under managed care.

An interesting question arises whether positive attitudes toward managed care relate to physician age. We expected that physicians who have only recently finished their training and therefore not had much experience outside managed care settings would have more positive attitudes than physicians who got started in medicine long before the managed care revolution. Contrary to our expectation, we find that some older physicians in our sample considered managed care a desirable model. For example, the participant who argued that managed care only formalized cost-effective ways of practicing medicine that sensible physicians had always used was among the oldest in our physician sample. A potential reason for more favorable attitudes toward managed care among some older physicians is that before managed care came to dominate health-care markets, physicians self-selected into managed care. Those who chose to join a managed care practice may have had relatively positive attitudes toward managed care to begin with. These physicians may thus be stronger advocates for managed care than their younger counterparts.

Redefining the Patient-Physician Relationship

As physicians elaborated on precisely how the recent changes in the health-care system in the United States affected patient-physician trust, they often alluded to the dissolution of a traditional social contract between physicians and patients. This theme was among the more general ones, encompassing aspects of other, more specific themes. We therefore present it first in our list of findings pertaining to physicians' understandings of the specific mechanisms by which managed care affects patient-physician trust.

Physicians described how much managed medicine is replacing more traditional, individualized relationships between physicians and their patients. A family physician participating in the first focus group characterized HMO medicine as "faster medicine, expeditious medicine, versus actually caring for somebody." Another explained how under managed care, a physician-patient relationship more and more resembles a business relationship in which the patient is a consumer and the practice of medicine is governed by efficacy: "That medicine is becoming increasingly business- and consumer-oriented has had an impact on the doctor-patient relationship. The same as needing to see a certain number of patients and having a defined, relatively shorter and shorter period of time to deal with them. And the patient becoming more of a consumer of a service and seeing it as a business enterprise as much as a healing enterprise" (pediatrician, interview).

When describing how physicians' and patients' roles are shifting as the traditional physician-patient relationship is dissolving, physicians often brought up the role third parties represented by insurance companies played in this process. In almost all cases, the involvement of the third party was perceived negatively, as a factor that endangered physician-patient trust. Several physicians shared their desire to preserve the more traditional relations between physicians and patients that excluded these third parties. The following opinion is illustrative: "I mean, I'm old-fashioned . . . in the sense that I think the physician-patient relationship should be . . . that's where everything stems from. And I think by introducing the player of the insurance company in this way, that it really damages the physician-patient relationship" (internal medicine, interview).

Conflicts of Interest

A conflict of interest theme emerged strongly from our data. Apparently, physicians saw conflict of interest as an important factor in their relationships with patients. Their responses suggested that conflicts of interest forced them to examine and perhaps even redefine these relationships. For this reason, we present the conflicts of interest findings immediately after those relating to the physician-patient relationship.

Physicians often talked about aspects of their practice under managed care that are incompatible with a more traditional understanding of their ethical obligations toward patients. They explained that their understanding of these responsibilities conflict with cost-containment policies imposed by the insurance companies. A pediatrician said in an interview, "I used to feel as though I was working for my patients . . . and now I feel more as though I'm working for insurance companies."

Other interviewees elaborated on the specific aspect of managed care policies that contributed to their perceived conflicts of interest. A family physician, for instance, mentioned pressures to see more patients and explained that his decision to spend more time with each patient would have negative financial consequences for him. Another physician, who talked about a conflict between his desire to devote more time to each patient and the organizational policies preventing him from doing so, noted that some obstacles to spending more time with each patient go beyond financial pressures. These obstacles can prove especially difficult to overcome:

> Those are issues that are extremely difficult to talk about . . . the number of patients that one sees is absolutely tied to how much you're paid. If you see fewer patients, your salary will directly be decreased. If a person says, "well, that's great, I'll take a lower salary then, because it's really important to me to spend more time with my patients." Then there's another comeback, which is, "yeah, but we budgeted our staffing of the clinics around the assumption that you're going to have a certain level of productivity [that] meets the community standard, and that's what your salary is tied to." It makes a physician feel like there are very few choices

in that kind of a setting, that you have to abide by . . . a set of values that don't belong to me.

The apparent difficulty the physician found in talking about the impact of managed care on his practice suggests frustration, value conflict, and perceived disempowerment. A similar feeling of frustration emerged from an oncologist's description of the conflicts of interest that arose for her when she learned that ordering tests and services for a patient directly takes money out of the hospital's pocket. She remarked that she had never been in a similar situation. Her response suggested that she felt unprepared and stressed as a result:

> I took my position here last year . . . and I was told that my patients would be capitated. That means the funds are controlled here by [the organization I work for]. And so directly and indirectly . . . test ordering takes out of that fund. Not ordering a test, we get to keep the money. So to that direct level, which I never have before. What decision I made in ordering a test might take money out of the pocket of my hospital or me. You know, I mean, or services for the patients, down the road.

Physicians elaborated at length on their concern that their decisions are closely watched by patients, who are aware of the conflict of interest brought about by insurance policies. Such awareness and the resulting distrust may be especially likely among highly educated, well-informed patients, as a psychiatrist explained in an interview with us:

> I would say that especially among the kind of patients that we have here, who are very savvy, obviously highly educated, sophisticated people who, I mean . . . they're quite conscious of some of the restrictions that managed care has imposed. They're quite conscious of the sort of the burden that's put on doctors and they're also aware that the managed care creates something of a disincentive to get medical services, so I think to some degree it has eroded patients' confidence that the advice that they're getting from their doctors is entirely unbiased by the financial incentives or disincentives that the managed care imposes.

At the same time, participants noted that patients want a trusting relationship with their physicians. The psychiatrist provided textured insights into how patients might struggle to maintain a positive relationship with their physicians, yet at the same time are concerned about how managed care incentives might affect the physician's decisions about their care. He explained it this way:

> On one hand, the patient feels sympathetic to the physician, while on the other hand, the patient feels she has to look out for her own interests since the physician may withhold care. Both the patients' sympathy and critical atti-

tude represent a notable departure from the traditional, paternalistic patient-physician relationship. So, I mean, I think they actually have two minds. On one, they're sort of sympathetic, "Oh, god . . . you're a doctor, you have to work under [these conditions]." So there's part of that. Then, I think they kind of wonder, especially if there's something that they want that you don't immediately agree with, you don't immediately think is necessary, I think it certainly sometimes enters their mind, "am I not getting this thing that I, the patient, think I ought to get because that costs a lot of money?"

Another noteworthy finding involved physicians' concern that the conflicts of interest under managed care affect their ability to treat patients in ways that foster patient-physician trust. The following interview response from an internist illustrates the worry that incentives provided by managed care might disrupt loyalty to patients:

The patients need to know the physicians are on their side, and that we can both battle the insurance companies together if need be. But with the insurance companies transferring, with managed care transferring the financial risk to the physicians, then the physicians might find themselves not necessarily on the patient's side. And again, that might be on a subconscious kind of level; but you have to worry how that alters the fundamental relationship between patient and physician.

Experiencing and Expressing Ambivalence Toward Managed Care

Physicians relating experiences of shifting roles and conflicts of interests in physician-patient relationships often suggested that they are ambivalent about managed care. The tension between recognizing that managed care can have both benefits and a deleterious effect on physician-patient relations emerged as one source of this ambivalence. Ethical issues surrounding physicians' medical decisions under managed care seemed to further complicate the situation. One participant, a family physician, talked during our interview about being rewarded for withholding referrals: "Primary care doctors got a bonus if they didn't refer patients to other departments. So you can tell they really felt ambivalent about it. And I guess conversely if you made a lot of referrals to other departments then you didn't get these bonuses. So there was a built-in reward for managing things yourself."

Contradictions in some responses express physician ambivalence poignantly. One family physician from the first focus group, for instance, contradicted himself as he struggled to express loyalty to both HMOs and patients:

Well, I think for some patients you can be seen as being on their side, not against the HMO, but if you, well, I guess if when you talk with them and

> if you let them know that . . . you're on their side . . . almost in some ways has fostered a bit of trust, because they realize you're not just going to go with whatever the HMO says. So if you are able to go to bat for them and get something turned around, it fosters a bit of trust.

Sometimes physicians' feelings about managed care were construed, explored, and clarified even as the physicians spoke. One family physician stressed that she adopted a strategy of being uninfluenced by insurance rules, yet admitted that sometimes she was influenced in managing a patient's medication. This contradiction illustrates her ambivalence:

> The health care system nowadays is an HMO system and there's a lot of frustration, specifically this trust. . . . And I specifically say to my patients, "Listen, I take care of my patients that are PPO and HMO, Medical and Medicare all the same. I don't even know what kind of insurance you have. And so I don't withhold medication, I don't try to manage their medication differently, *or sometimes I do,* but basically I say that up front and that, I think makes them feel a little bit better. (italics added)

Making Trust Judgments Under Managed Care

Role ambiguity, conflicting interests, and ambivalent attitudes toward managed care create a context in which patients and physicians negotiate their relationship over time. Our data suggest that physicians were greatly concerned with how much their patients trust them. Three categories of these responses emerged from our data: perceptions of lower a priori trust among patients, perspectives on patients' experiences with the organization of health care, and understanding of patients' experiences with the technical aspects of care.

The first category involves physicians' experience with patients whose trust is low from the beginning of the relationship. Participants were concerned that negative images of managed care disseminated by the media, whether accurate or not, might decrease a priori trust or even lead to active a priori distrust among patients. A family physician in the first focus group expressed it this way: "I think some of the trust has been eroded by negative press against HMOs. These images seem to powerfully shape patients' initial attitudes toward the physician and toward the health services they are about to receive, in spite of the fact that these images may be inaccurate." Another suggested in an interview that patients' suspicions might be rooted in experiences with their local HMO and the representations of managed care in the media, which may not accurately reflect other types of managed care practices:

> I have a lot of patients that are very skeptical, like is this an HMO thing. . . . I think the thing with [names a local HMO] that was a lot different was the

> productivity issues. . . . All their office visits were fifteen minutes no matter what they were. . . . Whether it was a physical or a broken leg or an earache, it was all fifteen minutes. Lot of perceptions of HMOs have come out of [this] experience for a lot of patients and a lot of doctors and I'm not sure it's applicable to what HMO medicine definitely is.

That patients tend to have little choice under managed care about which physician they see may also lead to low a priori trust, a family physician suggested in our interview: "The people who think they were assigned to me by an insurance company . . . from the beginning they tend to have bitter feelings, that this is not the place they'd choose. . . . Then, in those . . . circumstances, the trust is a little bit less than patients who decided to come [on their own]."

Discontinuity of care is still another factor, as one oncologist explained in an interview: "I started out with a lot of very distrustful patients. Patients had a whole list of questions: What were my grades in school, what . . . you know what I mean, I had never been asked those things like that before. They were so angry that they were looking for any reason to call health firms to say I don't want this doctor, this doctor's not acceptable, and her credentials are not as good. So managed care has had a huge impact."

A neurologist suggested that patients who were discontinued from their previous physicians and were assigned to a new one might doubt the professional competency of the new physician: "My friends who work in all HMO organizations . . . run into people who don't trust that the organization will do everything for them or have some very outdated ideas that you can't be a good doctor if you work for an HMO organization."

Patient experiences with the organization of care was the second major factor physicians pointed out as particularly informative about the level of trust they can expect from a patient. Certain experiences, according to our participants, may be especially vulnerable to managed care effects. One is the time with the physician. Physicians commented extensively on their own time pressures and the consequences for their physician-patient relationships. Physicians were concerned that sending a patient away without addressing every health concern might be frustrating for the patient and lead to lack of trust. A family physician from the first focus group explained it this way:

> One thing . . . the HMOs have done is change our time with the patient. "You're here for one problem, come back for your wart another day. You know, I don't want to hear that problem today," and I don't do that. I don't think most of us do that. But some of us, some people have done that and immediately it takes the trust. "I don't want to hear about your abdominal pain. You're here today because you want a refill, and I have ten minutes for you." Bad news.

Another expressed the same concern:

> I think that it takes a fair amount of time for the real issues to come out and that people have sort of superficial issues for which they come to the doctor, and then the real things that are going on, and the interest to drum up those underlying things. . . . I went into medicine hoping to work on all of that, and that is a lot of the psychosocial stuff, and psychosomatic. But if you get into it in fifteen minutes and you end up shutting the door on them, which regardless I don't think any of us would literally shut the door and say, "oh, sorry I don't have any time." But you have to speed them up or something. I mean, you can't survive [otherwise]. You can't spend an hour with each patient.

Another, a family physician, observed in an interview that under managed care, patients might be exposed to fewer physicians' behaviors that help develop a trusting relationship, because such behaviors are time consuming:

> I can tell you that I feel like time crunch pressure gets in the way of . . . developing good relationships and part of developing a good relationship, part of that is trust. And maybe trust is a result of developing the relationship. So just it's harder because I feel stressed. I feel like I'm always sort of under the gun . . . to see more patients and get through quickly so I don't really, I can't sort of sit in a room in a relaxed way open up the discussion to anything. I think that having the space to do that, like walk into a room, sitting down in a relaxed way and saying, so, you know, what's going on? That allows people to feel like they're really listened to, that they're being heard, that they can really open up. . . . So anyway, that I think has an impact on trust, I'm sure it has an impact on trust.

That patients cannot always reach their physicians when they would like to speak to them, whether in an office or on the telephone, is another experience that, according to our participants, may decrease patient trust under managed care. Physicians were worried that their patients may perceive the lack of the availability of the physician as a lack of caring. The following interview replies from a family doctor exemplify this theme:

> Another thing that affects trust as well is that you feel they can't get a hold of me afterwards, like say we have an exam, a problem on a day that I'm not here or during a day I'm working and they call my nurse and this is a direct line into my nurse's, it's not even a voice mail to the main office. If they can't get through, they begin to feel that the quality of their care is not good. They can't express their concerns, they can't get a medication refilled, they can't get a quick appointment, and so I felt that patients have definitely been not [only frustrated] but [it] actually affected my relationship with them, do they really trust me to take care of them if I can't, they can't get a hold of me?

The third set of factors related to patient trust included experience with the technical aspects of care, including diagnosis, treatment, and referrals. An internist spoke in an interview about how patients may react with distrust when they are given a prescription for generic drugs instead of brand name drugs, that they "are sometimes suspicious that generic medication will be different from brand-name medication." Patients may also be suspicious that economic motives play a role in physician's decisions about selecting a particular prescription or a test, a family physician remarked during an interview: "When a patient will ask if a test or a treatment is being suggested because their insurance company picks the test or the drug. That most commonly comes up as a patient asking that I make sure that a drug I write a prescription for is covered by their insurance. . . . Patients will question, rightly so often—is there an economic reason for what you're doing?"

One participant mentioned an interesting consequence of the lack of information about the power physicians have in ordering procedures and treatments, especially nonstandard ones. Insurance companies may, in some instances, misrepresent the physicians' power and thus contribute to the erosion of trust. A family physician explained this during the second focus group: "Well, the insurance companies do the same thing. They'll say, 'your doctor just needs to give you an okay to see the acupuncturist.' And so, what they do is, they erode the trust because you actually do not have that power. . . . I mean, the medical director of the insurance company has the power where you don't, so the insurance erodes trust."

Although most physicians were concerned that managed care constraints might erode patient trust, some suggested this might not always be the case. One internist suggested in an interview that patients separate their attitudes toward the physician from those about the system as a whole. He said that managed care does lead to distrust in the medical system, but does not necessarily have a negative effect on trust among his patients because he has good relationships with most of them.

The following responses reveal a novel theme concerning managed care and trust. Physicians observed that patients' expectations were not limited to a physician's medical and interpersonal competence, but also included the administrative side of care. These expectations became harder to meet under managed care. Patients may feel that a physician should be able to work with the system in such a way that the patient obtains the best possible care regardless of systemic and structural obstacles. One family physician explained this during our interview:

> I've had patients leave our clinic, in fact it's because of inability to access and, although I don't know if it was clearly stated, I certainly felt that there was, it was almost, they felt it was my responsibility to get the system work-

ing for them. And if I couldn't get the system to do the job, then they didn't have trust in me. I don't think it was really a trust of the medical diagnosis or my medical management as much as helping them get their care taken care [of], their needs cared for.

A similar theme of trust in a physician's administrative and management skills also surfaces in a description of an incident in which a patient's trust was disrupted because an administrative shortage resulted in a mistake. A family physician described in an interview how a patient placed the responsibility for the mistake on a physician, and expressed low trust in the physician's ability to run the office:

I have had a couple of sort of bad, not really bad things, things happen where lab results went out without my seeing them. It's a staff sort of issue and . . . really erodes trust. . . . I know that two patients received these lab results. One is a very sort of litigious [and] high-powered woman who was horrified, understandably. I would have been horrified. . . . It just had the results and no doctor's signature, no comment, no nothing. She [said something] like, 'What kind of office are you running?' So but the reality is . . . I think . . . purely a financial thing. I don't think we pay people enough to get good people and so in general. There are some good people, I don't mean to say everyone's bad, but to run a really good operation, you have to have people who are good, who are paid enough, who take . . . who have pride in their jobs and everything.

Coping with Conflicting Interests and Pressures

The data presented so far suggest that physicians working under managed care are faced with conflicting interests and pressures, ambivalent attitudes, and role conflicts. These experiences are often stressful. Here we explore how physicians cope with these experiences. Two common types of cognitive and behavioral coping strategies emerged from physicians' comments.

"Us Versus Them" One commonly expressed strategy involved actively opposing HMOs as agents preventing proper care, even while forming alliances with patients. Physicians who used this strategy believed it was an effective way to build trust. An ophthalmologist summarized this strategy during an interview: "I think it becomes an us-versus-them kind of thing, because we both want to treat the condition appropriately and [patients] understand that it's something that is being placed on the physician as well as the patient. So I don't think it—most of them don't really see it as us, they recognize it's an insurance issue, it's a business issue, and I don't find it affecting . . . our relationship."

Another participant, an internist, elaborated on fighting with the insurance companies and strategizing on behalf of patients. He seemed to take pride in taking extra steps to serve as an advocate for patients, making sure they eventually receive medications and procedures he had recommended:

> Oftentimes we have to fight with the insurance companies and make multiple phone calls and things like that, but I actually have never had a medication refused. . . . And the same with testing. . . . So, yeah, and I mean that's a lot of strategy, and that's part of the strategy of HMOs is that if they deny everything up front, then a lot of people won't have the staff time or they'll decide not to go through with the appeal. But if you persevere, the squeaky wheel definitely gets the grease.

"I Don't Know What Your Insurance Is" The second commonly mentioned strategy is to make medical decisions independently of insurance rules and financial concerns. This involves resisting any alliances with the insurance companies and rejecting open opposition. It implies a positive or neutral attitude toward patients. One participant, a cardiologist, said in our interview that he made his strategy explicit to his patients to preempt any suspicions about economic motives of his medical decision making: "One of the big trust builders I say is, 'I don't make any money when I order all those tests, I don't know what your insurance is,' and that helps establish the boundaries."

A similar approach, which a family physician in the second focus group offered, stresses resisting alliances: "I think they respect that, because you don't align yourself. I basically say I don't know what your insurance allows because that's not how I'm treating you. This is what I think is best for you, and then we can work it out with the insurance company."

Two additional strategies cannot be considered themes, but include interesting insights into how some physicians cope with job-related stress and how they understand their relationships with patients and with managed care organizations. We present these strategies for the sake of completeness and a full range of coping strategies.

"It Makes Sense, After All" One participant argued that HMO care is in fact consistent with the interests of both patients and physicians because it is efficient and allows the delivery of high quality medicine. He seemed to have internalized the managed care cost containment efforts as desirable and consistent with his ideal of providing the best care regardless of economic incentives. He pointed out that a part of his job, radiology, was to educate other physicians about how to determine whether some forms of care were appropriate. His conflict resolution strategy thus involved maintaining loyalty to the managed care philosophy of cost containment while remaining positive or neutral toward the patients:

> I've also been of the philosophy that the best possible care for somebody is the same, regardless of who's paying, and how it's being paid. . . . So now

> that health care, managed care say, well, you know, you're not supposed to do that, it's not cost effective. Well, we've always known it's not cost effective. So, we've never done things that have been . . . to generate revenue, or for the sake of doing it; and we've always been able to do things internally, without having to go through a lot of health plan organizations. . . . my job is to educate the physicians as to when one gets an MRI, when one gets a CT, when one doesn't do anything but bed rest for three weeks, and see if they respond.

"It's Against Me" The last coping strategy suggests rejecting alliances with patients and with managed care organizations. Instead, the physician who expressed this approach, a dermatologist, looked at the problems systemically, as reflecting the demands of the consumers:

> I think they often think that it's me and them against the system. I think that's the major feeling. And my problem is that I've realized that we charge it to the insurance, but if the insurance doesn't pay for it then it comes out of our pocket. So it's really not against the system, it's me. It's against me. And the other thing is that I feel that insurance is really difficult, and it has put up a lot of barriers and made things a lot more difficult, but it's the people that buy the insurance. So if we want the system to change, I think that people need to get . . . [to] just kind of realize that they're in control. I don't think the doctors are in control of the system.

This physician shifted the responsibility for the barriers to patients' satisfaction in managed care settings back to the purchasers of insurance plans. In her view, patients and employers who buy insurance have power over the insurance market and it is therefore incumbent on them to pressure insurance companies to change their products in such a way to make more satisfactory health care possible. The failure to do so (so far) leaves the physician no choice but to play by the rules of the insurance company, albeit grudgingly. This may mean providing less than ideal care for patients, but, at the same time, it protects physicians against financial loss.

Most physicians seemed motivated to resolve the conflicts of interest they experienced under managed care in ways that helped preserve good relationships with their patients, and chose a coping strategy accordingly. The first two strategies, which involved partnering with patients against managed care companies or resisting the influence of insurance companies on their practice, were often mentioned as physicians spoke of their efforts to build patients' trust. A similar trust-building motive did not surface as part of the remaining two strategies, even though these strategies did not necessarily seem incompatible with the goal of building patients' trust, should the physician choose to pursue it.

Discussion and Conclusions

Our findings offer textured insights into how physicians in two practice settings in northern California understand the impact of managed care on their patients' trust and on their practice generally. They reveal complex, often ambivalent attitudes toward managed care. Physicians acknowledged some benefits of managed care for the technical quality of care, but also felt that managed care endangered patient-physician relationships, an effect generally perceived as stressful. Another source of stress included conflicts of interest. Physicians felt pressured by the rules and incentives to decrease the cost of care by limiting the services they provide their patients.

Physicians also spoke of the role ambiguity they experienced in their encounters with patients. This seemed linked to the broader reorganization of the roles and responsibilities of physicians and patients, which was in part propelled by the rise of managed care, and in part reflected trends in health-care system development that preceded the managed care revolution, such as health-care consumerism and patient empowerment. Physicians talked about how the traditional patient-physician relationship is being replaced with a new ethic, in which the role of a patient resembles that of a consumer in the business world, and the primary responsibility of physicians is no longer to their patients, but to the organizations for which they work. As a result of these changes, physicians found themselves in an uncertain situation in which they could no longer rely on the traditional understanding of physicians' and patients' roles. Some felt unprepared and struggled to form a set of expectations and behaviors that fit the new realities of the health-care system. The inconsistency between their values and their job demands sometimes led to ambivalence toward managed care organizations.

Our data suggest that some physicians were ambivalent toward their patients as well. This seemed to originate in part from physician perceptions of negative patient attitudes. Physicians were concerned that working in managed care practices might reflect poorly on how some patients evaluated their competence, because some patients believed that only mediocre physicians work in managed care settings. Physicians also noted that some patients, especially the highly educated, were aware of the conflicts of interest inherent in managed care arrangements and worried that this awareness endangered patient trust. In fact, some physicians suggested that patients might see them as adversaries partnered with managed care companies against patients' interests. This finding can be compared to that of Debra Feldman, Dennis Novack, and Edward Gracely, who reported that the belief that patients perceive physicians as adversaries because of their gatekeeper roles is widespread among physicians (1998).

Possibly prompted by the perception of the fragility of patients' trust under managed care, physicians appeared to put considerable cognitive effort into evaluating how much or how little their patients trusted them. Noting the instances of high and low trust, physicians reflected on their understanding of mechanisms through which managed care might influence patient-physician trust. Some comments reflected patient-level factors and centered mainly on patient experiences with health care from other physicians. Physicians discussed how some new patients come to their offices with low initial levels of trust. Such low trust may be difficult to remedy. Others elaborated on organization-level factors, such as difficulties in access to physicians that some patients may interpret as lack of caring. Another set of responses reflected physician-level factors. These responses represented physicians' perceptions of patients' experiences with physician time management, clinical skills and decision making, and general provision of patient services. Physicians worried that patients might interpret the negative effects of managed care on their time management and on their clinical discretion as reflecting a lack of competency in working within the system. Patient trust may be especially endangered if patients suspect that physicians refrain from providing care for economic reasons. Significantly, physicians' responses revealed that they see the patient-level, organizational-level, and physician-level sources of patient-physician trust as interconnected.

Several of the themes identified in our data are consistent with those proposed in published theoretical and empirical studies. In particular, the organizational-level factors in patient-physician trust, including limited time for each patient, disruption in the continuity of the relationship, and poor access to physicians, have been widely discussed (see, among others, Scott et al. 1995; Mechanic and Schlesinger 1996; Mechanic and Rosenthal 1999). Our study contributes empirical evidence concerning the meanings physicians attach to these organization-level factors as well as their understanding of how these factors affect their relationships with their patients.

Physician-level factors have received less attention in the existing research on managed care. An exception is the theme of conflicts of interest, a topic of numerous prior discussions (Emanuel and Dubler 1995; Goold 1998; Kao et al. 1998; Mechanic and Schlesinger 1996; Pearson and Hyams 2002). We add an important layer to this work by identifying beliefs held by physicians about how their patients receiving their care under managed care systems perceive their physicians' conflicts of interest, and how physicians understand the impact of these patients' understanding on the physician-patient relationship. It is clear from our study that physicians engage in complex interpretive work when trying to see themselves through the eyes of their patients.

One theme that has received little or no research attention is the patient's trust in the physician's administrative and management skills.

Some physicians in our study felt that patients expected them to oversee their staff to prevent administrative or other mistakes, and to overcome the resource constraints imposed by managed care through superior time management, organizational skills, and effective negotiations with insurers. These responses illustrate the changing roles of physicians and patients. Patients now have similar expectations for the quality of service as paying customers in the nonmedical world. Our findings suggest that patient trust may depend increasingly not just on the physician's technical competency, communication, and agency, but also on the physician's ability to negotiate with third parties to provide appropriate services.

Lower a priori trust or distrust caused by patients' negative images of managed care is another theme that has received little attention in research. Physicians commented on how some patients prejudge them, often on the basis of negative media images about managed care. One example was the physician who suggested that some patients believe that good physicians do not work for HMOs. Physicians suggested that such low a priori trust might be overcome if they establish and sustain good long-term relationships with the patients. Yet low a priori trust may put considerable strain on the physician-patient relationship in its beginning stages. To increase this trust, physicians need considerable resources that are scarce under managed care, including time.

One compelling conclusion of this study is that physicians are neither passive victims of the conflicting pressures imposed on them under managed care, nor bystanders who disinterestedly or passively watch trust levels plummeting among their managed care patients. On the contrary, we identified several cognitive and behavioral strategies that physicians actively use to cope with the conflicting interests and pressures they experience. In earlier research, we discussed a number of physician behaviors that physicians as well as patients linked to higher patient trust, such as high quality, unhurried physician communication characterized by active listening, and nonverbal behaviors that express empathy and respect (Cook et al. 2004). In this study, we moved a step further to explore more complex cognitions that ground such understanding among physicians. We were interested in how physicians actively manage their cognitions and behaviors to achieve adaptation goals. Our research adds to the literature on how individuals adapt to changing organizational environments by showing that physicians often understand these adaptive strategies and use them in turn to build the patient-physician relationship and trust, which, in their view, are endangered by the same circumstances.

One such coping strategy involves attitudinal opposition to managed care organizations while forming an alliance with patients. Physicians using this strategy say they see themselves as teaming up with their patients to fight managed care as the common enemy, one that prevents the physician from doing what is best for the patient. One behavioral component of this strategy is contacting insurance companies to advocate for the patient, so that the patient may obtain a referral or receive coverage for costly or nonstandard procedures or medication. Interestingly, although physicians suggested they use this strategy to build patient trust, it is also possible that existing trust in the physician-patient relationship influence the likelihood that the physician will use this strategy. Physicians who do not have a good relationship with a patient may be less motivated to provide services above and beyond the call of duty. In the absence of mutual trust, physicians may not be inclined to exert extra effort to advocate and help the patient maneuver through the clinical and insurance bureaucracies. Ironically, managed care may make trusting patient-physician relationships less likely and may therefore decrease physician motivation to advocate for patients. The situation may be worsened by disruptions in the continuity of care that commonly occur under managed care. When the relationship is brief, the physician may simply not have enough information about the patient to justify the extra effort.

The second commonly used coping strategy that emerged from our data involves the conscious effort on the part of physicians to make medical decisions independently of insurance rules and financial concerns. Physicians using this strategy strive to practice medicine as if managed care were not a factor. They try to blind themselves to the insurance status of their patients, believing that this strategy will result in better medicine. They also believe it will make their patients see them as nonpartisan and thus enable patient trust.

The first of the two remaining coping strategies involved accepting managed care as a desirable model of care while maintaining a positive or neutral attitude toward the patients. The physician using this strategy interpreted the effects of the cost-containment efforts of managed care on the overall quality of care as positive and identified with the emphasis on efficiency as characterizing managed care. Managed care organizations strive to maximize the impact of medical interventions while minimizing costs. This goal may appeal to physicians who have internalized the values of efficiency as an important part of medical culture.

The last strategy involves rejecting loyalty to patients as well as to HMOs and taking a more systemic view of the problems with managed care. It is based on the recognition that managed care is driven largely by consumer demands for health care the consumers do not pay for out of pocket, and for low premiums. To change managed care requires that consumers, either directly or indirectly through their employers, demand and pay for a different system. The physician holding this view felt that health-care consumers must pressure insurance companies to change the ways in which the health-care system is organized so that the insurance companies loosen constraints on the physician's ability to deliver high-quality care, both technical and interpersonal. This more systemic outlook may have been prompted by the managed care backlash. Debra Draper and Gary Claxton concluded that though "the move toward greater consumer engagement is clear, the impact on costs and consumer willingness to assume these new responsibilities remain to be seen" (2004, 1). Other possible impacts of these changes, including effects on physician-patient relationships and trust, await further research.

It is important to address the limitations of this study. Our data address physicians' understandings of the linkages between managed care and patient-physician trust. They represent physicians' experiences and interpretations as physicians shared them with us. They are not based on what happens when physicians talk to patients. Many factors not examined in this study are likely to contribute to physicians' interpretations of physician-patient encounters and to the ways they present their experiences in focus group or interview situations. To understand these factors, future research, preferably comparing experiences of physicians practicing in a wider sample of health-care settings, supplemented by the observations of physician-patient encounters, is needed.

Another limitation concerns the size of our study. It is relatively small, consisting of two focus groups with ten physician participants and twenty-one interviews with physicians practicing in an academic setting and in a large not-for-profit health-care organization in California. Selection bias cannot be ruled out. When first approached with an invitation to participate in the study, physicians were informed that the study was about patient-physician trust and managed care. It is possible that some physicians responded to this invitation because they had particularly strong opinions on these topics. Some of them may have had more negative experiences with managed care than others and wanted to share them with the research team. In principle, physicians with unusually positive experiences with managed care could be just as motivated to voice their experiences as physicians with unusually negative experiences, but because our findings revealed mainly negative attitudes toward managed care, particularly regarding its impact of managed care of physician-patient relationship and trust, we must assume that if selection bias operated, it weighted our data more in the direction of negative attitudes.

Our data do not enable us to say how the experiences of physicians outside these practice settings would compare. Compared to other parts of the United States, California health-care markets have unique characteristics, most notably, the high degree of penetration of managed care and more common use of external incentives to improve the quality of health care (Gillies et al. 2003). These unique characteristics affect physicians' practices and may make physicians' experiences with their patients dissimilar from physicians practicing outside California. In addition, the site-based variation in the ways medicine is practiced is considerable, even when we compare practice sites within a single region or single health-care plan (Solomon et al. 2002). More research is needed to determine the degree to which our findings are unique to the settings in which our participants practiced and the degree to which they generalize to other settings in the United States or in other countries. Future research using cross-national comparisons of physicians' understandings of patient-physician trust could be informative, especially in countries that have widely adopted cost-containment policies similar to those used by managed care organizations in the United States.

Our study provided a snapshot of experiences of physicians practicing in managed care settings in a specific time and place. Since our study was conducted in 2000, managed care has continued to evolve. There now appears to be less concern about the impact of physician incentives for cost containment for managed care patients and more emphasis on adopting evidence-based guidelines for all patients that include cost-benefit considerations. Financial incentives based on quality of care, including patient satisfaction, have, to a large extent, replaced incentives based on cost containment. Direct-to-consumer advertising and access to medical information through the Internet has grown and is now an accepted part of the medical landscape. New models of patient care have become more common, including group visits (Jaber, Braksmajer, and Trilling 2006; Kirsh et al. 2007), primary medical care teams (Bodenheimer and Laing 2007), and new modes of communication using secure e-mail and other forms of online communication (Katz and Moyer 2004). How doctors and patients are responding to these changes is not known in any systematic way.

Many of these changes have the potential to increase patient trust. For example, national, evidence-based guidelines can provide a more rational basis for testing and treatment that has decreased concerns about the effects of financial incentives. Better channels of communication between doctor and patient can strengthen their relationship. Freeing the physician from more routine aspects of care through group visits or medical teams may allow more time to focus on the patient relationship. On the other hand, group visits and team models of medical care could dilute the doctor-patient relationship, resulting in a transfer of trust to the clinic or medical team that the doctor is part of. As managed care has become more established, we expect that expressions of direct opposition to it would become less frequent. Although some doctors have left managed care behind, practicing so-called boutique medicine for direct payment from patients (May 2006), the majority, finding themselves firmly embedded in some form of managed care, are finding ways to partner with their patients to meet patient expectations and provide quality care within existing resources constraints. The stresses of practicing primary care medicine in this environment has resulted in a sharp decline in physicians choosing primary care (Bodenheimer 2006), suggesting that the current system will be forced to evolve further to meet the needs of both patients and physicians.

Appendix: Focus Group Questions

Understanding of trust: What does trust mean to you in the context of your relationships with your patients? What do you think are the different dimensions involved in trust?

Consequences of patient's trust: Why is trust between you and your patients important? What are the concrete consequences of a trusting relationship?

Physician's trust in a patient: What makes you trust a patient? Do you ever have to wrestle with not trusting a particular patient because of something they are doing or not doing? What kind of patient do you find it hard to trust? What did the patient do or say that lessened trust?

Factors in patient's trust: What experiences come to mind when you think about specific incidents, behaviors, and the like that have led to the development of a good, mutually trusting relationship between you and a patient? What kinds of things do you do, or have you seen other physicians do, that help trust develop? What are some of the differences between the patients that you have felt high and low trust for? What factors do you think are important for patients in generating trust in their physicians? In other words, what do you think patients are concerned about in their relationship with you?

References

Altice, Frederick L., Farzad Mostashari, and Gerald H. Friedland. 2001. "Trust and the Acceptance of and Adherence to Antiretroviral Therapy." *Journal of Acquired Immune Deficiency Syndromes* 28(1): 47–58.

Anthony, Denise. 2003. "Changing the Nature of Physician Referral Relationships in the U.S.: The Impact of Managed Care." *Social Science and Medicine* 56(10): 2033–44.

Baker, Laurence C. 2003. "Managed Care Spillover Effects." *Annual Review of Public Health* 24: 435–456.

Baker, Laurence C., and Joel C. Cantor. 1993. "Physician Satisfaction under Managed Care." *Health Affairs (Millwood)* 12(suppl.): 258–70.

Barber, Bernard. 1983. *The Logic and Limits of Trust.* New Brunswick, N.J.: Rutgers University Press.

Blendon, Robert J., Tracey S. Hyams, and John M. Benson. 1993. "Bridging the Gap between Expert and Public Views on Health Care Reform." *Journal of the American Medical Association* 269(19): 2573–578.

Bodenheimer, Thomas. 2006. "Primary Care: Will It Survive?" *New England Journal of Medicine* 355(9): 861–64.

Bodenheimer, Thomas, and Brian Y. Laing. 2007. "The Teamlet Model of Primary Care." *Annals of Family Medicine* 5(5): 457–61.

Bourgeault, Ivy L., S. Lindsay, Eric Mykahalovskiy, Pat Armstrong, Hugh Armstrong, Jacqueline Choiniere, Joel Lexchin, Suzanne Peters, and Jerry P. White. 2004. "At First You Will Not Succeed: Negotiating Care in the Context of Health Reform." In *Research in the Sociology of Health Care,* vol. 22, *Chronic Care, Health Care Systems and Services Integration,* edited by Jennie J. Kronefeld. Amsterdam: Elsevier.

Brody, Howard. 1992. *The Healer's Power.* New Haven, Conn.: Yale University Press.

Center for Studying Health System Change. 2001a. Community Tracking Study Household Survey, 1998–1999 and Followback Survey 1998–2000. [Computer file]. ICPSR version. Washington, DC: Center for Studying Health System Change. Distributed by Inter-university Consortium for Political and Social Research.

———. 2001b. "Managed Care and Costs: Perspectives from Plans and Employers." *Emerging Health Care Market Trends: Insights from Communities* Conference Proceedings. Washington, D.C. (December 10, 2001). Available at: http://www.hschange.com/CONTENT/394 (accessed October 2005).

Cook, Karen S., Roderick Kramer, David Thom, Irena Stepanikova, Stefanie B. Mollborn, and Robin M. Cooper. 2004. "Trust and Distrust in Patient-Physician Relationships: Perceived Determinants of High and Low Trust Relationships in Managed Care Settings." In *Trust and Distrust Across Organizational Contexts,* edited by Roderick Kramer and Karen S. Cook. New York: Russell Sage Foundation.

Cook, Karen S., Russell Hardin, and Margaret Levi. 2005. *Cooperation Without Trust.* New York: Russell Sage Foundation.

Draper, Debra A., and Gary Claxton. 2004. "Managed Care Redux." *Issue Brief, Center for Study of Health Systems Change* 70(1): 1–4.

Draper, Elaine. 2003. *The Company Doctor: Risk, Responsibility, and Corporate Professionalism.* New York: Russell Sage Foundation.

Einbinder, Lynne C., and Kevin A. Schulman. 2000. "The Effect of Race on the Referral Process for Invasive Cardiac Procedures." *Medical Care Research and Review* 57(suppl. 1): 162–80.

Emanuel, Ezekiel J., and Nancy N. Dubler. 1995. "Preserving the Physician-Patient Relationship in the Era of Managed Care." *Journal of the American Medical Association* 273(4): 323–29.

Feldman, Debra S., Dennis H. Novack, and Edward Gracely. 1998. "Effects of Managed Care on Physician-Patient Relationships, Quality of Care and the Ethical Practice of Medicine: A Physician Survey." *Archives of General Internal Medicine* 158(1998): 1626–632.

Forrest, Christopher B., Leiyu Shi, Sarah von Schrader, and Judy Ng. 2002. "Managed Care, Primary Care, and the Patient-Practitioner Relationship." *Journal of General Internal Medicine* 17(4): 270–77.

Gambetta, Diego, and Heather Hamill. 2005. *Streetwise: How Taxi Drivers Establish Their Customer's Trustworthiness.* New York: Russell Sage Foundation.

Gillies, Robin R., Kate E. Chenok, Stephen M. Shortell, Gregrory Pawlson, and Julian J. Wimbush. 2006. "The Impact of Health Plan Delivery System Organization on Clinical Quality and Patient Satisfaction." *Health Services Research* 41(4p1): 1181–199.

Gillies, Robin R., Stephen M. Shortell, Lawrence Casalino, James C. Robinson, and Thomas G. Rundall. 2003. "How Different is California? A Comparison of U.S. Physician Organizations." *Health Affairs* 10(W3)(suppl.): 492–502.

Goold, Susan D. 1998. "Money and Trust: Relationships between Patients, Physicians, and Health Plans." *Journal of Health Politics, Policy and Law* 23(4): 687–95.

Grembowski, David E., Karen S. Cook, Donald L. Patrick, and Amy E. Roussel. 2002. "Managed Care and the U.S. Health Care System: A Social Exchange Perspective." *Social Science and Medicine* 54(8): 1167–180.

Grembowski, David E., Paula Diehr, Louise Novak, Amy E. Roussel, Diane Martin, Donald L. Patrick, Barbara Williams, and C. M. Ulrich. 2000. "Measuring the Managedness and Covered Benefits of Health Plans." *Health Services Research* 35(3): 707–34.

Groenewegen, Peter P., and Jack B. F. Hutten. 1999. "The Influence of Supply Related Characteristics on General Practitioners' Workload." *Social Science and Medicine* 40(3): 349–58.

Grumbach, Kevin, Dennis Osmond, Karen Vranizan, Deborah Jaffe, and Andrew B. Bindman. 1998. "Primary Care Physicians' Experience of Financial Incentives in Managed-Care Systems." *New England Journal of Medicine* 339(21): 1516–521.

Hadley, Jack, Jean M. Mitchell, Daniel P. Sulmasy, and M. Gregg Bloche. 1999. "Perceived Financial Incentives, HMO Market Penetration, and Physicians' Practice Styles and Satisfaction." *Health Services Research* 34(1p2): 307–21.

Hardin, Russell. 1993. "The Street-Level Epistemology of Trust." *Politics and Society* 21(4): 505–29.

———. 2002. *Trust and Trustworthiness.* New York: Russell Sage Foundation.

Hoff, T. J. 2003. "How Physician-Employees Experience their Work Lives in a Changing HMO." *Journal of Health and Social Behavior* 44(1): 75–96.

Jaber, Raja, Amy Braksmajer, and Jeffrey Trilling. 2006. "Group Visits for Chronic Illness: Models, Benefits and Challenges." *Family Practice Management* 13(1): 37–40.

Kao, Audiey, Diane C. Green, Alan M. Zaslavsky, Jeffrey P. Koplan, and Paul D. Cleary. 1998. "The Relationship between Method of Physician Payment and Patient Trust." *Journal of the American Medical Association* 280(19): 1708–714.

Katz, Steven J., and Cheryl A. Moyer. 2004. "The Emerging Role of Online Communication between Patients and Their Providers." *Journal of General Internal Medicine* 19(9): 978–83.

Kirsh, Susan, Sharon Watts, Kristina Pascuzzi, Mary Ellen O'Day, David Davidson, Gerald Strauss, Elizabeth O. Kern, and David C. Aron. 2007. "Shared Medical Appointments Based on the Chronic Care Model: A Quality Improvement Project to Address the Challenges of Patients with Diabetes with High Cardiovascular Risk." *Quality and Safety in Health Care* 16(5): 349–53.

Kitzinger, Jenny. 1995. "Qualitative Research: Introducing Focus Groups." *British Medical Journal* 311(July): 299–302.

Kramer, Roderick M. 1996. "Divergent Realities and Convergent Disappointments in the Hierarchic Relation: Trust and the Intuitive Auditor at Work." In *Trust in Organizations: Frontiers of Theory and Research,* edited by Roderick M. Kramer and Tom R. Tyler. Thousand Oaks, Calif.: Sage Publications.

Kramer, Roderick M., and Karen S. Cook. 2004. "Trust and Distrust in Organizations." In *Trust and Distrust in Organizations: Dilemmas and*

Approaches, edited by Roderick M. Kramer and Karen S. Cook. New York: Russell Sage Foundation.

Lawrence, David. 2001."Gatekeeping Reconsidered." *New England Journal of Medicine* 345(18): 1342–343.

Levinson, Wendy, Audiey Kao, Alma M. Kuby, and Ronald A. Thisted. 2005. "The Effect of Physician Disclosure of Financial Incentives on Trust." *Archives of Internal Medicine* 165(6): 625–30.

Linzer, Mark, Thomas Konrad, Jeffrey Douglas, Julia E. McMurray, Donald E. Pathman, Eric S. Williams, Mark D. Schwartz, Martha Gerrity, William Scheckler, and Elnora Bigby. 2000. "Managed Care, Time Pressure, and Physician Job Satisfaction: Results from the Physician Worklife Study." *Journal of General and Internal Medicine* 15(7): 441–50.

Mainous, Arch G. III, Richard Baker, Margaret M. Love, Denis P. Gray, and James M. Gill. 2001. "Continuity of Care and Trust in One's Physician: Evidence from Primary Care in the United States and the United Kingdom." *Family Medicine* 22(1): 22–27.

May, Jonathan. 2006. "The Cost of Care: Boutique Practices Offer an Alternative to Fast-Paced Healthcare Delivery." *Journal of Medical Practice Management* 22(3): 171–74.

Mechanic, David. 1998a. "The Functions and Limitations of Trust in the Provision of Medical Care." *Journal of Health Politics, Policy and Law* 23(4): 661–86.

———. 1998b. "Managed Care, Rationing, and Trust in Medical Care." *Journal of Urban Health* 75(1): 118–22.

Mechanic, David, and Marsha Rosenthal. 1999. "Responses of HMO Medical Directors to Trust Building in Managed Care." *Milbank Quarterly* 77(3): 283–303.

Mechanic, David, and Mark Schlesinger. 1996. "The Impact of Managed Care on Patient's Trust in Medical Settings." *Journal of the American Medical Association* 275(21): 1693–697.

Mintzes, Barbara, Morris L. Barer, Richard L. Kravitz, Ken Bassett, Joel Lexchin, Arminée Kazanjian, Robert G. Evans, Richard Pan, and Stephen A. Marion. 2003. "How Does Direct-to-Consumer Advertising (DTCA) Affect Prescribing? A Survey in Primary Care Environments with and without Legal DTCA." *Canadian Medical Association Journal* 169(5): 405–12.

Pearson, Steven D. 2003. "Patient Reports of Coverage Denial: Association with Ratings of Health Plan Quality and Trust in Physician." *American Journal of Managed Care* 9(3): 238–44.

Pearson, Steven D., and Tracey Hyams. 2002. "Talking about Money: How Primary Care Physicians Respond to a Patient's Question about Financial Incentives." *Journal of General Internal Medicine* 17(1): 75–79.

Reschovsky, James D., Peter Kemper, and Ha Tu. 2000. "Does Type of Health Insurance Affect Health Care Use and Assessments of Care among the Privately Insured?" *Health Services Research* 35(1): 219–37.

Safran, Dana G., Jana E. Montgomery, Hong Chang, Julia Murphy, and William H. Rogers. 2001. "Switching Doctors: Predictors of Voluntary Disenrollment from a Primary Physician's Practice." *Journal of Family Practice* 50(2): 130–36.

Safran, Dana G., Mark Kosinski, Alvin Tarlov, William H. Rogers, Deborah A. Taira, Naomi Lieberman, and John E. Ware. 1998. "The Primary Care

Assessment Survey: Tests of Data Quality and Measurement Performance." *Medical Care* 36(5): 728–39.

Schifrin, Emily, Amy E. Jacobs, Martha Romans, David Cruess, and Rebecca Kelly. 2001. "Impact on Managed Care on Obstetrician Gynecologists' Practice: The Providers' Perspective." *Women's Health Issues* 11(6): 461–70.

Scott, Robert A., Linda H. Aiken, David Mechanic, and Julius Moravcsik. 1995. "Organizational Aspects of Caring." *Milbank Quarterly* 73(1): 77–95.

Shi, Leiyu. 2000. "Type of Health Insurance and the Quality of Primary Care Experience." *American Journal of Public Health* 90(12): 1848–855.

Solomon, Leon S., Alan M. Zaslavsky, Bruce E. Landon, and Paul D. Cleary. 2002. "Variation in Patient-Reported Quality among Health Care Organizations." *Health Care Finance Review* 23(4): 85–100.

Sommers Lucia S., Trevor W. Hacker, David M. Schneider, Perry A. Pugno, and James B. Garrett. 2001. "A Descriptive Study of Managed-Care Hassles in 26 Practices." *Western Journal of Medicine* 74(3): 175–79.

St. Peter, Robert F., Marie C. Reed, Peter Kemper, and David Blumenthal. 1999. "Changes in the Scope of Care Provided by Primary Care Physicians." *New England Journal of Medicine* 341(26): 1980–985.

Stoddard, Jeffrey J., Lee Hagraves, Marie Reed, and Alison Vratil. 2001. "Managed Care, Professional Autonomy, and Income: Effects on Physician Career Satisfaction." *Journal of General Internal Medicine* 16(10): 712–23.

Strunk, Bradley C., and James D. Reschovsky. 2002. "Kinder and Gentler: Physicians and Managed Care, 1997–2001." Tracking Report 5. Washington, D.C.: Center for Studying Health System Change. Available at: http://www.hschange.com/CONTENT/486/ (accessed October 2005).

Sturm, Roland. 2002. "Effect of Managed Care and Financing on Practice Constraints and Career Satisfaction in Primary Care." *Journal of American Board of Family Physicians* 15(5): 367–77.

Thom, David H., Kurt M. Ribisl, Anita L. Stewart, and Douglas A. Luke. 1999a. "Further Validation of a Measure of Patients' Trust in their Physician: The Trust in Physician Scale." *Medical Care* 37(5): 510–17.

———. 1999b. "Validation of a Measure of Patients' Trust in their Physician." *Medical Care* 37(5): 510–17.

Thom, David H., Richard L. Kravitz, Robert A. Bell, Edward Krupat, and Rahman Azari. 2002. "Patient Trust in the Physician: Relation to Patient Requests." *Family Practice* 19(5): 476–83.

Chapter 7

Neighborhood Networks and Processes of Trust

ROBERT J. SAMPSON AND CORINA GRAIF

TRUST IS WIDELY thought to promote a variety of positive societal outcomes (Alesina and La Ferrara 2002; Fukuyama 1995; Knack and Keefer 1997), helping explain why reports of its decline set off alarms (for example, Paxton 1999; Putnam 2000). Much of the attention has centered on generalized trust in others as a proxy for harmonious societal functioning. In one of the best-known trends, a number of surveys reveal a long downward trajectory of Americans' trust in fellow citizens. Leading scholars have pointed to the decline in generalized trust as evidence that social capital is eroding and causally linked to a host of increasing social ills (for example, Putnam 2000).

A more contextualized approach is seen in efforts to specify what might be termed *grounded* or *working* trust. From this viewpoint, trust is specific to contexts of social action and must be conceptualized and measured accordingly. The Russell Sage Foundation's Program on Trust has spearheaded this move in a number of ways. One has been to conceptualize the emergence of trust within specific contexts such as immigrant communities, police departments, social service agencies, unions, and politics (Braithwaite and Levi 1998; Cook 2001; Tyler and Huo 2002). A second and related move has been to conceptualize trust in relational terms, leading to a view of trust as embedded within particular parties and substantive action—what Russell Hardin called "encapsulated interest" (2002, 7). A third move has been to conceptualize trust at a macro or social-organizational level, including the idea that societies and organizations, and, by implication, local communities, vary in cultures and structures of trust (Kramer 1999; Kramer and Cook 2004).

This chapter integrates all three moves of the broad intellectual framework of the Russell Sage program by studying the community and social-network predictors of trust in the city of Chicago. Capitalizing on a long-term project of original data collection, we examine variations in trust among residents, leaders, and institutions across time and community contexts. Between 1995 and 2002, a two-wave panel study was conducted of more than 1,000 positional leaders sampled from six institutional domains—law, politics, business, community organizations, education, and religion—and across thirty Chicago communities. Among other innovations, this study developed an instrument assessing working trust in relationships defined by networks of action among community leaders, along with an assessment of the extent to which local residents trust their leaders and institutions. In addition, in two independent studies of residents of the same communities, the trust and shared expectations of local residents in each other were also assessed.

We combine these new sources of data to contextualize the conditions under which trust emerges. As a result, we set aside legitimate and fundamental questions about how individuals appropriate social capital to achieve intended outcomes (for example, Coleman 1988; Portes 1998). We also set aside debates over aggregate outcomes thought to flow from trust-related dimensions of social capital. Instead we focus on a simple idea, that trust is endogenous and consists of multiple dimensions that vary by neighborhood and institutional-level contexts (Sampson 2002; Sampson, Morenoff, and Earls 1999). We assess this notion at the neighborhood level by using a variety of measures that tap different aspects of trust and shared expectations more generally. We specifically examine the measurement properties of between-neighborhood variations in trust, with a focus on how different measures hang together (or not) across communities. Is there one big dimension or context-specific components? Perhaps most important, we examine the structural predictors of trust with a focus on long-term processes that appear to generate durable *mistrust traps.*

Conceptual Framework

Although there are conflicting definitions, most agree that trust plays a central role in the constitution of social capital. Robert Putnam, for example, defined social capital as "features of social organization, such as networks, norms, and trust, that facilitate coordination and cooperation for mutual benefit" (1993, 36; see also Dasgupta 1988; Luhmann 1979). Social capital in this view stems not from the attributes of individuals but rather the structure of social organization (Coleman 1988). In the words of Karen Cook, Russell Hardin, and Margaret Levi, "evaluations of trustworthiness thus depend more on the nature of the relationship involved, the network in which that relationship is embedded, and other features of the social context or environment than on our initial judgments of the actors involved, which in some instances may be quite misleading" (2005, 32). Yet the empirical base of most studies so far remains quite limited when we consider variations in dimensions of trust or social capital at the neighborhood level (Sampson, Morenoff, and Earls 1999; Sampson, Morenoff, and Gannon-Rowley 2002).

Neighborhood-level research in particular is dominated by studies of poverty and other sociodemographic characteristics drawn from census data and government statistics that provide very little information on the collective properties of administrative units. Although important as an initial step, administrative studies fail to tap the social interactional or trust mechanisms of theoretical interest directly. These mechanisms may help explain the salience of community demographic attributes. As part of the social process turn in recent research, the community literature has therefore focused more directly on factors such as the density of local ties, exchange, voluntary associations, and trust (Sampson, Morenoff, and Gannon-Rowley 2002). In many urban communities, strong ties among neighbors are no longer the norm because friends and social support networks have become decreasingly organized in a parochial, local fashion (Fischer 1982; Wellman 1979). To address these changes in the nature of contemporary relationships, Robert Sampson, Jeffrey Morenoff, and Felton Earls highlighted a focus on neighborhood-linked mechanisms that facilitate social control without requiring strong ties or associations, emphasizing the combination of trust and shared willingness of residents to intervene in social control (Sampson, Morenoff, and Earls 1999; Sampson, Raudenbush, and Earls 1997).

This linkage of trust and cohesion with shared expectations for control was defined as neighborhood *collective efficacy.* Just as self-efficacy is situated rather than global (one has self-efficacy relative to a particular task), a neighborhood's efficacy exists relative to specific tasks, such as maintaining public order. Distinguishing between the resource potential represented by personal ties, on the one hand, and the shared expectations for social control and the working trust represented by collective efficacy, on the other, helps clarify disputes about social capital. Namely, social networks may foster the conditions under which collective efficacy flourishes but network ties are not enough to exercise control (Bursik 1999).

Viewed through this theoretical lens, collective efficacy is a task-specific construct that highlights shared expectations rooted in trust and mutual engagement by residents with respect to issues of social control (Sampson, Morenoff, and Earls 1999). Moving from a focus on private ties to social efficacy signifies an emphasis on shared beliefs and trust in neighbors' conjoint capability for action to achieve an intended effect, and hence an active sense of engagement on the part of residents. As Albert Bandura argued, the meaning of efficacy is captured in expectations about the exercise of control, elevating an agential aspect of social life over a perspective centered on the accumulation of resources (1997). This conception is consistent with Alejandro Portes and Julia Sensenbrenner's redefinition of social capital as "expectations for action within a collectivity" (1993, 1323).

Sources of Neighborhood Social Trust and Efficacy

A number of studies have hypothesized that collective efficacy and social trust are predicted by residential instability, concentrated disadvantage, and racial or ethnic heterogeneity. Clifford Shaw and Henry McKay, for example, argued that rapid population turnover, heterogeneity, and poverty undermine a community's capacity for formal and informal social control (1942/1969). More recently, Sampson, Stephen Raudenbush, and Felton Earls argued that concentrated disadvantage and racial exclusion foster a climate of economic dependency, alienation, fear, and distrust that obstruct collective efficacy even in the potential presence of strong personal ties (1997; see also Ross, Mirowsky, and Pribesh 2001).

The connection between neighborhood disadvantage and individual mistrust may be accounted for by social-psychological processes set off in routine interactions between individuals and alienating physical environments permeating their lives. In a study of Illinois residents, Catherine Ross, John Mirowsky, and Shana Pribesh showed that disadvantage predicts mistrust through its impact on individual perceptions of neighborhood disorder, such as abandoned buildings, graffiti, noise, vandalism, drug activities, and crime (2001). Such perceptions are thought to impair the sense of personal control and to beget feelings of alienation (Massey 1996). Although such findings suggest an effect of neighborhood poverty on mistrust within a relatively short time frame, the long-term effect of neighborhood poverty on contemporary mistrust remains unknown.

Migration and residential instability as reflected in the flux of population in and out of a neighborhood have been hypothesized to induce disruptions of institutional continuity, existing social networks, and social cohesion (Coleman 1990). In contrast, high rates of stability and home ownership, reinforced by correlated personal and financial investments, are thought to promote more vigorous efforts to maintain social control (Bursik and Grasmick 1993; Kornhauser 1978).

Finally, diversity of the population has been hypothesized to undermine the emergence and maintenance of social capital due to the difficulties of communication in a context of linguistic and cultural heterogeneity (Kornhauser 1978). Large gaps are reported between ingroup ethnic trust and interethnic trust levels (see chapter 2, this volume). Studies in both the United States and other countries find that ethnic and racial diversity result in lower levels of trust in others, but the results are not consistent for all dimensions of trust or across all contexts. The neighborhood-level literature on these hypotheses has been reviewed extensively elsewhere (Sampson, Morenoff, and Gannon-Rowley 2002).

Social Dynamics

Surprisingly, studies of community social capital are also largely static, examining cross-sectional associations rather than pathways of social trust or efficacy through time. However, as Charles Tilly (1998) and others have argued, categorical distinctions based on nativity, ethnic origin, or race can lead to enduring systems of social closure, exclusion, and control. Such systems, if left unchallenged, tend to imprint a pattern of durable inequality within the larger social structures. How changes in such social structures predict changes in trust and efficacy is largely unknown. We believe that the long-term durability of structural inequalities is fundamentally interwoven with differences in the learning of trust and mistrust across time (Hardin 2002). A major goal in this chapter is therefore to examine how cross-sectional hypotheses translate into longer-term patterns.

Moreover, research to date has largely neglected the mid-range processes whereby structural configurations of local networks and community and power elites influence the creation and maintenance of trust (see also chapter 5, this volume). More than two decades ago, Mark Granovetter advanced the highly influential idea that various forms of social and economic transactions are embedded in larger structures, which by themselves can generate and amplify trust (1985; Uzzi 1996). Although numerous case studies of community elite networks were conducted in the 1950s, 1960s, and 1970s (Knoke 1990), there are very few systematic comparative studies of such leadership structures and their collective capacity to broker internal and external resources and the collective trust critical for community well-being. Hypotheses turning on the density or cohesiveness of networks at the community level are thus largely unexplored.

Analytic Strategy and Hypotheses

We begin to investigate these and related issues by treating communities as social-ecological units, where the extent and focus of social organization is treated as an empirical question (see also Tilly 1973, 212). This theoretical perspective focuses on the ways in which neighborhoods are socially constituted and organized across a number of dimensions (Matsueda 2006; Sampson 2002). We conceptualize collective efficacy, like social capital, as endogenous to structural and cultural contexts (Bourdieu 1986; Sampson, Morenoff, and Earls 1999). We hypothesize that extreme resource deprivation and racial exclusion act as a centrifugal force that hinders trust and the broader concept of collective efficacy. Even when personal ties are strong in areas of concentrated disadvantage, daily experiences with uncertainty, danger, and economic dependency are likely to reduce expectations for taking effective collective action (Woolcock 1998, 207). William Julius Wilson's "socially isolated" areas, for example, are thought to be characterized by dense personal ties that are nonetheless disconnected from the capacity to capture resources from the larger society (1987). Lack of collective capacity in turn renders a neighborhood vulnerable to further decay and a relative lack of desirability in the pecking order of places to live (Sampson and Raudenbush 2004).

In other words, we suggest that if concentrated poverty serves as a sort of trap (Sampson and Morenoff 2006), it does so partly through a vicious circle whereby mistrust is reinforced, setting in motion a cascading set of disadvantages, such as out-migration and violence, that contribute to deepening and reinforcing poverty. We are not able to model these feedback processes, but we can take a first step by looking at the predictive role of initial conditions and change in poverty on later collective efficacy. In doing so, we adjust for the hypothesized effects put forth in past studies for racial diversity and residential stability. If the concentrated poverty relationships prove durable despite population and housing change over time, there is reason to explore more deeply the connection of declines in collective efficacy and trust with reciprocal declines in the social position of neighborhoods and ultimately the stratification of places.[1]

We propose a further structural focus on how institutionally based networks foster contextual settings of trust. In the organizational and social networks literature (for example, Burt 2005; McEvily, Perrone, and Zaheer 2003; Uzzi 1996), trust is often hypothesized as being closely grounded in the structural characteristics of a network, particularly its density and closure (Granovetter 1985; Portes and Sensenbrenner 1993), and shaped by actors' relative positioning in such structures (see also chapter 3, this volume). In a dense network, actors are more likely to know and trust each other based on past or repeated interactions (relational embeddedness, as defined by Granovetter 1985). They are more likely to know the same third actors, enhancing trust arising from "structural equivalence" (Burt 1992) or "structural embeddedness" (Granovetter 1985). Through a multiplier effect, we hypothesize that the more connected key actors are with multiple local leaders (egos), the more likely the whole local network and eventually the community is to be characterized by higher trust.

To our knowledge, how network structures of leadership vary across communities, much less predict trust, is largely unknown. The typical network study is based on a single or a handful of case studies, precluding comparative variations. In a comprehensive survey of studies on community power structures, John Walton concluded that more critical research was definitely needed to "allow a closer look at the cohesiveness of leadership groups and the conditions under which they effectively exercise power" (1970, 454). Almost forty years later, however, little progress in this direction has been made (for exceptions, see Gould 1989; Knoke 1990). We therefore present in this study a preliminary look at how a key characteristic—the centralization or density of leadership networks—

varies across Chicago communities and in turn predicts variations in contextualized trust independent of compositional features.

To summarize, this chapter has two primary goals. We first identify the major empirical dimensions of trust, whereby neighborhoods are differentially socially organized. How these vary over time and space—the social epidemiology of trust—is the main focus. Second, we examine the structural and spatial predictors of variations in dimensions of trust and efficacy. Here we move outside the black box of poverty and network structures to consider their connections to important social processes such as mutual trust among neighbors, shared expectations, and trust in community leaders and institutions. If the path dependence of resource- or network-based disadvantage has causal relevance at the neighborhood level, presumably it is because it generates self-reinforcing processes that further lock in self-defeating cycles of mistrust, cynicism, and apathy (Bowles 2000; Pierson 2000). To test such models requires the kind of dynamic models and data that no one, to our knowledge, has assembled. Nevertheless, we can examine some reasonable first approximations that may be generative of future research.

Data Sources

This study uses data from the Project on Human Development in Chicago Neighborhoods (PHDCN). The extensive racial and ethnic diversity of the population was a major reason Chicago was selected for the study. We examine local community areas, a collection of both people and institutions occupying a spatially defined area influenced by ecological, cultural, and sometimes political forces (Park 1915, 147–54). Although larger than what are traditionally considered neighborhoods, these areas often have well-known names and borders such as freeways, parks, and major streets. In particular, Chicago has seventy-seven local community areas with an average population of about 37,000, designed to correspond to socially meaningful and natural geographic boundaries. Although some boundaries have changed over time, these areas are widely recognized by administrative agencies, local institutions, and residents alike, and thus prove important when considering organizational aspects of social capital and leadership networks. The names of some have also changed over the years but the distinctiveness of the areas and their borders has remained remarkably stable (Suttles 1990).

Our first data source was the Community Survey (CS). In total, 8,782 individuals eighteen years of age or older were interviewed in their homes in 1995, with an average of 25 per original neighborhood sampling unit and more than 100 in each community area. The survey had three stages. At stage 1, city blocks were sampled within each neighborhood; at stage 2, dwelling units were sampled within blocks; at stage 3, one adult resident (eighteen or older) was sampled within each selected dwelling unit. Abt Associates carried out the screening and data collection in cooperation with research staff of PHDCN, achieving a final response rate of 75 percent. The design produced a representative probability sample of Chicago residents and a large enough within-cluster sample to create reliable between-neighborhood measures. The samples within areas were designed to be approximately self-weighting, and thus the between-community analysis is based on unweighted data (Sampson, Raudenbush, and Earls 1997, 924). Participants rated their neighborhoods on a number of dimensions, including trust, social cohesion, and informal social control (Raudenbush and Sampson 1999; Sampson, Morenoff, and Earls 1999).

A second Community Survey was conducted in 2001–2002 with a new (repeated) cross-sectional sample of all persons aged eighteen or older living in the Chicago. In collaboration with PHDCN, the University of Michigan's Institute of Social Research carried out 3,105 randomly selected, in-person, adult interviews. The probability sample was nested within the sampling clusters defined by PHDCN's earlier study of social environments. The 3,105 completed interviews mean that approximately forty cases within each community are available to construct contextual measures. The sample is racially and ethnically diverse: 1,240 non-Hispanic blacks, 983 non-Hispanic whites, 802 Hispanics, and 80 people of other races or ethnicities. The second community survey was conducted with a response rate of 72 percent, which comes close to matching the first even though in-person surveys are becoming harder to conduct.

Preliminary analysis has examined response bias and the reliability and validity of a core set of neighborhood-level constructs derived from prior PHDCN-related research. Sampson, Raudenbush, and Earls developed a three-level hierarchical model to assess the theoretical construct of collective efficacy (1997). They studied item inconsistency within scales, inter-rater agreement on each scale, and an overall estimate of the reliability of measurement of each scale. Extending this strategy, major constructs with accompanying intraclass correlations (ρ) and multilevel reliabilities were examined by linking waves 1 and 2 of the community survey (Sampson et al. 2007). Distinct from individual-level reliability (for example, Cronbach's alpha), neighborhood reliability (λ_2) is defined as: $\Sigma [\tau 00/(\tau 00 + \sigma^2/nj)] / J$, which measures the precision of the estimate, averaged across the set of J neighborhoods (for further details, see Raudenbush and Sampson 1999). With the exceptions noted in a later section, we are able to reliably tap parameter variance in social trust across neighborhood units.

The Key Informant Study

A weakness of research so far has been its inattention to organizations and the social networks of trust and affiliation among positional leaders at the center of social action for communities. Indeed, although interviewing residents and observing public areas has proven insightful, the organizational and institutional life of communities is equally if not more important from the perspective of understanding trust. We thus turn attention in this chapter to the institutional basis of trust invested in particular working relationships among institutional leaders for the purposes of getting things done in community settings. Our multipronged approach permits the partitioning of trust into network, institutional, and community components.

The KI (key informant) study designed to ask systematic questions of multiple key informants (leaders or experts) who were expected, based on their position, to have specialized knowledge of, and responsibility for, community social action. This method draws on a distinguished history in cultural anthropology and organizational sociology of using key informants to report on the social and cultural structure of collectivities (Campbell 1955; Tremblay 1957). The systematic use of positional informants to gather quantitative data on context has proved a reliable, although underused, methodology in the social sciences (Houston and Sudman 1975). Here we focus on the observed network structure of community leaders within and between communities from a positional perspective (Knoke 1990; Laumann and Pappi 1976), using informants to define, through both nominations of key actors in their network and through snowball sampling, the community-wide context of social organization relevant to a community's health.

Phase I Design

The initial KI design was based on a systematic sampling plan that targeted six institutional domains: education, religion, business, politics, law enforcement, and community organizations. Within each domain a list of positional leaders was constructed from public sources of information. Matched to areas already randomly selected for intensive investigation in other parts of the PHDCN study, the KI design focused on forty-seven of Chicago's seventy-seven community areas. In Chicago, most organizations representing the six institutional domains recognize the official boundaries of the city's community areas and many rely on them to provide services (Suttles 1990). The sampled areas were stratified by socioeconomic status (SES) and race-ethnicity to represent the full spectrum of Chicago's communities, from ethnically diverse Rogers Park on the far north side to black working-class Roseland on the far south, from exclusive Lincoln Park to the devastated ghetto of Garfield Park, from Mexican American (Little Village/South Lawndale) to Puerto Rican (Humboldt Park), and from white middle class (Clearing) to black middle class (Avalon Park). The Loop was also included.

The design required the construction of a geo-coded list of more than 10,000 positional leaders in Chicago from public sources of information. Of these, 5,716 were located in the forty-seven sampled communities. Target informants were defined by nature of who they were, what they did, and where they were. Examples of key informants are listed by domain:

- religion: Catholic priest, protestant pastor, mosque imam, synagogue rabbi
- education: school principal, local school council (LSC) president
- business: community reinvestment officer (banking), realty company owner/manager
- law enforcement: district commander, neighborhood relations sergeant
- political: alderman, ward committeeman, state representative, state senator
- community organization: housing organization president, health agency director

Approximately 2,500 cases were stratified by community and domain before random release for study, with 10 percent turning out to be ineligible (for example, moved, business closed). The National Opinion Research Center (NORC) at the University of Chicago carried out data collection in 1995, completing 1,713 interviews with sampled leaders in official positions.

Following the research tradition established in cultural anthropology and social-network analyses of community influence structures, a snowball sample was also incorporated as an important addition to the KI design. We suspected that many of the key actors in a community were new to the position or did not appear on official lists and hence were not sampled. Moreover, some of the influential actors in a community may hold nontraditional positions. To capture the full range of community informants, the KI interview asked respondents to nominate knowledgeable or influential persons in each of the six core domains of business, law enforcement, religion, education, politics, and community organizations. To elicit information on nontraditional persons who might be able to report on the community, we asked each respondent, "Now, other than the people and organizations that we've already discussed, is there any one else in [community name] that we should speak with, to really understand this community? This could include a long-time resident, a leader of a youth club or gang, a mentor of youth in the community, and so on. Who else would you recommend we talk to?"

The sampled positional leaders generated 7,340 reputational nominees, about 3,500 of whom were duplicate nominations—the same individual nominated more than once, or a nominee already in the sample.

This finding is an important validation of the design. In all, 1,105 reputational interviews were completed, bringing the final sample size to 2,822. The interviews averaged just under an hour in length and the overall completion rate was 87 percent of eligible cases.

Phase II KI Panel Study

Just as it is not enough to study individual development at one point in time, so too is it misleading to rely on snapshots of community-level processes—communities change as well. A panel-based positional approach to the study of community dynamics allows for the measurement of changes in community leadership (whether there is a new leader in the same position, for example), organizational change (such as whether the institution survived), changes in the dimensions of social-network structure (the density of ties, for instance) and changes in the content of action (such as crime prevention or health promotion). The KI panel study was thus designed to capture re-interviews of 1995 leaders still in the same position, new leaders in the same position or organization as in 1995, leaders in newly formed organizations and positions, and where leaders who exited from 1995 positions went. Organizational and positional sampling frames were updated and pretest interviews with fifty-two leaders were carried out in the summer of 2000.

The final sample was constructed as a random selection of original positional leaders in 1995, stratified by institutional domain, plus snowball sample nominations designed to capture both new organizations and new leaders. To contain costs, a representative subsample of thirty of the original forty-seven communities was selected for the panel sampling frame. NORC at the University of Chicago was selected to carry out all aspects of contacting respondents and conducting interviews. More than 1,000 ($N = 1{,}113$) interviews were completed over the summer and fall of 2002 at a response rate of 76 percent of eligible leaders. Approximately 60 percent of the interviews were conducted with new respondents holding the same position as 1995 respondents, indicating considerable personal turnover in fairly stable network positions. Overall, the final sample yielded an average of almost forty interviews per community, enough to construct reliable between-community measures.

The Chicago KI Study advances the science of networks by going beyond the personal and egocentric ties of residents to allowing the examination of cross-level ties between community elites and various subgroups of citizen residents, an understudied aspect of the community structure relevant for well-being (Knoke 1990). More important, unlike the vast majority of network studies, which are case studies of single settings (Faust and Skvoretz 2002), the KI study's comparative design is uniquely designed to allow us to examine how network structures vary across communities. The only parallel we know of in the literature is the Rang Nong study of fifty-one village networks in Thailand (Entwisle et al. 2007).

Constructing Measures

Using the community survey, we first defined several dimensions of neighborhood social organization from the perspective of residents. The specific goal was to assess the measurement properties and interrelationships among a number of trust-related indicators.

Collective efficacy is defined in as the combination of two scales—cohesion and social control (Sampson, Raudenbush, and Earls 1997, 919–20). *Control* is a scale composed of five items: "If a group of neighborhood children were skipping school and hanging out on a street corner, how likely is it that your neighbors would do something about it?" "If some children were spray-painting graffiti on a local building, how likely is it that your neighbors would do something about it?" "If a child were showing disrespect to an adult, how likely is it that people in your neighborhood would scold that child?" "If there were a fight in front of your house and someone was being beaten or threatened, how likely is it that your neighbors would break it up?" "Suppose that because of city budget cuts the library or fire station closest to your home was going to be closed down by the city. How likely is it that neighborhood residents would organize to try to do something to keep the fire station or library open?" The *cohesion* scale includes four items: "People in this neighborhood generally get along with each other. This is a close-knit neighborhood." "People around here are willing to help their neighbors." "People in this neighborhood share the same values." A trust item was also included: "People in this neighborhood can be trusted." All items were coded on a five-point scale such that a higher value signifies higher cohesion and control.

Collective efficacy has been shown to exhibit excellent ecometric properties that define the ability of a measure to capture between-area as opposed to between-individual variations (Raudenbush and Sampson 1999). In this study, collective efficacy yielded a community-level reliability of .92 in 1995 and .76 in 2002.[2] Although trust in neighbors is conceptualized as part of the larger construct of collective efficacy, based on theoretical interests central to this chapter we examined both the overall scale and the single trust items (λ_2 = .90 and .74 in 1995 and 2002, respectively). Trust and collective efficacy were measured the same way in both surveys.

In 2002 residents were asked the about *trust in police:* "The police in your local community can be trusted" (coded from strongly disagree to strongly agree; neighborhood reliability, or λ_2 = .72). They were also asked whether they agreed with the classic generalized trust items: "Now, I want to ask you some questions about how you view other people. Generally speaking, would you say that most people can be trusted or that you can't be too careful in dealing with people? 'Most people can be trusted' and 'You can't be too careful in dealing with people.'" From these we created a three-point general trust scale that is reliable across communities ($\lambda_2 = .76$).

Key Informant Measures

Leaders' general trust is composed of answers to two questions: "Generally speaking most people can be trusted" and "Generally speaking most people try to be helpful." The scale is coded on a three-point scale on which higher values reflect higher trust. Neighborhood reliability is .48.

Leaders' trust in residents is conveyed by their answers to one question: "People in [community] can be trusted?" The item was coded on a five-point scale on which higher values signify higher trust. Neighborhood reliability (λ_2) is .69. This question is a direct parallel to the question put to community residents on whether neighbors trust one another.

Indices of institutional trust draw on key informants' answers to questions about the most important institutions for the community in six domains: church, schools, political organizations or officials, business, law enforcement organizations or officials, and community organizations (Laumann and Pappi 1976). After the informants identified up to three organizations in each domain, they evaluated the residents' trust in the most important of the three with answers to the following question: "Would you say [organization/official] is trusted by residents of the community?" The items are coded on a three-point scale with higher values for higher trust. The neighborhood reliability for law enforcement and political trust was .64 and for schools .60; the rest of the institutional trust measures had reliabilities under .5, reflecting less meaningful area variation.

Institutional trust or trust in authorities has been shown to significantly predict individual performance, citizenship behavior or altruism, turnover intentions, commitment to the organization, and leaders' decisions in a variety of contexts, from financial institutions to manufacturing firms, military units, and public institutions (Dirks and Ferrin 2002). Institutional trust in authorities is also associated with individuals' feelings of obligation to obey the law (Tyler 1990), political participation, contributions of time and money to campaigns, and voting (Tyler and Huo 2002). Despite the widely accepted significance of institutional trust, the processes underlying its formation, persistence, or disruption are not well understood.

Socioeconomic and Temporal Predictors

We next focused on three dimensions of a community's structural position that have been shown to be important in previous research predicting neighborhood dimensions of social capital (Sampson, Morenoff, and Earls 1999, 633–60). Concentrated poverty is defined by the proportion of the population below the poverty line and measured in each decade from

1970 to 2000. We measured racial diversity as a Herfindahl concentration index equal to one minus the sum of squares of the proportions of the neighborhood population made up by a racial-ethnic group: whites, blacks, and others (Blau 1977; Massey and Denton 1988). The index has higher values the more racially diverse a neighborhood is and reflects the probability of any two randomly drawn individuals from a neighborhood to belong to different subgroups. In supplementary analyses, we also examined linguistic diversity and percentage foreign born but with similar results.

Consistent with a long line of urban research, the third major index captures neighborhood residential stability, defined as the percentage of residents (five years old and older) who lived in the same house five years earlier (Bursik and Grasmick 1993; Kornhauser 1978). We also examined a factor-weighted scale that combined the percentage of owner-occupied homes, with similar results. To better capture change we rely on the raw stability measure across three decades.

Structural Networks

To establish the network structure of leadership ties, the KI study developed a modified version of Ronald Burt's name generator, aided by focus groups and formal pretests in both the 1995 and 2002 studies (1992). Each KI respondent was asked to identify up to five people they went to in order to "get things done" in the community. The names and addresses of each key contact were recorded, along with their positions and organizational affiliations. The net result is a rich source of information that, because of the systematic and replicable sampling procedures, allows us to construct network measures for Chicago and for each of its communities, permitting comparative analysis of network structures. We have constructed an initial set of network measures including density, path distance (or higher-order) density, *alter* density, and leadership inequality.

For simplicity, we focus here on the *centralization of the leadership power network,* a measure of the concentration of nominations coming from all sampled key informants in a given community toward a small number of alters. It also indicates hierarchy or inequality in alters' nominations, that is, the tendency for a few alters to get most of the nominations. For the overall index of centralization, we count all alters, those living in the community of interest or outside it, though the nominations can come only from respondents within that community.

The main index of centralization is based on the Herfindahl formula, traditionally used as a measure of industry concentration, which formally is equal to $\Sigma\pi_r^2$, where π_r, refers to r^{th} alter's share of all the nominations coming from a given community. In this study, the centralization index captures the extent to which all nominations go to a smaller rather than larger number of alters, as well as the variation in the degree of inequality in the number of citations received by all alters nominated by respondents in a community:

$$\text{PWCON} = \Sigma_j\left[\left(\Sigma_i X_{ij}\right)/TNOM\right]^2, \text{ where } TNOM = \Sigma_i\Sigma_j X_{ij}$$

where i indicates a respondent from community k; j refers to all alters nominated by respondents from community k, and X_{ij} represents a tie sent from respondent i from community k to those alters j nominated by respondents from community k. If a tie exists, X_{ij} equals 1. If one does not, it equals 0. The index reflects the probability that two nominations randomly selected from all nominations generated by the KI within a certain community are directed toward the same rather than different alters. The index has a maximum statistically possible score of 1 when all KIs nominate the same alter and a minimum of $1/n$ when all alters receive the same number of nominations, where n is the number of all alters nominated by the KIs from a given community. For instance, a community distributing its nominations equally to only three alters will have a higher power concentration score than one distributing its nominations equally toward ten distinct alters. George Stigler suggested that squaring the nomination shares decreases the influence of errors due to the possible lack of precise data on very small groups (1968). Given its properties, this index can also be reversed and used as a diversity measure.

Finally, using the network name generator we found that about a third of key informants (303) reported a network contact with someone they trusted in the work setting but who was not a personal friend. We operationalize this configuration as a key dimension of *working trust*, where a 1 indexes a trusting contact with a nonfriend, and 0 indexes primarily *strong tie* contacts characterized by friendship and nontrusting ties. This type of formal working trust varies significantly across communities.

Dynamics and Dimensionality of Trust

We begin the analyses by examining the stability in community trust across time ($r = .62$) at the community level (figure 7.1). An important component of community trust seems to be transmitted across years, even as residents fluctuate in or out of the community. This pattern occurs despite the fact that the trust indicator is based on one item and is measured with error. Collective efficacy, based on a multi-item scale, is correlated at $r = .73$ over time. These results indicate persistence in the part of a community's character that is related to residents' trust and shared expectations for social action. Although there is no information about the levels of community trust from earlier than 1995 in Chicago, both the 1970 poverty rate and changes in poverty across three decades have a significant and durable association with contemporary trust levels. A long-ranging cumulative

Figure 7.1 Scatterplot of Trust in Chicago Communities over Time ($N = 77$)

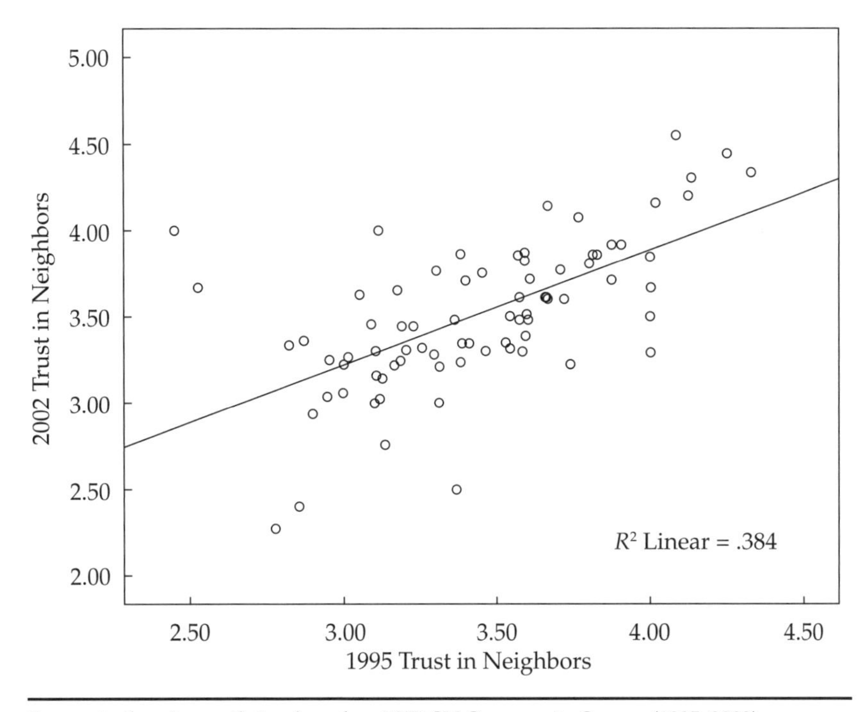

Source: Authors' compilation based on PHDCN Community Survey (1995, 2002).

effect of poverty on trust is further suggested by the fact that 1970 poverty has an even stronger association with later mistrust than the 1990 poverty rate. Neighborhood traces are apparently not easily overcome.

Figure 7.2 maps this pattern in geographic space. With few exceptions, most of the high poverty communities appear in the lowest trust quartile. Although there is some indication of high 1970 poverty levels in communities that also have a high level of trust in 1995, these communities seem to have experienced some of the highest decreases in poverty between 1970 and 2000 and the highest increases in trust levels between 1995 and 2002. The maps in figure 7.2 further reflect a remarkable pattern of spatial clustering, where communities with similar levels of mistrust are ecologically positioned near each other and overlap with poverty clusters, combining into what appear to be unfortunate traps of spiraling vulnerabilities and reinforcing spatial risks.

We turn now to dimensions of trust at different structural levels of the community by pooling data from the Chicago community survey and the KI panel survey. Table 7.1 shows that the three main structural dimensions

Figure 7.2 Geographic Distribution of 1995 Neighborhood Trust

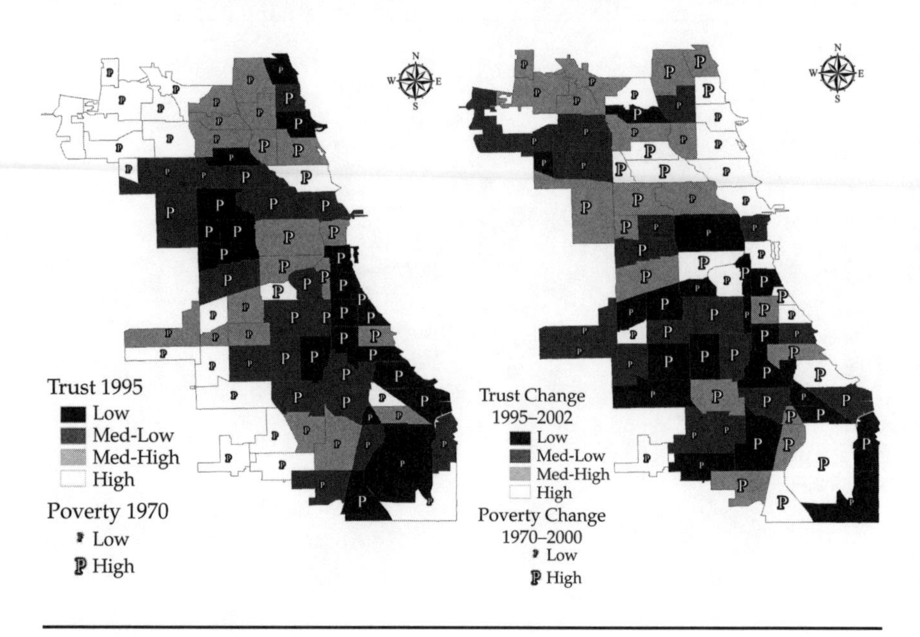

Source: Authors' compilation based on NCDB (GeoLytics 2003) and PHDCN Community Survey (1995, 2002.)

of trust correlate with each other differently. Whereas leadership trust correlates moderately to strongly with residents' trust items, trust in institutions does not correlate consistently with the other dimensions. The trust indices that correlate at the highest level with each other are those reported by residents. Although residents' trust in police would seem to fit better conceptually with the institutional trust items, and does covary strongly with residents' trust in law enforcement as reported by the key informants (itself an indicator of construct validity), both indices correlate surprisingly low with the rest of the institutional trust items and higher with residents' general trust and residents' trust in neighbors. Our findings do suggest, however, that trust includes a component related to personal security and law enforcement, a component that originates from, or makes reference to, community residents. Recall also that trust in law enforcement yields the highest between-community variance component of all the institutional trust measures, and thus is more reliably measured (at .64).

Consistent with table 7.1, a principal factor analysis (not shown) indicated that residents' general trust, trust in neighbors, and trust in police

Table 7.1 Correlations Among Trust Dimensions

	Residents' Trust			Leaders' Trust			Institutional Trust					
	General	Neighbor	Police	General	Resident	Working	LawEnf	ComOrg	Church	School	Politics	Busins
Residents' general trust	1.000											
Residents' trust in neighbors	.680	1.000										
Residents' trust in police	.683	.740	1.000									
Leaders' general trust	.595	.581	.412	1.000								
Leaders' trust in residents	.441	.741	.738	.440	1.000							
Leaders' working trust	.769	.493	.400	.512	.186	1.000						
Trust in law enforcement	.618	.762	.696	.395	.717	.371	1.000					
Trust in community organizations	.082	.025	.265	.026	.248	.131	.143	1.000				
Trust in churches	–.095	.155	.020	.005	.219	–.135	.235	.023	1.000			
Trust in schools	–.044	.173	.089	–.115	–.030	–.140	.168	.091	.380	1.000		
Trust in politicians	.228	.355	.304	.265	.338	.076	.544	.297	.319	.460	1.000	
Trust in business organizations	.018	.243	.415	–.090	.379	–.051	.376	.328	.364	.227	.383	1.000
Collective efficacy (residents' reports)	.453	.811	.636	.326	.616	.168	.450	.134	.132	.226	.260	.062
Collective efficacy (leaders' reports)	.516	.783	.738	.562	.869	.315	.715	.288	.131	.053	.454	.260

Source: Authors' compilation based on PHDCN Community Survey and Key Informant Studies 2002 (Sampson 2002).

load strongly on a single component. In the next steps in the analyses we therefore use a weighted factor score of the three items, called residents' "overall trust scale." In a different principal component analysis (PCA) of trust scores originating from the key informant reports, the three items most equivalent with the residents' also loaded on the first component but at a lower level. Note, too, the generally lower correlations among key informant measures (for example, the highest correlation of leaders' general trust with any other trust measure is .51). We thus decided to continue analyzing the individual trust items of key leaders rather than constructing an overall trust scale.

Also consistent with table 7.1, the institutional trust items do not cluster strongly with each other in a principal component analysis. This suggests either that there is no overarching concept of institutional trust or simply too little between-community variance in most of the institutional trust measures to justify including them in multivariate analyses. We leave to future research further investigation of this issue.[3] In the next models, we concentrate on the most reliable measure of institutional trust, namely trust in law enforcement. The two independently measured collective efficacy indices, as reported by residents and the institutional informants, largely follow similar patterns of covariation with the trust measures: strongly associated with resident trust in neighbors, police and law enforcement, and with leader trust in residents.

Multidimensional Scaling of Trust and Change in Trust Across Time

As a final descriptive tool we conducted a multidimensional scaling (MDS) analysis of Chicago communities based on their score on residents' general trust, trust in neighbors and in police, and changes across time in neighborhood trust to produce a geometric distribution of each community relative to all others (see figure 7.3). Essentially this is a dynamic MDS that reflects both pairwise and global dissimilarities between communities according to their scores on the input indices. MDS systematically transforms information on the dissimilarity between communities according to their trust scores from an *n*-by-*n* distance matrix, into a geometric representation of the input stimuli in a lower dimensional multivariate space. Similar to a principal components analysis, MDS condenses the dissimilarity between the stimuli from *p* dimensions (the number of input variables), into a smaller number of dimensions that are easier to interpret (Steyvers 2002). However, compared to a PCA, the MDS entails a minimum set of assumptions, mainly that the interpoint distances are monotonically (in the case of nonmetric MDS) related to the dissimilarities between stimuli (that is, communities).

To help interpret the neighborhood pattern arrangement of the MDS, we next conducted a cluster analysis (Kruskal and Wish 1978). In contrast

Figure 7.3 Structural Cluster Configuration of Chicago Communities ($N = 77$), Overall Trust and Change in Trust, 1995 to 2002

(A)

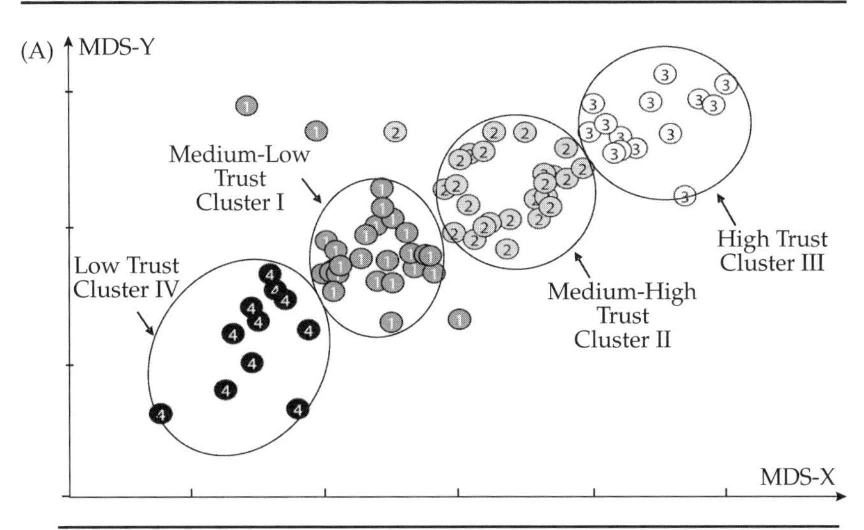

(B)

	Low Trust Cluster IV		Med-Low Trust Cluster I		Med-High Trust Cluster II		High Trust Cluster III	
	Mean		Mean		Mean		Mean	
Indices internal to the cluster analysis								
Residents overall trust 2002	−1.553	(.37)***	-.543	(.23)***	.442	(.29)***	1.478	(.31)***
Change in trust in neighbors 1995 to 2002	−.215	(.32)*	.098	(.45)	.130	(.30)*	.142	(.24)
Exogenous indices								
Percentage residents below poverty 1970	26.391	(8.93)***	14.996	(11.58)**	9.422	(6.55)*	5.295	(3.64)**
Change in percentage poor 1970 to 2000	12.729	(6.58)**	9.733	(6.27)**	5.156	(5.71)**	.750	(3.28)**

Source: Authors' compilation based on NCDB (GeoLytics 2003) and PHDCN Community Survey (1995, 2002).
Notes: (A) The shaded circles represent communities. Spatial location of communities relative to each other is based on multidimensional scaling (MDS). The shading and the loops around communities represent the corresponding cluster assignment based on a hierarchical cluster analysis (squared Euclidean distance, Ward method)
(B) Standard deviations in parentheses next to group means. * $p < .10$, ** $p < .05$, *** $p < .01$

to MDS, which identifies global structural positions, cluster analysis identifies more finely tuned patterns (Aldenderfer and Blashfield 1984). To reflect a balanced weighting of stability and change, we entered both the static and the dynamic components of overall community trust. The hierarchical cluster analysis using the pairwise squared Euclidean distance measure and the Ward method resulted in an assignment of communities to four main groups. The clusters are signaled in figure 7.3, panel A, by the loops and the shading of the smaller circles, which represent communities. The fairly compact loops suggest a good match between the community groupings yielded by the MDS configuration and the cluster solution (Kruskal and Wish 1978). The clustering results also indicate a good fit for the two-dimension MDS solution at the community level.

Panel B of figure 7.3 shows the mean characteristics of the communities within each of the four clusters. We name the clusters from low trust to high trust according to the rank order of their average scores on the indices used as input in the cluster analysis: residents' trust and change in trust across time. The group means for change in trust across time follow largely the same ordered distribution across clusters as the 2002 overall level of trust, indicating that communities with high levels in overall trust in 2002 also have experienced the highest increases in trust across time. The distribution pattern of the 1970 poverty scores (and change in poverty) across the low to high trust community clusters parallels the findings described earlier (see also table 7.1) indicating a robust negative association between poverty and trust across the three decades.

Poverty and Mistrust Traps

We now specify a set of multivariate regression models that account for spatial dependencies among communities in examining the prediction of community trust from poverty, diversity, and leadership structures. Including spatial lags is important because socioeconomic characteristics of a neighborhood tend to be associated with the characteristics of other spatially contiguous neighborhoods (see also Sampson, Morenoff, and Earls 1999).[4] In modeling panel data, the method of first differences is often used to eliminate fixed effects, a procedure we follow. Including serial lags is also important, however, because the observable population level response to changes in certain neighborhood characteristics often is delayed due to the natural duration that information takes to reach the relevant population, the time it takes for individuals to respond to the new information received and to negotiate normative, social, or institutional factors.

The analyses support the argument that the time-spanning durability of structural deprivation and inequalities is interwoven with sharp differences in the construction and maintenance of trust (Hardin 2002). Models 1 in tables 7.2, 7.3, and 7.4 show that even after controlling for residential mobility and population diversity, the level of community poverty from the 1970s has resilient negative associations with 2002 levels of resident overall trust and collective efficacy. Similarly, poverty predicts also lower leader trust in residents and institutional and working trust. To the extent that the 1970 level of poverty is highly associated with more recent levels of community poverty, this finding is not very surprising. Interestingly, however, the 1990 poverty levels are less strongly associated with trust

Table 7.2 Maximum Likelihood Spatial Regression of Residents' Overall Trust and Change in Trust in Neighbors

	Residents' Overall Trust 2002		Change in Trust in Neighbors 1995 to 2002	
	Coeff.	Std. Err	Coeff.	Std. Err
Constant	1.135	(.538)**	3.407	(.710)***
Percentage residents in poverty 1970	−.037	(.007)***	−.013	(.005)**
Change in percentage poor 1970 to 2000	−.067	(.010)***	−.029	(.008)***
Percentage residential stability	−.002	(.007)	.003	(.005)
Change percentage stability 1970 to 2000	−.002	(.008)	.004	(.005)
Racial diversity 1970	−.515	(.512)	−.383	(.295)
Change in diversity 1970 to 2000	.049	(.339)	.066	(.199)
1995 trust in neighbors			−.893	(.188)***
Spatial lag	.333	(.104)***	.060	(.147)
R^2	.735		.308	
N	77		77	

Source: Authors' compilation of NCDB (GeoLytics 2003) and PHDCN Community and Key Informant Surveys (1995, 2002; Sampson 1995, 2002).
***$p < .01$, **$p < .05$

Table 7.3 Maximum Likelihood Spatial Regression of Residents' Collective Efficacy and Change in Collective Efficacy

	Collective Efficacy 2002		Change in Collective Efficacy 1995 to 2002	
	Coeff.	Std. Err	Coeff.	Std. Err
Constant	1.776	(.386)***	2.383	(.484)***
Percentage residents in poverty 1970	−.004	(.002)**	−.005	(.002)**
Change in percentage poor 1970 to 2000	−.013	(.003)***	−.012	(.004)***
Percentage residential stability	.009	(.002)***	.010	(.002)***
Change percentage stability 1970 to 2000	.008	(.002)***	−.001	(.002)
Racial diversity 1970	−.105	(.136)	−.149	(.143)
Change in racial diversity 1970 to 2000	.082	(.091)	.081	(.096)
1995 collective efficacy			−.856	(.152)
Spatial lag	.330	(.117)***	.037	(.145)
R^2	.611		.371	
N	77		77	

Source: Authors' compilation based on NCDB (GeoLytics 2003) and PHDCN Community and Key Informant Surveys (1995, 2002; Sampson 1995, 2002).
***$p < .01$, **$p < .05$

Table 7.4 Regressions of Trust Dimensions in 2002 Among Key Informant Leaders: $N = 30$ Chicago Communities

	Leaders' General Trust		Leaders' Trust in Residents		Leaders' Working Trust		Trust in Law Enforcement	
	Coeff.	Std. Err	Coeff.	Std. Err	Coeff.	Std. Err	Coeff.	Std. Err
Constant	2.138	(.59)***	2.356	(.46)***	.874	(.25)***	1.834	(.34)***
Residents' trust in neighbors 1995	.084	(.16)	.451	(.12)***	–.159	(.07)**	.226	(.09)**
Percentage residents in poverty 1970	–.002	(.00)	–.010	(.00)**	–.004	(.00)**	–.007	(.00)**
Change in percentage poor 1970 to 2000	–.004	(.01)	.000	(.01)	–.008	(.00)***	–.006	(.00)*
Centralization of leader network 1995	1.246	(1.38)	–1.052	(1.08)	1.301	(.59)**	–.476	(.78)
Change in centralization of leader network 1995 to 2002	2.036	(1.77)	–1.635	(1.39)	2.423	(.76)***	1.813	(1.01)*
R^2	.263		.745		.494		.756	

Source: Authors' compilation based on NCDB 1970–2000 (GeoLytics 2003) and PHDCN Key Informant Panel Survey (1995, 2002; Sampson 1995, 2002).
$^{***}p < .01$, $^{**}p < .05$, $^{*}p < .10$

than the 1970 levels are. Moreover, the temporal fluctuations in community poverty across three decades from the 1970 to the year 2000 are also included in the estimated models and significantly predict lower levels of resident overall trust, trust in law enforcement, and more surprisingly, leader working trust.

Perhaps even more unexpected is the durable effect of the 1970 poverty level on recent decreases in residents' trust, controlling for changes in poverty over time (table 7.2). It appears that poverty and its associated pitfalls, disorder and violence, for instance, may have a lasting and cumulative effect on collective memories about urban communities affecting their reputation and perceived "local character" for a long time, in a downward spiral of disadvantage, which may increasingly undermine residents' trust in local institutions and possibly in each other as well (Molotch, Freudenburg, and Paulsen 2000; Suttles 1984). Reinforcing the importance of distinguishing between different dimensions of trust, however, note that 1970 poverty is not consistent in predicting all measures of trust. In particular, 1970 poverty does not predict leaders' general trust and the change in poverty across time does not seem to impact general trust by leaders or leaders' trust in residents. Contextual effects on trust are thus largely specific to grounded contexts rather than to global dimensions of general trust, in keeping with our hypothesis.

After controlling for poverty and residential stability, 1970 levels of diversity and change in diversity across three decades do not significantly predict trust or collective efficacy, suggesting that most of any zero-order negative association between racial diversity and trust is accounted for by the patterns of covariation between poverty and stability with trust at the community level. This set of findings implies that as the importance of the foreign born has grown in the United States and cities like Chicago, the negative effect of racial diversity on community social processes found in previous studies may have become outdated, changing into a nonsignificant effect. We are currently exploring these findings, using more extensive diversity measures, in greater detail.

Network Structure and Leadership Trust

Finally, we turn to the largely unexplored arena of the connection between community network structures and leadership trust. Figure 7.4 illustrates the range of variation in the centralization of community leadership structures by comparing two communities at different poles on this index, one with centralized and dense leadership structure and another with a sparse and decentralized community structure. The dots represent key informants and the thickness of the ties between informant pairs reflects the number of nominees they have in common, if any.

Figure 7.4 Decentralized and Centralized Leadership Networks

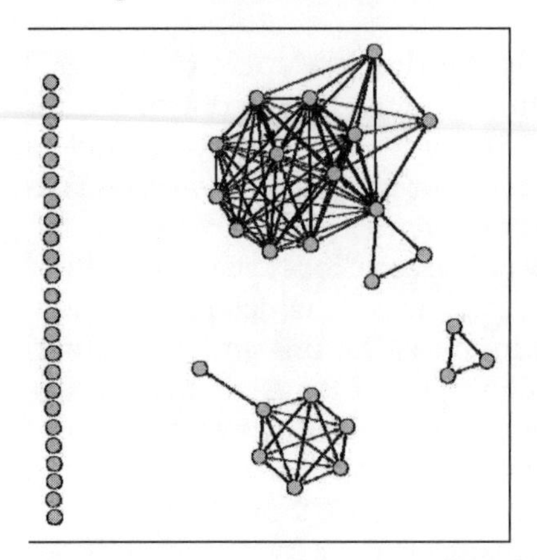

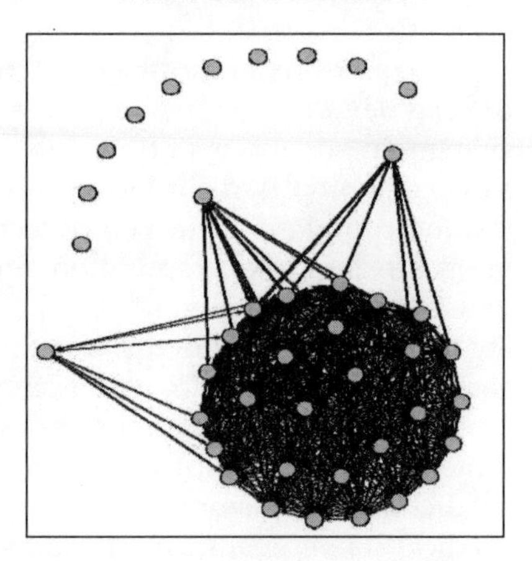

Source: Authors' calculations based on PHDCN Key Informant Network Study (1995; Sampson 1995)

Notes: N = 2,813 leaders, 47 communities. Degree of connectedness reflects the degree of centralization. Dots are key informants, and the thickness of the connecting ties represents the number of the same alters (if any) that two informants have nominated. Hence respondents are connected through alters.

The network concentration index simultaneously measures both the spread and evenness in the distribution of network ties within the social structure of a community (Ottaviano and Perri 2005; Parijs 2006). A high score reflects a relatively low number of alters nominated by the key informants. This indicates a high level of agreement among the respondents about the constituents of the leadership core, suggesting a relatively well-defined and small elite group instrumental in getting things done for the community. Furthermore, a high level of network concentration simultaneously suggests a relatively high inequality in the distribution of ties across all the nominated alters. This means that a few leaders receive nominations from a large number of respondents, whereas most other alters receive one or very few nominations.

Net of disadvantage and residential stability, network centralization yields a positive and strong association with leader working trust but not with leader general trust, their trust in residents, or trust in law enforcement (table 7.4). The nonsignificant coefficients at these higher structural levels might be affected by the small sample size (N = 30).[5]

Still, the negative sign of the centralization coefficient in predicting institutional trust indicates potentially opposite processes leading to some forms of trust compared to others. This raises yet another cautionary flag about the explicit or implicit assumption, frequently made in studies of trust and social capital, that individuals' general levels of trust reflect fairly well other specific dimensions of trust. In fact, the findings suggest that general trust may be more of a characteristic of the person than the context.

In contrast, working trust seems deeply embedded in the social and structural characteristics of the community and network contexts. One reason may be that a centralized network reflects perhaps a more cohesive leadership structure, whereby leaders agree more often with each other in naming the instrumental actors for the community. The more individuals are putting their hopes in a particular leader, the cost of monitoring his or her actions decreases and the level of trust likely increases in a self-reinforcing loop. Alternatively, when more key informants in a community nominate the same alters, it may be the result of shared perceptions among the members of the community leadership network that they form a cohesive elite group rather then multiple cliques or no group at all. If this is the case, the positive relationship between network centralization and working trust may be explained by an in-group heuristic based on expectations of generalized exchange. In chapter 1 of this volume, Margaret Foddy and Toshio Yamagishi present experimental results that support this hypothesis. Community leaders with high nomination scores seem to be more trustworthy (see chapter 3, this volume). A centralized network may also reflect a more condensed and smaller leadership core, making its members more visible and accountable to the community. Put differently, when the core leadership circle is relatively small and public attention more focused on them, the intensity of social control and the cost of deviance increases thereby creating a multilayered "enforceable trust" (Portes 1998).[6]

A common critique of indices of centralization or concentration brings to attention their inherent association with the size of the network or the community (Wasserman and Faust 1994). Using reports from key informants in fifty-one communities, Terry Clark suggested that that the population size of a community is positively related to the institutional decentralization of the decision making structure (1968). In contrast, Walton's (1970) review of community studies concluded that the size and the composition of the population are not related to the structure of the community power. In this study, we find that the leadership network concentration index is associated with the community size but the pattern of association between power concentration and other community characteristics remains significant independent of size.

Conclusions

We have found that mistrust and low collective efficacy are stubbornly persistent in terms of their neighborhood concentration, which is somewhat surprising when considered in relation to the common emphasis in urban sociology on social transformation (Wilson 1987). Low levels of trust and collective efficacy appear to beget cycles of further mistrust and ineffective institutional response. Neighborhoods also remain remarkably stable in their relative social standing despite the inflow and outflow of individual residents. There is something enduring about the poverty vulnerability of neighborhoods that is not simply a matter of the current income of residents (Sampson and Morenoff 2006; Sampson and Sharkey 2008).

Second, initial levels of concentrated poverty—those from 1970—predict multiple dimensions of (mis)trust some thirty years later. What change does occur reveals strong patterns of long-term increases in poverty from 1970 to 2000 being linked to decreasing trust, with the latter measured in the 1995–2002 period and thereby alleviating concerns about simultaneity. This finding suggests that increases in resource deprivation may have a substantial causal effect on reductions in trust. One way that historical connections between structural and individual level processes can expand across decades is by intergenerational transmission of what may be called "learned mistrust" (Hardin 2001). Even as the population composition changes within a chronically distrusting neighborhood, newcomers may learn not to trust others in the community, a rational reaction to a corrosive moral environment. This finding contributes to the midrange paradigm of trust Henry Farrell emphasizes in chapter 5 of this volume. We find that neighborhood poverty and the institutional deprivation it signifies have an enduring impact on trust across layers of the social fabric within a community. Not only does poverty predict resident mistrust of institutions such as law enforcement, it heightens leader mistrust of residents. Moreover, residents' mistrust of their neighbors seems to lead over time to mistrust of residents at the leadership level as well. At the structural level, the effect of concentrated disadvantage on communities at a given point in time may have snowballing effects on trust that amplify over time due to the cumulative weakening of their institutional and organizational base. Such processes may be reinforced by declines in opportunities for employment (Wilson 1996), deterioration of parks, schools, or medical services (LaGrange, Ferraro, and Supanic 1992; Robert 1998; Taylor and Hale 1986), the decline of formal services (LeClere, Rogers, and Peters 1997; Robert 1998), and the erosion of informal social controls (Sampson, Raudenbush, and Earls 1997). The deep imprint of cumulative disadvantage on collective mistrust appears to be difficult to overcome.

Third, decreases in poverty predict decreases in mistrust net of changes in racial diversity and residential stability. The latter itself has a strong association with collective efficacy but not trust in leaders or the overall trust factor. Because of statistical power constraints, we could not examine a large number of potential confounders at the time-varying covariate level, but racial change and changes in residential tenure are two of the most potent ecological characteristics in a long line of urban research. In line with those of Karen Cook, Russell Hardin, and Margaret Levi, our results support policies reducing economic, social, and political disparities by building a "social infrastructure that ensures a rupture with the past and that promotes substantial relearning of the likelihood of trustworthiness" (2005, 13).

Interestingly, however, a fourth result is that racial diversity is either positively correlated with trust or unrelated to trust once multivariate controls are introduced. Either finding contradicts common beliefs and theories arguing that ethnic heterogeneity plays a deleterious role for the community (for example, Shaw and McKay 1942/1969). Our findings instead are more in line with recent research that depicts a more optimistic image for communities increasing in immigration and diversity (Sampson 2008, 2009). Toward the beginning of the twenty-first century, diversity appears to be evolving from a marker of white-nonwhite hierarchies into a marker of increasingly complex cultural differentiations within a more amorphous ethnic hierarchy. Moreover, though racial heterogeneity is typically expected to increase problems of communication and mistrust (Putnam 2007), the weak link between diversity and trust we found here highlights the importance of drawing on alternative sociological frameworks to better understand contemporary diversity and its effects on neighborhoods. Conceptual frames such as Claude Fischer's subcultural theory of urbanism (1975) or Peter Blau's theory of heterogeneity and inequality (1977) predict both positive and negative social processes and outcomes stemming from diversity. For example, more diverse communities offer increased opportunities for both intergroup contact and intergroup conflict (Knight 2001) as well as increased tolerance and intermarriage.

A fifth finding is that spatial proximity to "mistrust traps" is related to lower levels of trust in focal neighborhoods despite indigenous characteristics. By contrast, proximity to neighborhoods with high levels of trust seems to have a protective effect on the focal neighborhood. Consistent with those of other studies on collective efficacy and social capital in Chicago, this finding highlights a remarkable, yet little documented, contextual characteristic of neighborhood trust—its spillover across space and time (see Sampson, Morenoff, and Earls 1999). Explanations for trust spillovers range from simple errors due to omitted variable bias to macro-level processes of what we call *mistrust contagion.* Systematic investigation of such processes will constitute a valuable area of further research.

Finally, structural networks among community leaders—both lagged and change—predict working trust among leaders *but not general trust.* In communities in which centralized and dense networks of leaders prevail and are increasing in number, contextual trust is thus higher (or increasing) despite controlling for concentrated poverty and racial diversity. This is one of the first empirical demonstrations we are aware of that indicates the role network structures can play in the formation of grounded trust. Of course, this model constitutes only a first glimpse at the enduring implications of complex local structures. Characteristics of social network structures can rarely be thought of as fully exogenous to outcomes generated within those structures (see also chapters 9 and 11, this volume). Accounting for potential feedback processes between contexts and trust would be highly valuable in further analyses. We emphasize, however, that in this chapter the predictors and outcomes were measured independently and time ordered, and that the finding holds regardless of the changing composition of the community population.

The consequences of durable and increasing poverty appear to be long lasting, at least with respect to predicting key social processes like relational trust. Controlling for stability and racial diversity, both persistent poverty and increases in poverty from 1970 to 2000 predict lower collective efficacy and higher mistrust by neighborhood residents in 2002. Although the time span is shorter, structural variations in dense networks among community leaders also predict future variations in trust specific to leaders in their communities. Ambiguities remain, of course, but our findings are consistent with the idea that the structural dynamics of concentrated urban poverty set systemic processes in motion that contribute to the marginalization of urban neighborhoods and a further deepening of poverty. On the more positive side, cohesive networks of leadership may signal hope as a viable lever of neighborhood social change.

Thanks go to the Russell Sage Foundation (Grant #82–05–01) and the National Institute of Child Health and Human Development (Grant #s HD38986 and HD050467) for funding support. Thanks especially to Bruce Carruthers and Susan Stokes for comments.

Notes

1. Interpretations of how neighborhoods become trapped in poverty vary, the most common one being the differential selection of individuals into and out of neighborhoods (Sampson and Morenoff 2006). In a recent examination of selection as a mechanism reproducing concentrated poverty, Robert Sampson and Patrick Sharkey found that even when selection decisions to move are explicitly modeled, inequality is replicated across racial-ethnic groups (2008).
2. Neighborhood reliability is a function of (1) the sample size (*N*) in each of the *j* neighborhoods and (2) the proportion of the total variance that is between

neighborhoods relative to that is within neighborhoods. Thus, the 2002 survey yields lower reliabilities overall given its substantially lower sample size.

3. Although one might expect evaluations of trust in different types of institutions to be strongly associated, some recent research questions this assumption by indicating that the strength of associations depends on variations in the information available or in individuals' differential experience with the respective institutions under evaluation (see chapter 10, this volume).

4. The significant Lagrange multiplier test (for example, LM-lag tests for a missing spatially lagged dependent variable) and the significant Robust Lagrange multiplier tests indicate that a spatial lag model is more appropriate than a spatial error model in predicting residents' overall trust and collective efficacy. Specifically, the spatial lag dependence is robust to tests for a missing spatial error term (Anselin 2005). Unlike those predicting time-lagged trust, models predicting change in trust or collective efficacy show no evidence of spatial dependence. The spatial dependence lag is not included in the models using network centralization or leader's reports on trust due to sample size limitations and to the fact that most of the sampled communities (thirty of the city's seventy-seven) are not contiguous.

5. Because of the small sample size at the community level (thirty), we specify only a small set of theoretically motivated control variables. Further sensitivity analyses revealed that the patterns remain once stability and change in poverty are in the model.

6. Conversely, one could also argue that tightly knit and centralized power structures can lead to lower trust and increased cynicism if these leaders become corrupt and monopolize access to community resources and power (Cook, Hardin, and Levi 2005).

References

Aldenderfer, Mark S., and Roger K. Blashfield. 1984. *Cluster Analysis.* Beverly Hills, Calif.: Sage Publications.

Alesina, Alberto, and Eliana La Ferrara. 2002. "Who Trusts Others?" *Journal of Public Economics* 85(2): 207–34.

Anselin, Luc. 2005. *Exploring Spatial Data with Geoda: A Workbook.* Department of Geography, Spatial Analysis Laboratory. Urbana: University of Illinois.

Bandura, Albert. 1997. *Self-Efficacy: The Exercise of Control.* New York: W. H. Freeman.

Blau, Peter. 1977. *Inequality and Heterogeneity: A Primitive Theory of Social Structure.* New York: Free Press.

Bourdieu, Pierre. 1986. "The Forms of Capital." In *Handbook of Theory and Research for the Sociology of Education,* edited by John G. Richardson. New York: Greenwood Press.

Bowles, Samuel. 2000. "Persistent Inequality in a Competitive World: Causes, Consequences, Remedies." Proposal to the Russell Sage Foundation and Santa Fe Institute.

Braithwaite, Valerie, and Margaret Levi, eds. 1998. *Trust and Governance.* New York: Russell Sage Foundation.
Bursik, Robert J. 1999. "The Informal Control of Crime Through Neighborhood Networks." *Sociological Focus* 32(1): 85–97.
Bursik, Robert J., and Harold Grasmick. 1993. *Neighborhoods and Crime: The Dimensions of Effective Community Control.* New York: Lexington Books.
Burt, Ronald S. 1992. *Structural Holes: The Social Structure of Competition.* Cambridge, Mass.: Harvard University Press.
———. 2005. *Brokerage and Closure. An Introduction to Social Capital.* Oxford: Oxford University Press.
Campbell, Donald. 1955. "The Informant in Quantitative Research." *American Journal of Sociology* 60(3): 339–42.
Clark, N. Terry. 1968. "Community Structure, Decision Making, Budget Expenditures, and Urban Renewal in 51 American Communities." *American Sociological Review* 33(August): 576–93.
Coleman, James S. 1988. "Social Capital in the Creation of Human Capital." *American Journal of Sociology* 94(S): 95–120.
———. 1990. *Foundations of Social Theory.* Cambridge, Mass: Harvard University Press.
Cook, Karen S., ed. 2001. *Trust in Society.* New York: Russell Sage Foundation.
Cook, Karen S., Russell Hardin, and Margaret Levi. 2005. *Cooperation Without Trust.* New York: Russell Sage Foundation.
Dasgupta, Partha. 1988. "Trust as a Commodity." In *Trust: Making or Braking Cooperative Relations,* edited by Diego Gambetta. Oxford: Blackwell Publishing.
Dirks, Kurt T., and Donald L. Ferrin. 2002. "Trust in Leadership: Meta-Analytic Findings and Implications for Organizational Research." *Journal of Applied Psychology* 87(4): 611–28.
Entwisle, Barbara, Katherine Faust, Ronald Rindfuss, and Toshiko Kaneda. 2007. "Networks and Contexts: Variation in the Structure of Social Ties." *American Journal of Sociology* 112(5): 1495–533.
Faust, Katherine, and John Skvoretz. 2002. "Comparing Networks Across Space and Time, Size, and Species." *Sociological Methodology* 32(1): 267–99.
Fischer, Claude S. 1975. "Toward a Subcultural Theory of Urbanism." *American Journal of Sociology* 80(6): 1319–341.
———. 1982. *To Dwell Among Friends: Personal Networks in Town and City.* Chicago: University of Chicago Press.
Fukuyama, Francis. 1995. *Trust: The Social Virtues and the Creation of Prosperity.* New York: Free Press.
GeoLytics. 2003. *Census CD Neighborhood Change Database from 1970–2002.* East Brunswick, N.J.: GeoLytics.
Gould, Roger V. 1989. "Power and Social Structure in Community Elites." *Social Forces* 68(2): 531–52.
Granovetter, Mark. 1985. "Economic Action, Social Structure, and Embeddedness." *American Journal of Sociology* 91(3): 481–510.
Hardin, Russell. 2001. "Conceptions and Explanations of Trust." In *Trust in Society,* edited by Karen S. Cook. New York: Russell Sage Foundation.
———. 2002. *Trust and Trustworthiness.* New York: Russell Sage Foundation.

Houston, Michael J., and Seymour Sudman. 1975. "A Methodological Assessment of the Use of Key Informants." *Social Science Research* 4(1): 151–64.

Knack, Stephen, and Philip Keefer. 1997. "Does Social Capital Have an Economic Payoff? A Cross-Country Investigation." *Quarterly Journal of Economics* 112(4): 1251–288.

Knight, Jack. 2001. "Social Norms and the Rule of Law: Fostering Trust in a Socially Diverse Society." In *Trust in Society,* edited by Karen S. Cook. New York: Russell Sage Foundation.

Knoke, David. 1990. *Political Networks: The Structural Perspective.* New York: Cambridge University Press.

Kornhauser, Ruth Rosner. 1978. *Social Sources of Delinquency: An Appraisal of Analytic Models.* Chicago: University of Chicago Press.

Kramer, Roderick M. 1999. "Trust and Distrust in Organizations: Emerging Perspectives, Enduring Questions." *Annual Review of Psychology* 50(February): 569–98.

Kramer, Roderick M., and Karen S. Cook, eds. 2004. *Trust and Distrust in Organizations: Dilemmas and Approaches.* New York: Russell Sage Foundation.

Kruskal, Joseph B., and Myron Wish. 1978. *Multidimensional Scaling.* Beverly Hills, Calif.: Sage Publications.

LaGrange, Randy, Kenneth Ferraro, and Michael Supanic. 1992. "Perceived Risk and Fear of Crime: Role of Social and Physical Incivilities." *Journal of Research in Crime and Delinquency* 29(3): 311–34.

Laumann, Edward O., and Franz Pappi. 1976. *Networks of Collective Action: A Perspective on Community Influence Systems.* New York: Academic Press.

LeClere, Felicia B., Richard G. Rogers, and Kimberly D. Peters. 1997. "Ethnicity and Mortality in the United States: Individual and Community Correlates." *Social Forces* 76(1): 169–98.

Luhmann, Niklas. 1979. "Trust: A Mechanism for the Reduction of Social Complexity." In *Trust and Power,* edited by Niklas Luhmann. New York: John Wiley & Sons.

Massey, Douglas S. 1996. "The Age of Extremes: Concentrated Affluence and Poverty in the Twenty-First Century." *Demography* 33(4): 395–412.

Massey, Douglas S., and Nancy A. Denton. 1988. "The Dimensions of Residential Segregation." *Social Forces* 67(2): 281–315.

Matsueda, Ross. 2006. "Differential Social Organization, Collective Action, and Crime." *Crime, Law and Social Change* 46(1): 3–33.

McEvily, Bill, Vincenzo Perrone, and Akbar Zaheer. 2003. "Trust as an Organizing Principle." *Organizational Science* 14(1): 91–103.

Molotch, Harvey, William Freudenburg, and Krista E. Paulsen. 2000. "History Repeats Itself, but How? City Character, Urban Tradition, and the Accomplishment of Place." *American Sociological Review* 65(6): 791–823.

Ottaviano, Gianmarco I. P., and Giovanni Perri. 2005. "Cities and Cultures." *Journal of Urban Economics* 58(2): 304–37.

Parijs, Phillippe Van. 2006. "Linguistic Diversity. What Is It? And Does It Matter?" Paper presented at the ECORE Conference on Challenges of Multilingual Societies. Brussels (June 9–10, 2006).

Park, Robert E. 1915. "The City: Suggestions for the Investigations of Human Behavior in the Urban Environment." *American Journal of Sociology* 20: 577–612.

Paxton, Pamela. 1999. "Is Social Capital Declining in the United States? A Multiple Indicator Assessment." *American Journal of Sociology* 105(1): 88–127.

PHDCN. 1995, 2002. *Community Survey.* Available at: http://www.icpsr.umich.educ/cocoon/PHDCN/SERIES/00206.xml?token=1.

Pierson, Paul. 2000. "Increasing Returns, Path Dependence, and the Study of Politics." *American Political Science Review* 94(2): 251–67.

Portes, Alejandro. 1998. "Social Capital: Its Origins and Applications in Modern Sociology." *Annual Review of Sociology* 24(1): 1–24.

Portes, Alejandro, and Julia Sensenbrenner. 1993. "Embeddedness and Immigration: Notes on the Social Determinants of Economic Action." *American Journal of Sociology* 98(6): 1320–50.

Putnam, Robert D. 1993. "The Prosperous Community: Social Capital and Public Life." *The American Prospect* 13(spring): 35–42.

———. 2000. *Bowling Alone: The Collapse and Renewal of American Community.* New York: Simon & Schuster.

———. 2007. "E Pluribus Unum: Diversity and Community in the Twenty-First Century: The 2006 Johan Skytte Prize Lecture." *Scandinavian Political Studies* 30(2): 137–74.

Raudenbush, Stephen W., and Robert J. Sampson. 1999. "'Ecometrics': Toward a Science of Assessing Ecological Settings, with Application to the Systematic Social Observation of Neighborhoods." *Sociological Methodology* 29(1): 1–41.

Robert, Stephanie. 1998. "Community-Level Socioeconomic Status Effects on Adult Health." *Journal of Health and Social Behavior* 39(1):18–37.

Ross, Catherine E., John Mirowsky, and Shana Pribesh. 2001. "Powerlessness and the Amplification Threat: Neighborhood Disadvantage, Disorder and Mistrust." *American Sociological Review* 66(August): 568–91.

Sampson, Robert J. 1995 and 2002. *Key Informant Panel Network Study.*

———. 2002. "Organized for What? Recasting Theories of Social (Dis)Organization." In *Crime and Social Organization: Advances in Criminological Theory,* edited by Elin Waring and David Weisburd. New Brunswick, N.J.: Transaction.

———. 2008. "Rethinking Crime and Immigration." *Contexts* 7(1): 28–33.

———. 2009. "Disparity and Diversity in the Contemporary City: Social (Dis)Order Revisited." *British Journal of Sociology* 60(1): 1–31.

Sampson, Robert J., and Jeffrey D. Morenoff. 2006. "Durable Inequality: Spatial Dynamics, Social Processes, and the Persistence of Poverty in Chicago Neighborhoods." In *Poverty Traps,* edited by Samuel Bowles, Steven N. Durlauf, and Karla Hoff. Princeton, N.J., and New York: Princeton University Press and Russell Sage Foundation.

Sampson, Robert J., and Stephen W. Raudenbush. 2004. "Seeing Disorder: Neighborhood Stigma and the Social Construction of Broken Windows." *Social Psychology Quarterly* 67(4): 319–42.

Sampson, Robert J., and Patrick Sharkey. 2008. "Neighborhood Selection and the Social Reproduction of Concentrated Racial Inequality." *Demography* 45(1):1–29.

Sampson, Robert J., Jeffrey D. Morenoff, and Felton Earls. 1999. "Beyond Social Capital: Spatial Dynamics of Collective Efficacy for Children." *American Sociological Review* 64(3): 633–60.
Sampson, Robert J., Jeffrey D. Morenoff, and Thomas Gannon-Rowley. 2002. "Assessing 'Neighborhood Effects': Social Processes and New Directions in Research." *Annual Review of Sociology* 28(2002): 443–78.
Sampson, Robert J., Stephen W. Raudenbush, and Felton Earls. 1997. "Neighborhoods and Violent Crime: A Multilevel Study of Collective Efficacy." *Science* 277(5328): 918–24.
Sampson, Robert J., Jeffrey D. Morenoff, Stephen W. Raudenbush, and Sapna Swaroop. 2007. "Ecometrics: The Use of Surveys and Observational Methods to Study Social Settings." In *Social Contexts of Pathways in Crime: Methods and Analytic Techniques,* edited by P. O. Wikstrom and Robert J. Sampson. Cambridge: Cambridge University Press.
Shaw, Clifford R., and Henry D. McKay. 1942/1969. *Juvenile Delinquency and Urban Areas.* Chicago: University of Chicago Press.
Steyvers, Mark, ed. 2002. "Multidimensional Scaling." In *Encyclopedia of Cognitive Science.* London: Nature Publishing.
Stigler, George J. 1968. *The Organization of Industry.* Homewood, Ill.: Irwin.
Suttles, Gerald D. 1984. "The Cumulative Texture of Local Urban Culture." *American Journal of Sociology* 90(2): 283–304.
———. 1990. *The Man-Made City: The Land-Use Confidence Game in Chicago.* Chicago: University of Chicago Press.
Taylor, Ralph B., and Margaret Hale. 1986. "Testing Alternative Models of Fear of Crime." *Journal of Criminal Law and Criminology* 77(1): 151–89.
Tilly, Charles. 1973. "Do Communities Act?" *Sociological Inquiry* 43(3–4): 209–40.
———. 1998. *Durable Inequality.* Berkeley: University of California Press.
Tremblay, Marc-Adelard. 1957. "The Key Informant Technique: A Non-Ethnographic Application." *American Anthropologist* 59(4): 688–701.
Tyler, Tom R. 1990. *Why People Obey the Law.* New Haven, Conn.: Yale University Press.
Tyler, Tom R., and Yen Huo. 2002. *Trust in the Law: Encouraging Public Cooperation with the Police and Courts.* New York: Russell Sage Foundation.
Uzzi, Brian. 1996. "The Sources and Consequences of Embeddedness for the Economic Performance of Organizations: The Network Effect." *American Sociological Review* 61(4): 674–98.
Walton, John. 1970. "A Systematic Survey of Community Power Research." In *The Structure of Community Power,* edited by Michael Aiken and Paul E. Mott. New York: Random House.
Wasserman, Stanley, and Katherine Faust. 1994. *Social Network Analysis: Methods and Applications.* Cambridge: Cambridge University Press.
Wellman, Barry. 1979. "The Community Question: The Intimate Networks of East Yorkers." *American Journal of Sociology* 84(5): 1201–231.
Wilson, William Julius. 1987. *The Truly Disadvantaged: The Inner City, the Underclass, and Public Policy.* Chicago: University of Chicago Press.
———. 1996. *When Work Disappears: The World of the New Urban Poor.* New York: Alfred A. Knopf.
Woolcock, Michael. 1998. "Social Capital and Economic Development: Toward a Theoretical Synthesis and Policy Framework." *Theory and Society* 27(2): 151–208.

PART III

INSTITUTIONS AND TRUST

Chapter 8

Trust and Credit

Bruce G. Carruthers

Many social interactions pose the issue of how much one person trusts another, but few seem to offer the clarity and ubiquity of credit transactions.[1] For many centuries and in almost all parts of the world, market exchanges have been accomplished on the basis of credit. Typically, this has meant that a seller extends credit to a buyer, who receives goods and gives in exchange a promise to pay in the future rather than cash. The two sides of the transaction occur at different times, and in the interim one party has extended credit to the other. For example, if one person ships lumber to a customer, who promises to pay in sixty days, then the seller has extended short-term trade credit to the buyer. Credit also arises through straightforward lending. Again, the two sides of the transaction are staggered in time: at one point the lender supplies a sum of money to the borrower, and at some other point (or points) in the future the borrower repays the sum (plus interest). At the first stage, the borrower receives money and makes a promise to the lender.

In both kinds of transactions, the seller or lender has to decide whether, or how much, they trust the buyer-borrower to complete their part of the transaction. Consistent with the definition Karen Cook, Russell Hardin, and Margaret Levi offer (2005, 7; see also Hardin 2001, 12–16),[2] trust in the matter of credit involves a three-way relation in which A, the creditor, trusts B, the debtor, to repay the loan. As we shall see, creditor expectations about the likelihood of debtor repayment are shaped by institutional as well as personal factors. The duration of credit transactions through time amplifies the element of uncertainty: who knows whether the buyer will pay in thirty days, or whether the borrower can repay the loan in ten years? Clearly the degree of uncertainty is generally greater for long-term as opposed to short-term debts. The exposure of the seller or lender also depends on the value of the goods sold, or on the size of the loan: the higher the worth, the greater the exposure. These two key aspects of credit, uncertainty,[3] and vulnerability, match exactly the two central elements of trust identified by Carol Heimer (2001). This is no surprise, for sellers (in the case of trade credit) and lenders (in the case of loan credit) must at the outset of the transaction consider how much they trust the other party to live up to their end of the bargain. Although creditors can adjust the terms of the transaction to reflect their concerns, such as charging higher interest rates to less trustworthy borrowers or making smaller loans, creditors ultimately make a simple choice—whether to lend. If they do not trust the buyer-borrower to repay, they do not lend. The stakes are relatively transparent and depend on the size and duration of the loan. And this trust problem occurs every time someone borrows money or seeks trade credit. It is a problem that has been posed and resolved one way or the other many, many times, and so we can use these ideas about trust to help understand how credit institutions operate.

In wondering how people deal with practical trust problems, it helps that credit is such a widespread and enduring feature of market economies, because this characteristic gives us an opportunity to survey the problem over time and space. In this chapter, I focus primarily on how credit institutions have changed over time, holding space constant by sticking to U.S. history.[4] American lenders in 1800 had to decide which borrowers they trusted, just as lenders do in 2009. But how they made that decision, and on what basis, changed dramatically. The problem of trust, insofar as it is manifested in credit, can be managed either by reducing the level of uncertainty or by reducing the degree of vulnerability, or both. Simply put, an entire apparatus has emerged to address the twin issues of uncertainty and vulnerability. This complex apparatus is more a loosely coupled assemblage than a monolith and has both private and public components, although the difference between them is fluid. Some parts are legal and formal, others are nonlegal (or extralegal) and informal. The components have also developed at different rates and at an unsynchronized pace. Furthermore, there are many types of credit, depending who is lending (banks, businesses, credit card companies, savings-and-loans, retailers), who is borrowing (individuals, businesses, nonprofits, governments), and the type of loan (trade credit, mortgage, consumer loan, business loan). In some cases, political interests motivated the creation of public institutions that supported particular kinds of credit (for example, home mortgages), and in other instances simple profit-seeking animated the creation of private institutions (for example, credit ratings, installment lending).

The overall result of these changes is that today, lenders have a much greater amount of information, and different kinds of information, than lenders had available to them circa 1800. Lenders also have more ways to protect themselves, and to reduce their vulnerability to borrower default. Consequently, the total volume of credit has grown tremendously. These two changes also altered what lenders focused on in their evaluation of debtors. Early on, lenders had to rely on informal information about the personal character of the borrower, and exploited the direct and indirect social networks in which borrowers were embedded, to assess trustworthiness. Over time, lenders have maintained their interest in character, but increasingly have been able to obtain greater amounts of quantitative information about the capacity of a debtor to repay a loan. This additional information has come from a variety of private and public sources, and its expansion has occurred in fits and starts. Furthermore, lenders now gather systematic information about large numbers of borrowers and can evaluate whole classes (or portfolios) of loans. To manage their vulnerability, lenders can use a variety of formal-legal devices that protect them from the possibility of debtor default, which include negotiability, security, securitization, debt covenants, and the like. Although the shift in sources of information and ways to manage vulnerability allowed credit to flourish, the process of change was uneven and haphazard.

Institutional development has affected the uncertainties and vulnerabilities lenders face, and consequently enhanced their willingness to trust debtors. For the overall economy, this has contributed to the vast increase in market activity. With so many transactions accomplished using credit rather than cash sales, greater trust means more exchange. The richness and density of market transactions has grown, as has their ability to reach across time and space. Over the nineteenth century, the United States went from a collection of separate regional economies, with selective connections between them, to become a nationally integrated economy with high volumes of interregional trade. The economy deepened temporally as well. More developed credit institutions allowed people, corporations, and government entities, to construct exchange relationships that unfolded over years and decades rather than months.

To organize my discussion of these developments in credit, and how they relate to the more basic issue of trust, I discuss a series of ten general factors that influence a lender's willingness to trust a debtor[5] and survey how each factor has evolved over time, roughly from the beginning of the nineteenth century to the middle of the twentieth. Each factor engages, in some fashion or other, the two fundamental problems of uncertainty and vulnerability. The factors range in scale from the individual, to the relational, to the institutional. They mostly operate in multiples, and a complex credit situation may involve all ten. But they also often send mixed or equivocal messages, with some factors signaling that a debtor is trustworthy and others suggesting not. Credit is a world with many shades of gray.

The first question faced by a lender concerns the authenticity of a promise. Even before wondering whether the borrower will keep her promise, a lender has to determine whether it is, in fact, an actual promise. Perhaps what looks like a promise is really an innocent joke. Anglo American commercial practice has generated a set of conventions that typically document the authenticity of a promise: is the promise made in writing, is it dated, witnessed, and signed? Has it been appropriately registered? Is the person making the promise eligible to make such a promise? (For example, is the person a legal minor? Can this person make commitments on behalf of the organization or firm?) Less formalized conventions govern the verbal expression of promises, but they too must be judged on their authenticity.

Let us assume, however, that someone has made a promise to pay (in the case of trade credit) or repay (in the case of a loan), and that their promise has been deemed authentic. Now the creditor must assess how willing and able the promise-maker is to keep their promise. The U.S. economy changed dramatically between 1800 and 1950, although credit was important throughout the period. Market transactions intensified and became more geographically dispersed as population grew in the midwestern and western regions of the country, and as national trade expanded. Industrialization and the emergence of large corporations increased the demand for large-scale borrowing. Over this period, ten basic factors entered into the assessments that creditors made about borrowers.[6] Their relative importance shifted over time, and varied from one type of credit to the next, but in some manner they all affected the level of information or vulnerability, or both, and so collectively shaped how willing creditors were to trust debtors. They range from microscopically individual to macroscopically institutional, with an intermediate social-network level. Similarly, they also vary in terms of how subject they are to individual control: social relations are relatively manipulable compared to legal institutions and financial systems. In the next section, I discuss them roughly in order from micro to macro.[7]

Individual Character

Credit practitioners and commentators have long believed that their personal character strongly affects people's willingness to keep the promises they make. Inner moral fiber, or some such psychological feature, was thought to distinguish genuine promise-keepers and so determine who is truly creditworthy. Such individuals can be relied on to keep their word, and because this propensity is an enduring trait, they will do so repeatedly. As one commentator put it, "the rock bottom foundation upon which the whole system of credit is based is character" (Skinner 1904, 91). Bankers' handbooks and manuals were filled with exhortations about the importance of character. In an article titled "Practical Banking," the *Bankers' Magazine* told its readers that "bankers, for their own interest, always have a regard to the moral character of the party with whom they deal; they inquire whether he be honest or tricky, industrious or idle, prudent or speculative, thrifty or prodigal, and they will more readily make advances to a man of moderate property and good morals than to a man of large property but inferior reputation" (*Banker's Magazine*, July 1884, 34). Character became enshrined as one of the Three C's—character, capacity, and capital—that bankers were always supposed to consider when making a loan (Kavanaugh 1921, 17).

Good character ensured that even flawed promises would be kept. It compensated for other deficiencies in a loan agreement or transaction. "As important as financial solvency in a mercantile community, is that strict integrity of purpose which guarantees reliance in the word, as well as the bond of the merchant. Were it necessary in all the transactions which take place between men of business to pass written guaranties, legally constructed and attested by witnesses, trade would be sadly hampered. The wheels of commerce would be clogged, and important time would be lost in gathering together the means requisite to guard against breaches of faith" (Hunt 1857, 241). In other words, good character could complete an incomplete contract, and ensure compliance with the spirit, and not only the imperfect letter, of an agreement.

Although creditors agreed that character mattered, it was no simple matter to discern it. What were the outward features that signified good character? To begin with, if inner character meant that someone kept their promises, then failure to keep such a promise sent a very strong message. A good reputation was a delicate thing that could be lost forever with a single mistake: "In no way, perhaps, can a young man destroy his business character more effectually than by obtaining the reputation of one who breaks his promises" (Hunt 1857, 118). In addition, there were no inconsequential promises: "Strict business integrity, in this particular, depends much on the general character. A person who pays little regard to slight promises, usually is somewhat careless of greater ones also" (119). Thus, a borrower's track record provided critical evidence about personal character.

Past behavior was not the only indicator of character, nor was it necessarily an adequate one.[8] Even more could be learned both directly and indirectly: "character is ascertained only by personal contact or references" (Fuller 1926, 379). Personal connections provided the intimate and ongoing contact needed to discern character. A lender might use her connections or draw on the experience of others. "Character is difficult to appraise. No precise unit of measurement exists. It is intangible and may easily be simulated. The credit man seeks to appraise character, yet in practice usually investigates reputation. Yet the two are distinct. Character lies within the man himself, while reputation exists in the minds of others" (Prendergast and Steiner 1931, 71). Clearly, this was a tacit or informal type of knowledge, not easily reducible to quantitative bottom lines. Hence something like looking someone in the eye was needed. "But the finer degrees of character such as perseverance, thrift, ingenuity—as well as weakness and purpose—may be appraised more accurately by word of mouth, the handshake, or a friendly moment with the applicant" (Haines 1936, 539). When it came to character, an experienced banker's instinct was deemed a valid measurement instrument.

Goals of the Debtor and Creditor

Why the debtor wants to borrow and why the creditor is willing to lend both affect how the creditor assesses the debtor's trustworthiness. For many years, banks avoided lending to individual persons because they recognized an important difference between personal and business loans: the purpose of the former was consumption, but of the latter to fund productive activity that would generate the cash flow necessary to repay the loan, among other things. Indeed, so important was the borrower's purpose that lenders found ways to earmark the money for specific purposes and to prohibit other uses. For example, a mortgage loan can be used to buy a particular house but not to fund a vacation trip to Las Vegas, and lenders use debt covenants to constrain how the money is spent. When the purpose of credit is to facilitate a sale, the connection to particular goals is direct. An installment loan, for example, gives credit to a buyer so that she can purchase a particular item (typically, a durable good like an automobile, piano, or sewing machine), and the credit cannot go to any other purpose. Such a tight linkage serves the lender's purpose of selling goods. The upshot is that lenders have long investigated the reasons why borrowers seek money, and have factored these into their decisions.

The lender's goals matter as well. We usually regard lending as a profit-seeking activity in which the lender is trying to optimize risk and rate of return. Loans can serve a variety of purposes, however, and these can attenuate the importance of repayment and make the other factors less critical. Sometimes, for example, loans are used for a philanthropic purpose and so though repayment may be desirable, it is not imperative (Ben-Amos 2000, 328–29). Loans may also be used to do favors, cultivate political constituents, support the local community, or develop the economy in a particular way (Fontaine 2001, 47; Muldrew 1998; Woo 1991). For example, many U.S. insurance companies were required in the nineteenth century to lend to state or municipal government, or to farmers, by investing in government bonds and farm mortgages (Keller 1963, 127). Again, repayment remains desirable but is not critical, and thus neither is the trustworthiness of the borrower. In fact, if loans are being used by lenders to do favors then it may be important that they not be repaid.

Informal Relationships Between Debtor and Creditor

Debtors and creditors often know each other through existing social relationships. These relationships can assume different forms and vary in intensity and duration. Perhaps they are cousins, or good friends, neighbors or mere acquaintances. But frequently they are not completely anonymous. Existing relations come with cognitive and normative baggage. Because of them, lenders may know a good deal about the personality, situation, and needs of the debtor. Likewise, debtors know a lot about their creditors. Depending on the relationship, the two sides may also have various expectations about and obligations to each other. These obligations will be relatively weak in the case of mere acquaintances, but can be strong when close kin are involved. A strong social connection between debtor and creditor can provide valuable private information about the debtor to the creditor and at the same time induce an obligation on the part of the creditor to lend to the debtor. One is expected to help friends and family, after all. But the obligations go both ways, and so it is also incumbent on debtors to meet their obligations to their friends and kin. Furthermore, ongoing social ties can offer to creditors a number of extralegal ways to enforce compliance with the loan agreement (Macaulay 1963).[9]

Existing social relations do not guarantee anything or provide absolute assurances, but their central role in credit was quite striking, particularly early on. In her study of early nineteenth-century New England banks, Naomi Lamoreaux found a distinctive pattern of lending that she termed *insider lending* (1994). This meant that bank funds were loaned either to bank directors or to people with a direct connection to the directors (friends, relatives, and so on). Insider lending was common and (at the time) not deemed problematic or corrupt. According to Lamoreaux, it made sense in a situation in which it was difficult to get reliable or accurate information about strangers. This pattern was not unique, for other studies of credit in premodern economies show how often it went through familial, religious, or friendship networks (Fontaine 2001; Lamoreaux 1994; Hancock 2005; Hanley 2004; Hunt 1996; Boyce 1995, 33).

Insider lending and its variants is constrained by the limited span of social networks. Even a very large family offers only a limited number of potential loan partners. With economic development, credit flowed increasingly outside such networks and so lenders had to devise different ways to manage their trust problems. In the United States, Lamoreaux argued, the end of the nineteenth century witnessed the development of specialized bank credit departments the job of which was to gather the information that before had flowed through informal social networks (1994, 105).[10] But even so, informal social relationships have not become irrelevant. In fact, for certain economic sectors the evidence suggests that social ties remain important in the extension of credit, for example, in contemporary U.S. bank lending to small and mid-sized firms (Akhavenin, Goldberg, and White 2004; Uzzi 1999; Uzzi and Gillespie 2002; Uzzi and Lancaster 2003).

Formal Contractual Relationship Between Debtor and Creditor

With a reliable and developed legal system, many of the creditor's concerns can be addressed using a formal contract. Depending on what kind of legal devices are available, a lender can enter into an enforceable agreement with the debtor that provides various protections (to reduce vulnerability) and types of information (to reduce uncertainty). A relatively complete and unambiguous contract (absolute completeness and specificity are unattainable) means that the creditor doesn't have to depend as much on the honesty and good character of the debtor. Such contracts also make it easier to transact with a wider range of individuals, including those who are strangers or who are outside existing social networks.

Financial contracts may contain provisions that require the debtor to provide information to the creditor, and even to specify the exact nature and timing of that information, such as audited balance sheets provided on a quarterly basis. Such provisions are termed *protective* or *restrictive* covenants and over time have become increasingly elaborate and sophisticated—witness the growing length of railway bond indentures between the early and late nineteenth-century (see Lister 1985; Smith and Warner 1979; Zinbarg 1975).[11] With such information, a creditor can monitor a debtor and intervene should the debtor fail to meet a critical financial threshold.

Contracts can also be used to reduce the creditor's vulnerability to debtor default. Two legal features have been particularly important in this respect, negotiability and security. The first allows creditors to exit the debt relationship before the loan has come to maturity, and the second gives creditors claim over debtor assets (the collateral) in the event of default.

Negotiability, as in negotiable securities, developed in English common law during the early eighteenth century and is significant because it makes debts liquid (Holden 1955). It allows people to transfer debts, trade them, pass them on, and in effect use them like money. Negotiability—and similar qualities like assignability, alienability, and transferability—means that debts do not necessarily bind the debtor and the creditor together until the debt is fully repaid. The original creditor can transfer the debt to a third party, to whom the debtor will be equally obliged, and therefore step out of the debt relationship and recover the capital invested in the loan. If, for example, A lends money to B, and B signs a promissory note to A or bearer then A can transfer the note to someone else, C, who as bearer will have a valid legal claim over B. Negotiability means that debtors may not know who their creditors are. It also means that A can use B's note to satisfy A's own debts to others, thus B's note functions like money. Finally, negotiability reposes the original trust problem: A may have decided that B is trustworthy enough to borrow money, but when A tries to transfer B's note to C, C now has to evaluate B's trustworthiness. Negotiability lifts trust out of the context of a specific debtor-creditor relationship and gives the issue greater generality and mobility. It also creates the possibility of a market for debt.

In traditional common law, debts could not be transferred (matters were different in the lex mercatoria). It was not until legal developments of the late seventeenth and early eighteenth century, like the Promissory Notes Act of 1704, that negotiability emerged as a stable and general feature of private and public debts (Carruthers 1996, chapter 5). Along with common law, negotiability was transplanted from England to its American colonies, but until the uniform law movement of the late nineteenth century state-by-state variation in how negotiability worked was considerable (Beutel 1940). Nevertheless, negotiability in whatever variant gave creditors the chance to stop being creditors even before the debtor repaid the loan, and so allowed them to protect themselves preemptively from debtor misbehavior. Negotiability also helped dislodge American debts from the ongoing social relations in which they were embedded, and allowed debt obligations to become more geographically and socially dispersed (Mann 2002, 4, 13).

If negotiability gave mobility to debts, security added "stickiness" to them. A secured debt grants to the creditor an interest in property owned by the debtor (the collateral). In the event of debtor default, the creditor is legally empowered to seize the property and use it to repay or offset the loan. The oldest version of a secured loan is the venerable mortgage, a loan secured by real estate.

The ability to seize and liquidate a valuable asset obviously helps lenders reduce their financial vulnerability. But the effectiveness of this type of protection depends on certain conditions. First, the identity of the collateral must be completely specific. For example, if a loan is secured by real estate, one must know exactly which piece of land is the collateral. Second, the borrower must have clear title over the collateral, that is, no shared ownership, competing interests, and so on. Third, title must be transferable to the creditor, because not all types of property are freely alienable.[12] Fourth, the value of the collateral must be estimable and relatively stable because, in practice, valuation can be quite a difficult undertaking (see Brief 1966). Finally, creditors prefer liquid collateral, that is, collateral that can be readily resold. They usually want to convert the collateral into cash rather than keep it in its original form (Wall 1919, 58).

Secured lending has developed with the emergence of new forms of collateral. Traditionally, land functioned as collateral for mortgage loans. Later, durable goods could be subject to a lien in a so-called chattel mortgage. Much nineteenth-century installment lending was secured by the tangible objects sold on credit: sewing machines, pianos, agricultural equipment, and so on. In time, intangible property could function as collateral: accounts receivable, stocks and bonds, or commercial paper (Kniffen 1915, 237, 389). Furthermore, valuation of collateral has changed dramatically with the development of general accounting standards, pricing models, and the entire apparatus of real estate valuation. Additionally, the issue of title over property is mostly resolved through various public registration and filing requirements.

Although the ideal of a complete and transparently unambiguous contract is unattainable, the complexity and sophistication of financial contracts has increased. Several important features, including negotiability, security, and protective covenants, address directly how credit is affected by the issues of uncertainty and vulnerability. Much of this has been made possible by the development of functioning U.S. commercial law, something that no single creditor or debtor has been able to control.

Some important interactions can occur between formal (contractual) relations and informal relations when they simultaneously conjoin the same debtor and creditor. These interactions may offset each other. For instance, the obligations and expectations that informal relationships entail can be very effective in compensating for the gaps, ambiguities, and inconsistencies that exist in a formal agreement. Informal relations help "grease the wheels" and fill in the gaps of formal structures. But the addition of a formal arrangement on top of an existing informal relationship can sometimes undermine the latter. Someone who borrows money from a close friend on a handshake basis may take offense if the friend subsequently insists on an exactingly formal loan contract. Formalizing an informal arrangement connotes distrust, and may subvert rather than bolster the informal arrangement. Of course, with a formal contract that bestows enough security, a creditor may not worry about offending debtors or signaling distrust, for they may think that the collateral offers enough protection.

As a formal contractual feature, negotiability has had a very special effect because it allows indebtedness to move outside the dyad that created the debt in the first place. In so doing, it creates new debtor-creditor dyads between parties who may be complete strangers, and so reduces the importance of informal social ties. Relationally based informal expectations and obligations cannot apply between anonymous parties. Negotiability confers mobility onto debts, and thereafter indebtedness becomes a more arms-length connection between socially and geographically distant parties. Given that social networks tend to be relatively narrow, with far fewer people inside the network than outside it, negotiability expands the set of potential partners on both sides of credit. So, for example, when banks kept home mortgages in their own loan portfolio, it was possible for a debtor in financial trouble to renegotiate the terms or to obtain some measure of forbearance from a banker with whom she had a long-standing personal relationship. But when banks simply originate mortgages, and then sell them off, as happens with mortgage securitization, the troubled debtor has no personal connection to the ultimate creditor, and so no social grounds on which to make an appeal.

Debtor's Network

A debt directly connects the debtor to the creditor. But debtors invariably have multiple economic and social ties to a number of others, as well. And networks outside of the debtor-creditor dyad can have an independent effect on trust within it, depending on what position the debtor occupies in the larger network. For example, consider that a debtor who enjoys high social status within a local community may suffer if she fails to honor her debts—her valuable status and reputation function as hostages, and fear of losing them will encourage her to behave in a more trustworthy fashion. Her status and reputation, however, exist only by virtue of her place within a particular social network that goes beyond the creditor, and by the ability of information about her default to circulate within that network. Other kinds of third-party networks insert debtors into webs of informal obligations that bolster creditworthiness. For example, someone from a wealthy family is connected to people who can act like informal guarantors of a loan: their familial obligations to the debtor bolster the debtor's own obligations to the creditor.[13] Or, someone who is obliged to care for others may behave more responsibly and be perceived to be a better risk: witness the long-standing belief that married men with children are more trustworthy than single men. Of course, creditors are also interested in other formal obligations that a debtor may have to other creditors, for example, your credit card company wants to know whether you owe a lot of money to a finance company, but these obligations are normally tracked as part of the assessment of a debtor's financial status (see the next section).

These social networks mostly form independently of the debtor-creditor connection, and they follow nonmarket logics. Systematic information about them is hard to obtain. In some settings, however, their value has been deliberately exploited, and the networks may even be cultivated on purpose. Consider participation in social networks that involve joint-liability for debts, as in many micro-credit arrangements. The structure of today's Grameen Bank and rotating credit associations, early twentieth-century credit unions and late nineteenth-century Hebrew free loan societies, and similar arrangements reflect deliberate social network engineering (see, for example, Biggart 2001; Ham and Robinson 1923; Light and Bonacich 1988, 243–72; Light, Kwuon, and Zhong 1990; Pitt and Khandker 1998; Tenenbaum 1993). Lateral social ties and obligations among a set of debtors make them all more creditworthy.

Debtor's Financial Status

Today, an entire institutional apparatus makes it possible to gather and process information, and so estimate a debtor's financial situation. Financial status determines the debtor's ability (but not willingness) to repay a loan. Will the debtor have enough resources to meet the payments? The ability of creditors to measure financial status has grown enormously with the general increase in systematic quantitative financial information, and such information helps them transform uncertainty into risk. Such information comes from many sources, both public and private, and its creation is very much a collective undertaking involving government agencies, regulatory bodies, professionals, and private for-profit firms, as well as the debtors themselves.

In the early nineteenth century, firms were generally small and opaque. Very little information about their inner financial dealings was available to outsiders. Indeed, the trained professionals who could provide such information did not yet exist (the accountancy profession had not yet formed), nor were there general standards for what such information should be or how it should be calculated (no generally accepted accounting principles). The development and creation of such information occurred in fits and starts. One very important first step came with the establishment of the U.S. credit rating industry. Starting in the 1840s, a number of firms, including the predecessor of today's Dun and Bradstreet, began systematically to assess the creditworthiness of tens of thousands, and later hundreds of thousands, of U.S. firms.[14] Before long, firms like Bradstreet's and the Mercantile Agency were publishing entire series of reference books listing firms by name and by location, and then appending a summary measure of their pecuniary strength and general credit.

The reference books rated firms in accordance with a specific category system, and were intended to help other firms decide whether to extend trade credit to the rated firm. Around 1880, for example, the Mercantile Agency measured pecuniary strength using an ordinal scale that estimated the capital in the firm, ranging from A+ ($1,000,000 or more) down to K (less than $2,000). General credit was also measured with ordered categories, from A1 (unlimited), through 1, 1½ (high), 2 and 2½ (good), down to 3 and 3½ (fair). In rating firms, credit raters used a national network of correspondents and reporters. These sources, who were often local attorneys, bankers, or business notables, submitted to the credit agencies unsystematic, qualitative information, of variable provenance and uncertain reliability. This confidential information was recorded, organized, and transformed into a quasiquantitative categorical rating. The latter were compiled into voluminous reference books and provided to subscribers, who could also commission specialized reports on a particular firm. Later in the nineteenth century, credit raters sought information directly from the rated firms themselves, usually in the form of a statement. The latter, in effect an unaudited simple summary of assets and liabilities, was often hard to obtain, and many firms simply refused to say anything about their own financial affairs.

As a business, credit rating was very successful and so, by the end of the nineteenth century, the Mercantile Agency, one of the two biggest credit raters, was rating more than 1 million firms and issuing reference books four times a year (Norris 1978, 110). Credit rating was a purely private operation and essentially unregulated. But it did provide systematic credit-relevant information about many, many small firms. In addition to their use by companies dispersing trade credit, credit ratings were also adopted at the end of the nineteenth century by credit insurance firms, who relied on the ratings to estimate their own risks and to price insurance policies (Federal Reserve Board 1922). Banks began to use credit ratings in the specialized credit departments they organized toward the end of the nineteenth century (Newfang 1912, 640), and John Moody explicitly emulated the credit raters when he began to rate railway and corporate bonds. The ratings done today by Moody's and Standard and Poor's are extremely consequential for the ability of corporations, governments, and even nation states, to borrow (Sinclair 2005). Credit ratings, as a privately created form of information, came to permeate the U.S. financial system.

New forms of information also emerged and circulated as a consequence of public regulatory reforms. The National Banking System set up during the Civil War required national banks to file standardized financial reports with the Comptroller of the Currency. Regulation of railroads involved setting rates that allowed them to earn a fair rate of return, which meant that regulators had to devise a set of accounting rules for calculating the rate of return (Yates 1989, 135). The establishment of the Federal Reserve System restricted the kinds of commercial paper eligible for the new discount facility, and so new accounting requirements had to be put in place to determine eligibility. This in turn pressured member banks to obtain financial statements from their corporate customers. The imposition of an income tax also helped standardize the reporting of financial information for both individuals and corporations (Edwards 1958). And the creation of the Securities and Exchange Commission (SEC) during the New Deal set filing and disclosure requirements for all publicly traded companies. Private regulation played a role as well. The New York Stock Exchange imposed disclosure requirements on the firms listed on the exchange. Finally, these various public and private imperatives for more financial information helped spur the development of the U.S. accounting profession, which came to specialize in creating and interpreting such information (Miranti 1986). In all these cases, new systems of public oversight or private accountability inadvertently created information that was very useful to potential creditors.

Even very simple information can be valuable: simply noting and recording a debtor's financial track record helps to determine who is trustworthy. Has this debtor ever defaulted on a loan or filed for bankruptcy? How many late payments have they made? What is their total debt burden? Have creditors ever taken the debtor to court? What debt load has the debtor been able successfully to service? Although haphazard and uneven, the century-length development of a high volume of quantitative information about the financial status of borrowers has certainly helped to address the problem of uncertainty for creditors. And yet, as the recent examples of Enron and WorldCom attest, accounting information is never 100 percent accurate, and in some circumstances can be completely subverted.

Creditor Networks

Creditors, like debtors, are frequently embedded in social networks that affect how they perceive and manage the trust problems they face. The networks that matter for credit are those joining the creditor to other debtors, and those connecting creditors to each other. How a creditor deals with a particular debtor depends not only on the merits of that particular loan, but also on all the other loans that the creditor has made to other debtors. Furthermore, lenders rely on their peers in deciding what to do. In other words, loans are made in a larger context. Two strategies have developed that deliberately consider particular loans in light of the entire loan portfolio—diversification and securitization. And linkages to peer groups often encourage heuristics that involve some kind of emulation.

Even without a statistical apparatus that would allow them to calculate correlations, covariances, or betas, bankers have for some time appreciated the value of not overconcentrating their assets. Banker's handbooks urged them not to put too many loans into the same industry or geographic region. Early conceptions of loan diversification seemed less informed by a sense that uncorrelated risks would reduce the overall variance of a bank's loan portfolio than by a concern over the balance of power between lenders and borrowers. The *Bankers' Magazine* commanded its readers: "Distribute your loans rather than concentrate them in a few hands. Large loans to a single individual or firm, although some times proper and necessary, are generally injudicious and frequently unsafe. Large borrowers are apt to control the bank, and when this is the relation between a bank and its customers, it is not difficult to decide which in the end will suffer" (August 1884, 113). Later on, readers were warned that "more than one bank has been wrecked by the unwise plan of 'putting too many eggs into one basket'" (*Bankers' Magazine,* June 1901, 815). The eggs-in-a-basket message was repeated in an article that went on to declare that "investment nowadays is coming to be a science, and one of its principles which is coming to be more and more clearly defined is that of diversification" (*Bankers' Magazine,* March 1910, 449). By the 1920s, the statistical aspects of diversification were becoming clearer, though the exact details were not. One article favoring diversification argued that investment in a variety of securities enabled the "law of averages" to operate and so protect the portfolio (*Harvard Business Review,* January 1927, 207).

Diversification meant that lenders stopped considering loans as stand-alone transactions. They had to be balanced against a larger context of all the other loans a lender had made or intended to make. Loans that seemed attractive strictly on their own merits might not be prudent if they were too much like all the other loans the bank had made, and seemingly unwise loans might make better sense as a way to diversify the larger portfolio. Diversification meant that even if it made good sense to trust a debtor of type A, it was not a good idea to trust too many debtors of type A.

Securitization refers to a process by which lenders make loans, group them into large pools, and then sell off the pools to third parties (Fabozzi and Modigliani 1992). It is very common in the home mortgage market where a variety of nonbank investors purchase mortgage-backed securities created by mortgage lenders (Carruthers and Stinchcombe 1999, 368–70). Lenders make loans, but do not hold those loans in their portfolios. The loans are grouped with large numbers of other similar loans and then sold to investors. Standardization of loans ensures that they are homogeneous enough to be grouped together. Securitization transforms how lenders and investors think about the loans into something close to how insurance companies think about risks—actuarially. If the loans in the pool are similar enough, good estimates of the probability that a borrower will default or a loan will become "nonperforming" are possible.[15] With such probabilities, uncertainties become risks and hence relatively tractable.

Both diversification and securitization alter how creditors assess trustworthiness. Their attention is shifted from single loan transactions to aggregates of loans. Rather than interrogate a particular case, lenders can assess overall trends and probabilities and simply add enough margin that the interest rate will cover expected losses. They will also be mindful of the variance as well as the average of loan performance. Rather than be deeply knowledgeable about a specific loan, lenders manage on the basis of statistical measures of portfolios of loans. For this to work, the loan pools must be statistically tractable, and the lenders must be able to generate and analyze statistical data. But when such information can be obtained, it enables lenders to manage their vulnerability in new ways.

Creditors are also connected to each other. Whether through direct personal relationships, business organizations, business school connections, corporate director interlocks, fraternal associations, or whatnot, creditors often have their own network of peers. When making loan decisions under conditions of uncertainty, lenders behave like other decision makers and often rely on various heuristics, rules of thumb, and shortcuts. One of the most common heuristics involves imitating others, and here peers form the relevant reference group for imitation. A contemporary banker who is concerned about the uncertainties of lending in a developing economy like Thailand will likely take note of the fact that "everyone is doing it." Certainly a number of lenders recently became active in the subprime mortgage market largely because other lenders were already active. Innovation introduced into a tightly connected community of lenders can set off cascades of imitation and through a diffusion process produce herd-like behavior (Strang and Soule 1998).

Intermediaries Between Debtors and Creditors

Transactions between debtors and creditors are not always conceived, negotiated, or consummated directly. Sometimes, a third party arises as an intermediary, standing between the other two and bringing them together much as a matchmaker brings couples together. Intermediaries can function like brokers, providing credible and confidential information to both sides about each other, and vouchsafing a debtor's reliability or a creditor's good faith. Investment banks (in the United States) and merchant banks (in the United Kingdom) have for many decades brought together investors and corporate borrowers. One thinks of J. P. Morgan and his ability to steer British capital into U.S. railroads in the nineteenth century. In such situations, the trust problem facing creditors is transformed by the intermediary's role: instead of worrying about whether to trust the borrower, the lender depends on the trustworthiness of the intermediary.

Intermediaries span what Ronald Burt called structural holes (1992). Such holes are gaps within economic networks where potential links do not exist. They could be there, but they are not. Someone who can span that hole, that is, who becomes connected to two parties who are not already connected to each other, can broker transactions and take advantage of that structural disconnection (on intermediaries and the corporate director interlock network, see Gulati 1995; Mizruchi 1996). The intermediary will have more information about the opportunities, needs, and constraints facing the two sides than they will know about each other. When brokers specialize in intermediation, they can build up the kind of reputation that can lead others to deem them trustworthy. Would-be transactors will first seek out intermediaries rather than each other, and will use the intermediaries to help them manage their own uncertainties and vulnerabilities. Although there has been little change in the fact of intermediation (intermediaries operated in 1800, in 1950, and in between), there has been some development in who functions as an intermediary. For example, the rise of the investment banking industry at the end of the nineteenth century institutionalized a set of intermediaries for corporate finance.

General Remedies for Debtor Insolvency

Contract law allows debtors and creditors to design, implement, and enforce their agreements using the coercive powers of the state. If a debtor defaults on a specific loan, the creditor can initiate legal proceedings to recover the money, seize the collateral, and so on. Sometimes, however, debtors are in such financial difficulty that they default simultaneously on all their loans—they are, in effect, insolvent. Total assets cannot satisfy total liabilities, and the firm is not paying its bills as they become due. Bankruptcy law provides a set of rules to deal with this kind of a situation, and sets a legal baseline for business failure, spelling out what happens when the entire nexus of contracts is not viable (Carruthers and Halliday 1998). Bankruptcy law covers both individual and corporate debtors, though the rules are usually different for the two groups, and through its operation affects the vulnerability of creditors to debtor failure.

Once a business bankruptcy filing has been set in motion, bankruptcy law typically does a number of things: suspends debt collection efforts against the bankrupt debtor (the so-called stay), collects all the debtor's assets into a single estate, and registers all the claims against the debtor and ranks them in priority. In the case of a corporate debtor, the pool of assets is capped by limited liability, so creditors cannot reach into the personal pockets of corporate shareholders. There are two general outcomes to business bankruptcy, liquidation and reorganization. In the case of liquidation, the assets are dispersed to the claimants in accordance with the priority rules, employees are laid off, and the firm is dissolved. The key issue is priority because in liquidation high priority creditors receive a greater proportion of their claims than do low priority creditors, who may get only pennies on the dollar. In the case of reorganization, the firm is restructured, its contractual obligations to suppliers, banks, and employees are modified or even suspended, and the firm is placed on a new financial and operational footing so that it can become successful again. The key issue here is the reorganization plan: Who can propose it?

Who can negotiate it? Who can veto it? And, within that plan, who bears the brunt of the costs of reorganization?

All bankruptcy laws provide for business liquidation, but they vary in how easy it is to attempt a reorganization. For both outcomes, bankruptcy law manages the conflicting interests of competing claimants. Every creditor or stakeholder wants someone else to bear the financial pain. In a liquidation, an insolvent firm's bank wants to see bank loans fully repaid, even if it means that trade creditors receive little. In a reorganization, workers would prefer to see bank loans refinanced at lower interest rates than big wage cuts.

Individual bankruptcies tend to be simpler matters. The debtor's assets are seized, liquidated, and used to pay off the creditors. The debtor receives a discharge from the balance of her obligations and gets a fresh start, and creditors receive some measure of repayment. Bankruptcy law can also make some debts nondischargeable, such as child support payments or income tax payments, and can protect certain types of property from seizure, homestead exemptions, for example. Thus the fresh start may not be entirely fresh and the liquidation may not be complete.

As stipulated by the U.S. constitution, bankruptcy law is federal law. However, the constitution does not require such a law and in fact for much of the nineteenth century there was none (Skeel 2001). Passage of a new bankruptcy law would be followed by a wave of bankruptcy filings, and then the law would be repealed. For example, the 1867 bankruptcy law was repealed in 1878, having been used by large numbers of southern debtors to settle their debts to northern creditors. With the repeated passage and repeal of bankruptcy laws, the legal baseline for failure proved to be quite unstable over time. Not until 1898 was a permanent bankruptcy law enacted. It was subsequently modified during the New Deal, and then again in 1978 and 2005.

Bankruptcy law sets a backdrop for lending. When debtors fail completely and are unable to meet their contractual obligations to creditors, bankruptcy law is activated. For lenders wondering how much they can trust borrowers, bankruptcy law sets limits around the vulnerability of creditors by setting the conditions for worst-case scenarios. Debtor-friendly bankruptcy laws will make lenders more cautious, ceteris paribus, whereas creditor-friendly laws will encourage them to lend more. A smoothly functioning bankruptcy law offers legal certainty and sets the level of financial vulnerability for creditors of failing firms. Bankruptcy law is not as readily manipulable as a contract is, but through political lobbying an interest group can shape the overall direction of legislative reform. North-South relations certainly shaped the Bankruptcy Act of 1867 (Thompson 2004), for example, and creditor groups were influential in pushing through the 1898 law (Skeel 2001, 26).[16] Overall, the legal uncertainties associated with repeated passage and repeal of bankruptcy laws over the nineteenth century has given way to a more stable framework, starting with the 1898 law. The legal backdrop for lending has become something that lenders and debtors could take for granted.

Overall Monetary Environment

Like commercial law, the monetary system is part of the context in which credit relationships operate. Because debts are eventually to be repaid in money, the status of the money supply can have a significant effect on debtor-creditor relations. Whether to lend to a debtor can be influenced by whether one trusts the money or legal tender that such a debtor would use to repay the loan (Moss 2002, 87). Dramatic changes in overall price levels or widespread uncertainty about the value of money can so favor debtors (in the case of inflation) or creditors (deflation) as to affect the overall willingness of people to lend money to others (Mann 2002, 172–74). Furthermore, the entire monetary system is occasionally subject to discontinuous shifts, as when the U.S. monetary system changed substantially during the Civil War, with the formation of the National Banking System, and again with the establishment of the Federal Reserve System in 1913. Before the Civil War, for example, individual banks issued their own bank notes, which then circulated along with the notes of all other banks. The real value of a bank note depended not only on the nominal sum printed on the paper, but also on the solvency of the issuing bank (Helleiner 2003). Furthermore, much less was known about the solvency of small out-of-state banks than about local institutions. Such nonstandardized and heterogeneous money (compounded by the problem of counterfeiting) made it hard for those receiving cash to know what it was they were getting, and complicated the trust problem lenders faced. After worrying about the debtor, lenders had to worry about the money. In addition, during the Civil War, the United States went off the gold standard and did not return to gold convertibility until much later. The return to gold was hardly an uncontroversial move, because it came to pass only after raging debates between bullionists (hard money) and greenbackers (soft money), and after much political contention that pitted debtor groups against creditor interests (Carruthers and Babb 1996). Not until the Federal Reserve System was established in 1913 did the United States have a central bank charged with managing the monetary system to avoid or ameliorate financial crises. And throughout this entire period, the U.S. banking system has, by international standards, depended much less on branch banks and much more on unit banks. This has made the system much more vulnerable to financial crises, and more difficult for individual banks to diversify their lending.

Like bankruptcy law, the monetary system is part of the overall backdrop for credit. As a system, it is not readily manipulable by individuals, except through large-scale political interventions. The latter do occur, and so, for example, money and banking became salient political topics during the postbellum period, after the 1907 financial crisis, and during the Great Depression, but such moments are relatively rare. The status of the monetary system affects the balance of vulnerability between debtors and creditors. Unstable or heterogeneous money increases the overall level of uncertainty, and money whose value is shifting over time in one direction or another (increasing or decreasing) can favor debtors over creditors, or vice versa. Inflation or deflation can also subvert the impact of the regulations that governments often impose on financial sector institutions to control or direct lending and savings (for example, interest rate caps, usury laws, dollar-denominated threshold points, and so on).

Complications of Credit

Credit situations need not involve all ten factors, though they typically involve more than just one or two. Whichever factors operate in a given situation, the more fundamental issues of uncertainty and vulnerability always appear. The basic elements of trust also happen to be the basic elements of credit. The ten factors are not equally important in all instances, and lenders clearly put more emphasis on some than on others, witness the particular stress placed on character. Lenders and borrowers tended to be more conscious of factors like formal contracts and informal social ties than of those like bankruptcy law, because the latter operated more in the background. And factors operated at varying levels of generality. The effect of the monetary system is pervasive, whereas the impact of a particular contract is felt mostly by the two parties it binds.[17] Furthermore, their relative importance has shifted over time following various legal and institutional developments. But each factor affected either knowledge or vulnerability and so influenced a creditor's willingness to lend, or a debtor's eagerness to borrow.

Obviously life is simplest when everything lines up in the same direction, making the lending decision an easy one (that is, the debtor is of good character, signs an airtight formal contract, has a strong informal relationship with the creditor, would lose her reputation in the event of default, and so on) or, conversely, that all factors go in the other direction. Matters are seldom so clear cut, however. Often some aspects signal a higher level of trustworthiness while others indicate less, giving the creditor a mixed picture to sort out.

One reason for mixed pictures is that various trade-offs and linkages exist among the factors: they do not operate independently. Bolstering one can weaken another, or two factors can positively reinforce each other. For example, a creditor's goals will often depend on what kind of informal relationship he or she has with the debtor: loans to strangers are more likely to be purely profit-seeking transactions than loans made to siblings. There may be less obligation to repay fully and promptly loans among close relatives or intimate friends. In this way, social relations shape goals, which in turn affect the importance of contractual completeness, diversification, and so on.

If the goal of lending is to earn a profit, lenders and borrowers may be motivated to seek third-party intermediaries when formal law is unreliable and credible financial information is scarce. In such cases, both borrowers and lenders consciously adapt to legal or informational deficiencies. Similarly, strong informal social ties can be used to obtain confidential information about a borrower, just as elaborate contracts can. Strong social ties can also provide credible sanctions to punish would-be defaulters.

Although some factors are clearly connected bilaterally, others have a more unilateral significance. They affect credit, obviously, and some of the other factors as well, but they are not themselves shaped by the other factors. The functionality of a bankruptcy law, for example, influences what kind of contracts creditors will use, but neither debtor character, informal social ties, intermediation, nor diversification strategies influence bankruptcy law. Factors operating at higher levels of generality (for example, bankruptcy law, monetary system) help set the terms for the other factors, but the effects are not reciprocal.

In weighing all the relevant factors, the creditor comes to some overall assessment of the would-be borrower and the likelihood of repayment. And then the creditor extends the loan, or not, and if the former adjusts the terms of loan (interest rate, maturity) to reflect that overall judgment. Interdependencies among the ten factors mean that change in one factor does not just directly change lending, for indirectly it influences other factors that also affect lending.

The development of one basis for trust made some other bases less problematic. One particularly important institutional development had to do with the law. In eighteenth-century New York, improved functioning of the legal system meant that courts, commercial law, and formal contracts substituted for personal relationships in the extension of credit (Rosen 1997, 72–73). Effective legal sanctions can replace the informal sanctions that social relationships make possible. A similar change occurred across the United States over a broader period as domestic commercial law became more effective. During the nineteenth century, American local and regional markets became integrated at a national level, and along with long-distance trade came national credit information (supplied by credit reporting firms like R. G. Dun), and the development of laws that enforced the property rights involved with commercial paper and other forms of negotiable instruments (Freyer 1982; Weinberg 1982). These formal legal means allowed for more anonymous borrowing, and made it easier for people to lend to strangers, outside the context of personal relationships, social networks, and intermediaries.[18]

Systematic credit information has developed considerably since the nineteenth century, and is now widely used not only in the United States but also around the globe to facilitate exchange among strangers (Olegario 2003; Sinclair 2005). In general, lenders have much more standardized, detailed, quantitative information about borrowers than they did in the past, and they use that information to make assessments about individual borrowers and entire groups of borrowers. Quantitative information connotes science and objectivity, even when such information is created out of messy and unreliable sources (Porter 1995). Furthermore, much of this information was created in response to public policy or various regulatory interventions, and not necessarily because of private demand. Consequently, both the format of the information and its intended purposes may not perfectly suit the narrow concerns of lenders.

At a macro-institutional level, the domestic U.S. money supply became much more standardized after the Civil War and so postbellum credit relationships were less troubled by concerns about the heterogeneity and variable value of bank-issued paper currency. More effective bank regulations, deposit insurance, and (eventually) the spread of branch banking across the entire country have made banks less vulnerable to financial crises. Public policy, and thus politics, also played a very large role in the expansion of specific forms of credit. For example, starting in the 1930s and 1940s a number of public measures directly encouraged the flow of money into home mortgages and helped reshape the geography of American society. These included providing credit insurance for home mortgages, setting underwriting standards, providing housing loans, establishing a secondary market for mortgages, and involved a number of public and quasi-private agencies like the FHA (Federal Housing Administration), FNMA (Federal National Mortgage Association, or Fannie Mae), and the VA (U.S. Department of Veterans Affairs). These measures specifically addressed both the uncertainties and the vulnerabilities of would-be mortgage lenders. The average maturity of mortgages grew with the institutionalization of fifteen-year, twenty-year, and later thirty-year mortgages, making monthly mortgage payments increasingly affordable to average families. In addition, the conventional loan-to-value ratio grew as home buyers were able to finance a larger proportion of their home. In other words, the minimum requirement for a down payment shrank to 5 percent and is now even lower in some circumstances. Together these policy changes helped steer much more money into mortgage loans that were increasingly available to larger numbers of borrowers. Basically, they encouraged lenders to trust homeowners more. They also helped boost the housing market and construction industry, and so enjoyed widespread political support.

The changes that have occurred to the problem of trust as it is posed in U.S. credit markets do not reflect the unfolding of some master process like modernization or a single logic like rationality. Nor are the causes of change solely technological, economic, social, or political. The key elements of trust may be simple, vulnerability and uncertainty, but their manifestation is complex and evolving, and the factors that have engaged them were only loosely coupled with each other. Credit remains highly differentiated, varying by lender, borrower, type of loan, purpose of loan, regulatory oversight, conventions, and so on. Nevertheless, techniques developed in one arena diffused to others. Credit rating, for example, first emerged in the nineteenth century as a way to help New York City wholesalers and suppliers manage their short-term trade credits with strangers. But as a method for gathering, processing, and summarizing information in a quasinumerical format, credit rating spread from trade credit to bank loans, credit insurance, railway bonds, corporate bonds, and, eventually, individuals (for example, FICO scores). To give another example, secured lending starting first with mortgages, and then spread to other types of credit as people brought other types of tangible and intangible assets into the category of collateral. The imperative to increase sales by lending to the customer led to installment lending, where the durable good being sold functioned as collateral. In general, the development of new types of credit has been an important part of market growth.

Despite these many institutional and legal developments, creditors still mistakenly trust the untrustworthy and lend to borrowers who cannot or do not repay (witness the recent problems in the subprime mortgage market). The elaborate legal and economic machinery governing credit has not led to the disappearance of failure, but it has allowed credit to spread across time, space, and social distance. Failure persists but credit has grown. Today's economy depends far more on credit than it did in the past, and the complexity and durability of credit relationships has increased. Lenders now have both multiple sources of information and many ways to reduce their vulnerability. Consequently, credit markets involve more trust, at least as it involves the three-way relation Karen Cook, Russell Hardin, and Margaret Levi discussed (2005, 7, 20). It is also clear that that the expansion of credit has not depended on greater personal virtue, stiffer moral fiber, or any such psychological characteristic or propensity.

Conclusion

Overall, there has been a definite shift away from personal bases for trust to more impersonal ones. In 1800, creditworthiness largely grew out of direct knowledge of someone's personal character, or direct social connections through personal and familial relations. By the middle of the twentieth century, these personal bases had been supplemented, though not entirely superseded, by impersonal formal institutions that provided new information about debtors or reduced the vulnerability of creditors. And though there have been substantial reductions in both uncertainty and vulnerability, the overall change has been more dramatic on the side of uncertainty: much more information is available than before.

To a great extent, the new information was quantitative, not qualitative. Quantitative information is manipulable in unique ways: one can calculate differences and ratios, set numerical thresholds, estimate averages, standard deviations, and correlations, and measure both individuals and groups. But quantitative information also has some particular biases, one of which we might call the fallacy of misplaced specificity to denote the tendency of users to treat quantitative information as more accurate and specific than is justified (see, more generally, Porter 1995). With specific numbers in hand, lenders are tempted to suppose that what they face are risks rather than uncertainties (a more profound form of ignorance). These limits are worth careful scrutiny given that credit evaluation has the quality of a self-fulfilling prophecy: in an economy where credit is essential, those deemed creditworthy receive credit and therefore thrive and those deemed unworthy are denied it and therefore more likely to fail. The continued functioning of informal credit arrangements like rotating credit associations (Biggart 2001) suggests that for all their computational prowess and decision-making rigor, modern institutions like banks, finance companies, and credit card companies continue to overlook types of lending that do not conform with their numerically based procedures.

Impersonal decision making does not mean that lenders no longer consider borrowers on an individual basis. Indeed, quite the opposite is true. The massive amounts of information now available allow lenders to know a great deal about a prospective borrower's individual credit history: credit limits, late payments, overall indebtedness, bounced checks, bankruptcies, defaults, and payments on time and in full. New decision protocols are individualized and impersonal at the same time. Within a specified range of quantitative information, modern lenders have a great deal of information about individual borrowers. Outside of that range, however, things are not so different.

Once computing power became cheap and widespread, algorithmically based credit assessment was possible, and credit decision making became much quicker and cheaper (if not wiser). However, the inner workings of such mechanical decision making remained opaque to most people. Today's banks create their own confidential rating systems, and the ones used by the major rating agencies and credit scorers—Moody's, Standard and Poor's, Fair Isaac—are proprietary, though the resulting ratings are circulated widely (Treacy and Carey 1998). A striking (and somewhat ironic) historical development has been the extent to which credit now depends on a complex set of social, legal and economic institutions whose own internal operations are mostly nontransparent. And, thanks to the dominant status of the United States in the world economy, these institutions now reach around the globe.[19] As Timothy Sinclair noted, Wall Street–based rating agencies wield considerable influence over the ability of corporations and governments worldwide to borrow, and on what terms (2005).

As the U.S. experience demonstrates, the institutional basis for credit can change substantially over time. The extent to which credit-as-trust is now more institutionally than personally embedded suggests that trust is not so much a matter of enduring national character or innate psychological propensity. Rather, with effective design and implementation, institutions dealing with uncertainty and vulnerability can be put in place that greatly enhance the willingness of lenders to trust borrowers, and thus expand the overall volume of credit. In addition, that key institutions, such as credit rating, have spread throughout first the U.S. economy and later the world economy suggests that institutional change can start out in one place on a small scale and grow to be decidedly consequential. Robust and effective institutions offer templates that can be established in one place and then transplanted to other sectors and spheres, creating virtuous cycles of change. The result is that a particular kind of trust, the willingness of creditors to believe that debtors will repay their loans, has been established on a massive scale and pervades the operation of the modern market economy. At the same time, however, older credit methods continue to function within the gaps and interstices that large-scale formal institutions leave behind. Personal character and small-scale social networks, for example, still affect credit (Newburgh 1991; Uzzi 1999). And however elaborate these new institutions have become, they can and do still fail.

My thanks to Henry Farrell, Margaret Levi, and other conference participants for their helpful feedback, and to the Russell Sage Foundation, the Radcliffe Institute for Advanced Study, and the Lochinvar Society for their support.

Notes

1. In stressing the value of credit for the study of trust, I strongly agree with Philip Hoffman, Gilles Postel-Vinay, and Jean-Laurent Rosenthal (chapter 9, this volume). My definition of trust, however, is broader than theirs. For example, I want to include formal legal institutions as causes of trust, whereas they exclude such institutions. Furthermore, their formal model combines a number of factors that I keep separate, and their quantitative analysis overlooks others I highlight.

2. My own notion of trust embraces the three-way formulation of Cook, Hardin, and Levi, but I do not confine it strictly to the interpersonal level, nor do I equate it with social capital (for example, Putnam 1993).
3. Uncertainty here means unknown outcomes whose probability of occurrence is also unknown. Thus, uncertainty differs from risk.
4. I also focus on private rather than public debts (for an analysis of public debts, see Carruthers 1996; Levi 1988).
5. I discerned these ten factors on the basis of my own previous research on financial and monetary history (see Carruthers 1996, 2005; Carruthers and Halliday 1998; Carruthers and Babb 1996).
6. Of course, any given single credit decision can involve additional idiosyncratic issues, but these are sufficiently ad hoc as to not require further discussion.
7. My discussion of these factors is necessarily very summary; an entire chapter could be devoted to each one.
8. "It used to be considered enough to know that a man paid his bills promptly. His private life, his character, were not investigated. That is not true to-day" (*Youth's Companion*, June 27, 1901, 330).
9. Credit rating agencies privately recognized the effect that the strength of social relationships could have on credit. In particular, credit agency ledgers sometimes recommended that strangers not extend trade credit to a firm, even though friends could. In the agency's judgment, stronger social connections made a debtor more creditworthy, but only with respect to the creditors the debtor was linked to. General creditworthiness was not enhanced.
10. Banks in other parts of the United States did not have the same insider lending pattern (see Wright 1999, 41).
11. Rodgers notes the growing complexity of bond indentures. The Philadelphia, Germantown, and Norristown Rail Road Company Indenture, devised in 1833, was three pages long. In 1898, the Baltimore and Ohio First Mortgage indenture took 121 pages, and the Wabush Securities Corporation Mortgage of 1962 was 298 pages long (Rodgers 1965, 552–55).
12. Consider how nineteenth-century state laws restricting foreign ownership of land affected British investment in farm mortgages (Clements 1955).
13. The Mercantile Agency often noted such relations in evaluating the creditworthiness of small businesses during the nineteenth century. Its ledgers recorded the presence of rich uncles and well-to-do fathers-in-law.
14. Before long, they were rating many foreign firms as well.
15. As the current trouble in the subprime mortgage loan market suggests, securitization may make it possible to derive good estimates, but it is still possible to derive bad estimates and, in effect, to underestimate the probability of default.
16. Similar political forces affected laws that were relevant to bankruptcy. For example, as farm foreclosures became more common during the 1920s and

1930s, various states passed laws enacting moratoria on creditor foreclosure (Alston 1984).

17. I set aside the issue of externalities.

18. It seems that six degrees of separation may be enough to connect almost any two people, but not necessarily enough for them to trust each other.

19. Although I cannot pursue the matter here, a proper comparison between the United States and Britain could shed some useful light on the important question of why credit rating developed in the United States but not elsewhere.

References

Akhavein, Jalal, Lawrence G. Goldberg, and Lawrence J. White. 2004. "Small Banks, Small Business, and Relationships: An Empirical Study of Lending to Small Firms." *Journal of Financial Services Research* 26(3): 245–61.

Alston, Lee J. 1984. "Farm Foreclosure Moratorium Legislation: A Lesson from the Past," *American Economic Review* 74(3): 445–57.

Ben-Amos, Ilana Krausman. 2000. "Gifts and Favors: Informal Support in Early Modern England." *Journal of Modern History* 72(2): 295–338.

Beutel, Frederick K. 1940. "The Development of State Statutes on Negotiable Paper Prior to the Negotiable Instruments Law." *Columbia Law Review* 40(5): 836–65.

Biggart, Nicole Woolsey. 2001. "Banking on Each Other: The Situational Logic of Rotating Savings and Credit Associations." *Advances in Qualitative Organization Research* 3(1): 129–52.

Boyce, Gordon H. 1995. *Information, Mediation and Institutional Development: The Rise of Large-Scale Enterprise in British Shipping, 1870–1919.* Manchester, U.K.: Manchester University Press.

Brief, Richard P. 1966. "The Origin and Evolution of Nineteenth-Century Asset Accounting." *Business History Review* 40(1): 1–23.

Burt, Ronald S. 1992. *Structural Holes: The Social Structure of Competition.* Cambridge, Mass.: Harvard University Press.

Carruthers, Bruce G. 1996. *City of Capital: Politics and Markets in the English Financial Revolution.* Princeton, N.J.: Princeton University Press.

———. 2005. "The Sociology of Money and Credit." In *Handbook of Economic Sociology*, 2nd ed., edited by Neil Smelser and Richard Swedberg. Princeton, N.J., and New York: Princeton University Press and Russell Sage Foundation.

Carruthers, Bruce G., and Sarah Babb. 1996. "The Color of Money and the Nature of Value: Greenbacks and Gold in Postbellum America." *American Journal of Sociology* 101(6): 1556–591.

Carruthers, Bruce G., and Terence C. Halliday. 1998. *Rescuing Business: The Making of Corporate Bankruptcy Law in England and the United States.* Oxford: Oxford University Press.

Carruthers, Bruce G., and Arthur L. Stinchcombe. 1999. "The Social Structure of Liquidity: Flexibility, Markets, and States." *Theory and Society* 28(3): 353–82.

Clements, Roger V. 1955. "British Investments and American Legislative Restrictions in the Trans-Mississippi West, 1880–1900." *Mississippi Valley Historical Review* 42(2): 207–28.

Cook, Karen S., Russell Hardin, and Margaret Levi. 2005. *Cooperation Without Trust.* New York: Russell Sage Foundation.

Edwards, James Don. 1958. "Public Accounting in the United States from 1913 to 1928." *Business History Review* 32(1): 74–101.

Fabozzi, Frank J., and Franco Modigliani. 1992. *Mortgages and Mortgage Backed Securities Markets.* Watertown, Mass.: Harvard Business School Press.

Federal Reserve Board. 1922. "Credit Insurance." *Federal Reserve Bulletin* 8(June): 667–78.

Fontaine, Laurence. 2001. "Antonio and Shylock: Credit and Trust in France, c.1680–c.1780." *Economic History Review* LIV(1): 39–57.

Freyer, Tony. 1982. "Antebellum Commercial Law: Common Law Approaches to Secured Transactions." *Kentucky Law Journal* 70(3): 593–608.

Fuller, Carlton P. 1926. "Modernizing Bank Credit Methods." *Bankers' Magazine* 1926(March): 379–83.

Gulati, Ranjay. 1995. "Social Structure and Alliance Formation Patterns: A Longitudinal Analysis." *Administrative Science Quarterly* 40(4): 619–52.

Haines, Howard. 1936. "Small Loan Technique." *Bankers' Magazine* 1936(June): 533–41.

Ham, Arthur H., and Leonard G. Robinson. 1923. *A Credit Union Primer.* New York: Russell Sage Foundation.

Hancock, David. 2005. "The Trouble with Networks: Managing the Scots' Early-Modern Madeira Trade." *Business History Review* 79(3): 467–91.

Hanley, Anne. 2004. "Is it Who You Know? Entrepreneurs and Bankers in São Paulo, Brazil, at the Turn of the Twentieth Century." *Enterprise and Society* 5(2): 187–225.

Hardin, Russell. 2001. "Conceptions and Explanations of Trust." In *Trust in Society,* edited by Karen S. Cook. New York: Russell Sage Foundation.

Heimer, Carol A. 2001. "Solving the Problem of Trust." In *Trust in Society,* edited by Karen S. Cook. New York: Russell Sage Foundation.

Helleiner, Eric. 2003. *The Making of National Money: Territorial Currencies in Historical Perspective.* Ithaca, N.Y.: Cornell University Press.

Holden, J. Milnes. 1955. *The History of Negotiable Instruments in English Law.* London: Athlone Press.

Hunt, Freeman. 1857. *Worth and Wealth: A Collection of Maxims, Morals and Miscellanies.* New York: Stringer & Townsend.

Hunt, Margaret R. 1996. *The Middling Sort: Commerce, Gender, and the Family in England 1680–1780.* Berkeley: University of California Press.

Kavanaugh, Thomas J. 1921. *Bank Credit Methods and Practice.* New York: Bankers Publishing.

Keller, Morton. 1963. *The Life Insurance Enterprise, 1885–1910: A Study in the Limits of Corporate Power.* Cambridge, Mass.: Harvard University Press.

Kniffen, William H. 1915. *The Practical Work of a Bank.* New York: Bankers Publishing.

Lamoreaux, Naomi. 1994. *Insider Lending: Banks, Personal Connections, and Economic Development in New England.* Cambridge: Cambridge University Press.

Levi, Margaret. 1988. *Of Rule and Revenue.* Berkeley: University of California Press.

Light, Ivan, and Edna Bonacich. 1988. *Immigrant Entrepreneurs: Koreans in Los Angeles, 1965–1982.* Berkeley: University of California Press.

Light, Ivan, Im Jung Kwuon, and Deng Zhong. 1990. "Korean Rotating Credit Associations in Los Angeles." *Amerasia* 16(1): 35–54.
Lister, R. J. 1985. "Debenture Covenants and Corporate Value." *The Company Lawyer* 6(5): 209–14.
Macaulay, Stuart. 1963. "Non-Contractual Relations in Business." *American Sociological Review* 28(1): 55–69.
Mann, Bruce H. 2002. *Republic of Debtors: Bankruptcy in the Age of American Independence.* Cambridge, Mass.: Harvard University Press.
Miranti, Paul J. Jr. 1986. "Associationalism, Statism, and Professional Regulation: Public Accountants and the Reform of the Financial Markets, 1896–1940." *Business History Review* 60(3): 438–68.
Mizruchi, Mark S. 1996. "What Do Interlocks Do? An Analysis, Critique, and Assessment of Research on Interlocking Directorates." *Annual Review of Sociology* 22(1996): 271–98.
Moss, David A. 2002. *When All Else Fails: Government as the Ultimate Risk Manager.* Cambridge, Mass.: Harvard University Press.
Muldrew, Craig. 1998. *The Economy of Obligation: The Culture of Credit and Social Relations in Early Modern England.* Houndmills, U.K.: Macmillan Press.
Newburgh, Conrad. 1991. "Character Assessment in the Lending Process." *The Journal of Commercial Bank Lending* 73(8): 34–39.
Newfang, Oscar. 1912. "The Essentials of Commercial Credit." *Bankers' Magazine* 84(5): 639–46.
Norris, James D. 1978. *R. G. Dun & Co. 1841–1900: The Development of Credit-Reporting in the Nineteenth-Century.* Westport, Conn.: Greenwood Press.
Olegario, Rowena. 2003. "Credit Reporting Agencies: A Historical Perspective." in *Credit Reporting Systems and the International Economy,* edited by Margaret J. Miller. Cambridge, Mass: MIT Press.
Pitt, Mark M., and Shahidur R. Khandker. 1998. "The Impact of Group-Based Credit Programs on Poor Households in Bangladesh: Does the Gender of Participants Matter?" *Journal of Political Economy* 106(5): 958–96.
Porter, Theodore. 1995. *Trust in Numbers: The Pursuit of Objectivity in Science and Public Life.* Princeton, N.J.: Princeton University Press.
Prendergast, William A., and William H. Steiner. 1931. *Credit and Its Uses.* New York: D. Appleton and Co.
Putnam, Robert D. 1993. *Making Democracy Work: Civic Traditions in Modern Italy.* Princeton, N.J.: Princeton University Press.
Rodgers, Churchill. 1965. "The Corporate Trust Indenture Project." *The Business Lawyer* 20(3): 551–71.
Rosen, Deborah A. 1997. *Courts and Commerce: Gender, Law, and the Market Economy in Colonial New York.* Columbus: Ohio State University Press.
Sinclair, Timothy J. 2005. *The New Masters of Capital: American Bond Rating Agencies and the Politics of Creditworthiness.* Ithaca, N.Y.: Cornell University Press.
Skeel, David A. Jr. 2001. *Debt's Dominion: A History of Bankruptcy Law in America.* Princeton, N.J.: Princeton University Press.
Skinner, Edward M. 1904. "Credits and Collections in a Wholesale House." In *Credit and Collections: The Factors Involved and the Methods Pursued in Credit Operations: A Practical Treatise by Eminent Credit Men,* edited by T. J. Zimmerman. Chicago: The System Company.

Smith, Clifford W. Jr., and Jerold B. Warner. 1979. "On Financial Contracting: An Analysis of Bond Covenants." *Journal of Financial Economics* 7(2): 117–61.
Strang, David, and Sarah A. Soule. 1998. "Diffusion in Organizations and Social Movements: From Hybrid Corn to Poison Pills." *Annual Review of Sociology* 24(1998): 265–90.
Tenenbaum, Shelly. 1993. *A Credit to Their Community: Jewish Loan Societies in the United States 1880–1945.* Detroit: Wayne State University Press.
Thompson, Elizabeth Lee. 2004. *The Reconstruction of Southern Debtors: Bankruptcy after the Civil War.* Athens: University of Georgia Press.
Treacy, William F., and Mark S. Carey. 1998. "Credit Risk Rating at Large U.S. Banks." *Federal Reserve Bulletin* November: 897–921.
Uzzi, Brian. 1999. "Embeddedness in the Making of Financial Capital: How Social Relations and Networks Benefit Firms Seeking Financing." *American Sociological Review* 64(4): 481–505.
Uzzi, Brian, and James Gillespie. 2002. "Knowledge Spillover in Corporate Financing Networks: Embeddedness, Network Transitivity, and Trade Credit Performance." *Strategic Management Journal* 23(7): 595–618.
Uzzi, Brian, and Ryon Lancaster. 2003. "Relational Embeddedness and Learning: The Case of Bank Loan Managers and Their Clients." *Management Science* 49(4): 383–99.
Wall, Alexander. 1919. *The Banker's Credit Manual.* Indianapolis: Bobbs-Merrill.
Weinberg, Harold R. 1982. "Commercial Paper in Economic Theory and Legal History." *Kentucky Law Journal* 70(3): 567–92.
Woo, Jung-En. 1991. *Race to the Swift: State and Finance in Korean Industrialization.* New York: Columbia University Press.
Wright, Robert E. 1999. "Bank Ownership and Lending Patterns in New York and Pennsylvania, 1781–1831." *Business History Review* 73(1): 40–60.
Yates, JoAnne. 1989. *Control Through Communication: The Rise of System in American Management.* Baltimore, Md.: Johns Hopkins University Press.
Zinbarg, Edward D. 1975. "The Private Placement Loan Agreement." *Financial Analysts Journal* 31(1): 33–35.

Chapter 9

The Role of Trust in the Long-Run Development of French Financial Markets

PHILIP T. HOFFMAN, GILLES POSTEL-VINAY, AND JEAN-LAURENT ROSENTHAL

USING HISTORICAL DATA, we test whether social capital generates trust in past financial markets and whether the effects of trust persist across time. The evidence for the tests comes from 108 credit markets in France over nearly two centuries. We find that social capital had no significant effect on trust in these credit markets and that this trust must have changed over time. The implication is that trust in financial markets is an intermediate variable that evolves rather quickly so long as societies are not pathological.

Trust, it has long been argued, can facilitate economic transactions that make people better off and thereby have an enormous impact on economic growth (Arrow 1972). Trust ought to have such an effect, if it means that people can invest without spending a great deal to keep from being defrauded. And its consequences should be particularly important in financial markets, for investors inevitably put their money in other people's hands.

There is some evidence that trust does work this way. A measure of trust taken from questionnaires is correlated with more rapid economic growth (Knack and Keefer 1997). It also seems to explain individuals' willingness to invest in financial markets that cannot be traced back to differences in their wealth or their attitudes toward risk and ambiguity (Guiso, Sapienza, and Zingales 2005). But what in turn determines trust? It is usually presumed to reflect some form of social capital, such as norms that discourage abuses of trust or social networks that facilitate punishment of untrustworthy behavior. The usual (though not universal) assumption is that this social capital will change very slowly, if at all, in a given society, but it will vary a great deal from place to place.[1] The same will therefore be true of trust. And there is considerable evidence from surveys and experiments that social capital and trust do in fact vary across societies and even within regions of a single country (Putnam, Leonardi, and Nanetti 1993; Henrich et al., 2004; Guiso, Sapienza, and Zingales 2004, 2006). There is also evidence that the two are linked in financial markets (Guiso, Sapienza, and Zingales 2004, 2005).

If trust is generated by social capital and if it does in turn significantly affect financial markets, then its effects should be visible both today and in the past. More social capital, be it stronger norms to discourage fraud or more effective networks to punish deviants, will mean more trust and hence—if other things are equal—more lending and investment, no matter what the year. And if social capital changes slowly, then so will trust, and the effects of trust on lending or investment will remain the same over long periods.

As yet, no one has subjected this argument to a thorough statistical test.[2] In particular, no one has verified—at least quantitatively—that the relationship between trust and social capital holds in the past or that the effects of trust persist over time. The statistical evidence usually advanced in favor of trust mattering and of its being generated by enduring social capital simply cannot speak to this issue, because it all comes from current day observations—experiments, modern surveys, and cross-sectional regressions—and thus cannot answer questions about the past or about change over time. Historical evidence would be an obvious way to see whether the relationships observed today bear up over long periods, but no one has ever subjected them to the right sort of statistical scrutiny.

The omission is hardly a matter of mere antiquarian interest, because it raises fundamental questions about trust, social capital, and even about policy. If the sort of relationship between social capital and financial development that we see today were to end up disappearing in the past, we would in fact have to rethink what trust in financial markets might be. We would have either to admit that in the long run trust does not matter in financial markets, or to conclude that it is not generated by fixed or slowly changing social capital. It would have to come from some other source, at least in financial markets.

Historical evidence is critical here. Without it, we cannot tell how durable the effects of trust are, a matter that is essential for policy. Simply knowing that trust and lending are linked at one moment in time is not enough. If, for instance, the relationship between trust and lending does not vary across the centuries, then trust is unfortunately not a variable that can be changed to promote better social outcomes. At the other extreme, if trust is simply the way individuals respond to the returns on a certain form of human capital, then it is an effect, not a cause, and the connection will run from anemic loan demand through trust to a low level of lending, making policies about trust as such unnecessary. Finally, if trust and its effects are persistent, but the effects decay over time, then it will be an important policy variable.

Analyzing how trust, credit, and time interact requires a panel of observations with historical data. It also requires eliminating as many other sorts of variations in transactions costs as possible. The best way to do that would be to examine different markets within a single country. The legal costs of discouraging untrustworthy behavior will be virtually the same throughout the country, and hence trust, and the social capital that generates it, will have more of a role in explaining variations in the level of lending or investment between different markets. If trust and social capital change slowly, their effect on lending or investment should remain the same over long periods. And the relationship between trust and social capital should hold in the past too.

Testing whether social capital generates trust in past financial markets and whether the effects of trust persist across time is therefore essential, and we perform such a test in this paper. We focus on lenders' trust in borrowers. Although it is not the only form of trust, it is essential for nearly all financial transactions, which typically involve a lender or other investor advancing money in return for a promised payment in the future, and all of our tests will concern this form of trust. The evidence for the tests comes from 108 credit markets in one country—France—over nearly two centuries. The markets we look at are precisely the kind that are stepping stones to economic development in poorer countries, and, because they all lie within the same country, we can hold constant the judicial and political institutions that affect lending and in particular the legal costs of preventing or punishing fraudulent behavior. The next two sections develop the model of lending that underlies our statistical tests and present our data. We then carry out the tests and discuss their implications. We find that social capital has no significant effect on trust in the past, or at least the trust in borrowers that we consider here: it does not explain levels of lending that cannot be accounted for by economic variables. Furthermore, although there are persistent differences in the level of lending that can conceivably be interpreted as trust, they have no relationship to social capital, and may well derive from other causes (such as informal institutions or the acquired expertise of financial intermediaries) and have nothing to do with trust at all. The implication, which we take up in our conclusion, is that trust in financial markets may be generated by something other than social capital; alternatively, it and social capital may matter only in certain settings. In particular, trust becomes important in societies where formal support for credit is low because of civil conflict, widespread corruption, or ethnic discrimination. The evidence from France suggests that one might be better off treating the root of the problem rather than seeking to improve trust.

A Simple Model of Trust

How then should we conceive of trust in financial markets? Perhaps the easiest way to think of it is in the context of an extremely simple economic model, one that helps pin down what it means when we say that trust should encourage more lending and investment. Like all models, this one does gloss over a number of complexities; in particular, it lumps together the many ways in which trust can be established, as Bruce Carruthers shows in the previous chapter. It does capture the essence of trust in financial markets, however, and makes simple tests of our hypotheses possible.

The model requires a few simple equations, and readers who prefer can simply jump to the end of the section because the underlying idea is quite simple. It is in fact merely the claim that, other things being equal, more trust ought to translate into more lending. Precisely how much money is lent will of course depend on many things, including interest rates, borrowers' demand, and collateral. But if these other factors are held constant, then more trust ought to mean that lenders are willing to advance more money to borrowers. Such willingness is a prerequisite for most financial transactions, and it is essentially what is measured in experiments on trust. Using our model we can see whether this trust changes over time and whether it is related to social capital.

Imagine, then, a society in which individuals can either borrow or lend; such a society is not too far removed from reality when financial markets are underdeveloped, as in the past or in developing countries today, particularly when lending moves beyond the narrow confines of a family or village. Each individual in this society has some wealth w. The amount may be small or large. He can either lend this money and earn interest i on the loan, or use it as collateral to borrow and set up a small business. If he sets up the small business, he will earn a rate of return r, which will depend on local demand and his talents as an entrepreneur. This rate of return r will be the same no matter how much he borrows; if he takes out a loan of size x, he will therefore end up with $(1 + r) x$. We assume a large number of individuals, so that any one of them will take the interest rate i as given (see the appendix for a formal version of what follows).

Having earned this sum from his business, the entrepreneur will have to decide whether to default on his loan or repay it. To keep things simple, let us assume that he has only these two possibilities—default or repayment—and that if he defaults, he will face a penalty Tw that will be proportionate to his wealth w. If T is larger than 1, then a default will cost him far more than the assets he owns. Such a penalty, which goes beyond his wealth alone, could be interpreted as evidence of trust, as would be the case if borrowers who defaulted not only lost all their assets but faced social sanctions for violating social norms. Similarly, a T smaller than 1 might be interpreted as a lack of trust, although it could reflect other causes as well. A legal system that allowed a defaulting borrower to retain a large fraction of his assets would lead to a small T for reasons having nothing at all to do with trust.

When it comes time for the borrower to repay, he thus faces a choice between giving his lender $(1 + i)\,x$ or defaulting and forfeiting the penalty Tw. The borrower will default if $(1 + i)\,x > Tw$; knowing this, lenders will limit their loans to an amount $x = Tw/(1 + i)$. Individuals who can set up businesses that will earn a rate of return $r > i$ will borrow up to their credit limit of $Tw/(1 + i)$; individuals with lower rates of return will lend their wealth out at the interest rate i. If the distribution of rates of return r among individuals in the market is given by the distribution $G(r)$ and the distribution of wealth among the same individuals is given by $F(w)$, then the fraction of individuals who lend money out when the market interest rate is i will be $G(i)$, and the average amount lent per person will be

$$G(i)\,E(w|r \leq i), \tag{1}$$

where $E(w|\,r \leq i)$ is the average wealth of individuals with rates of return less than i. Similarly, the average amount borrowed per capita will be

$$(1 - G(i))\,TE(w|r > i)/(1 + i), \tag{2}$$

where $E(w|\,r > i)$ is the average wealth of individuals with rates of return higher than i. To avoid complications, we assume that F and G are independent; in other words, an individual's skill as an entrepreneur has nothing to do with his wealth. For our simple model, this is not an unreasonable assumption, provided we think of the return r as innate talent as an entrepreneur.[3] Because F and G are independent, the average amount lent per person will be

$$G(i)\,E(w), \tag{1'}$$

and the average borrowing per person will be

$$(1 - G(i))\,TE(w)/(1 + i), \tag{2'}$$

where $E(w)$ is simply average per capita wealth. Average borrowing per person will therefore be a function of the interest rate, average wealth, the distribution G of rates of return (which will reflect both the supply of entrepreneurial skills and the demand for entrepreneurs' services), and last but not least T (which is our trust measure but could reflect other factors as well, such as the legal system). A higher T implies—other things being equal—more credit per capita: the same fraction $1 - G(i)$ of people take out loans, but loan sizes increase. In practice, T will end up being something of a residual, because we will measure it using a regression to filter out the amount of per capita lending that cannot be accounted for by the economic variables or by legal institutions, which will be held constant if we remain in one country. But T is nonetheless what trust in financial markets ought to be—lending that goes beyond what collateral alone would justify.

So far we have dealt only with a single market and made the interest rate i exogenous. What happens when there are several such markets, each of different size and each with its own measure of trust and its own distribution of wealth and entrepreneurial talent? These distributions of wealth and talent may differ from market to market, but once again we assume that in each market they are independent. If we suppose that funds can be transferred between markets, there will be an equilibrium interest rate i^* that will equate the supply of funds to lend and the demand for loans and that will be common to all markets. Funds will flow from markets with low trust to markets with high trust, and if we measure average borrowing per person in each market, in market j it will be

$$y_j = \left(1 - G_j(i^*)\right) T_j E_j(w)/(1 + i^*), \tag{3}$$

where G_j is the distribution of talent in the market, $E_j(w)$ is the average value of wealth in the market (calculated using the market's distribution of wealth F_j), and T_j is the market's trust measure. Note that the logarithm of y_j will be

$$\ln(y_j) = \ln(1 - G_j(i^*)) + \ln(T_j) + \ln E_j(w) - \ln(1 + i^*) \tag{4}$$

The first term, $\ln(1 - G_j(i^*))$, will depend on the interest rate, the supply of talent, and local demand conditions, and in a regression we would expect it to be a linear function (at least to a first order approximation) of the logarithms of variables such as the interest rate, measures of local talent (such as literacy rates), and local indexes of demand (such as urban populations and the number of banks). Similarly, $\ln(T_j)$ will at least approximately be a linear function of the logarithms of measures of social capital embodied in norms or social networks, if trust is in fact related to social capital. Even if T_j is also affected by the legal system, the portion of T_j that is a function of legal or political variables will presumably be constant and hence swept into the constant term if we confine ourselves to data from one country, because legal and political institutions will then be the same for all markets.

The model is most easily interpreted as explaining what we would observe at one point in time in a cross-sectional regression. In such a regression, the equilibrium interest rate will also be a constant, and the coefficients of the social capital measures will reveal whether trust T_i is related to social capital. But the model can easily be extended to observations of the same markets at different times, with the trust T_i in each market either being fixed or varying over time. We can test whether T_i is fixed using panel data, which can also tell us whether the relationship between trust and social capital persists across time. Both sorts of regressions can easily be run using the historical data we have collected.

Data for 108 French Credit Markets: 1740 to 1899

The data we have gathered concern more than 200,000 loans drawn from 108 credit markets scattered through France (see figure 9.1 for a map and table 9.1 for summary data on their populations). The markets were chosen to yield a stratified sample of towns and cities that would reflect the French population as a whole. The markets included Paris, other large cities such as Lyon; medium-sized urban centers with 10,000 to 70,000 inhabitants such as Grenoble, and smaller towns with populations as low as 500. The loans in each market were drawn up by notaries (semiprivate court officers who preserved records and provided legal and financial advice) and subject to a tax. The notaries had to register the loans at the local tax office, where officials collected the tax and recorded information about the debts. We gathered information from the offices' archives, which covered lending in the municipality where the office was located and in surrounding towns and villages. Although there were certainly some small debts that did not appear in these archives, most lenders had a powerful incentive to report their loans to the offices and do so truthfully, for otherwise they would have had difficulty pursuing defaulting debtors in court. Unregistered debt was therefore likely to be minimal, though the exact amounts at stake cannot be measured precisely.[4]

For this chapter, we leave aside information about the identities of the parties involved in the loan contracts and focus on the number of new loans, average loan sizes, and loan durations; we then use this information to estimate the stock of outstanding debt in each market for six years: 1740, 1780, 1807, 1840, 1865, and 1899 (for details about the data collection and the estimation process, see the appendix). The dates of these estimates were chosen to be roughly a generation apart, with two dates—1780 and 1807—bracketing a devastating bout of hyperinflation during the French Revolution. The first date, 1740, was the earliest for which we could collect data on lending and explanatory variables for all of our markets;

Figure 9.1 Credit Markets in Sample

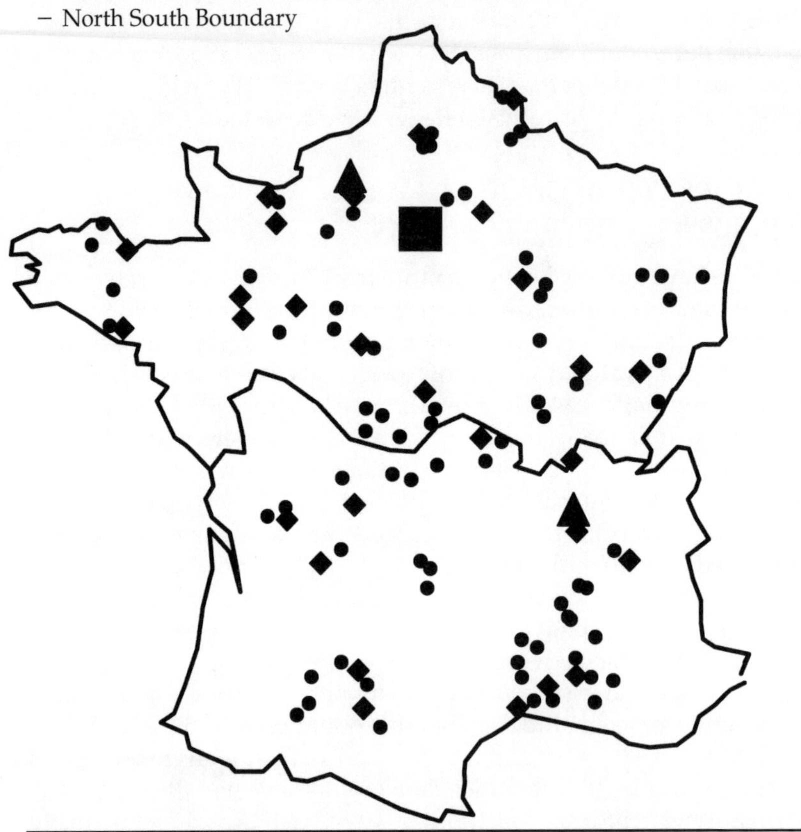

Source: Authors' compilation based on sources described in the appendix.

the last date, 1899, was the most recent for which we could get access to the records needed for the data collection.

One might naturally worry whether the French Revolution altered legal and political institutions so greatly that our data might be affected after 1807. Institutions did certainly change, but not enough to distort our data. The court system was reorganized, which perhaps reduced the costs of litigation, but the law governing credit contracts remained much the same. The same was by and large true for notaries, and it held as well for the officials who collected the tax on loans and registered them. Indeed,

Table 9.1 Descriptive Statistics

1. Loan Characteristics (Values in 1840)

Characteristic	All Markets	Without Paris
Average loan size (francs)	3,860	1,847
Median loan size (francs)	—	500
Average loan duration (years)	4.62	4.68

2. Variables and Measures of Trust and Social Capital

Variable Name	Description/Units	Mean	SD
Dependent variables (values in selected periods)			
Per capita stock of loans in 1740	livres	54.00	110.22
Per capita stock of loans in 1780	livres	70.03	159.90
Per capita stock of loans in 1807	francs	53.09	82.76
Per capita stock of loans in 1899	francs	270.69	294.68
Social capital measures			
Oath scale	Index of fraction of priests taking oath of loyalty to the revolutionary constitution in 1791, with higher score on 1-to-6 scale meaning more priests took the oath	3.29	1.52
Intermediate score	Dummy variable equaling 1 if score on 1-to-6 oath scale was 2, 3, or 4; variable equals 0 otherwise.	0.59	0.49
Turnout 1849	Vote turnout in 1849 (percentage eligible voters)	70.59	8.32
Resist draft: self-mutilate	Local draftees (per 1,000 recruits) exempted 1820–1830 for loss of a finger, presumably due to self-mutilation. Because it could be zero, what was entered in the regressions was the logarithm of this variable plus 0.01.	1.10	0.88

(Table continues on p. 258.)

Table 9.1 Descriptive Statistics (*continued*)

2. Variables and Measures of Trust and Social Capital			
Variable Name	Description/Units	Mean	SD
Resist draft: fail to report	Local draftees (per 1,000 recruits) who failed to report in 1820–1830. Because it could be zero, what entered the regressions was the logarithm of this variable plus 0.01.	6.13	12.59
Verdicts (value in 1840)	Verdicts against defendants in civil and criminal trials (per 100 inhabitants)	0.85	0.61
Verdicts (value in 1865)	Verdicts against defendants in civil and criminal trials (per 100 inhabitants)	0.67	0.23
Verdicts (value in 1899)	Verdicts against defendants in civil and criminal trials (per 100 inhabitants)	0.83	0.83
Trust measures			
Annuity share 1740	Share of perpetual annuities in total stock 1740	0.72	0.27
Annuity share 1780	Share of perpetual annuities in total stock 1780	0.50	0.31
Other variables (value in selected periods)			
City population (in 1840)	Population of city where registration office located	19,853	85,734
Banks (number in 1840)	Number of banks; because it could be zero, what was entered in the regressions was the logarithm of this variable plus 1.	4.46	21.06
Wealth (value in 1840)	Property tax per 1,000 people (francs)	4.69	1.35
Voters	Number of men eligible to vote in 1840	213.00	1,113.22
Illiteracy	Percentage of draftees who are illiterate, 1820 to 1830	49.82	19.62

Source: Authors' compilation based on sources described in the appendix.
Notes: For detailed description of the variables, see text and appendix. Table shows per capita stock of loans for 1740, 1780, 1807, and 1899. Values for other variables are shown for the first and last dates they are available only. Monetary amounts in 1740 and 1780 were in livres, which equaled 0.989 francs, the currency unit created during the French Revolution. To get a sense of the value of the value of the amounts involved, in 1740 an unskilled day laborer earned 1 livre a day in Paris; in 1840, his wages had climbed to roughly 2.4 francs a day; and by 1899, they were nearly 5 francs a day. We did not compute median loan sizes for all markets including Paris because of the different sampling strategy used with the Paris records. The average loan duration is calculated weighting durations by loan sizes.

the nature of the tax and the size of the areas covered by each office hardly changed (for the relevant legal, political, and administrative reforms under the revolution and Napoleon, see Woloch 1994). In any case, we can check whether the revolutionary turmoil made a difference by running our regressions for the period between 1840 and 1899, when the legal and political institutions were all in place and uniform across the entire country. It turns out that results do not depend on whether we use the data from 1840 to 1899 or the entire sample.

The loans in our 108 markets were mortgages and business loans with durations running from a few months to several years or more (for summary data on the loans and on the variables used in our analysis, see table 9.1). In 1740, 30 percent of them took the form of life or perpetual annuities, which lenders invested in for support in old age or to create a stream of income that profligate heirs could not dissipate. The rest were term loans with an average duration of slightly over two years. The annuities disappeared in the nineteenth century, but loan durations grew to almost nine years by 1899. The sums involved were in total very large. If we extrapolate from our sample to France as a whole, the outstanding stock of this debt was perhaps 21 percent of gross domestic product (GDP) in 1740 and 23 percent of GDP a century later. By 1899, it reached 44 percent of GDP. Even so, many of the loans involved only modest sums. Outside Paris, for example, the median loan size was 500 francs (F) in 1840, roughly a year's earnings for a day laborer. The records are full of smaller loans: F 100 that the vintner François Meunier and his wife borrowed in 1840 from their neighbor, the laborer François Gressin, or F 160 that the laborer Etienne Desgens owed the landowner François Poubeau the same year.[5]

Unfortunately, the tax records we used to gather our data often omitted the interest rate charged on the loans.[6] Eighteenth-century term loans were particularly likely to leave out the interest rate, though it was usually 5 percent when it was indicated. Mention of the rates was more common in the nineteenth century, with 5 percent being the modal figure. The gap in rates between different markets was greatest in the 1899 cross section, when 90 percent of the records give an interest charged on the loan. At first glance, the figures from 1899 might seem to cast doubt on our assumption that our loan markets were integrated, because the average interest rates in distinct markets differed by as much 1 percent. Yet in 80 percent of the markets the averages fell in a narrow range between 4.22 and 4.73 percent, which suggests that the assumption is not unreasonable, particularly given that the gap in rates between markets was smaller in our other cross sections. Furthermore, lenders participated in multiple markets, yet another sign of integration. Even in Lunel, the market with highest average interest rate in 1899—4.97 percent—there were in fact lenders who came from the cities of Montpellier and Nîmes. Such piecewise integration was in fact the norm in our credit markets.[7]

What about the collateral backing the loans, which is also an important part of our model? The original contracts preserved in the notarial archives describe the collateral in great detail, because providing such information was essential part of the notaries' service. But our fiscal records often gloss as well over that information, which was not needed for collecting the tax, and going back to the original contracts to gather it would have slowed our data collection to a crawl.

We have, however, been able to examine the original contracts in several specific markets. In them, loans with a duration of a year or more almost always involved real estate as collateral. In 1740, for example, annuities were nearly always collateralized on specific pieces of land or other real property, but shorter term loans (with a typical duration of three to twelve months) mention no specific collateral. By 1780, specific real collateral did begin to appear in these term loans, which came to resemble modern day mortgages with balloon payments, and in the nineteenth century more than three-quarters of all contracts involved mortgaged real estate of some sort. As for the remaining loans without any mention of specific collateral, they did usually give a general claim to the borrower's assets in case of default, but loans backed by liens on specific collateral were paid off first, leaving lenders with general claims to share what was left.

The per capita stock of outstanding loans in each market is our measure of y_j, borrowing per person in our model. It was calculated by dividing our estimates of the loan stock by the population in the surrounding canton, a small region that included the municipality where the loans were registered plus nearby towns and villages.[8] The calculation thus yields a panel of data, with a y_j for each market j and for each of our six cross sections from 1740 to 1899.

Trust and Social Capital

Our model implies that the y_j can be regressed on social capital measures and economic variables to see whether a persistent effect can be interpreted as trust and, if so, whether it is related to social capital. The regressions can either be panel regressions or cross-sectional regressions for one of the six individual years. A panel regression addresses the question of trust's persistence and can also be used to explore the relationship between trust and social capital. But a series of cross-sectional regressions at different times can do the same; if one finds an effect that seems like trust in one cross section but not others, then it is difficult to maintain that trust is persistent. Normally, the panel regression is preferable to the cross sections, but the lack of data for certain periods makes it worth examining the cross sections too.

To make it clear how the regressions will be specified and what hypotheses will be tested, let us return to our model. Whether we are using panels or cross sections, our regressions will always be based on equation (4). For the cross sections, the regressions to estimate will have the form

$$\ln(y_j) = a + b\,x_j + c\,z_j + u_j \tag{5}$$

Here j is the index for each of the 108 markets; u_j is the error term; a, b, and c are matrices of regression coefficients; x_j is a matrix of logarithms of measures of wealth and local demand conditions, which come from a first order expansion in logarithms of the terms $\ln(1 - G_j(i^*))$ and $\ln E_j(w)$ in (4); and z_j is a matrix of logarithms of social capital measures or other variables correlated with trust, which are derived similarly from the term $\ln(T_j)$ in (4).

The panel regression will be similar except that the interest rate i^* will enter the regressions too, as a variable that varies over time but not from market to market.[9] The panel regression will also include fixed (or random) effects w_j that measure persistent characteristics of market j; because a persistently larger $\ln(T_j)$ in market j might yield a larger w_j in a first-order expansion, these fixed or random effects could be interpreted as long-lasting trust. All the other variables in the panel regression can depend on both the market j and the date of the cross section t; formally, the panel regression will be

$$\ln(y_{jt}) = a + b\,x_{jt} + c\,z_{jt} + d\,v_t + w_j + u_{jt} \tag{6}$$

Here v_t is a matrix of dummy variables for each time period (except one) that captures changes in the interest rate, and x_{jt} and z_{jt} are analogous to the corresponding matrices of variables in (5).

Regression equations (5) and (6) will be used to test two hypotheses: first, that trust was related to social capital in the past, and second, that trust is persistent across time. If the first hypothesis is true, then the coefficients of the social capital variables in z_j should have large and significant coefficients with appropriate signs when the cross-sectional regressions (5) are run with our historical data. If the second hypothesis is true, then either the w_j in the panel regressions should be large or the correlates of trust in z_{jt} should have large and significant coefficients with the appropriate signs.[10] If both hypotheses hold, then the social capital variables in z_{jt} should have large and significant coefficients with the expected sign in the panel regressions.

To see what these expected signs are, let us introduce all of our variables. The per capita value of the property tax serves as our wealth measure; it is available only for the 1840, 1865, and 1899 cross sections (for a description of the sources for these and the other explanatory variables, see the appendix; for summary data, see table 9.1). If a wealth measure is included in the panel regressions, they can therefore only be run for these three periods.[11] The local demand measures include the population of the municipality where the loans were registered, and the number of banks, which was not available for 1740 and 1780. Presumably migration would have swelled the population of the cities where demand was strong; note that these municipal populations are different from the canton population that was used to figure per capita wealth and the per capita loan stock. Banks would have opened in such cities as well, making their number yet another index of demand. The banks specialized in providing short-term mercantile credit, and because banking was essentially unregulated, they tended to open in markets where merchants were thriving, making their presence a good index of demand.[12] By the 1830s, hundreds of firms or individuals (many of whom were wholesale merchants who offered trade credit on the side) were providing such commercial banking services. About one-third were in Paris and the rest primarily in the largest cities. As the century wore on, the banks spread rapidly through France's smaller cities. In 1829, two of every three cities with populations greater than 20,000 had a bank office; by 1851, all of them did. For cities between 5,000 and 10,000, the fraction with banks jumped from one-third in 1829 to 87 percent in 1862.

Of these three variables, wealth is exogenous (at least in our simple model), and because the number of banks and the city populations are likely to be endogenous, we have used their lagged values in all of our regressions. We also have one measure of entrepreneurial talent—namely, literacy rates, which were measured from 1820 to 1830. Like the demand measures, literacy will affect the expression $\ln(1 - G_j(i^*))$.

We have several social capital measures, each one indexing a particular form of social capital. It proved impossible to find other useable measures of social capital.[13] Only one of the social capital indices varies over time; the others capture social capital at one specific date. Two of the measures concern Catholicism, which was, at least nominally, the religion of most French people. The first religious indicator measures the extent to which local Catholic priests took an oath of allegiance to the French revolutionary constitution. The oath was required of all clergymen in 1791, but substantial numbers refused, and this opposition varied considerably from place to place (Tackett 1986). The higher the numerical score in scale, the greater the proportion of priests who took the oath, and the regions where most did so tended to be those where ties to orthodox Catholicism were weak and remained weak throughout the nineteenth century. By contrast, the regions where the clergy refused the oath were so strongly attached to Catholicism that all sorts of behavior was affected for decades—in particular, the use of birth control. The reasons for the differences were historical. In many areas where the clergy took the oath, not only had religious devotion faded away by the outbreak of the revolution, but shortly thereafter the clergy was removed during the revolutionary campaign against Catholicism. Parishes then went without priests for years. When the priests finally returned, often not until well into the Napoleonic empire or even later, after restoration of the monarchy in 1814, the by then anticlerical citizens were hardly inclined to listen to a priest's advice. Meanwhile, in the regions where the clergy spurned the oath, most priests had gone into hiding and ministered to the faithful in private. In these hotbeds of counterrevolution, the priests were hailed as heroes when orthodox Catholicism was restored, and parishioners faithfully heeded admonitions from the pulpit.[14]

Religious norms would thus exert more influence over behavior in the places where the clergy rejected the oath and where Catholicism remained robust—in other words, in areas where the oath score was low. What would the norms say about repaying debts? Worries about usury had long since withered away in Catholicism, at least at the level of daily life, and failure to pay a legitimate debt would presumably be tantamount to theft, provided of course that the borrower was not facing a dire emergency (Hoffman, Postel-Vinay, and Rosenthal 2000; Dumas 1953; Noonan 1957). If so, religious norms would pressure borrowers to uphold their end of the bargain, and logarithm of the oath scale would enter both panel and cross sectional regressions with a large, negative coefficient (for a list of the social capital measures and their expected sign in cross sectional and panel regressions, see table 9.2).

There is, however, a second and different way that the oath measure could conceivably enter the regressions. Where priests refused the oath, religious norms should have been effective, but the contrasting anticlerical regions should have had a strong attachment to the secular norms of the revolution and, later, the French Republic, which would entail respect for state courts and legal contracts. In areas with intermediate scores, however, it would not be clear whether either norm applied, and lenders would presumably have to exercise more caution. Such areas were likely to be divided between two mutually suspicious and even hostile camps: on one side, the royalist Catholics and, on the other, the anticlerical republicans.[15] Unfortunately, we cannot actually trace out the membership of camps because borrowers and lenders did not identify themselves as royalists, Catholics, republicans, or anticlericals. But we know that they did exist from realistic nineteenth-century novels. In Balzac's *Illusions perdues* (1843/1990), for instance, the clergy and royalist officials in Angoulême simply cease doing business with the printer David Séchard when rival printers falsely accuse him of atheism and republicanism; he nonetheless continues to work for the city's merchants, lawyers, and notaries, whose liberal opinions place them in the opposite camp. Should one trust such evidence? Dismissing it simply because it comes from a novel seems foolish. Balzac after all was describing a city and a business he knew well and was in fact striving for accurate detail.[16]

Members of these two camps would be leery of dealing with one another, particularly when something like lending was involved, for social networks would likely not cross the divide. How could, say, a republican lender pull strings in a royalist's social network to get a loan repaid? As a result, fewer loans would be made in places with such intermediate scores, because lenders would often have to rely on the legal system alone, not on social networks. If so, a dummy variable for places with such intermediate scores would have a negative sign in both the panel and cross-sectional regressions.

A third measure of social capital—voter turnout—is identical to one used in Luigi Guiso, Paola Sapienza, and Luigi Zingales's study of trust in financial markets (2004). For them, high voter turnout is a sign that behavior is guided by norms or by networks that punish aberrant behavior. One argument in favor of such a claim is that narrow economic self-interest alone cannot justify turning out to vote, because the time spent voting cannot be justified by the infinitesimal odds that one's ballot will sway the outcome. This is a classic example of a free rider problem, and high voter turnout suggests that it has been overcome. Norms or other punishment of misbehavior would be one way to achieve such a solution.

We have turnout for one election only. Many other elections were held, but to guarantee that the voting statistics would be comparable, we have restricted ourselves to instances where the voting met four conditions: the elections had to all be of the same type, the electoral districts had to be nearly identical to our markets, the suffrage had to be the same and as broad as possible, and voters must not have faced pressure to spurn the election and stay home. Concretely, these conditions limited us to general elections (and not local ones) with universal male suffrage. We further excluded cases in which the turnout was extremely low in some districts, which we took to be a mark of pressure on voters. We were left with the elections of May 1849, in which voters cast ballots for representatives in the Second Republic's new Assembly; in the future, however, we may include other elections as well.[17] If the arguments about norms are correct, a high turnout in the 1849 elections should boost T and thus have a large positive coefficient in both the panel and cross-sectional regressions.

Draft resistance provides a fourth measure of social capital. Conscription works when draftees trust their government or are at least committed to following its orders (Levi 1998). Conceivably, trust in the government or commitment to its rules might translate into respect for legal agreements, such as loan contracts. If so, indexes of draft resistance should enter into the regressions with a large negative coefficient.[18]

We have two such measures. The first is the proportion of the draftees who failed to report between 1820 and 1830. Although failure to report when called might appear an unambiguous sign of draft resistance, it could also reflect something quite different. The draftee could be dead, in prison, or away working as a migrant laborer, as often happened in regions where large numbers of young men left to work part of the year as itinerant masons. As a result, this measure captures other phenomena besides draft resistance, and it was in fact highest in areas with large populations of migratory laborers.

The second measure is much more clear cut. It is the percentage of the draftees between 1820 and 1830 who escaped service because they had mutilated themselves—typically by cutting off a finger. Apart from the occasional accident, the meaning of self-mutilation is unambiguous. And where such self-mutilation was common, *T* should have been low. The same should presumably be true for the other measure of draft resistance. Both variables should therefore have large negative coefficients in the panel and cross section regressions.

Our final measure of social capital is a legal one—the per capita number of verdicts against defendants in civil and criminal trials, which we can measure in 1840, 1865, and 1899; it is our one measure of social capital that varies over time. We count the guilty verdicts in criminal trials, add to that the number of civil judgments against defendants, and divide the total by the population. If the measure is high, then either there is a great deal of crime relative to the population or many legal transactions end up in court. Either way, trust would presumably be low, leaving a variable that should have a large negative sign in the regressions.

Those are our measures of social capital; their expected signs in the regressions (if trust is related to social capital) are shown in table 9.2. In addition, we have two independent measures of trust in borrowers that do not necessarily have any connection to social capital. They will be useful for testing whether trust in borrowers persists in credit markets even if it is unrelated to social capital. The first is the share of outstanding loans in 1740 that were perpetual annuities; the second is the same measure, only in 1780. Again, the perpetual annuities involved a lender's giving money to a borrower in return for an annual stream of payments, which (at least in theory) could continue forever given that it was the borrower alone (or his heirs) who decided when the principal was to be repaid. As we have noted, loans of this sort were common in 1740 and 1780, and required that a lender enter into an open-ended and long-term commitment to a borrower. Such a commitment was arguably a sign of trust, because it would be hard for a lender to know what would happen to a borrower's collateral in the years after the loan was first made. The share of such annuities in the total of outstanding loans, either in 1740 or in 1780, thus provides yet another measure of trust, but one that is not necessarily tied to social capital.

As a measure, it is a particularly interesting one because it allows a possible test of the persistence of trust. Consider the share of perpetual annuities in 1740. If it entered the regressions with a positive sign in periods after 1740, this could conceivably be taken as evidence that the same trust that allowed lenders to make a long-term commitment in 1740 was still working years later. If, however, the regression coefficient sign is zero or negative, then trust in 1740 apparently exercises no hold in later periods. In that case, trust, if it did play a role in financial markets, would simply not have any lasting effects; in other words, trust itself would vary. Similar arguments could be made about the share of perpetual annuities in 1780 if it is used as a variable in later periods.

For historical reasons, we might actually expect that this sort of trust shown in 1740 or 1780 might well fade away, particularly for the share of perpetual annuities in 1780. Lenders who entered into perpetual contracts in that year ended up losing heavily during the hyperinflation of the French Revolution (Hoffman, Postel-Vinay, and Rosenthal 2000). Their loans were all repaid in worthless paper money, and their long-term commitment, which could be taken as a sign of trust, was sorely abused. It would not be surprising if they and their descendants refused to make such commitments in the future; their reluctance would then register in the regressions as a lack of trust. But, as we shall see, this not the only possible test for the persistence of trust.

Results

Let us then examine the evidence from the regressions. Again, we have two hypotheses to test: first, that trust was linked to social capital in the past, and, second, that it persists across time. The first hypothesis requires nonfinancial measures of social capital to get around the problem that low levels of social capital in financial markets may reflect only low demand for loans. The second hypothesis requires panel data. We begin by assuming that the two hypotheses are both true, using panel regressions. We next move to repeated cross-sectional regressions to test the first hypothesis alone and explore the relationship between trust and social capital. We then return to panel regressions to test the second hypothesis by itself and see whether trust is persistent.

Let us first test whether both hypotheses are true. The test amounts to seeing whether the social capital variables in z_{jt} have large and significant coefficients with the signs shown in table 9.2. The dependent variable in the panel regressions is the logarithm of the per capita stock of outstanding debt; the other explanatory variables are logarithms of wealth (because our wealth measures are not available before 1840, it is omitted in regressions with cross sections before that year) and of measures of demand, including the number of banks and the population of the municipality where the loans are registered. Because at this stage we have no wealth measures for the first three periods and no count of banks for the first two, the regressions are run with all the variables for the period from 1840 to 1899, and without banks and wealth for 1740 to 1899 (tables 9.3 and 9.4,

Table 9.2 Hypotheses and Expected Signs of Regression Coefficients

If Trust Is Related to Social Capital	
Measure of Social Capital	Expected Sign of Coefficient
Intermediate score	Negative
Oath scale	Negative
Turnout in 1849	Positive
Resist draft: self-mutilate	Negative
Resist draft: fail to report	Negative
Verdicts	Negative
If Trust Is Persistent	
Measure of Trust	Expected Sign of Coefficient
Annuity share 1740	Positive
Annuity share 1780	Positive

Source: Authors' model and argument made in text.

regressions 1 through 7). The panel regressions are estimated using random effects when our social capital measures do not vary over time.[19] Some of these time-invariant social capital measures come from the revolutionary period and some from the middle of the nineteenth century, but each one is measured only once. All the coefficients have a simple interpretation: they measure by what percentage the dependent variable would change if the independent variable increased by 1 percent (in economic terms, they are elasticities).

The panel regressions show that our measure of lending per capita is clearly related to local conditions. Larger cities have large average outstanding debt, as do areas with more banks and markets where taxes per capita are higher—precisely what our model of credit rationing would suggest. As far as our two hypotheses are concerned, however, the regressions argue against them both. Only one of the social capital coefficients turns out to be statistically significant and have the sign we would expect if trust were persistent and linked to social capital (see tables 9.2 to 9.4). That one coefficient comes from *failure to report,* our somewhat ambiguous measure of draft resistance, which could well reflect something besides social capital. If it did reflect social capital—if, for instance, a willingness to serve meant people had confidence in formal institutions—then we would expect a negative coefficient not only for *failure to report,* but for our other, less equivocal measure of draft resistance, *self-mutilation.* But it in fact has a positive coefficient. As for the other social capital measures, *verdicts* has a coefficient with the wrong sign. Oath scale, the turnout in the 1848 elections, and our measure of religious divisions (*intermediate score*) do all have the expected sign, but not one is close to being significant.

Table 9.3 Test of Both Hypotheses: Selected Coefficients from Panel Regressions, 1840 to 1899

Variable	1	2	3	4	5	6	7
City population	0.38 4.99	0.37 4.82	0.36 4.85	0.36 4.91	0.39 5.34	0.37 5.05	0.06 0.28
Banks	0.15 1.71	0.15 1.73	0.15 1.77	0.15 1.82	0.15 1.84	0.13 1.57	–0.12 –0.98
Wealth	0.20 1.82	0.19 1.73	0.18 1.63	0.18 1.63	0.17 1.52	0.18 1.70	0.11 0.89
Social capital measure	intermediate score	oath scale	turnout 1849	resist draft: self-mutilate	resist draft: fail to report	verdicts	verdicts
Social capital coefficient	–0.13 –1.04	–0.11 –1.05	0.36 0.74	0.06 1.81	–0.06 –2.33	0.14 1.26	0.22 1.40
N	290	290	294	299	302	302	302
Specification of effects	random	random	random	random	random	random	fixed
Fraction of variance due to effects	0.32	0.31	0.33	0.31	0.31	0.32	0.66

Source: Authors' compilation based on sources described in the appendix.
Notes: Dependent variable is the logarithm of per capita stock of outstanding loans, and the explanatory variables are all logarithms, except for *intermediate score,* which is a dummy variable equal to 1 in markets that had intermediate scores on the oath taking scale. See table 9.1 and the text for details. *Banks* and *city population* are lagged. The regression also included dummy variables for the different cross sections to capture changes in the interest rate and other time varying effects. Coefficient estimates are on the top of each cell, *T*-statistics are below.

Table 9.4 Test of Both Hypotheses: Selected Coefficients from Panel Regressions, 1740 to 1899

Variable	1	2	3	4	5	6	7
City population	0.55 12.28	0.55 12.19	0.55 12.65	0.54 12.63	0.55 13.04	0.53 12.46	0.54 12.46
Social capital measure	intermediate score	oath scale	turnout 1849	resist draft: self-mutilate	resist draft: fail to report	verdicts in 1840	verdicts in 1865
Social capital coefficient	−0.02 −0.15	−0.06 −0.67	0.13 0.31	0.03 0.88	−0.04 −1.75	0.10 1.20	0.05 0.35
N	498	498	505	513	518	518	518
Specification of effects	random	random	random	random	random	random	random
Fraction of variance due to effects	0.31	0.31	0.30	0.30	0.29	0.30	0.30

Source: Authors' compilation based on sources described in the appendix.
Notes: Because the variable *verdicts* is not available before 1840, regression 6 was run using its value in 1840 for the entire panel; regression 7 did the same, using value in 1865. The other explanatory variables and the dependent variable are as in table 9.3, except that *banks* and *wealth* are omitted. Coefficient estimates are on the top of each cell, *T*-statistics are below.

Furthermore, virtually all of the coefficients are small, suggesting that even if a larger sample yielded more precise estimates the connection between trust and social capital would be economically trivial.[20] And the conclusions are the same whether we look at full panel or only the data from 1840 on; they are therefore not the result of institutional change during the French Revolution.[21]

Let us set aside the second hypothesis temporarily and focus on the first one, which asserts that trust is tied to social capital. The regressions here are cross sectional and resemble those run by other researchers in that they take a reduced form approach to evaluating trust, using instruments culled from nonfinancial measures of social capital. Our nonfinancial measures are in fact quite close to those others have used. But there are two differences between their work and ours. The first is that we have no direct measure of trust, such as the surveys that some contemporary researchers employ. That is perhaps a weakness, but it is offset by a second difference, which works in our favor. That second difference is that we follow financial development over a century and a half, something contemporary researchers cannot do.

Table 9.5 gives the results for a sample of our cross-sectional regressions. Like the panel regressions, they provide little evidence in favor of a close link between trust and social capital, even though we can augment the set of control variables for several regressions. If we run the cross-sectional regressions for 1865, for instance, we can add a measure of entrepreneurial talent (illiteracy, as measured among military recruits) and a measure of wealth inequality (the proportion of tax payers who had enough property to be eligible to vote in 1840).[22] The economic variables are jointly significant and generally have the predicted sign, except for banks once we control for wealth and inequality (through the number of males rich enough to vote in 1840 and illiteracy, which is correlated with poverty as well as entrepreneurial talent). Overall the economic variables explain 46 percent of the variance in the logarithm of per capita lending.

Yet even with these additional variables, the social capital measures still fail to have coefficients that are both statistically significant and have the expected sign for the 1865 cross section (table 9.5, regressions 2 through 7). The results are similar if we run the regressions for the other cross sections. Although we do not report all the results here, the only one that comes close to demonstrating a relationship between trust and social capital is the 1840 regression with *failure to report,* our ambiguous measure of draft resistance (table 9.5, regression 8). It has the right sign, and the odds that it is a statistical fluke are less than .082. But again the measure itself is questionable, the coefficient is small, and in any case, this single result is a weak reed on which to stand an argument about the connection between trust and social capital. In fact, it is remarkable that only one of several dozen coefficients (because we can run these regressions going all the way back to the revolution) is statistically significant.

Table 9.5 **Is Trust Related to Social Capital? Selected Cross-Sectional Regression Coefficients**

	1	2	3	4	5	6	7	8
Year of Cross Section	1865	1865	1865	1865	1865	1865	1865	1840
Variable								
City population	0.27	0.28	0.25	0.28	0.25	0.26	0.26	0.33
	1.66	1.64	1.48	1.65	1.53	1.61	1.65	2.10
Banks	–0.08	–0.09	–0.06	–0.06	–0.07	–0.08	–0.08	–0.01
	–0.59	–0.64	–0.43	–0.38	–0.49	–0.57	–0.57	–0.07
Wealth	0.38	0.41	0.37	0.36	0.35	0.34	0.35	–0.01
	1.39	1.40	1.30	1.23	1.26	1.23	1.29	–0.04
Voters	0.24	0.24	0.24	0.21	0.25	0.27	0.25	0.19
	1.83	1.72	1.81	1.51	1.84	2.03	1.88	1.40
Illiteracy	–0.34	–0.36	–0.34	–0.31	–0.34	–0.30	–0.39	–0.51
	–1.67	–1.71	–1.62	–1.45	–1.65	–1.48	–1.84	–2.26
Social capital measure	none	intermediate score	oath scale	turnout 1849	resist draft: self-mutilate	resist draft: fail to report	verdicts in 1840	resist draft: fail to report
Social capital coefficient		–0.05	–0.19	0.13	0.06	–0.05	–0.13	–0.07
		–0.28	–1.26	0.19	1.24	–1.26	–0.94	–1.76
N	90	86	86	87	89	90	90	91
R^2	0.46	0.45	0.46	0.45	0.47	0.47	0.47	0.47

Source: Authors' compilation based on sources described in the appendix.
Notes: There are two new explanatory variables in some of the cross-sectional regressions. The first is *illiteracy,* the logarithm of the illiteracy rate among local military recruits, as measured in the years 1820 through 1830. The second is *voters,* the fraction of tax payers in 1840 who were wealthy enough to meet the property requirements for voting; it is a measure of inequality, since it rises as the distribution of wealth becomes more unequal. Both of these new variables enter the regressions as logarithms. For further details about the two new variables, see table 9.1. The dependent variable in the regressions and all the other explanatory variables are as in table 9.3, with lagged values (from the previous cross section) of *banks* and *city population.* Regression also included a constant term. Coefficient estimates are on the top of each cell, *T*-statistics are below.

It thus seems that if trust does play a role in credit markets over the long term, it has little to do with social capital. Trust and social capital may be connected in certain markets today, but the connection is not universal and did not always hold in the past, even though the set of social capital variables was large. One could, of course, raise doubts about such a conclusion, arguing that our data are measured with error and that our regression coefficients are therefore biased toward zero. One could also make a similar argument about omitted variables. But if so, why do we continue to find no convincing evidence in favor of social capital in 1865 and in 1899, when the data are quite accurate, the relevant political institutions have long been in place, and we can include additional variables as well? Furthermore, our data avoid some of the obvious drawbacks of the surveys that other researchers on trust use. Our evidence comes from real transactions in which people had sizable sums of money at stake—a big difference from surveys. True, our measure of trust in borrowers is something of a residual, but the lack of any relationship between it and conventional measures of social capital suggests that social capital is simply not essential for generating financial trust. The results may of course be different for the sort of small consumer debts that never appear in our database, but that sort of credit was much less important than the lending in the markets we studied. In them, social capital was not related to financial trust.

If the evidence thus argues against the first hypothesis, what about the second one, that trust is persistent? There is at least some conceivable support for it. If we run the panel regressions without social capital measures, we can then use fixed effects to measure persistent differences between markets. The fixed effects turn out to be appreciable: they explain a significant fraction of the variance in the per capita stock of lending (between 63 and 67 percent), and an F-test shows that the odds of all the fixed effects being zero is less than .0001 (table 9.6, regressions 1 and 3).[23] The panel regressions thus imply that there are large and persistent differences between markets that our economic variables (wealth and the demand measures, banks and city size) cannot account for. The persistent differences may be interpreted as evidence that trust exists and endures over time, but it should be stressed they may also reflect other causes as well, such as geographic conditions that favor economic growth, informal institutions that have nothing to do with trust, or the learning and experience of local financial intermediaries that can be passed on to their successors.

Possible evidence that the differences may have been generated by something like trust comes from two further panel regressions, which add the share of perpetual annuities in either 1740 or 1780 and look at its effect over the years 1840 to 1899. The annuity share turns out to have a large positive and significant coefficient in both regressions. A market in which all loans in 1780 were perpetual annuities had, other things being equal, a

Table 9.6 **Is Trust Persistent? Selected Coefficients from Panel Regressions**

	1	2	3	4	5	6	7	8
Panel	1740 to 1899	1740 to 1899	1840 to 1899	1840 to 1899	1840 to 1899	1840 to 1899	1780 to 1899	1807 to 1899
Variable								
City population	0.005	0.54	0.03	0.36	0.34	0.36	0.50	0.51
	0.03	12.83	0.16	5.03	4.70	5.09	12.00	12.01
Banks			–0.12	0.15	0.13	0.14		
			–0.97	1.76	1.58	1.66		
Wealth			0.10	0.19	0.15	0.18		
			0.79	1.75	1.40	1.71		
Trust measure	none	none	none	none	annuity share 1740	annuity share 1780	annuity share 1740	annuity share 1780
Coefficient of trust measure	0.82	0.58	0.78	0.54	3.93	3.17	4.27	3.22
N	518	518	302	302	299	299	514	407
Specification of effects	fixed	random	fixed	random	random	random	random	random
Fraction of variance due to effects	0.63	0.30	0.67	0.32	0.28	0.29	0.26	0.29

Source: Authors' compilation based on sources described in the appendix.
Notes: Annuity share 1740 and 1780 are not entered as logarithms. All the variables are logarithms and are the same as in tables 9.3 and 9.4. Banks and city populations are lagged. Regression also included dummy variables for the different cross sections to capture changes in interest rate and other time-varying effects. Coefficient estimates are on the top of each cell, *T*-statistics are below.

58 percent higher per capita loan stock from 1840 to 1899; for the 1740 annuity share, the impact was even higher—an 82 percent jump in the per capital stock (table 9.6, regressions 5 and 6). Regressions run with the same annuity shares for longer periods (when we unfortunately lack data on banks and wealth) lead to similar results (table 9.6, regressions 7 and 8).

One might be tempted to interpret these findings as evidence that trust does have a lasting effect on financial markets. After all, that the annuity share in 1740 influences borrowing some 100 to 150 years later is a striking result, particularly given that it comes from regressions from 1840 to 1899, when the relevant legal and political institutions are not changing. Conceivably—so the explanation might go—individuals might have been inclined to lend money out in perpetual annuity contracts in those markets in which people had developed effective social sanctions against potential defaulters. If so, perhaps the trust formed in these markets might have became a perennial factor in the local lending culture and thus persisted for generations.

Yet though that interpretation may seem plausible at first glance, it has a fatal disadvantage: it cannot stand up to historical reality. In 1790, the French revolutionary government, which was falling short of revenue, embarked on an ambitious scheme to nationalize church properties and to issue paper currency (assignats) backed by the confiscated wealth (Hoffman, Postel-Vinay, and Rosenthal 2000). The printing presses churned out so many reams of assignats that the currency lost 99 percent of its value in five years. All that would be of little importance save that for ancient legal reasons all loan contracts were nominal and thus not indexed against inflation. Essentially, the loan contracts took two forms. One was a term loan with a short, specified maturity, typically under three years except in Paris. Lenders who had put out their money in these contracts were by and large able to get it back before the currency's value plunged. The second contract type, however, was the perpetual annuity, and repayment of the capital for these loans was at the discretion of the borrower, provided he continued to pay the interest due. For these contracts, borrowers could wait as inflation eroded the currency and then repay their annuities in worthless paper. The lenders could do nothing to force repayment. Our estimates for Paris are that more than 90 percent of the perpetual annuities were paid off and that the lenders lost on average 75 percent of the prerevolutionary value of their investments. The inflation, quite simply, was a dagger aimed at the trust shown by individuals who lent money out in annuities. The connection with trust is inescapable, because borrowers could have chosen not to repay in worthless assignats and then borne the full cost of their loans once the currency had been stabilized. Although markets with high annuity shares before the revolution might have been places where trust was high, they should have had very low trust afterwards.

If trust were important, we would expect lenders in markets with high annuity shares to shun lending after the revolution. But if that was how many lenders acted, we should have observed exactly the opposite in the regression—namely, a coefficient that was large and negative. The positive coefficient thus begs explanation, but fortunately a simple alternative makes sense of our results. Markets with large annuity shares in 1740 witnessed a great deal of lending in 1780 because they were the markets with more wealth and demand for credit. If the revolution left the distribution of economic activity intact and informal cultural variables were unimportant, we would expect markets with big annuity shares to recover swiftly and to again have sizeable demand for credit after the revolution. And that is precisely what happened. Although bloodshed and tumult during the revolution slowed the recovery, the redistribution of property (albeit considerable) was sudden and definitive and hence did not disrupt the economy greatly. The original property owners had little time to allow assets to depreciate much, and some of the church property that was auctioned off was actually converted to productive use—in particular, monastic buildings. The real economy quickly recovered and with it the large demand for loans in the markets with all the eighteenth-century annuities. With a delay, one that was a bit longer in Paris and other cities where annuities were popular, so did the supply of loans. By 1807, the stock of outstanding debts had already climbed to 72 percent of its 1780 value, if we use our figures to extrapolate to France as a whole.

This demand side story has an appealing consistency that the trust story lacks. For otherwise, we would have to believe that trust could somehow survive the social upheavals of an event like the French Revolution and persist without flinching for years—even though it was trust in annuities that had suffered the greatest damage from the revolutionary inflation. What could make it through such turmoil unbowed? It would simply be impossible for trust not to change. History mounts a powerful argument for persistent differences in demand and against differences in trust.

Conclusion

When we began this inquiry, we firmly believed that credit required trust and in particular that lenders had to trust borrowers, given that a debtor could affect a creditor's ability to recover his capital in many ways. In earlier work, we had emphasized the importance of informal institutions and human capital development in explaining the growth of lending in Paris (Hoffman, Postel-Vinay, and Rosenthal 2000). In extending our research to encompass not just Paris but a large sample of cities and towns as well, we encountered some startling differences in the institutions that sustained lending (Hoffman, Postel-Vinay, and Rosenthal 2004). It was our ambition to connect our analysis of institution with the study of trust and trustworthiness.

Yet, to our surprise, we found that trust was neither persistent nor firmly linked to conventional measures of social capital. At first glance, this result seems absurd, given the importance accorded to trust in financial markets. It seems doubly absurd given the weight many scholars have put on the role of informal networks in financial affairs. It may even seem ridiculous, given the emphasis individuals active in financial markets have always placed on trust and on reputation. After all, trust or its abuse has been advanced to explain aggregate fluctuations (in financial crises stemming from loss of confidence), individual success (of bankers such as Rothschild or Morgan, whose fortunes were built on trust), and individual failure (individuals denied credit because of a lack of trust) (Hoffman, Postel-Vinay, and Rosenthal 2007). That seemed true as far back as the eighteenth century and remains true today. Yet the contradiction here is more apparent than real. Although trust is critical, it is not hard to manufacture in adequate amounts in economies and societies that are not pathological. In the previous chapter of this volume, we can actually see the process involved, at least in the case of the United States. As a result, from a statistical perspective, trust in the financial arena is an intermediate variable that evolves rather quickly, at least from the sort of generational perspective that we have been investigating, in response to shocks to the demand for credit.[24]

Problems of trust do of course arise when societies have severe problems of racketeering. Indeed, in such societies—southern Italy, for example—participation in formal financial markets may well make one a target for thieves, extortionists, or embezzlers. What then should policymakers in such societies do? No policy they adopt will change an individual's trust unless it attacks the ultimate cause of the lack of trust—namely, racketeering. In this instance, as in cases of civil war or racial and ethnic discrimination, capital will spurn financial markets and flow only through peculiar channels. Individuals without access to these channels may well be shut out, and attempts to eliminate mistrust without treating the larger social problem will have little effect.

In economies that have escaped such intractable social and political problems, the problems for policymakers are different, even if the societies are poor. Capital markets in such economies may simply be underdeveloped, and the historical experience of France and other countries in the North Atlantic suggest that in this case two sets of institutions are worth nurturing: those that encourage savings and those that boost the flow of information between borrowers and lenders. Savings are important because even today most loans go to individuals or firms that have accumulated assets that can be used as collateral. Even unsecured debt is usually taken on by individuals and firms that are already rich. An important way for countries to increase lending is thus to reduce the cost of saving in the form of financial assets; once individuals have accumulated such assets, they can leverage them. Savings of this sort does require that individuals believe that their wealth is secure. That belief, which could be called trust in formal institutions, seems to have been prevalent early on in France.

The importance of institutions that help convey information is also clear, for if information flows are blocked, lenders cannot detect borrowers' misbehavior, and everyone will be encouraged to take advantage of everyone else. Reduced information can then quickly translate into generalized distrust. The institutions that facilitate the flow of information can thus heighten trust. If a country has both these institutions and the ones that foster savings, then our evidence suggests that the more informal institutions affecting trust will fall into place on their own.

Appendix: The Model

Our model abstracts from an economy in which the number of markets for credit is finite, and each market is large relative to the loans that any individual makes. It assumes N such markets, the j-th market having a continuum of individuals of positive mass m_j and the sum of the m_j equaling 1. The m_j are measures of the relative size of the markets, which would be relative populations if the number of actors in each market were finite. Capital flows from market to market as individuals borrow and lend; the equilibrium condition for the interest rate i is that average excess demand for loans is zero for the entire economy:

$$\Sigma_j m_j \left[\left(1 - G_j(i)\right) T_j E_j(w|r > 1)/(1+i) - G_j(i) E_j(w|r \leq i) \right] = 0$$

where the sum is taken over all N markets, G_j is the distribution of entrepreneurial rates of return talent in market j, $T_j > 0$ is trust in the market, and $E_j\ (w|r > i)$ is the expected value of wealth in the market for individuals with $r > i$. This expected value is calculated with respect to the market's distribution of wealth F_j. Because we assume that the distribution of wealth and entrepreneurial talent are independent in each market, this condition becomes

$$\Sigma_j m_j \left[\left(1 - G_j(i)\right) T_j E_j(w)/(1+i) - G_j(i) E_j(w) \right] = 0 \qquad \text{(A1)}$$

We assume that the distribution functions G_j are absolutely continuous and that there is a maximum feasible rate of return $R > 0$ such that $G_j\ (R) = 1$ for all markets j. The expression on the left hand side of A1, which we will call D, is therefore negative for $i = R$ and positive for when $i = 0$. Because D is a continuous function of i, there must therefore be at least one interest rate i^* for which A1 holds.

This i^* will be unique if there is at least one market j for which $G_j(i^*) < 1$, for then D, which is nonincreasing in i, will actually be decreasing in a neighborhood of i^*. If we assume that such a market exists and that the density functions for the G_j are all continuous, we can apply the implicit function theorem to i^* as a function of T_k, the measure of trust in market k. The equilibrium interest rate i^* will then be an increasing function of T_k. An increase in T_k will raise the average supply of funds $m_j\, G_j(i)\, E_j(w)$ from other markets ($j \neq k$) and reduce the average demand in these markets. Its effect on the demand in market k, however, will be ambiguous, because the rising interest rate may offset the effect of greater trust.

For our regressions, we are concerned with per-capita borrowing in each market, which in our model is $(1 - G_j(i^*))\, T_j\, E_j(w)/(1 + i^*)$. The logarithm of this expression is the dependent variable in our regressions, and to a first order approximation it will be a linear function of the interest rate, average wealth, and our indexes of demand and trust, if we assume that G_j and T_j are continuously differentiable functions of the demand and trust indices.

Sources for Data

Thanks to generous support from the Russell Sage Foundation, we have managed to gather data on more than 200,000 loans spread out over 160 years and 108 separate markets in six cross sections: 1740, 1780, 1807, 1840, 1865, and 1899. The markets were chosen to form a stratified sample of French towns and cities according to their population. The sample includes Paris, three other large urban centers (Lyon, Rouen, and Toulouse), thirteen medium-sized cities (populations between 20,000 and 50,000, such as Amiens), and forty smaller cities (populations between 5,000 and 20,000), and sixty-one towns (populations under 5,000). Our evidence, it should be stressed, comes not simply from the cities and towns themselves but from the surrounding countryside as well.

In addition to the credit data, we have also collected data on financial intermediaries, populations, economic development, bankruptcies, wealth, inequality, human capital, and social capital in each of the 108 markets. Here we describe our sources and how we estimated the per capita stock of outstanding debt in each market.

To estimate, we used records of loan registration that survive as far back as the early eighteenth century. Lenders had to have their loans registered with a local registration office and pay a tax on the transaction. If they did not do so, they would have difficulty enforcing their loans in court in case of default, and they therefore had a powerful incentive to register the loans and report truthfully the terms of the loan contract. The registration offices were located in towns and cities but registered transactions for the surrounding countryside as well. Although the registration was reorganized late in the French Revolution, the nature of the tax and the size of the areas covered by each office hardly changed over time.[25] Typically each office covered an area that was nearly the same as a nineteenth-century French canton, a small administrative unit averaging some 150 square kilometers.

For each market and cross section, the registration records gave us the number of new loans made, the types of loans, their size, and, in most cases, their duration. In the eighteenth century, data on durations in certain types of loans had to be gathered directly from the original loan contracts, which survive in the archives of notaries, the legal officials who drew up loan contracts and arranged loans.[26]

To calculate the outstanding stock of debt, we took the new loans registered in each market in the years of our six cross sections and multiplied the value of each loan by its duration. The sum of these products is our estimate for the loan stock. The calculation assumes that the market is in a steady state, but a detailed investigation of the credit market in Paris shows this method is a good approximation. We could also calculate the fraction of loans of each type and single out particular sorts of debt, such as annuities.

The dependent variable in our regressions was the logarithm of the outstanding stock per person, which we calculated by dividing the outstanding loan stock by the population of the district the office served.[27] Our regressions also used the population of the city where the registration office was located as an explanatory variable; again, this population was not the same as that used to compute the per capita loan stock.

As for our other explanatory variables, the wealth measure came from property tax records in 1840, 1864, and 1899. Tax records and the Bottin *Almanach*—a national guide that provided commercial, administrative, and personal information for all French cities, including those eligible to vote—also provided our measure of inequality, the proportion of taxpayers who had enough assets to be eligible to vote in 1840 (Bottin and Tynna 1840).[28] Literacy rates came from draft records for the years 1820 to 1830, which in addition furnished our two measures of draft resistance.[29] The religious measures of social capital were graciously provided by Timothy Tackett; they come from his data as published in the atlas of Claude Langlois and colleagues (1996). The judicial measures of social capital (the number of verdicts against defendants in civil and criminal trials in 1840, 1865, and 1899) come from *Compte général de l'administration de la justice criminelle en France pendant l'année 1840* (Ministere de la Justice 1841), table LXXVI ; *Compte général de l'administration de la justice criminelle en France pendant l'année 1865* (Ministere de la Justice 1866), table LXXVIII; and *Compte général de l'administration de la justice criminelle en France pendant l'année 1898* (Ministere de la Justice 1899), table XXX.

Finally, the number of banks was taken from the Bottin *Almanach* or *Annuaire* for the years of our nineteenth-century cross sections. If bank data was unavailable for that exact year, we used figures for the nearest available year: data from 1829 for 1807, from 1862 for 1865, and from 1898 for 1899 (Bottin and Tynna 1829, 1840; Bottin 1862, 1898).

Notes

1. Robert Putnam, Robert Leonardi, and Rafaella Nanetti argue that social capital in different parts of Italy has ancient historical roots; it thus must change very slowly, if at all (1993). More recently, however, Edward Miguel, Paul Gertler, and David Levine used repeated surveys to show that social capital does seem to have changed during industrialization in Indonesia (2006).
2. Although Miguel, Gertler, and Levine explored changes in social capital during industrialization, they did not investigate the relationship between social capital and the sort of trust in financial markets that is the subject of this chapter (2006). They did examine the number of credit cooperatives, but for them it is simply one of several measures of social capital, and not an index of financial trust.
3. The entrepreneur's return r could of course be related to his education, which a wealthy entrepreneur could purchase, but we can control for that in our regressions. A more complicated dynamic model could also introduce a correlation between w and r.
4. Unregistered debt included informal consumption loans and certain forms of merchant credit that were not subject to the registration requirements. For an individual merchant, the mercantile credit could be important, but because only a small number of people took out such loans, they would count for very little in our calculation of the per capita debt stock that is our dependent variable. They would count for even less given that such debt was short term (typically ninety days or less) and our dependent variable (as we explain in the appendix) takes into account the duration of the loans. As for the informal consumption loans, they too would be small, given the incentives that lenders had to register anything sizeable.
5. These examples come from the registration office records for Dun-sur-Auron at the Archives départementales du Cher, 1 Q 4025 (January 6, 1840).
6. Many of the original term loan contracts in the notarial archives also omitted the interest rate, simply saying, for instance, that a borrower owed a particular amount due on such and such a date.
7. The differences in interest rates could also reflect risk premiums and fees, which are not part of our simple model.
8. We used total loan stock rather than the volume of new loans because the loan stock comes closer to capturing the notion of total borrowing that is at the heart of the model. Imagine, for instance, that an entrepreneur can fund a three-year construction project to build a new factory by taking out a $1,000 loan for three years, or by taking out three successive $1,000 loans, each for one year. If we were only taking into account the volume of new loans in a single year (which is essentially what we would be doing in a one-year cross

section), then one of the one-year $1,000 loans would count for as much as three-year $1,000 loan; if, however, we weight by duration (as in the computation of loan stock), then the three-year loan is worth three times as much.

9. The interest rate will not figure in the cross-sectional regressions because it will be constant in any single cross section. It will enter the panel regression via both the term $\ln(1 - G_j(i^*))$ and the term $\ln(1 + i^*)$. To a first-order approximation, we can expand $\ln(1 - G_j(i^*))$ as a linear function of $\ln(1 + i^*)$ and other variables, and thus the interest rate will appear in the panel regression simply as a coefficient times $\ln(1 + i^*)$, which we can capture by using time dummies in the panel regression. Because $(1 + i^*)$ is very close to i^*, we could also simply insert the average interest rate in the regressions.

10. Although one can try to test the persistence of trust by running successive cross-sectional regressions for different years, the results could well be misleading, because the effects of the w_j could be mixed in the constant term with the impact of varying interest rates and other time dependent variables. One could therefore not tell for sure whether trust was changing. In the panel regression, the interest rate and the other time-varying variables can be captured by dummies for the periods.

11. If it is left out of the regressions, there is of course the problem of omitted variables bias, as when any other variables are omitted.

12. This short-term bank credit was usually not registered with the tax offices and so does not figure in our data. But as we have explained, the omission is not likely to affect our per capita loan stocks y_i significantly, because the mercantile loans were short term and only a relatively few merchants were involved.

13. As we explain, finding useable voting data was difficult, and it is even harder to gather reliable data on guilds. The sort of information about associations often used to measure social capital was not available until the 1870s or later. Conceivably, distance from a given market to Paris might be considered a proxy for social capital, because Paris was the source of political and cultural change, but it was not correlated in any plausible way with our social capital measures and in any case had no significant effect when inserted in our panel regressions. Finally, we do have some evidence on professional and familial ties linking borrowers and lenders in a few selected markets; such ties (which were important in Paris in the seventeenth century, though not thereafter) might be considered yet another proxy for social capital. Gathering similar information for even a reasonable sample of our markets, though, would have been prohibitively time consuming.

14. Donald Sutherland addresses the relationship between the oath and the use of birth control through the effect the French Revolution had on Catholicism (2003, 193–94, 242–45, 345). In unpublished research, David Weir (personal communication to Philip T. Hoffman) has also noticed the connection between the oath and birth control. As Sutherland pointed out, the revolutionary campaign against traditional Catholicism was far from uniform, and as a result, the correlation between rejecting the revolutionary oath and subsequent attachment to Catholicism is not a perfect one (2003, 186–98). But there is still a correlation.

15. For other examples of this social rift as a backdrop in novels, see Stendhal (1830/1963), *Le rouge et le noir*. The divisions here may in fact have reached back to eighteenth century (see, for instance, Vovelle 1973; Norberg 1985).

16. Balzac had himself worked in the printing business and he had made several extended visits to friends in Angoulême (1843/1990). He was also so attentive to detail that he even asked his friends there for information about place names and a city map, which he completed by reading guides to Angoulême.

17. We leave alternative elections for further research, in particular, those for the *Etats Généraux* in 1789 and various general elections during the Third Republic (on the May 1849 elections, see Dupeux 1962 ; Vigier 1963). The detailed results for 1849 are in the Archives nationales, C 1467–578.

18. Conscription can also be undermined by inequality, which is at least in part an economic variable. In an unequal society, average wealth will be a poor measure of collateral, because many people will have little or no collateral, and per capita lending may therefore be less than what the average wealth implies. The expected effect, again, will be a negative relationship between resistance to conscription and lending, though it may be in part economic.

19. Our panel regressions always use a random-effects specification when we have an explanatory variable (such as a measure of trust or social capital) that does not vary across time. Otherwise, we used a fixed-effects specification, though in some cases we have also shown the results with a random-effects specification for the sake of comparison. Fixed effects have certain advantages over random effects, but they are inappropriate when explanatory variables do not vary over time. The random-effects estimator assumes that the time invariant social capital or trust measures are not correlated with the economic variables; that may have been a problem for our trust measure *annuity share 1740*, for our social capital measure *election turnout 1849*, and for *verdicts* when its value in 1840 is used in a random-effects regression in table 9.4 (regression 6). On the other hand, one can argue that the random-effects estimator is more appropriate for all of our regressions because we are dealing with a sample of markets.

20. One might worry that the social capital measures could be jointly significant, but if they are all added to a random effects regression for the years 1840 to 1899, the null hypothesis that they jointly have no effect cannot be rejected at the 10 percent level ($P = 0.1038$). The test used *self-mutilate* rather than *fail to report* to measure draft resistance.

21. Because Miguel, Gertler, and Levine found out that migration eroded social capital in Indonesia, one might wonder whether our panel regressions would change if we took migration into account (2006). We can do so in a crude way by using changes in city populations as a yardstick of migration and adding an interaction term with our measures of social capital. If we do so, the results are unchanged, and the coefficients of the social capital measures are all statistically insignificant.

22. Wealth restrictions on male suffrage in France ended in 1848; earlier in the decade, only one of forty adult males had been eligible to vote.
23. Random effects regressions (table 9.6, regressions 2 and 4) also point to sizeable w_j.
24. Our claim here parallels what Miguel, Gertler, and Levine found about the relationship between industrialization and social capital (2006).
25. Before the revolution, the registration was known as the *contrôle des actes;* after the revolution, it was the *enregistrement des actes civils publics.*
26. In a small number of cases, where records were destroyed or unavailable, we had to seek other data in the notarial archives or in judicial records. That was the case, for example, in Caen, where the records were destroyed during the Normandy invasion, and in Paris, where registration did not exist in the eighteenth century.
27. For the population of the area served by each office, we used the canton population, or its geographic equivalent in the eighteenth century, which we calculated by summing the populations for the corresponding parishes (in the eighteenth century) or communes (in the nineteenth century). We thank Claude Motte for graciously making this population data available.
28. Unfortunately 1840 was the only year when the Bottin gave the list of taxpayers eligible to vote.
29. The sources here are Jean-Paul Aron, Paul Dumont, and Emmanuel Le Roy Ladurie (1972) and the *Comptes numériques et sommaires sur les jeunes gens* for each department, which are in the Archives nationales, F9 150–261.

References

Aron, Jean-Paul, Paul Dumont, and Emmanuel Le Roy Ladurie. 1972. *Anthropologie du conscrit français d'après les comptes numériques et sommaires du recrutement de l'armée (1819–1826).* Paris: Mouton.

Arrow, Kenneth J. 1972. "Gifts and Exchanges." *Philosophy and Public Affairs* 1(4): 343–62.

Balzac, Honoré de. 1843/1990. *Illusions perdues,* edited by Philippe Bertier. Paris: Flammarion.

Bottin, Sébastien. 1862. *Annuaire-Almanach du commerce et de l'industrie ou Almanach des 500000 adresses, Paris.* Paris: Didot-Bottin.

———. 1898. *Annuaire-Almanach du commerce et de l'industrie ou Almanach des 500000 adresses, Paris.* Paris: Didot-Bottin.

Bottin, Sébastien, and Jean de la Tynna. 1829. *Almanach du commerce de Paris, des départements de la France et des principales villes du monde by Jean de la Tynna continué et mis à jour par S. Bottin.* Paris: Didot-Bottin.

———. 1840. *Almanach du commerce de Paris, des départements de la France et des principales villes du monde by Jean de la Tynna continué et mis à jour par S. Bottin.* Paris: Didot-Bottin.

Dumas, Auguste. 1953. "Intérêt et usure." *Dictionnaire de droit canonique,* vol. 5, *1475–1518.* Paris: Librairie Letouzey et Ané.

Dupeux, Georges. 1962. *Aspects de l'histoire sociale et politique du Loir-et-Cher 1848–1914.* Paris: Mouton.

Guiso, Luigi, Paola Sapienza, and Luigi Zingales. 2004. "The Role of Social Capital in Financial Development." *American Economic Review* 94(3): 526–56.

———. 2005. "Trusting the Stock Market." *CRSP* working paper 602. Chicago: University of Chicago, School of Business.

———. 2006. "Does Culture Affect Economic Outcomes?" *Journal of Economic Perspectives* 20(2): 23–48.

Henrich, Joseph, Robert Boyd, Samuel Bowles, Colin Camerer, Ernst Fehr, and Herbert Gintis, eds. 2004. *Foundations of Human Sociality: Economic Experiments and Ethnographic Evidence from Fifteen Small-Scale Societies.* Oxford: Oxford University Press.

Hoffman, Philip T., Gilles Postel-Vinay, and Jean-Laurent Rosenthal. 2000. *Priceless Markets: The Political Economy of Credit in Paris 1660–1870.* Chicago: University of Chicago Press.

———. 2004. "Révolution et évolution: Les marchés de crédit notarié en France 1780–1840." *Annales: Economies, Sociétés, Civilisations* 59(2): 387–424.

———. 2007. *Surviving Large Losses: Financial Crises, the Middle Class, and the Development of Capital Markets.* Cambridge, Mass.: Harvard University Press.

Knack, Stephen and Philip Keefer. 1997. "Does Social Capital Have an Economic Payoff? A Cross-Country Investigation." *Quarterly Journal of Economics* 112(4): 1251–288.

Langlois, Claude, Timothy Tackett, Michel Vovelle, Serge Bonin, and Madeleine Bonin, eds. 1996. *Atlas de la révolution française,* vol. 9, *Religion.* Paris: École des Hautes Études en Sciences Sociales.

Levi, Margaret. 1998. "Conscription: The Price of Citizenship." In *Analytic Narratives,* edited by Robert H. Bates, Avner Greif, Margaret Levi, Jean-Laurent Rosenthal, and Barry R. Weingast. Princeton, N.J.: Princeton University Press.

Miguel, Edward, Paul Gertler, and David I. Levine. 2006. "Does Industrialization Build or Destroy Social Networks?" *Economic Development and Cultural Change* 54(2): 287–317.

Ministere de la Justice. 1841. *Compte général de l'administration de la justice criminelle en France pendant l'année 1840.* Paris: Imprimerie Nationale.

———. 1866. *Compte général de l'administration de la justice criminelle en France pendant l'année 1865.* Paris: Imprimerie Nationale.

———. 1899. *Compte général de l'administration de la justice criminelle en France pendant l'année 1898.* Paris: Imprimerie Nationale.

Noonan, John Thomas. 1957. *The Scholastic Analysis of Usury.* Cambridge, Mass.: Harvard University Press.

Norberg, Kathryn. 1985. *Rich and Poor in Grenoble 1600–1814.* Berkeley: University of California Press.

Putnam, Robert D., Robert Leonardi, and Raffaella Y. Nanetti. 1993. *Making Democracy Work: Civic Traditions in Modern Italy.* Princeton, N.J.: Princeton University Press.

Stendhal [Marie-Henri Beyle]. 1830/1963. *Le rouge et le noir* (*The Red and the Black*), edited by Henri Martineau. Paris: Garnier.

Sutherland, Donald M. G. 2003. *The French Revolution and Empire: The Quest for a Civic Order*. Oxford: Blackwell Publishing.

Tackett, Timothy. 1986. *Religion, Revolution, and Regional Culture in Eighteenth-Century France: The Ecclesiastical Oath of 1791*. Princeton, N.J.: Princeton University Press.

Vigier, Philippe. 1963. *La seconde république dans la région alpine: Etude politique et sociale*. Paris: Presses universitaires de France.

Vovelle, Michel. 1973. *Piété baroque et déchristianisation: Les attitudes devant la mort en Provence au XVIIIe siècle*. Paris: Librairie Plon.

Woloch, Isser. 1994. *The New Regime: Transformations of the French Civic Order 1789–1820s*. New York: W. W. Norton.

Chapter 10

Proxies and Experience as Bases of Trust in Courts

GABRIELLA R. MONTINOLA

EARLIER CHAPTERS IN this volume examine how individuals determine who is trustworthy. In this chapter, I focus on the bases of evaluations of institutions rather than coethnics or potential debtors, and examine how individuals determine whether government institutions are trustworthy.

Most work on trust in government centers on the conditions that promote high levels of trust rather than the bases under which judgments of trustworthiness are derived. But work on the sources of trust in government provides insight into the bases of trust evaluations of government institutions (for a comprehensive survey of the trust literature, see Levi and Stoker 2000). Research on attitudes toward specific government institutions shows that evaluations across institutions are linked. Support for the president, for example, has been shown to influence support for the Congress and the Supreme Court (Bernstein 2001; Caldeira 1986; Kimball and Patterson 1997), and trust in the federal government has been shown to influence trust in lower-level governments (Rahn and Rudolph 2005; Uslaner 2001). I argue that this link in evaluations across specific institutions is due to an information-processing strategy employed by individuals. This strategy directs individuals to use information on institutions with which they are familiar to make inferences regarding institutions about which they know little (Rahn and Rudolph 2002).

I use a research design that allows us to determine whether individuals with less information on a specific institution are more likely to use such proxies. This design centers on an analysis of local courts. Local courts are particularly suited to this purpose because a significant proportion of the population has direct experience in court that they can use as a basis for their assessments, a point I elaborate on shortly. We can thus compare court users with those who have had no court experience and determine whether individuals respond to experience-based information.

Determining the cognitive process underlying evaluations of specific government institutions has important implications for those concerned with low levels of trust or declining trust in government. If individuals evaluate institutions separately depending on the information they have, reforms need not be global to affect trust assessments. Reform of one institution would generate higher levels of trust even if other institutions remain problematic, as long as citizens have specific information with which to update their trust judgments.

Focusing on local courts is also of substantive importance given their role in establishing the rule of law. A substantial amount of foreign aid from Organisation for Economic Cooperation and Development (OECD) countries and international financial institutions is targeted toward establishing the rule of law in emerging democracies (Carothers 1998; McClymont and Golub 2000). Local courts are the first set of institutions on which the public must rely when conflicts arise between citizens and between citizens and government. The vast majority of these conflicts must be resolved at the local level if the judicial system is to work properly. Because courts have no direct control over how their decisions are implemented, their authority rests in large part on popular assessments (Caldeira 1986). Understanding the bases of trust in courts is thus a step toward understanding how the rule of law is established.

The data used in the following sections are from a survey conducted in an emerging democracy—the Philippines. Most work that demonstrates the link in evaluations across specific institutions focuses solely on the United States,[1] whereas most work on emerging democracies centers on government as an organic whole (for example, Chang and Chu 2006; Mishler and Rose 1997, 2001; Seligson 2002). Work that does investigate specific institutions in emerging democracies centers on high courts but does not consider the basis for linked evaluations across specific institutions (Gibson, Caldeira, and Baird 1998; Gibson and Gouws 1997). Focusing on an emerging democracy is particularly interesting because many are undergoing judicial sector reforms. This study will have implications for the impact of such reforms.

The results of my analyses show that individuals' bases of trust do differ depending on the information they have. Trust assessments of court users are based mainly on their judgments about court performance, whereas those of noncourt users are based on evaluations of other institutions as well. These results support my information-processing approach to linked evaluations. Those with specific knowledge about a particular institution rely on that knowledge to assess the institution, whereas those lacking specific information use proxies.

Issues and Methods

Research on the formation of public opinion shows that individuals use mental shortcuts when asked to evaluate topics about which they know little (for a comprehensive review of the literature, see Taber 2003). These shortcuts, it is argued, are used because individuals have limited cognitive capacities and, consciously or subconsciously, deem it irrational to invest time and effort to become fully informed. One shortcut, in particular, entails classifying specific cases in terms of general categories and using what is known about those cases to make inferences about newly observed cases in the same category. Many studies show, for example, that American voters use political party as a general category, and when asked to evaluate a candidate, use the candidate's party affiliation to infer his or her positions, if those positions are relatively unknown (for example, Campbell et al. 1960, Conover and Feldman 1989; Kam 2005; Rahn 1993). American voters have also been shown to rely on other informational cues, such as trusted experts, interest groups, and candidates' demographic characteristics (for example, Kuklinski and Hurley 1994; Lupia 1994; Mondak 1993; Page and Shapiro 1992; Popkin 1991; Zaller 1992).

This information-processing perspective is a framework for understanding linked evaluations across different government institutions. Few if any citizens have information on the performance of each distinct institution within government. Citizens are likely instead to view different institutions as specific instances of the general category—government. Thus, when asked to evaluate an institution with which they are not familiar, citizens are likely to infer that its performance is similar to other government institutions with which they are familiar. In contrast, citizens who are familiar with the institution have less need to make inferences about it. Their evaluations of other government institutions are thus less likely to affect their assessments of the institution in question. From this perspective, views across government institutions covary because individuals use information on institutions with which they are familiar to make inferences regarding institutions about which they know little (Rahn and Rudolph 2002).

Focusing on local courts is particularly useful for identifying whether individuals use this information-processing strategy because a significant proportion of the population has direct experience in court while the rest do not. First-hand experience provides a basis for court performance that the former can use for their trust assessments. Court users may believe, for example, that they were treated fairly by a judge and infer that most judges would behave similarly. This assessment would then serve as a basis for trust assessments of judges or courts in general. Note that court users may have positive or negative experiences, which will affect their level of trust in courts. But in either case, their personal experience provides readily accessible information that can be used as a basis for their trust assessments.

In contrast to court users, the rest of the population is likely to have little direct information on local courts. The media would be one likely source of information for noncourt users. But local court performance is unlikely to be widely publicized. Given their lack of direct information, noncourt users are more likely to use their knowledge of other more visible government institutions as a basis for their assessments.

In his work on advanced industrial countries, Robert Rohrschneider similarly argues that experience with one government institution shapes evaluations of other institutions (2005). In particular, he maintains that personal contact with what he calls arbitrating institutions—bureaucracies and judiciaries—shapes citizens' evaluations of how well parliaments and governments represent their interests. He shows that national-level measures of institutional quality, each of which refers explicitly or implicitly to bureaucracies or judiciaries, are associated with evaluations regarding the representativeness of government. However, because Rohrschneider's data do not allow him to distinguish between citizens who have had personal experience with arbitrating institutions and those who have not, the bases for the linked evaluations he finds is still unclear. In a number of studies on U.S. courts, Tyler and his coauthors show that experience-based judgments of distributive and procedural fairness influence citizens' evaluations of legal authorities in general (Tyler, Casper, and Fisher 1989; Tyler 1990, 2001). They do not investigate the issue of linked evaluations between specific government institutions.

By comparing the bases of trust in courts between those who have had experience in court and those who have not, we have the opportunity to determine whether individuals with experience-based information on an institution are less likely to use other institutions as proxies when evaluating the institution in question. If links between assessments across institutions are due to the varying degrees of information that individuals have, then court users' bases of trust assessments should differ from those of noncourt users. When evaluating courts, court users should rely more on their specific knowledge about court performance, and their evaluations of other institutions should be less likely generalize to courts. In contrast, noncourt users will be more likely to use other institutions as proxies when evaluating courts. I thus test the following hypotheses:

> Hypothesis 1. Individuals without court experience are more likely than those with court experience to use proxies when evaluating local courts.
>
> Hypothesis 2. Among noncourt users, the impact of court performance judgments on trust in local courts is smaller than the impact of assessments of more visible government institutions.
>
> Hypothesis 3. Among court users, the impact of court performance judgments on trust in local courts is larger than the impact of assessments of other government institutions.

Support for these hypotheses would indicate support for the information-processing perspective.

I test these hypotheses with data from a survey conducted in the Philippines during November and December 1999.[2] The face-to-face survey focused on a stratified random sample of voting-age adults. The questionnaire was translated into six of the languages used in the Philippines. Individuals familiar with each language were then trained to interview and record responses. A multistage probability sampling procedure was used to select respondents. If selected respondents were unavailable, substitutes with the same qualities in terms of gender, age bracket, and socioeconomic class were taken from other households in the sample precinct. Of the 2,927 respondents contacted, 1,200 were interviewed, for a response rate of 41 percent.

The dependent variable, trust in local courts, is based on responses to the following item on the survey: "How much confidence do you have in local courts? Would you say that your trust in local courts is very high, somewhat high, undecided if high or low, somewhat low, or very low?" Responses were coded on a 5-point scale from 0 to 4, 4 representing the highest level of trust.

In the survey, the response of "undecided if high or low" as to one's degree of trust is distinct from responses of "don't know." The latter response was an option if respondents chose not to specify any of the alternatives in the survey question. Because responses of "don't know" were less than 2 percent, they are coded as missing data.

Responses of "undecided if high or low" were more numerous—29.3 percent. Respondents could have interpreted this option in one of two ways. First, they were truly uncertain of their level of trust in courts despite adequate information. In this case, "undecided" would indicate that their level of trust in courts was between those who had "somewhat high" trust in courts and those who had "somewhat low" trust. It is also possible, however, that respondents simply felt they did not have enough information with which to respond to the question. To account for both possibilities, I first consider responses of "undecided if high or low" as an intermediate category and then treat the "undecided" responses as missing data.

For robustness, I also use as the dependent variable a similar survey question on trust in judges. In the Philippines, the title *judge* is applied to all trial court judges up to the regional level, but is generally associated with local courts. Assessments of local courts and judges are not identical but are highly correlated (Pearson's $r = 0.65$). Moreover, the number of responses of "don't know" and "undecided if high or low" on this item are similar to the question on courts. Around 29 percent of respondents chose the "undecided if high or low" option, and fewer than 1.5 percent of respondents chose "don't know."

Tables 10.1 and 10.2 provide more detailed information on the dependent and the key independent variables. Table 10.1 lists the survey questions, answer options, and the frequency of responses for each answer option as a percentage of the total sample. Table 10.2 provides summary statistics and shows that more than 98 percent of respondents provided an evaluation of local courts and judges, and their responses varied substantially. The mean score for trust in local courts is 2.17 with a standard deviation of 1.02, and that in judges is 2.21 with a standard deviation of 1.03.

Assessments of Other Government Institutions

As observed, linked evaluations across institutions may be related to how one used information about one institution to develop evaluations of another. Although proxies may differ in each country depending on government structure, they are likely to be institutions that are highly visible and that citizens are likely to view as responsible for overall government performance. For example, in countries with strong presidents, individuals are likely to associate government performance with presidents. In parliamentary systems, the party or parties in government are more likely to be associated with government performance.

Arguably, the institution most likely to be used as a proxy in the Philippines is the presidency because of the strength of the president in relation to the other branches of government (Rocamora 1997; Thompson 1995). The Philippine government is highly centralized. Local governments depend on the national government for essential resources. Effective line item veto power over budgetary matters gives the president substantial control over legislators. Many legislators attempting to secure resources for their districts deem being a member of the president's party so important that they are willing to switch allegiance to the incoming president's party shortly after election results are tallied (Montinola 1999). The president also dominates the selection process for Supreme Court justices. Each justice is appointed by the president from at least three individuals nominated by a Judicial and Bar Council (JBC). Five of the eight JBC members are appointed by the president (Haynie 1998). In large part because of these and other prerogatives, the president receives much greater media coverage than any other government institution. Thus, when Filipinos are asked to evaluate a government institution with which they are not familiar, they are most likely to use their assessments of the president as a basis for their evaluations.

To determine whether Filipinos use the president as a proxy when evaluating local courts, a measure of satisfaction with the performance of the president is included in the analyses. The variable is measured using responses to the following question: "How do you feel about the performance of [name], the president of the Philippines? Are you very satisfied,

Table 10.1 Survey Questions and Responses

Questions	Frequency (%)	Coded
"How much confidence do you have in local courts? Would you say that your trust in local courts is very high, somewhat high, undecided if high or low, somewhat low, or very low?"		
Very high	5.5	4
Somewhat high	37.8	3
Undecided if high or low	29.3	2
Somewhat low	18.9	1
Very low	6.5	0
Don't know	1.7	—
"How much confidence do you have in judges? Would you say that your trust in local courts is very high, somewhat high, undecided if high or low, somewhat low, or very low?"		
Very high	6.5	4
Somewhat high	38.8	3
Undecided if high or low	29.0	2
Somewhat low	17.3	1
Very low	6.9	0
Don't know	1.3	—
"How do you feel about the performance of [name], the president of the Philippines? Are you very satisfied, somewhat satisfied, undecided if satisfied or not, somewhat dissatisfied, or very dissatisfied?"		
Very satisfied	8.9	4
Somewhat satisfied	36.5	3
Undecided if satisfied or not	16.5	2
Somewhat dissatisfied	21.6	1
Very dissatisfied	16.1	0
Don't know	0.1	—
"Whether rich or poor, people who have cases in court receive equal treatment. Do you strongly agree, somewhat agree, are undecided if you agree or disagree, somewhat disagree, or strongly disagree with this statement?"		
Strongly agree	4.5	4
Somewhat agree	22.0	3
Undecided if agree or disagree	19.8	2
Somewhat disagree	23.0	1
Strongly disagree	19.7	0
Don't know	0.7	—
"How much corruption do you think is there in our judiciary? None, a little, somewhat much, or very much?"		
None	19.2	3
A little	17.9	2
Somewhat much	34.8	1
Very much	27.2	0
Don't know	0.7	—

Source: Author's compilation, based on Social Weather Survey (Social Weather Stations 1999).

Table 10.2 Summary Statistics

Variable	Obs	Mean	SD	Min	Max
Trust in local courts	1179	2.172	1.021	0	4
Trust in judges	1184	2.209	1.034	0	4
Satisfaction with president	1198	.501	.315	0	1
Equality of treatment	1190	.536	.281	0	1
Judicial corruption	1191	.568	.356	0	1
Age	1200	42.3	15.6	18	88
Class	1200	1.986	.628	1	4
Gender (male = 1)	1200	.500	.500	0	1
Religious affiliation (Muslim = 1)	1200	.017	.129	0	1

Source: Author's calculations, based on Social Weather Survey (Social Weather Stations 1999).

somewhat satisfied, undecided if satisfied or not, somewhat dissatisfied, or very dissatisfied?"

For ease of interpretation, the responses to these questions are coded on a scale from 0 to 1, 1 representing the highest satisfaction. The measure shows substantial variation, with a mean of .50 and a standard deviation of .31. As in the survey question on courts and judges, "don't know" was an option if respondents chose not to specify any of the choices. Because only two of 1,200 respondents did so, their responses were coded as missing data.

Observe that this item measures satisfaction with the performance of the president, not trust in the president. Because the survey does not have an item on trust in the president, I cannot test directly whether individuals transfer their trust from one institution to another. However, my purpose is to test whether individuals link their evaluations of institutions, not simply their trust assessments, so this is not a problem for my analysis.

Assessments of Court Performance

If individuals update their judgments when provided with specific information, court users should rely more heavily on their knowledge of court performance when evaluating courts than on information regarding the president. In his work on U.S. courts, Tom Tyler shows that confidence in courts is a function of beliefs regarding the fairness of the procedures that courts use when they exercise their authority (1990, 2001). By procedural fairness, he means concerns about the equality of treatment that different societal groups are afforded by legal authorities as well as about the honesty, dignity, respect, politeness, and sensitivity with which courts treat people (1990). Two measures for judgments regarding procedural fairness are thus included in the analyses.

The first measure is based on the statement and question, "Whether rich or poor, people who have cases in court receive equal treatment. Do you strongly agree, somewhat agree, are undecided if you agree or disagree, somewhat disagree, or strongly disagree with this statement?" The 5-point responses are then coded on a scale from 0 to 1, with 1 representing the highest level of procedural fairness.

The second measure is based on the question, "How much corruption do you think is there in our judiciary? None, a little, somewhat much, or very much?" The 4-point measure based on this question is recoded on a scale from 0 to 1, with 1 representing the highest levels of corruption.

Court Experience

To gauge whether the bases of trust differ between those with court experience and those without, I divide the sample into those who identified themselves as having had direct court experience and those who did not. In particular, respondents were asked whether they had ever filed a complaint in court or been charged in court, or if they had experience in the village court mediation system as a complainant or respondent. Although village courts are not formally part of the Philippine judicial system, they play an important role in the administration of justice. They serve as a primary screening mechanism for referral to the trial courts.

Of the 1,200 survey respondents, a sizeable minority—295 or nearly 25 percent of the sample—reported having direct experience in the formal or village court system. Some reported having experience in more than one capacity or venue. Of the 212 respondents who reported having formal court experience, 118 identified as only having filed complaints, fifty-six as only having been charged in court, and thirty-eight as having filed complaints and been charged.[3] Of the 139 who reported having experience with the village court system, 144 identified as having filed complaints and fifty-five as having been respondents. None of the complainants in the village court system identified as having also been respondents. However, 116 of those who had village court experience identified as also having experience in the formal court system. Thus, the number of individuals with direct experience in either the formal or village court systems was 295. I coded the variable 1 if the respondent indicated that she or he had experience in the formal or village court system, and 0 otherwise. I then created interactions terms—the products of the experience variable and evaluations of the president and court performance—to determine whether the impact of these evaluations on trust in courts differ between those with experience and those without.

In the subsequent analyses, I did not distinguish individuals by the role they played in the court system, complainant or respondent, or by venue, formal or village court, because I have no theoretical reason to think that these differences would affect the degree to which they use their

Figure 10.1 Trust in Courts and Judges

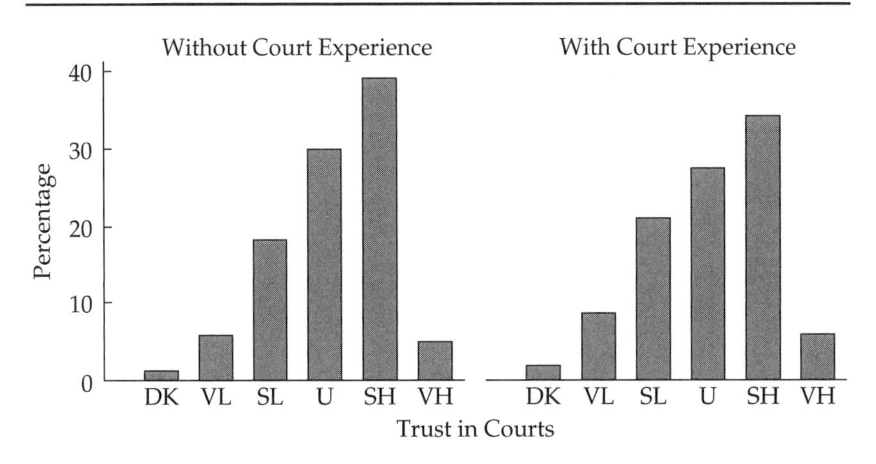

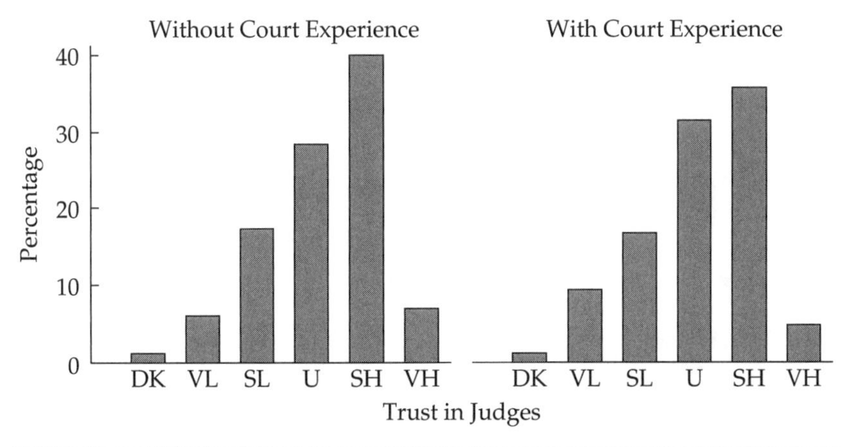

Source: Author's calculations, based on Social Weather Survey (Social Weather Stations 1999).
Note: DK = don't know; VL = very low; SL = somewhat low; U = undecided if low or high; SH = somewhat high; VH = very high.

experience as a basis for evaluating courts. One might argue that complainants are likely to trust courts more than respondents. However, the focus of this study is not on levels of trust, but on whether individuals use information from their experience, or rely on proxies, when evaluating courts. Thus, what should matter is simply whether one has had experience with courts.

Figure 10.1 provides the frequency distribution of responses on trust in courts and judges by experience. Observe that lack of court experience does not substantially affect respondents' ability to express an evaluation of courts. When asked how much trust or confidence they had in courts, only 1.5 percent of noncourt users responded "don't know," as opposed

Table 10.3 Respondents' Demographic Characteristics by Court Experience

Variable	No Experience	Experience
Mean age	41.5	44.8
Percentage male	47.0	58.9
Percentage Muslim	2.4	—
Class (percentage of sample)		
Upper (AB)	2.8	3.0
Middle (C)	9.5	12.8
Poor (D)	69.6	68.1
Destitute (E)	18.0	15.9

Source: Author's calculations, based on Social Weather Survey (Social Weather Stations 1999).

to 2.4 percent of their counterparts. Thus respondents without court experience were slightly more likely to express an evaluation of courts. Moreover, the difference in percentages of respondents with and without court experience who indicated that they were "undecided" as to whether they had high or low trust in courts is not large. Around 30 percent of noncourt users and 27 percent of their counterparts chose the "undecided" category.

The corresponding figures for evaluations of judges were similar to those for courts. When asked how much trust or confidence they had in judges, 1.33 percent of noncourt users and 1.36 percent of their counterparts responded "don't know." The percentages for "undecided" responses were 28 percent for noncourt users and 31.5 percent for court users. Thus there appears to be little difference in level of conviction in views on trust between court users and noncourt users.

Demographic Controls

Because I am interested in whether court users are less likely than their counterparts to link their evaluation of the president to courts, I control for demographic characteristics that may influence an individual's likelihood of having court experience. In this way, I ensure that any variation I find is not due to differences in the composition of court users. For robustness, I also split the sample into respondents with and without court users, and run analyses on the split samples. Table 10.3 provides respondents' demographic characteristics by court experience.

In particular, I control for age, gender, and class status. Respondents' age ranges from eighteen to eighty-eight. Gender is coded as 1 for males, 0 otherwise. Class status is an indicator of wealth. Respondents are classified as (AB) upper class, (C) middle class, (D) poor, and (E) destitute. The classification is based on self-reported income, land ownership, and the quality of one's home and appliances (Arroyo 1990). The variable is coded from 1 to 4, with 1 representing the lowest class (E) and 4 the upper class (AB).

I also control for respondents' religious affiliation because this is a particularly salient social cleavage in Philippine politics. More than 80 percent of Filipinos are Roman Catholic, 5 percent are Muslim, and the rest either identify with other Christian denominations or claim no religious affiliation. Although they are a small minority of the population, Muslims are geographically concentrated in the southern part of the country, and Muslim organizations have been fighting for independence from the Republic of the Philippines since the early 1970s. Muslims may therefore evaluate courts differently from the rest of the population.[4]

Empirical Analyses

I estimate the determinants of trust in local courts and judges with ordered probit regression models, because the dependent variables—trust in courts and trust in judges—have five ordered categories. Table 10.4 presents the main results of the analyses. The first model uses evaluations of trust in local courts as the dependent variable, while the second uses evaluations of trust in judges. Bearing in mind that all variables of interest are scaled from 0 to 1, the size of the coefficients in table 10.4 provides an indication of the relative impact of evaluations of the president and court performance on trust in courts and judges. After a discussion of the relative size and statistical significance of these coefficients, I present more precise estimates for the variables of interest in the form of predicted probabilities.

In both models, the coefficient for the measure of satisfaction with the president is positive and statistically significant, indicating that noncourt users' evaluations of the president and courts (judges) are linked. Among noncourt users, the more satisfied one is with the performance of the president, the more likely one is to trust local courts (judges). More important for the purpose of this study, the interaction term between presidential satisfaction and court experience is negative and statistically significant in both models. This result supports hypothesis 1. The impact of satisfaction with the president on trust in courts is smaller for court users than for noncourt users. It suggests that individuals without court experience are more likely than those with it to use proxies when evaluating local courts.

The estimates in table 10.4 also support hypothesis 2. Among noncourt users, the impact of court performance judgments on trust in local courts is smaller than the impact of assessments of more visible government institutions. The coefficients for the court performance variables—equality of treatment and corruption—are significant and in the expected direction in both models. They indicate that noncourt users who believe courts to be fair are more likely to trust courts and judges, and that those who assess levels of corruption among the judiciary to be high are less likely to trust courts

Table 10.4 Trust in Local Courts and Judges, Ordered Probit Estimates, Full Samples

	Local Courts	Judges
Experience	.095	.126
	(.218)	(.216)
Satisfaction with president	.608**	.588**
	(.117)	(.117)
Experience × satisfaction with president	–.315*	–.436**
	(.230)	(.229)
Equality of treatment	.234**	.369**
	(.108)	(.108)
Experience × equality of treatment	.512**	.428**
	(.218)	(.218)
Corruption	–.205**	–.235**
	(.102)	(.101)
Experience × corruption	–.299*	–.263
	(.219)	(.217)
Controls		
Class	–.066*	–.056
	(.050)	(.049)
Age	–.001	–.003*
	(.002)	(.002)
Gender (male = 1)	–.085*	.010
	(.062)	(.062)
Religious affiliation (Muslim = 1)	.256	–.070
	(.243)	(.237)
N	1,165	1,168
Likelihood ratio $x^2(11)$	83.60	89.79
Prob > x^2	.000	.000

Source: Author's compilation, based on Social Weather Survey (Social Weather Stations 1999).
Notes: Standard errors in parentheses; cut-points not shown for ease of presentation.
$^{*}p < .10$, $^{**}p < .05$, one-tailed test

and judges. Notably, the coefficients for court performance judgments, which range from an absolute value of .20 to .36, are much smaller than the estimates for presidential satisfaction, which range from .58 to .60. This suggests that, for noncourt users, assessments of court performance are less important than those of the president when evaluating courts.

In contrast, the analysis indicates that court users rely more heavily than their counterparts on their assessments of court performance when evaluating courts. The coefficients for the interaction terms between experience and the court performance variables are all in the expected direction. The estimates for the interaction term between experience and equality of treatment are positive, indicating that judgments regarding equality of treatment in court have a larger positive impact on trust in courts for individuals with court experience than those without. The coefficients for the interaction term between experience and corruption are negative, indicating that judgments regarding corruption in the judiciary have a larger negative impact on trust in courts for court users than for noncourt users. With only one exception, these coefficients are statistically significant, indicating that the bases of court users' evaluations differ from those of noncourt users. Moreover, by summing the coefficients for the court performance variables and the interactions between court performance and experience, we find support for hypothesis 3, which states that among court users, the impact of court performance judgments on trust in local courts is larger than the impact of assessments of other government institutions. Among court users, the impact of court performance evaluations on trust in courts and judges ranges from an absolute value of .50 to .80, whereas the impact of presidential satisfaction ranges from only .15 to .29.

To ensure the robustness of these initial findings, I perform two additional tests. First, I drop from the sample respondents who indicated that they were undecided as to whether they had high or low trust in local courts and judges. As table 10.5 shows, the results of the analyses with the smaller samples are similar to those with the full samples. The coefficients for the presidential satisfaction variable are positive and highly significant, indicating that satisfaction with the president is positively associated with trust in courts and judges for individuals without court experience. The coefficients for the interaction term between experience and satisfaction with the president are significantly negative, indicating that the impact of satisfaction with the president on trust in courts and judges is smaller for court users than for noncourt users. Conversely, though the coefficients for the court performance variables are statistically significant, they are small compared to the presidential satisfaction variable, indicating that for noncourt users, evaluations of court performance have a smaller impact on trust in courts and judges than assessments of the president. Moreover, the absolute values of the coefficients for the interaction terms between experience and court performance variables are larger than the coefficients for the court performance variables, indicating that assessments of court performance have a larger impact on trust in courts and judges for court users than noncourt users.

I probe the robustness of these findings further by splitting the sample between court users and noncourt users. The results of the split-sample analyses support my initial results and convey additional information. First, as shown in table 10.6, the coefficients for satisfaction with the president are positive and statistically significant in the models of noncourt users. This indicates, as also presented in tables 10.4 and 10.5, that presidential satisfaction is associated with trust in local courts and judges among individuals without court experience. Second, note that the coefficients for

Table 10.5 Trust in Local Courts and Judges, Ordered Probit Estimates, No Undecided Respondents

	Local Courts	Judges
Experience	.108	.267
	(.266)	(.278)
Satisfaction with president	.778**	.789**
	(.142)	(.142)
Experience × satisfaction with president	−.425*	−.727**
	(.283)	(.285)
Equality of treatment	.208*	.360**
	(.134)	(.133)
Experience × equality of treatment	.727**	.610**
	(.264)	(.267)
Corruption	−.284**	−.308**
	(.126)	(.126)
Experience × corruption	−.362*	−.412*
	(.271)	(.282)
Controls		
Class	−.096*	−.091*
	(.064)	(.064)
Age	−.001	−.001
	(.002)	(.002)
Gender (male = 1)	−.114*	−.001
	(.078)	(.077)
Religious affiliation (Muslim = 1)	.546*	−.053
	(.335)	(.282)
N	817	825
Likelihood ratio $x^2(11)$	90.30	93.57
Prob > x^2	.000	.000

Source: Author's calculations, based on Social Weather Survey (Social Weather Stations 1999).
Notes: Standard errors in parentheses; cut-points not shown for ease of presentation.
*$p < .10$, **$p < .05$, one-tailed test

satisfaction with the president are not statistically significant in the models of court users. This suggests not only that the impact of presidential satisfaction on trust in courts and judges is smaller for court users than noncourt users, but that satisfaction with the president has no effect on court users' trust in courts and judges. Table 10.6 thus makes it clear that survey respondents with court experience do not link their evaluations of the president on one hand, and courts and judges on the other. Finally, table 10.6 shows that the absolute values of the coefficients for the court performance variables are statistically significant and larger in the court user models than in the noncourt user models. Consistent with the results of tables 10.4 and

Table 10.6 Trust in Local Courts and Judges by Experience, Ordered Probit Estimates, Split Samples

	Without Experience		With Experience	
	Local Courts	Judges	Local Courts	Judges
Satisfaction with president	.622**	.589**	.220	.136
	(.118)	(.118)	(.199)	(.199)
Equality of treatment	.243**	.368**	.773**	.801**
	(.109)	(.108)	(.193)	(.194)
Corruption	−.203**	−.242**	−.505**	−.510**
	(.102)	(.102)	(.195)	(.194)
Controls				
Class	−.020	−.047	−.224**	−.092
	(.057)	(.057)	(.100)	(.098)
Age	−.003*	−.003*	.008**	−.001
	(.002)	(.002)	(.004)	(.004)
Gender (male = 1)	−.049	.048	−.223**	−.110
	(.072)	(.071)	(.128)	(.127)
Religious affiliation (Muslim = 1)	.252	−.073		
	(.244)	(.237)		
N	879	880	286	288
Likelihood ratio $x^2(10)$	5.00	54.42	38.81	31.93
Prob > x^2	.000	.000	.000	.000

Source: Author's calculations, based on Social Weather Survey (Social Weather Stations 1999).
Notes: Standard errors in parentheses; cut-points not shown for ease of presentation.
*$p < .10$, **$p < .05$, one-tailed test

10.5, this indicates that the impact of court performance evaluations on trust in courts and judges is larger for court users than noncourt users.

Although tables 10.4 though 10.6 indicate that the data support the hypotheses outlined, for precise estimates of the impact of key variables, I calculate changes in the predicted probabilities of trust in courts and judges given changes in the key variables of interest. I present these estimates in figure 10.2. The height of each bar represents the change in predicted probability of high trust in courts (judges) as one moves from the minimum to the maximum evaluation score (0→1) on the variables measuring respondents' satisfaction with the president, assessment of equal treatment before courts, and assessment of judicial corruption. The darker bars represent results for the sample without court experience, while the lighter bars represent those for the sample of court users. The estimates are based on the ordered probit regressions in table 10.4.

Figure 10.2 Change in Predicted Probability of High Trust as Key Variables Move from Maximum to Minimum

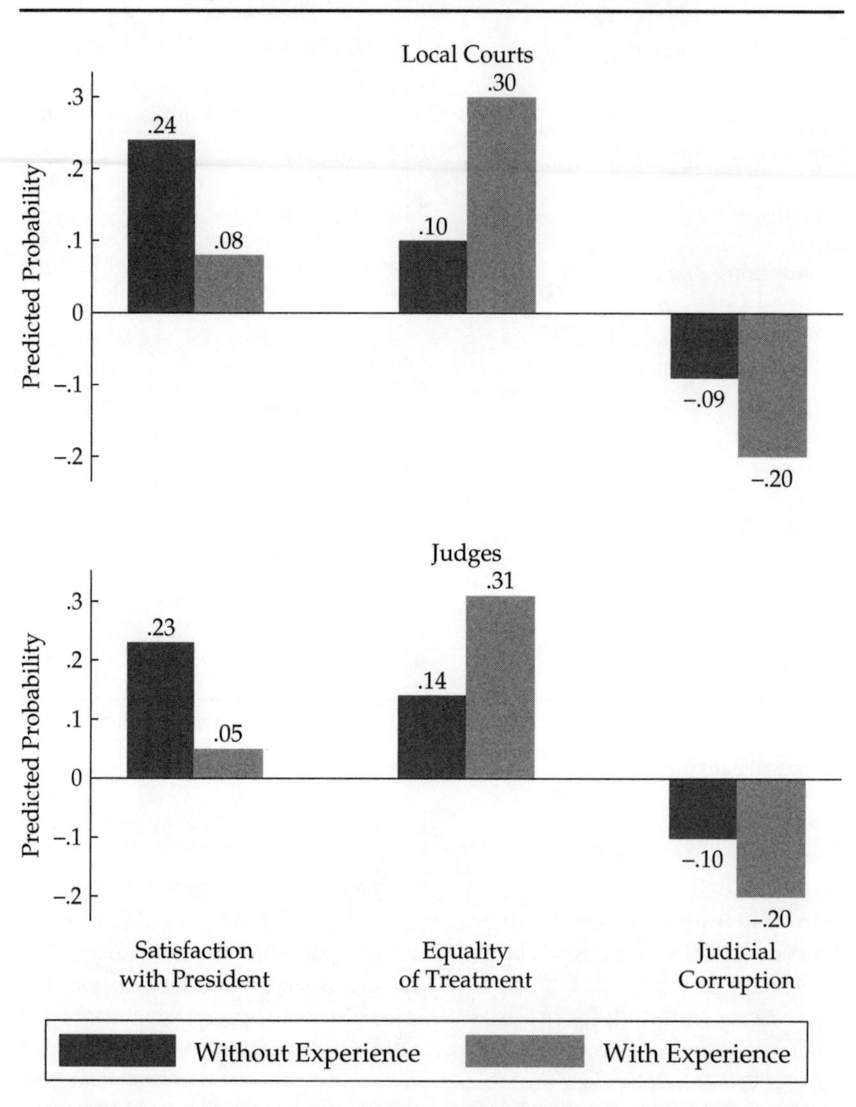

Source: Author's calculations, based on Social Weather Survey (Social Weather Stations 1999).

As shown in figure 10.2, the impact of satisfaction with the president on the probability of high trust in courts and judges is much larger for noncourt users than for court users. Among noncourt users, moving from the minimum level of satisfaction with the president to the maximum level increases the probability of trust in courts and judges by .24 and .23 respectively, whereas the corresponding change for court users is at most .08. In contrast, the impact of court performance variables on the probability of high trust in courts and judges is much smaller for noncourt users than court users. A change from 0 to 1 in noncourt users' evaluation regarding equal treatment before the court increases the probability of their trust in courts and judges by only .14 at most.

The corresponding changes for court users are more than twice as much at .30 and .31 respectively. Similarly, a change from 0 to 1 in noncourt users' evaluation of judicial corruption leads to a decrease in the probability of trust in courts and judges by only .10 at most, and the corresponding change for court users is .20. These results suggest, as hypothesized, that individuals without court experience are more likely than those with it to use proxies when evaluating institutions with which they have no personal experience.

Conclusion

Comparing the bases of trust in local courts of individuals with and without court experience, we see that the two groups' bases of trust differ in important respects. Assessments of the president are more likely to generalize to local courts for those without court experience, whereas those with direct court experience rely more heavily on their judgments on court performance when evaluating courts. These results support an information-processing approach to understanding linked evaluations across government institutions. The approach states that when assessing institutions, individuals evaluate them separately depending on the information they have. Those with experience-based knowledge rely more heavily on that knowledge when assessing an institution, and those who do not use proxies.

This analysis highlights differences between individuals with and without experience-based knowledge of specific government institutions. Whether these differences would be present if the information were from less direct sources is an open question. It would be interesting, for example, to determine whether information on specific government institutions from media sources or social networks would have a similar effect, that is, whether individuals with information from these sources would be less likely to use proxies as a basis for their evaluations than those with no information. Knowledge from media sources and networks might be captured with carefully worded questions in future surveys, and analogous to the analysis in this study, one could then investigate whether the bases of trust differs between respondents with and without such knowledge.

The analysis also highlights a methodological issue that Matthew Cleary and Susan Stokes raise in the chapter that follows. They argue that the survey questions used to measure trust in government institutions are problematic because respondents are unlikely to have had any experience with the institutions in question, and therefore have little ability to evaluate them. They maintain that because of this lack of context, respondents are likely to be influenced by any number of circumstances that have little to do with judgments of the trustworthiness of the institutions in question. Consistent with this criticism, my work suggests that when a respondent has no direct experience with an institution, his or her evaluation of a more familiar institution is likely to provide the basis for evaluation of the less familiar one. This calls into question the construct validity of the standard trust measures when they are asked of respondents unfamiliar with the institutions in question.

Finally, this study suggests that government reform need not be global to have an impact on trust assessments. Assessments of a specific institution can be changed as long as citizens have specific information on the performance of the institution. Assessments of one institution need not generalize to all others. Whether such information will promote trust is of course likely to depend on the nature of the information. If, for example, individuals with court experience perceive that they did not receive fair treatment, they are less likely to perceive courts in general as trustworthy. Conversely, if they had a favorable experience, they are likely to evaluate courts in general favorably. That said, this study implies that recent reforms focusing primarily on judicial sectors in emerging democracies have the potential to elicit higher levels of trust in courts and consequently, greater respect for the rule of law, despite ongoing problems in other government sectors. This conclusion is especially encouraging for emerging democracies, which generally have limited resources and therefore cannot reform all government institutions simultaneously. It should also be of interest to organizations, including USAID and the World Bank, that have been targeting their assistance toward restructuring judicial systems with the aim of strengthening the rule of law in emerging democracies.

Notes

1. One exception is work by Robert Rohrschneider, who examined the impact of bureaucratic and judicial performance on evaluations of parliaments and governments in advanced industrial democracies (2005).
2. The survey was conducted by Social Weather Stations, a nongovernmental institute in the Philippines.

3. It is possible that individuals who experienced the court in both capacities were involved in suits and countersuits in court. The survey does not provide enough information, however, to determine whether individuals experienced the court system in both capacities over the same issue.

4. Muslims are underrepresented in the sample as a whole, as well as among court users. The group constitutes only 2.4 percent of the total sample, and none of the court users identified themselves as Muslim. Because my concern is simply to control for the impact of religious affiliation, the underrepresentation of Muslims should not be a problem for my analyses; however, the estimates regarding the impact of religious affiliation on trust in courts and judges should be interpreted with caution.

References

Arroyo, Dennis M. 1990. "The Usefulness of the ABCDE Market Research System: A Means to Check Social Welfare and Class Attributes." *Social Weather Bulletin* 90(11/12): 1–16.

Bernstein, Jeffrey L. 2001. "Linking Presidential and Congressional Approval During Unified and Divided Governments." In *What Is It About Government that Americans Dislike?* edited by John R. Hibbing and Elizabeth Theiss-Morse. New York: Cambridge University Press.

Caldeira, Gregory A. 1986. "Neither the Purse nor the Sword: Dynamics of Public Confidence in the Supreme Court." *American Political Science Review* 80(4): 1209–226.

Campbell, Angus, Philip E. Converse, Warren E. Miller, and Donald E. Stokes. 1960. *The American Voter.* Chicago: University of Chicago Press.

Carothers, Thomas. 1998. "The Rule of Law Revival." *Foreign Affairs* 77(2): 95–107.

Chang, Eeric C. C., and Yun-han Chu. 2006. "Corruption and Trust: Exceptionalism in Asian Democracies?" *Journal of Politics* 68(2): 259–71.

Conover, Pamela J., and Stanley Feldman. 1989. "Candidate Perception in an Ambiguous World: Campaigns, Cues, and Inference Processes." *American Journal of Political Science* 33(4): 912–40.

Gibson, James L., and Amanda Gouws. 1997. "Support for the Rule of Law in the Emerging South African Democracy." *International Social Science Journal* 49(2): 173–91.

Gibson, James L., Gregory A. Caldeira, and Vanessa A. Baird. 1998. "On the Legitimacy of National High Courts." *American Political Science Review* 92(2): 343–58.

Haynie, Stacia. 1998. "Paradise Lost: Politicization of the Philippine Supreme Court in the Post-Marcos Era." *Asian Studies Review* 22(4): 459–73.

Kam, Cindy D. 2005. "Who Toes the Party Line? Cues, Values, and Individual Differences." *Political Behavior* 27(2): 163–82.

Kimball, David C., and Samuel C. Patterson. 1997. "Living up to Expectations: Public Attitudes Toward Congress." *Journal of Politics* 59(3): 701–28.

Kuklinksi, James H., and Norman L. Hurley. 1994. "On Hearing and Interpreting Political Messages: A Cautionary Tale of Citizen Cue-Taking." *Journal of Politics* 56(3): 729–51.

Levi, Margaret, and Laura Stoker. 2000. "Political Trust and Trustworthiness." *Annual Review of Political Science* 3(1): 475–507.

Lupia, A. 1994. "Shortcuts Versus Encyclopedias: Information and Voting Behavior in California Insurance Reform Elections." *American Political Science Review* 88(1): 63–76.

McClymont, Mary, and Stephen Golub, eds. 2000. *Many Roads to Justice.* Washington, D.C.: Ford Foundation.

Mishler, William, and Richard. Rose. 1997. "Trust, Distrust and Skepticism: Popular Evaluations of Civil and Political Institutions in Post-Communist Societies." *Journal of Politics* 59(2): 418–51.

———. 2001. "What are the Origins of Political Trust? Testing Institutional and Cultural Theories in Post-Communist Societies." *Comparative Political Studies* 34(1): 30–62.

Mondak, Jeffrey J. 1993. "Source Cues and Policy Approval: The Cognitive Dynamics of Public Support for the Reagan Agenda." *American Journal of Political Science* 37(1): 186–212.

Montinola, Gabriella R. 1999. "Parties and Accountability in the Philippines." *Journal of Democracy* 10(1):126–40.

Page, Benjamin I., and Robert Y. Shapiro. 1992. *The Rational Public: Fifty Years of Trends in Americans' Policy Preferences.* Chicago: University of Chicago Press.

Popkin, Samuel L. 1991. *The Reasoning Voter: Communication and Persuasion in Presidential Campaigns.* Chicago: University of Chicago Press.

Rahn, Wendy M. 1993. "The Role of Partisan Stereotypes in Information-Processing About Political Candidates." *American Journal of Political Science* 37(2): 472–96.

Rahn, Wendy M., and Thomas J. Rudolph. 2002. "Trust in Local Governments." In *Understanding Public Opinion,* edited by Barbara Norrander and Clyde Wilcox. Washington, D.C.: CQ Press.

———. 2005. "A Tale of Political Trust in American Cities." *Public Opinion Quarterly* 69(4): 530–60.

Rocamora, Joel. 1997. *The Constitutional Amendment Debate: Reforming Political Institutions, Reshaping Political Culture.* Manila: Institute of Popular Democracy.

Rohrschneider, Robert. 2005. "Institutional Quality and Perceptions of Representation in Advanced Industrial Democracies." *Comparative Political Studies* 38(7): 850–74.

Seligson, Mitchell A. 2002. "The Impact of Corruption on Regime Legitimacy: A Comparative Study of Four Latin American Countries." *Journal of Politics* 64(2): 408–33.

Social Weather Stations. 1999. Social Weather Survey 1999 [dataset]. Available at: http://www.sws.org.ph.

Taber, Charles S. 2003. "Information Processing and Public Opinion." In *Oxford Handbook of Political Psychology,* edited by David O. Sears, Leionie Huddy, and Robert Jervis. New York: Oxford University Press.

Thompson, M. R. 1995. *The Anti-Marcos Struggle: Personalistic Rule and Democratic Transition in the Philippines.* New Haven, Conn.: Yale University Press.

Tyler, Tom R. 1990. *Why People Obey the Law.* New Haven, Conn.: Yale University Press.

———. 2001. "Public Trust and Confidence in Legal Authorities: What Do Majority and Minority Group Members Want from the Law And Legal Institutions?" *Behavioral Sciences and the Law* 19(2): 215–35.
Tyler, Tom R., Jonathan D. Casper, and Bonnie Fisher. 1989. "Maintaining Allegiance Toward Political Authorities: The Role of Prior Attitudes and the Use of Fair Procedures." *American Journal of Political Science* 33(3): 629–52.
Uslaner, E. M. 2001. "Is Washington Really the Problem?" In *What Is It About Government that Americans Dislike?* edited by John R. Hibbing and Elizabeth Theiss-Morse. New York: Cambridge University Press.
Zaller, John R. 1992. *The Nature and Origins of Mass Opinion.* New York: Cambridge University Press.

Chapter 11

Trust and Democracy in Comparative Perspective

Matthew R. Cleary and Susan C. Stokes

Social scientists have become obsessed with trust. Interpersonal, social, political, institutional, intra-elite, generalized, network-specific, vertical, horizontal, or however the term *trust* is qualified, recent scholarship has lamented the lack of it, advocated for more of it, and (where it can be found) given it credit for any number of positive social outcomes. Nowhere is this more apparent than in the study of democracy, broadly conceived. Trust is said to facilitate transitions to democracy, to help consolidate democratic regimes once they exist, and to "make democracy work"—to improve the quality of democratic governance in some tangible sense. And, it follows, scholars blame the absence of trust for authoritarianism, weak democratic institutions, and poor democratic performance.

Hence Ronald Inglehart writes that societies endowed with "a syndrome of tolerance, trust, political activism, and Post-materialist values" are more likely to become democratic (2003, 51; see also 1988, 1999). Robert Putnam and many others link the quality of democracy to social capital, which usually incorporates interpersonal trust in its definition (1993). Marc Hetherington argues that "trust matters" because the lack of it in the United States has impeded "progressive public policy" (2005, 3). Other studies link a lack of trust to low levels of civic participation (Almond and Verba 1963; Uslaner 2002), alienation from the political system (Anderson and Tverdova 2001; Anderson et al. 2005), or a "crisis of democratic representation" (Mainwaring 2006).[1] These studies, and the larger literatures they represent, vary widely in terms of their theoretical approaches and conceptualizations of trust. Yet they share a claim that, on some basic level, trust is important for democratic politics; where trust is absent, democracy is in trouble.

But some recent scholarship has begun to treat the presumptive relationship between trust and democracy with much more caution. This new perspective challenges many of the central claims of the more traditional literature. Regarding the *theory* of trust and democracy, some scholars have asked whether trust is a cause or a consequence of participation in civic organizations, whether competing trust networks might heighten divisions within a society rather than moderating them (Armony 2004), and whether high levels of trust in government, perversely, produce bad outcomes and governments that are not trustworthy. Regarding the *evidence* on trust and democracy, critics have questioned both the measures used to gauge levels of trust and the broad set of inferences that scholars have drawn from this small set of ambiguously worded survey questions (Jackman and Miller 1996; Seligson 2002; Seligson and Booth 1993).

In this chapter we examine some of these criticisms, both theoretical and empirical, focusing on the claim that trust (interpersonal or institutional) improves the quality of democracy. We show that, at least in Latin America, much of the literature linking trust to the quality of democracy is misguided; even where such a link might exist, low levels of trust are best interpreted as a symptom of underlying social and political problems, rather than a cause of weak democratic performance (see Mainwaring 2006). We conclude with some suggestions regarding the proper interpretation of common survey-based measures and the possibility of future theoretical development.

The Case for Trust

Much recent scholarship on trust and democracy rests on naked empiricism rather than sound theory. For decades, public opinion surveys have asked questions that include the word *trust.* The most common question is designed to measure interpersonal trust, and asks respondents whether "most people can be trusted," or some variant on the theme. Another common battery of questions ask whether the respondent "trusts" a list of social and political institutions, like political parties, the congress, the church, or the media. Responses to these questions, either at the individual level or aggregated by country, tend to correlate with measures of other factors that social scientists care about, such as democratization, the level of development, support for democracy, favorability toward a particular government, reported activity in civic organizations, and much more. The wealth of data and the statistical significance of the correlations are too tempting to resist, and thus trust has become a focus of scholarly attention and a presumptive cause of various desirable political outcomes.

Often these accounts fail to provide any sound theoretical grounding for the empirical link between trust and democracy. There are two clear exceptions, in which scholars have developed thoughtful theoretical underpinnings: political culture and social capital. We have criticized this literature in earlier work and do so again in this chapter (see Cleary and Stokes 2006). But these two approaches offer the best hope for scholars who aim to establish a causal relationship between trust and democracy. The political-culture approach, classically represented by Gabriel Almond and Sidney Verba (1963), and developed more recently in a series of publications by Inglehart (1988, among others), posits that mass attitudes and social norms matter for democratic outcomes, and that widespread interpersonal trust is one of the most important social norms. The social-capital approach, classically represented by Putnam but greatly enhanced by further theoretical work (including Putnam's own), is closely related (1993; see also 2000; Boix and Posner 1998; Paxton 2002). This theoretical tradition posits that societies have varying levels of social capital, which individuals can draw on to promote cooperative ventures. Although taxonomies may (with reason) place this theory within the political culture paradigm, we treat it separately here because it relies on a different causal mechanism.

No serious political culture theorist makes the simplistic claim that interpersonal trust causes democracy. Rather, trust functions as one part of a more complex concept. For Almond and Verba, the relevant concept is the *civic culture,* a pattern of political attitudes conducive to democratic forms of government (1963). In contrast to how many subsequent scholars use the term, Almond and Verba defines it as a "mixed political culture," in which most citizens remain passive and disengaged, and in which only some people, some of the time, actively participate in politics. To use their language, in the civic culture "the roles of subject and parochial have not been displaced. . . . Actually, these two orientations do more than persist: they play an important part in the civic culture" (339). Nevertheless, most scholars read Almond and Verba to mean that political engagement and participation are more frequent in societies that have civic political cultures.

Interpersonal trust is clearly a component of the civic culture, as an attitude that helps to foster solidarity and cooperation. For example, Almond and Verba blame low levels of trust in Germany, Italy, and Mexico for reducing "the ability of citizens to cooperate with each other in their relations with the government" (1963, 361). But at other points, Almond and Verba find trust to be important because it restrains participation rather than fostering it. Where interpersonal trust is high, citizens can remain passive and disengaged without worrying that their fellow citizens will take advantage of them or harm their interests. Consider this: "Attitudes favorable to participation within the political system play a major role in the civic culture, but so do such *nonpolitical attitudes as trust in other people* and social participation in general. The maintenance of these more traditional attitudes *and their fusion* with the participant orientations lead to a balanced political culture in which political activity, involvement, and rationality exist but are balanced by passivity, traditionality, and commitment to parochial values" (Almond and Verba 1963, 30, first emphasis added). Thus, the exact mechanism linking trust to democratic stability is open to interpretation in Almond and Verba's theory.

Ronald Inglehart also uses the term civic culture, but characterizes it as a "syndrome of political cultural attitudes" that includes interpersonal trust, subjective well-being, and "postmaterialist values" (1988, 1203). Interpersonal trust is more central to Inglehart's account than to Almond and Verba's. But the two approaches are equally imprecise in identifying the causal mechanisms that link cultural factors to democratic stability. Inglehart suggests that the syndrome is important because it lends legitimacy to democratic systems and produces moderation among regime opponents (see especially 1988, 1214). In other work, Inglehart focuses on trust among elites: democracy requires that "the opposition is trusted to play by the rules of the democratic game. This means that if the opposition wins an election, the ruling elite will turn power over to it, confident that they will not be executed or imprisoned for doing so" (1999, 98).[2]

Thus the political-culture literature contains several working hypotheses about the relationship between interpersonal trust and democracy. Trust encourages moderation in political conflicts; it fosters cooperation among citizens, who are then better able to hold their governments accountable; it lends legitimacy to democratic institutions; it engenders compromise among political elites. Critics often point to these varying suppositions as evidence of theoretical ambiguity; one might more charitably interpret them as evidence of theoretical complexity and development over time. We prefer to take these statements as working hypotheses, and later in the chapter evaluate some of them with a variety of available evidence.

Social capital represents the second major theoretical approach that links trust to democracy. According to Robert Putnam, the term "refers to . . . social networks and the norms of reciprocity and trustworthiness that arise from them" (2000, 19). There are many similarities between the social-capital approach and civic-culture theories: both rely on arguments about social norms, both trumpet the ability of interpersonal trust to foster cooperation among citizens, and more. One important difference, in our view, is that social capital is best understood as a characteristic of societies rather than individuals. Patterns of political attitudes are less important than networks, norms of reciprocity, and reserves of goodwill that exist in the social realm, rather than the psychological. Citizens can tap into these norms, networks, and reserves, but they do not "have" them. Furthermore, social capital theorists have made significant advances in generating clear explanations linking social capital to the adoption or (especially) successful maintenance of democratic institutions, whereas this link remains obscure in political-culture studies.

Pamela Paxton offers an example of this greater theoretical precision. She argues that social capital can facilitate democratization, by creating "a way for active opposition to the regime to grow" (2002, 257). Social capital also helps citizens to disseminate information, generate new ideas, and make opposition publicly known. Authoritarian regimes frequently maintain power by keeping potential opponents isolated and unaware of their common antiregime sentiment (Kuran 1991). Social capital erodes this isolation, which may explain why societal organizations like Solidarity in Poland or the Alianza Cívica in Mexico are often in the vanguard during authoritarian openings and transitions to democracy.

In sum, there may be some reason to believe that social capital contributes to democratization. Yet most social-capital theorists focus not on transitions but on improving the performance or responsiveness of democratic governments. This was Putnam's original intention in *Making Democracy Work* (1993). His early theoretical effort, however, did not provide a well-grounded explanation for democratic performance. Although he theorized that social capital might help to solve collective action problems among citizens, he did not offer a compelling account for why overcoming collective action problems necessarily improved government performance. Subsequent scholarship has attempted to explain how social capital might aid in solving not only the collective action problem among citizens, but also the principal-agent problem that typically exists between citizens and government functionaries.

There are many ways in which social capital might enhance the quality of democracy. One common view is that social capital generates an active civil society, and that people who are actively engaged in civic organizations learn skills that make them more capable of pressing demands on the government (Sandel 1996; Rosenblum 1998; Warren 2001). A rich associational life might also nurture civic consciousness, or a decision-making process in which the deliberators consider the general good, rather than narrow self-interest (Cohen and Rogers 1995).

Interpersonally trusting communities might also free the government from the need to enforce compliance and therefore allow it to spend time and resources on other activities. Putnam argues that in societies endowed with social capital, people are better able to cooperate with government (2000). In a similar vein, Carles Boix and Daniel Posner posit that "by giving citizens more optimistic expectations about the behavior of their fellow citizens, social capital can relieve the government from the burden of enforcing compliance and free up resources that can be applied towards increasing the efficiency or expanding the range of the services that it provides" (1998, 691).

A final potential link between social capital and democracy is that, for democracy to work well, citizens must monitor their government, and they will monitor it better if they trust one another. Putnam finds that democracy works better in some regions of Italy, where people trust each other more, than in others, where they distrust each other. The connection between interpersonal trust and democracy is that citizens have a collective interest in getting their government to be more responsive to them: carrying out public services more efficiently, not stealing public monies, and so on. If civil society monitors and pressures government enough, it can induce this higher degree of responsiveness, and the quality of regional democracy improves. But monitoring and pressuring are costly and the benefits of a more responsive government cannot be confined to those who expend the effort. People therefore have an incentive to let someone else do the monitoring and pressuring, with the predictable result that few participate. In some communities, people interact intensively, observe one another a lot, and believe, even when they do not observe each other, that others are acting cooperatively. Such communities encourage everyone to act for the common good, and thus citizens monitor government more closely. By this account, a well-functioning democracy is the consequence of a trusting society.

Theoretical Objections

From among the many potential objections to the explanations we have outlined, we focus on three that are particularly relevant to the way that Inglehart, Putnam, and others have integrated trust into their theoretical accounts. First, trust is not the only, and probably not even the most important, source of social and political cooperation (Cook, Hardin, and Levi 2005). Second, even in settings in which aggregate levels of trust can be empirically linked to social cooperation or desirable political outcomes, trust is usually better viewed as a symptom, rather than a cause (Hardin 2002). And, third, trust in political institutions is often unwarranted. When political officials or institutions are not trustworthy, citizens are better off when they remain skeptical or even outright distrustful. Skepticism, rather than (unwarranted) trust, can improve the quality of democracy (Cleary and Stokes 2006).

Theories linking political culture or social capital to democracy rely on the claim that interpersonal trust facilitates cooperation and coordination. This is clearest with respect to social capital theory, which is centrally concerned with how social groups solve collective action problems. Scholars do not typically assert that trust is a necessary condition; claims like Almond and Verba's or Putnam's are that interpersonal trust makes social cooperation easier, or more common. Other authors, however, dispute that trust plays such an important role. The Cook, Hardin, and Levi thesis can be distilled simply by striking the question mark from the book's title: cooperation without trust (2005). In part, their critique relies on Hardin's definition of trust, which requires an exchange between two or more individuals and excludes what we and others have called institutional trust (Hardin 2002; Cleary and Stokes 2006; Uslaner 2002). For example, Hardin is unwilling to say that a citizen might trust a government bureaucracy and prefers to describe the citizen's view as a belief about "government reliability" (see, for example, Cook Hardin, and Levi 2005, 152–55).

But even when we put this issue aside, it is far from clear that interpersonal trust is a major determinant of broad social cooperation. Cooperation is frequently achieved simply through narrow considerations of self-interest (Axelrod 1984). It might also be achieved through nonmaximizing psychological mechanisms such as kinship ties or other networks that have little to do with other-regarding interpersonal trust. As many of the authors in this volume argue, institutional structures can generate different levels of cooperation, either by generating trust (thus making trust endogenous), or through other mechanisms that have nothing to do with trust (see chapters 4, 5, and 9). Margaret Levi argues that cooperation, at least in the domain of compliance with government regulations, can be achieved through transparency and perceived fairness, rather than trust (1997). Finally, even when trust facilitates social cooperation, it may do so in ways that hinder responsive governance: interpersonal trust is a salient feature of mafias, cartels, and patron-client networks, which use trust relationships to achieve undemocratic ends (Armony 2004; Cleary and Stokes 2006; Cook, Hardin, and Levi 2005).

An additional criticism takes issue with the importance of trust in government. We have argued, in the context of a study of Mexico and Argentina, that democracy functions best in settings in which citizens adopt a skeptical attitude toward government (Cleary and Stokes 2006). Rather than trusting government institutions to work toward their interests, citizens in regions of these two countries where democracy works best are generally suspicious of government institutions, and trust them primarily when they believe that politicians and bureaucrats are constrained by horizontal accountability (for example, when executives are constrained by courts) and third-party monitoring (such as when government actions are closely observed by interest groups or the press). Thus, we offer both theoretical and empirical reasons to discount the importance of trust in government. On the theoretical side, the failure of some strains in the literature to explain how trust in government leads to improved government performance is especially relevant to developing parts of the world, where governments repeatedly prove themselves untrustworthy. On the empirical side, our evidence from the two Latin American democracies shows that, if anything, a trusting citizenry is a feature of subnational regions where democracy functions particularly badly.

Trust should not be the central focus in efforts to determine the causes of or to remedy democratic deficiencies. Where it occurs, the lack of interpersonal trust or trust in government is best viewed as a symptom of deeper structural or political problems, rather than a problem in its own right. This may seem to be a simple issue of how we frame our discussion. In fact, however, we argue that the focus on trust, especially within political culture theory, is a direct result of theoretical underspecification and a misunderstanding of how attitudes of trust are generated.

As an example of how a failure to specify the causes of trust can produce confusing inferences, consider two prominent studies of political trust from the recent literature. Marc Hetherington identifies low levels of trust in government as one of the major obstacles to progressive policymaking in the United States (2005). He notes the contrast between high levels of trust in government in the 1960s, which (he argues) allowed Lyndon Johnson to produce the Great Society, and low levels of trust in government in the 1990s, which forced Bill Clinton to dismantle it (Hetherington 2005, 153). Similarly, Scott Mainwaring notes a lack of political trust in many Andean countries (2006). Some of the governments of these countries are ineffective almost to the point of state failure, and have little legitimacy. Strong majorities—between 69 percent and 95 percent of respondents—in the five countries Mainwaring studied "agreed that corruption had increased greatly in the last five years" (2006, 299–300). The percentage of survey respondents expressing trust (confianza) in institutions like political parties, the national assembly, the police, the judiciary, and the presidency hovers in the mid-twenties (Mainwaring 2006, 309).[3]

The two authors present similar evidence, but draw contrasting inferences. Hetherington writes that

> If progressives desire a change . . . they must start by finding a way to resuscitate the federal government's image. . . . If [Americans] do not trust the federal government, they will want to limit the number, size, and scope of its programs. The key for the Left, then, is to take necessary steps to effect a sustained increase in political trust. To do this, progressives must make efforts to redefine what government means in the public mind, have the courage to praise the things it does well, and fight the urge to criticize its unpopular elements for political gain. (2005, 145–46)

In other words, what the federal government needs is a good public-relations campaign. Get people to trust government more, and government will be able to do more good things for people.

Mainwaring views the relationship between political trust and government performance quite differently. "The low confidence in parties and assemblies in the Andes stems above all from state deficiencies" (2006, 329–30). Andean states are widely perceived to be corrupt, and have "failed to resolve the policy [and economic] concerns of the vast majority of citizens" (2006, 330). This poor performance is the root cause of low trust in democratic institutions. "Better state performance is key to promoting greater confidence in the institutions of representative democracy and greater satisfaction with democracy. When democratic governments fail to produce what citizens need for a long time, most citizens will distrust the institutions of representative democracy" (331). Given poor performance, Latin American citizens are wise to judge their governments as untrustworthy. If citizens were to invest greater trust in their governments, this trust would almost surely be abused. Thus Mainwaring's conclusion is the opposite of Hetherington's: get government to do more good things for people, and people will begin to trust it more.

Our own view, based on both theoretical considerations and the available empirical evidence, to which we turn shortly, clearly favors Mainwaring's interpretation. This does not mean that trust in government is unimportant. It means, rather, that our analytical focus should be trained on the factors that would make trust in government reasonable and rewarding for citizens. For example, Margaret Levi believes that trust in government can increase compliance (1997), and John Ferejohn notes that trust in government allows government to expand its power and authority (1999). Both authors are clearly willing to say that trust matters, but for them the real action is in the factors that create conditions for trust—namely fairness, transparency, and efficiency. In other words, these authors focus on trustworthiness rather than trust (see Hardin 2002).

Concepts and Measures

In addition to the theoretical doubts we have outlined, many of the central findings linking trust to democracy are also open to empirical objections. We now focus on the most commonly used measures of trust—both interpersonal and institutional—and identify several weaknesses in the way the literature has employed available measures. We then turn to the causal inferences that scholars have suggested between trust, on the one hand, and cooperation, social capital, and democracy, on the other. In so doing, we broaden the discussion to include additional measurement and inferential problems that are common in the literature, and show that the statistical evidence does not support trust hypotheses as strongly as is often claimed. These charges are especially damning because of the problematic survey questions that have factored so heavily in most attempts to measure trust.

We are not the first to register doubt that responses to the most common survey questions about interpersonal trust actually measure people's propensity to trust. One issue is that interpersonal trust can only be understood as a contextual attitude (Hardin 1998, 2002, 2006). For example, we trust our spouses to consider our interests across a wide array of daily actions and decisions; but we would not trust them to perform surgery on us. Questions like "do you think most people can be trusted?" have no capacity to represent this sort of context (see also Cook, Hardin, and Levi 2005, 164). It remains unknown what sorts of images or hypothetical situations respondents conjure up in their minds when deciding how to answer these questions.

Another potential problem with survey measures of interpersonal trust is the high level of variation in responses over time. Inglehart's syndrome of attitudes and Putnam's concept of civic community are supposed to be enduring and relatively stable. But measures of interpersonal trust often show significant short-term variation, suggesting that responses are generated by time-specific evaluations of how people perceive their current social situation, rather than a more basic attitude of social trust, toleration, or willingness to cooperate (Newton 2001, 203). Inglehart offers one example of this when he shows that interpersonal trust in the United States fell from 58 percent to 35 percent between 1960 and 1995, with changes as high as 8 to 10 percentage points in the two-year intervals between surveys (1999, 95).

Trust attitudes are also highly variable within individuals over time. We are not aware of any panel survey data from Latin America that would speak to this point, but the National Election Studies (NES) in the United States did include questions on interpersonal and institutional trust in a three-wave panel survey conducted in 2000, 2002, and 2004 (NES 2005). Analysis of these data shows a high level of inconsistency. Of those who responded in 2000 that "most people can be trusted," only 70 percent offered the same response when asked again in 2002 and 2004. Among those two expressed distrust in 2000 ("you can't be too careful"), only 58 percent maintained a consistent answer in the subsequent two studies. In all, 65 percent of respondents in the panel maintained a consistent answer in all three surveys.[4] In other words, a respondent's own previous answers are not always reliable predictors of how she will answer the same question in subsequent surveys.

One might argue that we have simply identified random error, and that the survey question still provides a noisy, but ultimately accurate, measure of cultural civicness or social capital. In our view this is unlikely. If the standard trust indicators tapped into a stable, enduring characteristic of societies like civicness or social capital, we would expect variability over time in the interpersonal trust question to be similar to the variability observed for other enduring attributes. An illuminating comparison is to party identification, which is known to be quite stable over time in the United States (Campbell et al. 1960, 148–49; Green and Palmquist 1994). As with previous research, the NES panel study shows a pattern of stability. Among those who identified as Democrats in 2000, 84 percent maintained their response in 2002 and 2004; for Republicans, the figure is

Table 11.1 Almond and Verba: Social Trust and Distrust

Percentage Who Agree That	United States	United Kingdom	Germany	Italy	Mexico
Statements of distrust					
"No one is going to care much what happens to you, when you get right down to it."	38	45	72	61	78
"If you don't watch yourself, people will take advantage of you."	68	75	81	73	94
Statements of trust					
"Most people can be trusted."	55	49	19	7	30
"Most people are more inclined to help others than to think of themselves first."	31	28	15	5	15
"Human nature is fundamentally cooperative."	80	84	58	55	82
Total number of respondents	970	963	955	995	1,007

Source: Almond and Verba 1963, 213, table IX.2.

87 percent. And though some of the variability here may result from random error as well, these responses are clearly more stable over time than those to the standard trust question discussed earlier. Thus, interpersonal trust (or more accurately, whatever characteristics, attitudes, or circumstances respondents tap when answering the standard trust question) is not the result of any deeply held core beliefs or enduring cultural syndromes. Rather, the evidence suggests that the standard survey measures of trust are responsive to contemporary circumstances and short-term fluctuations in attitudes or beliefs.

Nor can we be confident that these survey questions tap into some diffuse or general attitude of trust. Consider five questions about trust and distrust that come from the original *Civic Culture* survey (see table 11.1). The cross-national pattern is certainly striking. But what underlying attitudinal or psychological processes have generated this pattern? A reasonable look at the data should make any researcher cautious about interpreting these data as a clear indication of cross-country variability in trust. For instance, whereas 55 percent of U.S. respondents agree that "most people can be trusted," a much larger proportion (68 percent) agrees that "people will take advantage of you." The proportion of trusters in the United States appears to be as low as 31 percent or as high as 80 percent, depending on which question we consult. Other contradictions are even starker: the overwhelming majority of respondents agree both that "people will take advantage of you" (78 percent, all countries combined), and that "human nature is fundamentally cooperative" (72 percent). These discrepancies suggest either that each question taps a distinct set of attitudes, which may or may not be related to interpersonal trust, or that the questions introduce significant biases in the responses, perhaps by cueing different emotions or reactions in different subsets of respondents.

The problem of construct validity is even more serious when scholars use interpersonal trust to measure social capital. Robert Putnam conceives of interpersonal trust as an integral part of social capital, but clearly does not believe that social capital is simply reducible to interpersonal trust (1993). His compound measure of civic community in the Italian regions, which forms the basis of some of the most influential empirical findings ever produced in this literature, has no trust component whatsoever (91–97). We suspect this is no mistake. Social capital is a complex characteristic that inheres within societies or communities; as a characteristic of social groups it does not correspond directly to individual attitudes; and it is not reducible to an aggregate proportion of agreement with the statement that "most people can be trusted." In our view, it is just plain wrong to use aggregate data on interpersonal trust as an indicator of social capital.

To summarize, in spite of impressive illustrations that show bivariate relationships across an array of countries between survey measures of interpersonal trust and democratic outcomes (Inglehart 1988, 2003), the proper interpretation of such patterns remains murky.

Questions about trust in government are equally ambiguous. The most commonly used survey question asks how much trust respondents have in particular political and social institutions, like the congress, parties, the church, or the courts. Figure 11.1 shows how the question is typically asked; this version is from the questionnaire for the 2004 Latinobarometer survey.[5] As we can see, the question lacks any context. Even if the individual institutions are rotated randomly, the respondent is still left with a battery of questions about political institutions with which he or she may have no experience and little ability to evaluate. For example, most citizens have never been directly involved in litigation of any sort, let alone in front of the national judiciary. What might it mean for such citizens to say that they trust (or distrust) el poder judicial? With such lack of context, responses to these questions are likely to be influenced by recent political events, the respondent's general feelings about the state of the economy, his approval (or disapproval) of the institution, and his or her own personal well-being. Or, as Gabriella Montinola suggests in the previous chapter, respondents may simply use their experience with one branch or office of government to generate expectations about the trustworthiness of other government institutions.

Of course, data gathered with these questions can be useful for many purposes, but our concern here is whether they are appropriate for the uses to

Figure 11.1 Sample Institutional Trust Question

P34ST. (Show card 07). Please, look at this card and tell me, how much trust (*confianza*) do you have in each one of these groups/institutions (READ EACH ONE OF THE INSTITUTIONS AND ASK) Would you say you have a lot (1), some (2), little (3), or no (4) trust (confianza) in…
(MARK A RESPONSE FOR EACH ONE) (ROTATE)

	A Lot	Some	Little	None	DK	NR
P34STA. Large Businesses........	1	2	3	4	8	0
P34STB. The Judiciary..............	1	2	3	4	8	0
P34STC. The President..............	1	2	3	4	8	0
P34STD. Political Parties...........	1	2	3	4	8	0
P34STE. Newspapers	1	2	3	4	8	0
P34STF. The National Congress/ Parliament............................	1	2	3	4	8	0
P34STG. The Stock Exchange...	1	2	3	4	8	0
P34STH. Municipalities............	1	2	3	4	8	0

P34ST. **(MOSTRAR TARJETA 07)** Por favor, mire esta tarjeta y dígame, ¿cuánta confianza tiene en cada uno de estos grupos/instituciones? **(LEA CADA UNA DE LAS INSTITUCIONES Y PREGUNTE)** ¿Diría que tiene mucha (1), algo (2), poca (3), o ninguna (4) confianza en....? **(MARQUE UNA RESPUESTA PARA CADA UNA) (ROTAR)**

	MUCHO	**ALGO**	**POCO**	**NINGUNA**	**NS**	**NR**
P34STA. Grandes Empresas........	1	2	3	4	8	0
P34STB. El Poder Judicial...........	1	2	3	4	8	0
P34STC. Presidente......................	1	2	3	4	8	0
P34STD. Los partidos políticos...	1	2	3	4	8	0
P34STE. Diarios...........................	1	2	3	4	8	0
P34STF. El Congreso Nacional/ Parlamento	1	2	3	4	8	0
P34STG. Bolsa de comercio.........	1	2	3	4	8	0
P34STH. Municipalidades...........	1	2	3	4	8	0

Source: Authors' translation of Latinobarometer 2004 Questionnaire.
Notes: DK = Don't know
NR = No response

which scholars of trust have put them. It seems unlikely that these questions accurately gauge institutional trust, or the belief that the named institution acts (or would act) in the respondent's interest.[6] As we have mentioned, this is partly due to the questions' lack of context, which makes it difficult for respondents to understand what they might be trusting the institution to do. Taking the definition of trust seriously also forces us to recognize that governments cannot engender universal trust when faced with controversial decisions—in at least a myopic sense, policies in favor of labor necessarily harm the interests of employers; policies in favor of gay rights necessarily harm those opposed to such rights. In this sense, employing aggregate levels of institutional trust as an indicator of cultural favorability toward democracy is clearly at odds with basic democratic theory.

In addition, even if we accepted that these measures capture institutional trust in some sense, they would be of little practical use in studies of trust because they do not give us any insight into the underlying motivation or belief structure of the respondent. Elsewhere we have distinguished between "weaker" forms of trust, in which the trust results from expectations regarding effective monitoring or third-party enforcement, and "stronger" forms, which result from beliefs about the character or predisposition of the trustee (Cleary and Stokes 2006). One weakly trusts a town mayor when one expects her to behave well because she is under close scrutiny by the local press; one strongly trusts her when one believes that she is deeply committed to the public good and personally incapable of corruption. This distinction is important because the different forms of trust have different implications for the quality of democracy. But survey questions such as those illustrated in figure 11.1 cannot capture these types of distinctions, and thus are not very useful for understanding the origins or effects of institutional trust.

Neither does it seem likely that aggregate responses to these questions serve well as a measure of legitimacy or support for the underlying political system, which is what some scholars seem to mean by terms like *political trust* or *trust in government*. These scholars argue that trust in government is important because a lack of such trust indicates a willingness to support nondemocratic regime change. Although we agree that mass support can be helpful for democratization and democratic consolidation, we do not believe that these questions measure regime support. What seems more likely is that they are influenced by respondents' views on recent political events and the performance of current incumbents; they may serve better as approval ratings or feeling thermometers than as measures of trust (Citrin 1974). In what follows, we subject this conjecture to an empirical test. If we are correct, we should notice fluctuations in the trust responses based on partisan differences, political events, and the like; other interpretations of the measures would not predict such differences.

Review of the Evidence

Keeping our theoretical and empirical skepticism in mind, we turn to an array of evidence that helps us evaluate several common hypotheses about interpersonal and institutional trust. Our discussion focuses on data from Latin America, our region of expertise, but we suspect that

Table 11.2 Interpersonal Trust and Civic Participation in Mexico and Argentina

	Mexico			Argentina		
		(100.0)	(1,155.0)		(100.0)	(1,900.0)
	No Trust	Trust	Total	No Trust	Trust	Total
Does belong	157	86	243	329	133	462
(one or more)	(15.8)	(21.1)	(17.4)	(22.1)	(32.3)	(24.3)
	(64.6)	(35.4)	(100.0)	(71.2)	(28.8)	(100.0)
Does not	834	321	1,155	1,159	279	1,438
belong	(84.2)	(78.9)	(82.6)	(77.9)	(67.7)	(75.7)
	(72.2)	(27.8)	(100.0)	(80.6)	(19.4)	(100.0)
Total	991	407	1,398	1,488	412	1,900
	(100.0)	(100.0)	(100.0)	(100.0)	(100.0)	(100.0)
	(70.9)	(29.1)	(100.0)	(78.3)	(21.7)	(100.0)

Source: Authors' compilation based on Cleary and Stokes (2006).
Note: Each cell lists the number of responses, followed by the column percentage and the row percentage.

most of the claims we offer here apply more generally. For clarity, we maintain the organizational framework of the theoretical discussion and review the evidence that can be brought to bear on our three main propositions: that interpersonal trust is merely one source of, and at best a partial explanation of, cooperative behavior; that trust (interpersonal and institutional) is usually best understood as a symptom, rather than a cause; and in particular that institutional trust is not a cause of democratic outcomes, and in fact is often unwarranted in democratic settings.

Trust Is Not the Only Source of Cooperation

We have already offered theoretical reasons to doubt the centrality of interpersonal trust to social cooperation. The empirical record also suggests that interpersonal trust is no more than a partial determinant of political participation or social cooperation, even if many studies identify a statistical relationship. For example, in our work on Mexico and Argentina, we found that interpersonal trusters are more likely to belong to civic associations, and to report having worked with others to solve a common problem in their neighborhood (Cleary and Stokes 2006, 139–40). As part of a broader study of social capital and participation in four Latin American countries, Joseph Klesner found that interpersonal trusters were more likely than nontrusters to be politically active (2007, 12).[7] But the size of the relationship needs closer scrutiny. In the data from our study, reported here in table 11.2, the differences are moderate. In Mexico, 21 percent of trusters, but only 16 percent of nontrusters, reported membership in civic organizations.

Table 11.3 Interpersonal Trust and Political Participation in Four Latin American Countries

	No Trust	Trust	Total
Does participate (one or more activities)	1,198 (31.5) (78.7)	325 (40.7) (21.3)	1,523 (33.1) (100.0)
No participation	2,604 (68.5) (84.6)	473 (59.3) (15.4)	3,077 (66.9) (100.0)
Total	3,802 (100.0) (82.7)	798 (100.0) (17.3)	4,600 (100.0) (100.0)

Source: Authors' compilation based on Klesner (2007, 12), based on data from World Values Survey.
Notes: Data are pooled responses from four Latin American countries (Argentina, Chile, Mexico, and Peru). Each cell lists the estimated number of responses (calculated from the bottom panel of table 2 in Klesner 2007, 12), followed by the column percentage and the row percentage. The *N* reported in each cell is calculated from the cell percentages offered by Klesner, and might be slightly inaccurate due to rounding.

In Argentina, 32 percent of trusters, but only 22 percent of nontrusters, report membership. In table 11.3, we use data reported in Klesner to look at a similar relationship (2007). Here, trusters were somewhat more inclined to participate than nontrusters (40.7 percent versus 31.5 percent).

These differences are real, in that they are statistically significant, substantively important, and commonly found across various public opinion datasets. But they also demonstrate how limited the relationship between trust and political participation is. Our data show that a strong majority of those who belonged to civic organizations (65 percent in Mexico and 71 percent in Argentina) did not express interpersonal trust. Similarly, most trusters (79 percent in Mexico and 68 percent in Argentina) did not belong to any civic groups. According to Klesner's data, the overwhelming majority of participants (78.7 percent) did not report interpersonal trust, and most (59.3 percent) interpersonal trusters did not report political participation. These findings do not refute the empirical relationship between trust and participation, but they do put it in context: if most trusters do not participate and most participants are not trusters, then clearly interpersonal trust can be only a small part of the equation in determining why individuals participate.

To attribute even this limited causal impact to interpersonal trust, furthermore, would require us to ignore serious questions about the direction of the causal relationship between trust and participation. Most empirical studies, including ours and Klesner's, are cross sectional, and are thus unable to determine whether trust is a cause or a product of the political and civic activity to which it correlates. Theory offers no clear guidance on this point. Most scholars working in the literature on trust assume that the direction of causality runs from attitudes toward behavior, and interpret statistical correlations accordingly. There is, however, no persuasive reason to favor this view. It seems at least plausible, for instance, that those who participate (for whatever reason) in collective efforts to solve community problems or alter government policies might gain a sense of trust in their fellow citizens, whom they observe, interact with, and get to know through the experience of political activity. Indeed, this was our argument in Cleary and Stokes (2006). In such a scenario, the behavior is the cause of the attitude. It is important to emphasize that the cross-sectional evidence provided in numerous studies, including our own, cannot distinguish between these two theoretical explanations.[8]

Trust Is Best Viewed as a Symptom, Not a Cause

As the discussion of interpersonal trust and political participation indicates, attitudes of trust can easily be seen as a consequence of social and institutional processes, rather than a cause. If this is true, then the literature's focus on mass attitudes is misplaced. Assuming (for now) that low levels of interpersonal or institutional trust are evidence of some sort of problem, there are two ways to view it. The first is as an attitudinal problem, in which individuals' beliefs about their social world happen to form patterns that generate suboptimal outcomes, such as a lack of cooperation or scant support for democracy. This approach would lead researchers to recommend strategies aimed at directly changing people's beliefs, as Hetherington has advocated (2005). The second is as a structural or institutional problem, in which some specifiable social or institutional condition generates suboptimal outcomes. In this view, mass attitudes simply reflect actual political conditions; changing mass beliefs becomes less important than changing the underlying causes of those beliefs. Although the discussion regarding interpersonal trust and political participation was unable to adjudicate between these two views, it is easy to identify additional examples in which the attitudinal explanation is implausible and the institutional explanation makes more sense. Our view is that low levels of interpersonal or institutional trust are not evidence of a crisis in mass attitudes, but rather a symptom of poor institutional performance—or as others have described it in the context of Latin America's weak democracies, a "crisis of democratic representation" (Mainwaring, Bejarano, and Leongómez 2006, 1).

One example involves the relationship between standard measures of institutional trust and corruption in Latin America. As many studies have shown, perceptions about official corruption tend to correlate with attitudes of trust, subjective well-being, and government approval. In figures 11.2

Figure 11.2 Corruption and Trust in Congress

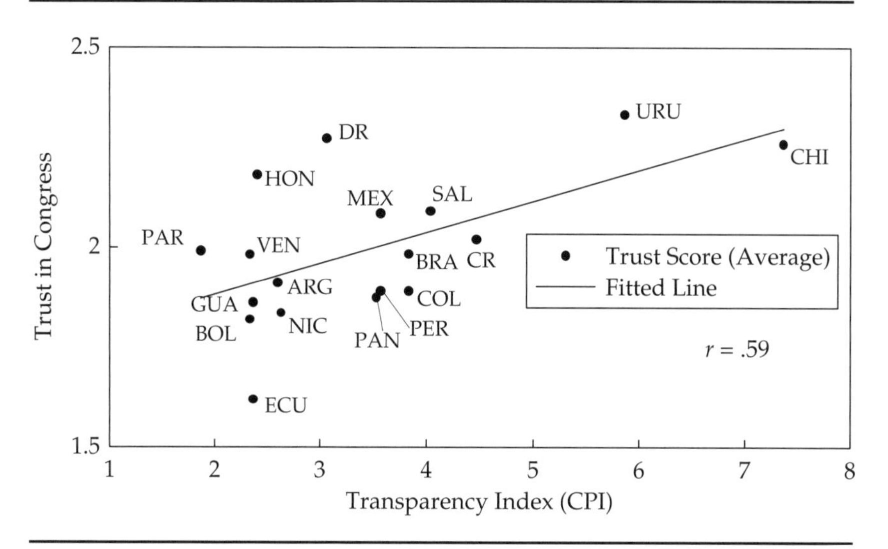

Source: Authors' compilation based on data from Latinobarometer and Transparency International datasets.
Note: See note 9 for country codes.

through 11.5, we show that at the aggregate level, institutional trust is also related to estimated levels of corruption across countries. To construct these illustrations, we use country-level indicators of corruption and institutional trust across eighteen Latin American countries.[9] The corruption indicator is Transparency International's well known Corruption Perceptions Index (CPI), an estimate of the severity of official corruption based on surveys of business people and country experts.[10] Higher numbers correspond to increased transparency, and lower numbers to greater corruption. The scale ranges from 1 to 10, and actual values can be found close to both extremes. In 2005, for example, Iceland scored a 9.7 and both Chad and Bangladesh a 1.7. Here, we use the average score for the three-year span from 2003 to 2005. To construct indicators of institutional trust, we take data from the Latinobarometer, years 2003 to 2005. As shown in figure 11.1, the Latinobarometer asks respondents "how much trust (confianza)" they have in particular institutions, and offers four responses indicating decreasing levels of trust. We reverse the scale so that larger numbers indicate higher levels of trust, and compute the average score per country, pooling across years.[11] From among the many institutions about which respondents are asked, we selected four that are most relevant to official corruption (both in fact and in public perception): the congress, the president, the public administration, and the government. Figures 11.2 through 11.5 illustrate the bivariate relationship between

Figure 11.3 Corruption and Trust in the President

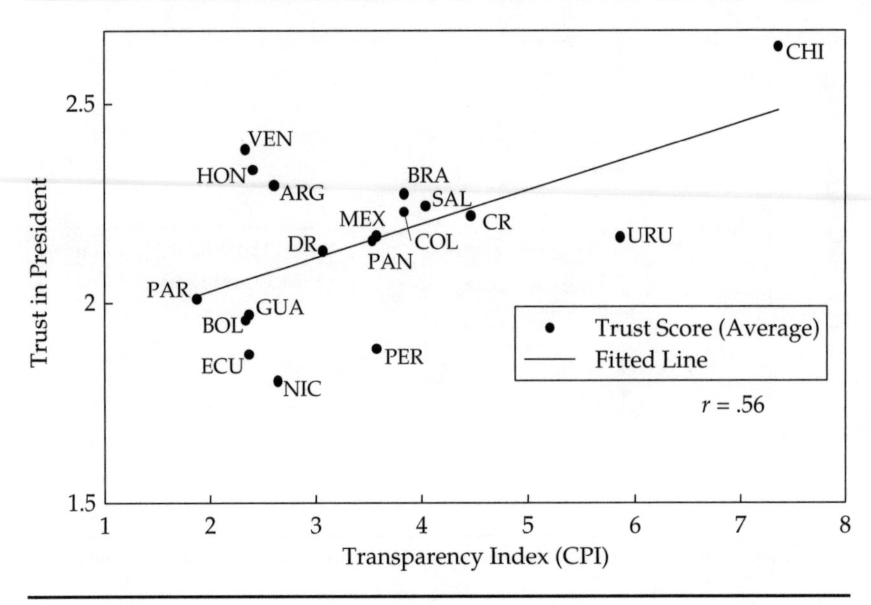

Source: Authors' compilation based on data from Latinobarometer and Transparency International datasets.
Note: See note 9 for country codes.

Figure 11.4 Corruption and Trust in Public Administration

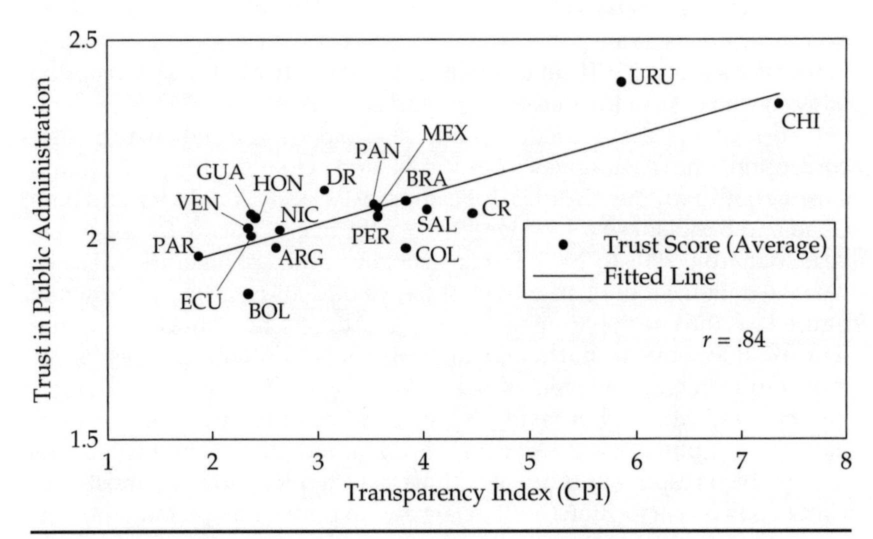

Source: Authors' compilation based on data from Latinobarometer and Transparency International datasets.
Note: See note 9 for country codes.

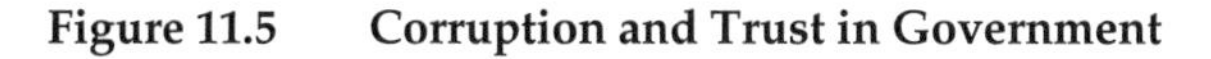

Figure 11.5 Corruption and Trust in Government

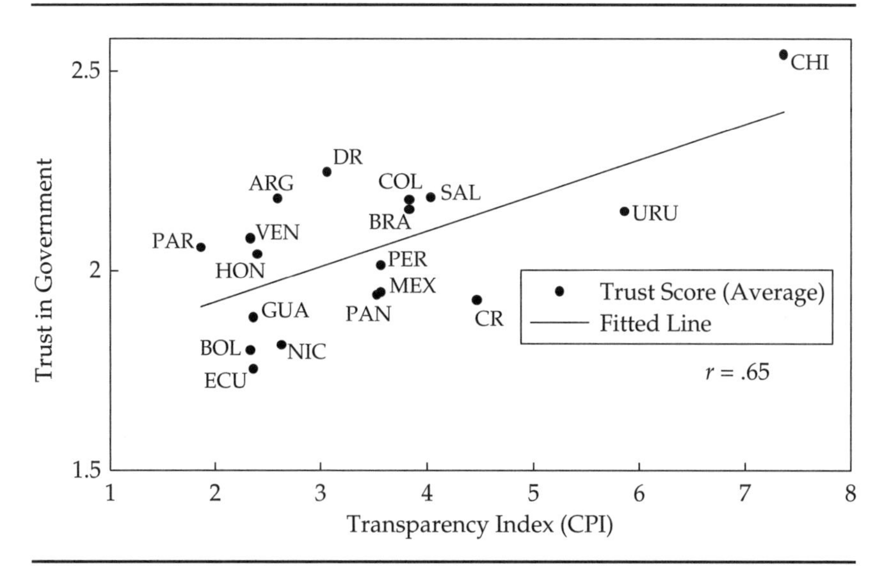

Source: Authors' compilation based on data from Latinobarometer and Transparency International datasets.
Note: See note 9 for country codes.

expert assessments of actual corruption and aggregate levels of confianza in these four political institutions.

The data show a clear relationship between corruption and institutional trust, as measured by the Latinobarometer and many other surveys. In all four cases, higher transparency scores coincide with higher levels of confianza in public institutions. The two countries with the highest CPI scores, plotted in the northeast section of each of the figures, are Uruguay and Chile. Chile in particular drives much of the pattern, as we might guess by noting that the remaining countries have much less variation on their CPI scores. Excluding Chile from the analysis renders the correlation coefficients statistically insignificant at standard levels, but in all cases the estimated coefficient remains positive. This is particularly true with respect to trust in the public administration, which might be the institution most closely related to corruption in the minds of many Latin Americans, where small bribes are routinely used to ease progress through driver's license bureaus and many other street-level institutions of government.

The statistical relationship is quite strong, as is the relationship between institutional trust and perceived corruption at the individual level.[12] But how should we interpret this empirical finding? It is notoriously difficult to establish causal direction when studying the relationship among mass attitudes. In this case, however, the measure of corruption comes from a separate source, and is intended as a measure of actual levels of corruption rather than of mass perceptions. It would be convoluted to argue that Latin American governments are more corrupt because citizens do not trust them. The far more plausible interpretation is that citizens express low confidence in government institutions because they observe and perceive official corruption.

Consider the counterfactual scenario in which citizens of Argentina or Brazil suddenly became more trustful of their governments, expressing full faith that their governments would work hard in the public interest. It would be foolish to believe that the governments of these two countries (which score 2.6 and 3.8, respectively, on the 10-point transparency indicator) would actually behave with greater transparency because of the vote of confidence. If anything, we might suspect that governing officials would use the public's (unwarranted and misplaced) trust to further enrich themselves at public expense. On the other hand, it is easy to conceive of a scenario in which institutional performance generates increased trust over time. Assume that a government, like Brazil's or Argentina's, begins to act with more transparency and to punish corrupt officials when they are exposed. Although publicity of malfeasance might lead to greater distrust in the short term, we would expect serious and lasting improvements in government performance to generate higher levels of institutional trust. The data offer equal support to both arguments, but logic and common sense speak clearly in favor of the latter.

Note also that our explanation of the empirical relationship between corruption and trust in political institutions has consequences for the interpretation of standard institutional trust measures. Because we reinterpret the standard indicators to be a result of institutional performance, there is no need to tie these measures to specific and conceptually rigorous definitions of trust, or to a theory that claims institutional trust as an important causal factor in institutional performance—fortunately so, because the measures are not well suited for this purpose. Rather, responses about how much trust respondents have in political institutions amount to approval ratings (see also Citrin 1974). In fact, the indicators we discuss here correlate strongly with standard questions about satisfaction with democracy and views on the state of the economy.

These indicators also show certain forms of short-term variation that we would not expect to see if they were valid measures of the broader, more diffuse sets of attitudes that are central to most political-culture explanations of democracy. The standard political culture account posits that societies have stable (though not permanent) attitudinal or cultural characteristics that make them more or less suitable for certain types of government. Setting aside the validity of the argument, if institutional trust questions are a valid measure of political culture, we would expect relative stability over time. What we see instead are changes in institutional trust based on partisanship and other political factors.

Table 11.4 Partisanship and Trust in Congress in Venezuela

	1995 to 1998			2000 to 2005		
	Right	Left	Total	Right	Left	Total
No trust	1,479	857	2,336	1,352	875	2,227
	74.3%	79.2%	76.0%	67.3%	58.3%	63.5%
Trust	513	225	738	658	625	1,283
	25.8%	20.8%	24.0%	32.8%	41.7%	36.6%
Total	1,992	1,082	3,074	2,010	1,500	3,510
	100.0%	100.0%	100.0%	100.0%	100.0%	100.0%

Source: Authors' compilation based on data from Latinobarometer.

One excellent opportunity to illustrate these changes comes from Venezuela, because of the transition from a center-Right administration in the mid-1990s to the leftist administration of Hugo Chávez in early 1999.[13] In table 11.4, we show the relationship between partisanship and trust in congress by generating two dummy variables from Latinobarometer data.[14] The row variable represents trust in congress, where we separate Venezuelan respondents who reported much or some trust from those who reported little or none. The column variable is based on Left-Right self-placement. The original survey question asks respondents to rank themselves on a scale from 0 (for Left) to 10 (for Right). A large proportion of respondents choose 5, presumably to indicate nonpartisanship. We drop those cases, and collapse the remaining respondents into Left and Right categories. The table shows that, before 1999, those who self-identified on the Left side of the political spectrum were significantly less likely to report trust in congress (20.8 percent, versus 25.8 percent for those on the Right). But after 1999, the relationship is reversed, with those on the Left being far more likely (41.7 percent) than those on the Right (32.7 percent) to express trust in congress. This may not be surprising, given Chávez's explicit partisanship and the widespread hopefulness that existed for the "Bolivarian revolution" at that time. But the radical swing in both the overall amount of trust, and in its partisan composition, shows that the standard trust measure is better understood as a product of government approval and other political factors than of cultural proclivities or enduring social attitudes, as many scholars claim.

Trust Does Not Cause Democracy

As much of the preceding analysis has already implied, we do not believe that either interpersonal or institutional trust should be viewed as a cause of democratization, democratic consolidation, or improved institutional performance of democratic governments, even though they are often observed to be correlates of such outcomes. In our view, the evidence in favor of such propositions is quite limited even when we set aside the types of theoretical and empirical objections we have already outlined. We also summarize evidence that directly contradicts these propositions.

One finding that scholars have cited in favor of trust and democracy arguments is a correlation between interpersonal trust and support for democracy at the individual level. For example, Timothy Power and Mary Clark argues that trust matters based on an empirical relationship between interpersonal trust and support for democracy among survey respondents in Chile, Costa Rica, and Mexico (2001). But the authors do not offer a causal explanation that takes us from interpersonal trust to mass support for democracy, or from mass support for democracy to the installation and consolidation of democratic institutions. Although most scholars would agree that mass support cannot be a bad thing for democracy, there are good reasons to doubt that it is decisive. Even Inglehart questioned whether mass support for democracy, as measured in polls, can be a critical factor, given that expressions of support are uniformly high across countries, regardless of regime type (2003). According to data from his World Values Surveys, support for democracy is highest in Albania and Egypt (where 99 percent of respondents are favorable), and is above 80 percent in seventy-five of the seventy-seven countries for which data exist (Inglehart 2003, 52). Obviously, those seventy-five countries are not all democracies. If aggregate levels of support for democracy do not coincide with actual levels of democracy across countries, then the correlation between interpersonal (or institutional) trust and favorability toward democracy at the individual level should not be cited in support of the hypothesis that trust causes democracy.

In our 2006 study, *Democracy and the Culture of Skepticism,* we attempted to shed light on several other hypotheses about trust and democracy by comparing more- and less-democratic regions within Mexico and Argentina. Here, we summarize the design of that research and discuss two of the crucial findings regarding trust and democratization.

Our research strategy was to identify regions within each country both where democracy was relatively consolidated and functioned relatively well, and where it was less consolidated and functioned poorly. To select for variation on the level of democracy and to produce our rankings, we consulted a wide array of information, including regional histories, voting patterns, levels of clientelism, leadership patterns, and data on political violence. After selecting four cases in each country, we also confirmed our rankings with information gleaned from public opinion surveys we conducted in 2001. For example, the Argentine surveys revealed that respondents in regions we had identified as more democratic were generally less likely to support the Peronist party, more likely to split their tickets, better informed, and more willing to talk openly about their vote choice. Similar patterns held for Mexico. In the end, from among the cases we selected in Mexico, we identified Baja California Norte as the most democratic state, followed by Chihuahua, Michoacán, and finally Puebla. In Argentina, we identified Mar del Plata as our most democratic case, followed by the provinces of Buenos Aires, Córdoba, and Misiones (see Cleary and Stokes 2006, chapters 2–3).[15]

Our study did replicate some of the literature's common empirical findings, such as the correlation between political participation and interpersonal trust. But we also found important patterns that would not have been predicted by any of the standard theoretical accounts linking trust to democracy. For example, we asked a battery of questions about what kinds of organizations existed in the neighborhoods where people lived, what organizations they belonged to, and whether they took part in other, less organized forms of civic life. Although we found that respondents who reported these types of civic involvement were indeed more trusting, we also found that they are more likely to live in the most clientelistic regions, where democracy functions worst. For instance, in Argentina, the only important difference in rates of participation between more and less democratic regions was that people in the less democratic regions reported working with neighbors to solve a common problem significantly more frequently. They also reported higher rates of attendance at religious services. In Mexico, respondents from Baja California, our most democratic state, were less likely than those of any other state to have attended a public meeting or to report membership in a civic organization. They were less likely than respondents from Chihuahua and Michoacán to have worked with others to solve a common problem. Interpersonal trust and participation remain related in our data, but aggregated at the state level, neither correlate with the quality of democracy.[16] To the extent, then, that we find regional differences in social capital, they run against the grain of the social-capital theory of democracy.

Our findings also contrast with the conventional wisdom regarding trust in government. In the more democratic regions of Mexico and Argentina, people tend to trust government less (in the strong, traditional sense of that term). To the extent that political trust exists, it takes the form of what we have called weak institutional trust. Citizens tend to believe that politicians are responsive and efficient only when they are under institutional constraints to act responsively and efficiently. And a form of interpersonal trust becomes important in one specific sense: citizens in the more democratic regions are more likely to believe that their fellow citizens do actually monitor government activity and hold government accountable for its performance (rather than being bought off or voting based on personalistic ties). In other words, citizens in the more democratic regions are skeptical of government. Still, they are willing to invest in a weak form of political trust, in that they tend to believe that institutional mechanisms of accountability effectively constrain the behavior of politicians.

To gauge this skepticism in the Argentine and Mexican contexts, we asked survey questions meant to elicit from our samples whether they attributed good governance to institutional incentives or to the character of the people staffing governments. We asserted, for instance, that politicians sometimes perform well—provide good public services, pay attention to the opinions of constituents—and then asked respondents to choose between alternative explanations for this good performance. In each case, one option attributed good performance to the personal qualities of politicians ("they are committed people," "they care about constituents' opinions"). The other option attributed good performance to mechanisms of accountability ("they're under the watch of the courts," "if they perform badly they'll lose the next election"). Accountability explanations imply a more skeptical view of government responsiveness and efficiency.

In both Argentina and Mexico, people from our least democratic region tended to attribute good government to the individual qualities of officeholders. To give a sense of how large the regional differences are, consider a typical respondent in our Argentine sample, one with an average household income, education level, and quality of housing, and who lived in an average-sized city. Simulations show that if she lived in Mar del Plata (most democratic), this typical respondent had a 65 percent chance of saying that governments provide good services "because they're monitored." But if she lived in Misiones (least democratic), the chance dropped to 38 percent.[17]

The greater skepticism of people in more democratic regions comes out clearly in responses to the following survey question: "Thinking in general about people who hold public office, how many of them do you think are trustworthy and will behave well without being monitored—all, a majority, a minority, or none?" In figure 11.6, we have subtracted the percentage responding "all" or "a majority" from the percentage responding "none." Thus larger differences indicate a greater degree of skepticism about officeholders. In all four Argentine regions, more people answered "none" than "all" or "most." In both countries, the more democratic the region, the more skeptical its residents. Thus, as with previous evidence, we see here significant differences in political culture across more and less democratic regions. But the differences are not those that would have been predicted by the trust theories examined in this chapter.

To summarize, our data from Argentina and Mexico lead us to doubt explanations of democratic consolidation that rely on social trust. We did find that people in regions where democracy functioned relatively smoothly showed a type of interpersonal trust, in that they believed others would hold politicians accountable rather than being bought off with personalistic favors. We also found that people who participated in civic life were more personally trusting than those who did not. But, contrary to the theory, the more democratic regions did not have higher levels of inter-

Figure 11.6 Regional Levels of Institutional Trust, Mexico and Argentina

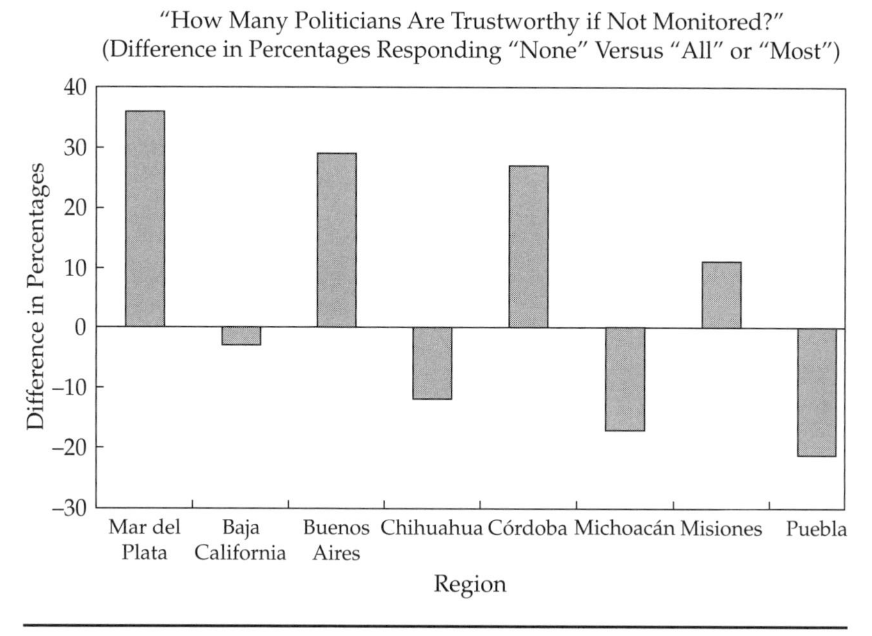

Source: Authors' compilation based on survey data reported in Cleary and Stokes (2006).

personal trust or civic participation. We do find robust differences in the political cultures of our more and less democratic regions, but social capital has little to do with these differences.

Conclusion

In this chapter, we have raised a number of objections to recent trends in the scholarship on trust and democracy. We value this literature, and have attempted to contribute to it. But we also worry that some attempts to link democratic outcomes to the previous existence of interpersonal or institutional trust rest on weak theory and ambiguous empirical evidence. Among our theoretical concerns is the presumption that trust is necessary for cooperation, a benefit to society in general (rather than narrow trust networks), or a cause of democratic responsiveness. Our empirical concerns are manifold, beginning with doubts about the most common measures of trust. We have shown that common survey questions probably do not capture what most social scientists mean by trust, which is a relational and domain-specific attitude rather than a general character trait. If common measures are not good indicators of trust, they are even less appropriate as measures of a certain type of political culture or of social capital. According to evidence presented in this chapter, measures of both interpersonal and institutional trust are almost certainly influenced by short-term fluctuations in the political arena and in respondents' personal lives. They do not accurately reflect any enduring culture or syndrome.

Furthermore, even when we suspend our doubts about the utility of the measures, we find little empirical evidence to support a causal link from trust to democracy, and much empirical evidence to contradict such a link. Interpersonal trust is not a good predictor of the quality of democracy, either in the Mexican and Argentine regions we studied or in general. Our evidence showed that interpersonal trust is unlikely to be an unmediated underpinning of democratic participation. Nor would an exogenous jump in trust—if one could imagine such a jump as truly exogenous—improve the quality of democracy. Institutional trust is a product of the quality of democracy, rather than a cause; the only form of institutional trust that might actually cause democratic responsiveness is a belief, grounded in skepticism, that government can be trusted when it is monitored closely and held accountable. This insight, which should not sound foreign to anyone familiar with Putnam's 1993 argument, may point the way toward further theoretical development: our evidence suggests that any theory linking trust and democracy will have to focus on the institutional conditions (like effective monitoring) that make trust rational. Trust is not a cause of democracy or democratic responsiveness. Rather, interpersonal trust, and trust in public institutions, tends to arise from social and political practices that make public institutions trustworthy.

Notes

1. Most of these studies characterize trust as a causal factor. Several, however, view trust primarily as a symptom (Anderson and Tverdova 2001; Anderson et al. 2005; Mainwaring 2006).
2. Adam Przeworski offers a nearly identical account, but sees the type of compromise described here as the result of rational calculations rather than a cultural predisposition to trust opponents (1991).
3. Confianza in the military, the press, and the church are all significantly higher.
4. This excludes nonresponses like "don't know" or a refusal to answer; inclusion of these responses would produce a consistency figure even lower than 65 percent. Trust in government shows a similar pattern: of those who expressed trust in government in 2000, only 56 percent maintained the answer in the two subsequent waves.
5. The Latinobarometer version also illustrates the fact that the only translation for *trust* in Spanish is *confianza,* which also means confidence. Although trust and confidence are synonyms in lay English, scholars such as Hardin have drawn important conceptual distinctions between the two terms.

6. Recall that Russell Hardin considers *institutional trust* oxymoronic (2002). As we define the term, institutional trust amounts to an individual's belief that the institution will act in her interest. This would require us to assume either that institutions can be conceived as actors, or that in our definition, *institution* amounts to shorthand for "the actors who control institutional output."
7. Specifically, Klesner shows that interpersonal trusters are more likely to have reported doing one or more of the following: signing a petition, joining a boycott, attending a demonstration, joining an illegal strike, and occupying a building (2007, 7–9).
8. In a study based on time series data from the United States, Luke Keele suggests that trust in government does not cause either civic engagement or interpersonal trust, but that interpersonal trust does cause trust in government over time (2007). The strongest predictor of trust in government is civic engagement, as our alternative theoretical account might predict. Keele does not test whether civic engagement causes interpersonal trust, as we suggest here.
9. Within Latin America, we selected all countries for which data were available: Argentina (ARG), Bolivia (BOL), Brazil (BRA), Colombia (COL), Costa Rica (CR), Chile (CHI), Dominican Republic (DR), Ecuador (ECU), El Salvador (SAL), Guatemala (GUA), Honduras (HON), Mexico (MEX), Nicaragua (NIC), Panama (PAN), Paraguay (PAR), Peru (PER), Uruguay (URU), and Venezuela (VEN).
10. We accessed the data from Transparency.org in December 2007; more information on the data sources and coding criteria can also be found at this website.
11. Trust in the public administration was asked only in 2005; trust in the president was asked only in 2003 and 2004.
12. Latinobarometer has not asked respondents about their perception of corruption since 2001. Pooling all years from 1995 to 2001, and correlating with institutional trust measures, we find that among respondents who believe corruption had increased in the previous five years, 29 percent expressed trust in congress and 32 percent expressed trust in government—versus 40 percent and 53 percent, respectively, for those who did not perceive an increase.
13. Chávez was elected in December 1998 and inaugurated in February 1999.
14. We chose trust in congress because it is one of the only institutional trust questions asked every single year of the Latinobarometer survey. Results are similar (indeed, the differences are larger) if we use trust in government or trust in public administration.
15. Mar del Plata is not a province, but rather a city within the province of Buenos Aires. The other three Argentine cases are provinces (for the rationale behind our case selection, see Cleary and Stokes 2006).
16. Similarly, in a cross-national study with data from seventeen Latin American countries, Cynthia McClintock and James Lebovic find no relationship between

levels of interpersonal trust and democracy, as measured by Freedom House scores (2006).

17. We also found that Mexican respondents were much more likely to cite the personal qualities of politicians than were Argentines.

References

Almond, Gabriel A., and Sidney Verba. 1963. *The Civic Culture: Political Attitudes and Democracy in Five Nations.* Princeton, N.J.: Princeton University Press.

Anderson, Christopher J., and Yuliya V. Tverdova. 2001. "Winners, Losers, and Attitudes about Government in Contemporary Democracies." *International Political Science Review* 22(4): 321–38.

Anderson, Christopher J., André Blais, Shaun Bowler, Todd Donovan, and Ola Listhaug. 2005. *Losers' Consent: Elections and Democratic Legitimacy.* Oxford: Oxford University Press.

Armony, Ariel C. 2004. *The Dubious Link: Civic Engagement and Democratization.* Stanford, Calif.: Stanford University Press.

Axelrod, Robert. 1984. *The Evolution of Cooperation.* New York: Basic Books.

Boix, Carles, and Daniel Posner. 1998. "Social Capital: Explaining Its Origins and Effects on Government Performance." *British Journal of Political Science* 28(4): 686–93.

Campbell, Angus, Philip E. Converse, Warren E. Miller, and Donald E. Stokes. 1960. *The American Voter.* Chicago: University of Chicago Press.

Citrin, Jack. 1974. "Comment: The Political Relevance of Trust in Government" *American Political Science Review* 68(3; September): 973–88.

Cleary, Matthew R., and Susan C. Stokes. 2006. *Democracy and the Culture of Skepticism: Political Trust in Argentina and Mexico.* New York: Russell Sage Foundation.

Cohen, Joshua, and Joel Rogers. 1995. "Secondary Associations and Democratic Governance." In *Associations and Democracy,* edited by Joshua Cohen and Joel Rogers. London: Verso.

Cook, Karen S., Russell Hardin, and Margaret Levi. 2005. *Cooperation Without Trust.* New York: Russell Sage Foundation.

Corporación Latinobarómetro. Various years. Latinobarómetro, 2003–2005 [dataset]. Santiago, Chile: Corporación Latinobarómetro [distributor]. Available at: http://www.latinobarometro.org.

Ferejohn, John. 1999. "Accountability and Authority: Toward a Theory of Political Accountability." In *Democracy, Accountability, and Representation,* edited by Adam Przeworski, Susan C. Stokes, and Bernard Manin. New York: Cambridge University Press.

Green, Donald P. and Bradley Palmquist. 1994. "How Stable is Party Identification?" *Political Behavior* 16(4): 437–66.

Hardin, Russell. 1998. "Trust in Government." In *Trust and Governance,* edited by Valerie Braithwaite and Margaret Levi. New York: Russell Sage Foundation.

———. 2002. *Trust and Trustworthiness.* New York: The Russell Sage Foundation.

———. 2006. *Trust.* Cambridge: Polity.

Hetherington, Marc J. 2005. *Why Trust Matters: Declining Political Trust and the Demise of American Liberalism.* Princeton, N.J.: Princeton University Press.

Inglehart, Ronald. 1988. "The Renaissance of Political Culture." *American Political Science Review* 82(4): 1203–230.

———. 1999. "Trust, Well-Being, and Democracy." In *Democracy and Trust,* edited by Mark Warren. Cambridge: Cambridge University Press.

———. 2003. "How Solid Is Mass Support for Democracy and How Can We Measure It?" *PS: Political Science and Politics* 36(1): 51–57.

Jackman, Robert W., and Ross A. Miller. 1996. "A Renaissance of Political Culture?" *American Journal of Political Science* 40(3): 632–59.

Keele, Luke. 2007. "Social Capital and the Dynamics of Trust in Government." *American Journal of Political Science* 51(2; April): 241–54.

Klesner, Joseph L. 2007. "Social Capital and Political Participation in Latin America: Evidence from Argentina, Chile, Mexico, and Peru." *Latin American Research Review* 42(2): 1–32.

Kuran, Timur. 1991. "Now Out of Never: the Element of Surprise in the East European Revolution of 1989." *World Politics* 44(October): 7–48.

Levi, Margaret. 1997. *Consent, Dissent, and Patriotism.* New York: Cambridge University Press.

Mainwaring, Scott. 2006. "State Deficiencies, Party Competition, and Confidence in Democratic Representation in the Andes." In *The Crisis of Democratic Representation in the Andes,* edited by Scott Mainwaring, Ana María Bejarano, and Eduardo Pizarro Leongómez. Stanford, Calif.: Stanford University Press.

Mainwaring, Scott, Ana María Bejarano, and Eduardo Pizarro Leongómez, eds. 2006. *The Crisis of Democratic Representation in the Andes.* Stanford, Calif.: Stanford University Press.

McClintock, Cynthia, and James H. Lebovic. 2006. "Correlates of Levels of Democracy in Latin America during the 1990s." *Latin American Politics and Society* 48(2): 29–59.

National Election Study (NES). 2005. *National Election Study 2000-2002-2004 Full Panel File* [dataset]. Ann Arbor: University of Michigan, Center for Political Studies [producer and distributor]. Available at: http://www.electionstudies.org (accessed December 2007).

Newton, Kenneth. 2001. "Trust, Social Capital, Civil Society, and Democracy." *International Political Science Review* 22(2): 201–14.

Paxton, Pamela. 2002. "Social Capital and Democracy: An Interdependent Relationship." *American Sociological Review* 67(2): 254–77.

Power, Timothy J., and Mary A. Clark. 2001. "Does Trust Matter? Interpersonal Trust and Democratic Values in Chile, Costa Rica, and Mexico." In *Citizen Views of Democracy in Latin America,* edited by Roderic Ai Camp. Pittsburgh, Pa.: University of Pittsburgh Press.

Przeworski, Adam. 1991. *Democracy and the Market.* New York: Cambridge University Press.

Putnam, Robert D. 1993. *Making Democracy Work: Civic Traditions in Modern Italy.* Princeton, N.J.: Princeton University Press.
———. 2000. *Bowling Alone: The Collapse and Revival of American Community.* New York: Simon & Schuster.
Rosenblum, Nancy L. 1998. *Membership and Morals: The Personal Uses of Pluralism in America.* Princeton, N.J.: Princeton University Press.
Sandel, Michael. 1996. *Democracy and Its Discontents: America in Search of a Public Philosophy.* Cambridge, Mass.: Harvard University Press.
Seligson, Mitchell A. 2002. "The Renaissance of Political Culture or the Renaissance of the Ecological Fallacy." *Comparative Politics* 34(3): 273–92.
Seligson, Mitchell A., and John A. Booth. 1993. "Political Culture and Regime Type: Evidence from Nicaragua and Costa Rica." *Journal of Politics* 55(3): 777–92.
Transparency International. Various years. Corruption Perceptions Index, 2003–2005 [dataset]. Berlin: Transparency International [distributor]. Available at: http://www.transparency.org/policy_research/surveys_indices/cpi.
Uslaner, Eric M. 2002. *The Moral Foundations of Trust.* New York: Cambridge University Press.
Warren, Mark E. 2001. *Democracy and Association.* Princeton, N.J.: Princeton University Press.

Index

Boldface numbers refer to figures and tables

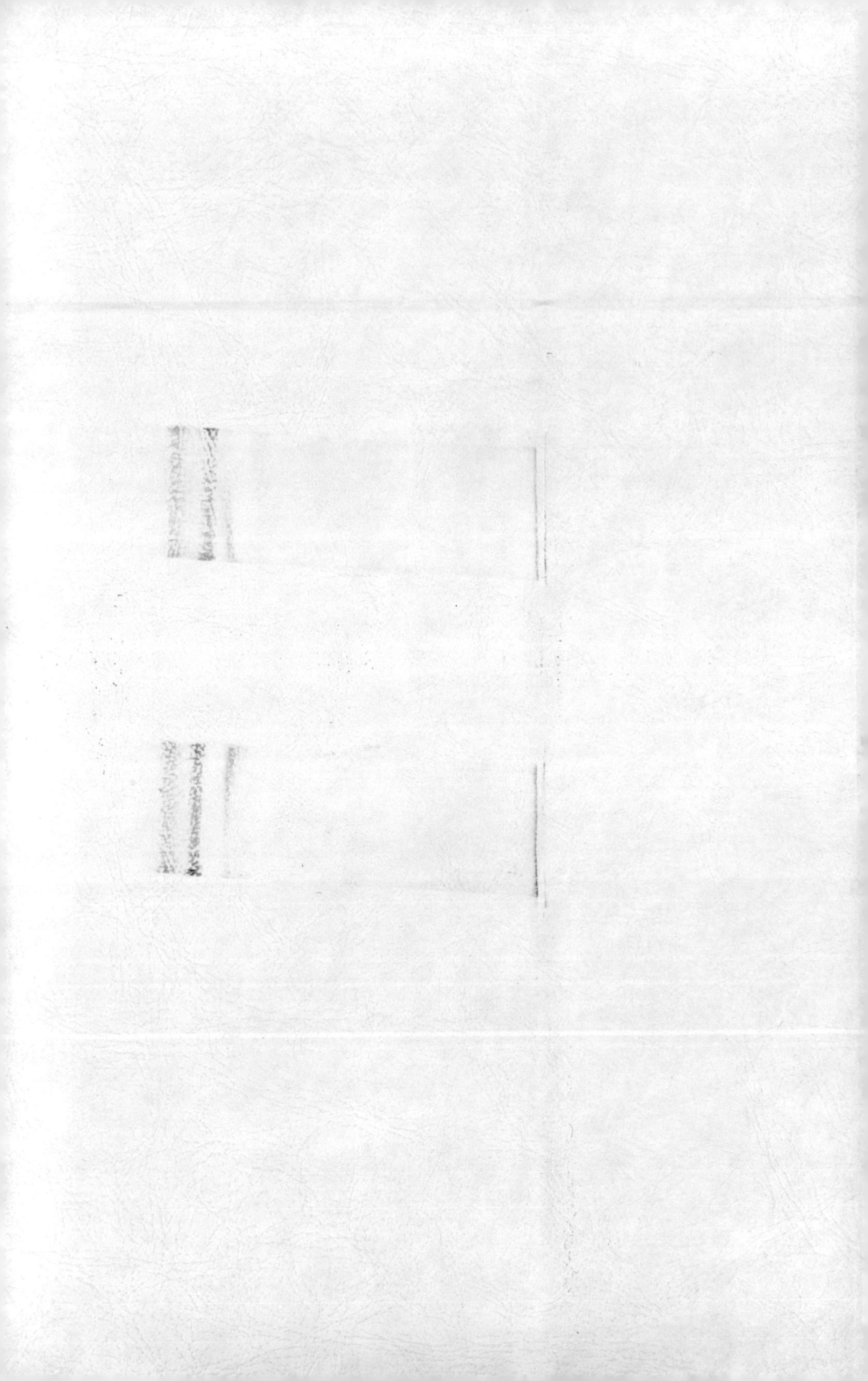